## Free French Africa in World War II
### *The African Resistance*

General de Gaulle's Free French may have been headquartered in London, but their base lay in Brazzaville. This book shows compellingly that the movement drew its strength from 1940 to 1943 from fighting men, resources, and operations in French Equatorial Africa and Cameroon. Territorially, Free France spanned from the Libyan border with Chad down to the Congo River, and to the scattered tiny French territories of the South Pacific and India. Eric T. Jennings tells the story of an improbable French military and institutional rebirth through Central Africa. *Free French Africa in World War II* provides a unique look at the long forgotten role Gaullist Africa played to help the Allied cause.

Eric T. Jennings is professor of history at Victoria College at the University of Toronto. His books include *Vichy in the Tropics*, *Curing the Colonizers*, and *Imperial Heights*, as well as an edited volume with Jacques Cantier entitled *L'Empire colonial sous Vichy*. Jennings has received a John Simon Guggenheim Fellowship; Social Sciences and Humanities Research Council of Canada grants; the Alf Andrew Heggoy, Jean-François Coste, and Fetkann book prizes; and the Palmes académiques.

# Free French Africa in World War II

## The African Resistance

ERIC T. JENNINGS
*University of Toronto*

CAMBRIDGE
UNIVERSITY PRESS

# CAMBRIDGE
## UNIVERSITY PRESS

University Printing House, Cambridge CB2 8BS, United Kingdom

One Liberty Plaza, 20th Floor, New York, NY 10006, USA

477 Williamstown Road, Port Melbourne, VIC 3207, Australia

314-321, 3rd Floor, Plot 3, Splendor Forum, Jasola District Centre, New Delhi - 110025, India

79 Anson Road, #06-04/06, Singapore 079906

Cambridge University Press is part of the University of Cambridge.

It furthers the University's mission by disseminating knowledge in the pursuit of education, learning and research at the highest international levels of excellence.

www.cambridge.org
Information on this title: www.cambridge.org/9781107696976



First published in 2014 by Perrin (Paris) as La France libre fut africaine
First English edition 2015

*A catalogue record for this publication is available from the British Library*

*Library of Congress Cataloging in Publication data*
Jennings, Eric T. (Eric Thomas), 1970– author.
Free French Africa in World War II : the African resistance / Eric T. Jennings,
University of Toronto.
pages cm
Includes bibliographical references and index.
ISBN 978-1-107-04848-5 (alk. paper)
1. France libre – History.   2. France combattante – History.   3. World War,
1939–1945 – Africa, French-speaking Equatorial.   4. World War, 1939–1945 –
Cameroon.   5. World War, 1939–1945 – Participation, African.
6. France – Colonies – Africa.   I. Title.
D766.96J47   2015
940.53´67–dc23      2015010599

ISBN   978-1-107-04848-5   Hardback
ISBN   978-1-107-69697-6   Paperback

# Contents

# Figures

# Maps

# Acknowledgments

I am deeply grateful to the Social Science and Humanities Research Council of Canada, which made possible the bulk of the research for this book, as well as the Victoria College Senate, which supported archival trips to Yaoundé and Washington. The Department of History at the University of Toronto generously covered the costs associated with using Rodger/Magnum photos. Victoria College defrayed costs for the index and the cover.

The Jackman Humanities Institute allowed me to focus on research thanks to a six-month teaching release fellowship. A visiting fellowship at Saint Andrews University, and Stephen Tyre's hospitality on location, proved fruitful during the writing phase. Chapter 3 owes them a hint of Scottish thistle that even the sharpest reader might miss.

I wish to thank the many colleagues who provided advice along the way. I am particularly grateful to Joseph Owona Ntsama and Kane Aliou, who kindly assisted me during my research trips to Yaoundé and Brazzaville, respectively. Other Africanists provided crucial advice especially early on in this project, among them Guillaume Lachenal, Florence Bernault, Tamara Giles-Vernick, Alexie Tcheuyap, Charlotte Walker-Said, Phyllis Martin, Alexander Keese, Jeremy Rich, Odile Goerg, Gregory Mann, Jean-Pierre Bat, François Dumasy, Nora Greani, Owen White, William Clarence-Smith, and Catherine Coquery-Vidrovitch. Archivists shaped this project in many ways; I wish to recognize the support provided by Jacques and Isabelle Dion and Marie-André Durand at the colonial archives in Aix-en-Provence, Jean-Marie Ntonta at the National Archives of the Republic of Congo, Eugène Loubou at the Brazzaville municipal archives, Valdimir Trouplin at the Ordre de la

Libération, Anne-Sophie Cras at the Nantes archives, Christine Lévisse-Touzé at the Mémorial Leclerc, Philippe Oulmont and Nathalie Sage Prachère at the Fondation Charles de Gaulle, Kerstin Meincke and Robert Knodt at the Folkwang Museum, and Captain Eric Warnant and Mrs. Icard at the CHETOM in Fréjus. Paule René-Bazin consistently shared fruitful information on military archives.

Katie Edwards generously took the time to photograph the Dudley Harmon papers at Smith College, Kirsten James did the same with relevant files at the British National Archives, Ruth Ginio at the National Archives of Sénégal, Françoise Passsera with the Boislambert papers in Caen, Matt Swagler with a file I missed in Brazzaville, and Dustin Harris with the Géraud collection that was deposited to the Aix-en-Provence archives as this project was being completed. Brett Lintott graciously shared some of his findings at the UK national archives derived from decrypted German signals. I am grateful for the input of those in attendance at several venues where drafts of chapters were presented, including Hélène Blais, Gregory Mann, Stephen Tyre, Pierre Singaravélou, Jean-François Muracciole, and Emmanuelle Sibeud.

I wish to express my gratitude to a large team at Cambridge University Press including Kate Gavino, Eric Crahan, William Hammell, Joshua Penney, Dona Hightower Perkins, and the copy editors at Aptara. Thanks to Celia Braves for taking on the indexing. Special thanks go out to those who patiently read part or all of the manuscript: Alice Conklin and Frederick Cooper helped immeasurably with matters of calibration, comparison, and chapter sequence; Olivier Wieviorka considerably improved the flow of the text; and Marc Olivier Baruch, Raphaëlle Branche, Ruth Ginio, Chantal Bertrand-Jennings, and Lawrence Jennings all provided helpful feedback. Thanks to Tina Freris for her careful reading and constant support. Finally, I wish to dedicate this book to our daughters Alexandra and Sophie.

# Archival Abbreviations

| | |
|---|---|
| ADN | Archives diplomatiques de Nantes |
| AFCF | Archives de la Fraternité des Capucins de France, Paris |
| AMB | Archives municipales de Brazzaville |
| AMC | Archives du Mémorial de Caen |
| AML | Archives du Mémorial du Maréchal Leclerc, Paris |
| ANC | Archives nationales de la République du Congo, Brazzaville |
| ANCMR | Archives nationales du Cameroun, Yaoundé |
| ANF | Archives nationales de France, Paris |
| ANOM | Archives nationales d'outre-mer, Aix-en-Provence |
| ANS | Archives nationales du Sénégal, Dakar |
| AOL | Archives de l'Ordre de la Libération, Paris |
| BD | Bodleian Archives, Oxford |
| CHETOM | Centre d'histoire et d'études des troupes d'outre-mer, Fréjus |
| CMA | Archives of the Christian and Missionary Alliance, Colorado Springs |
| CSE | Archives de la Congrégation du Saint-Esprit, Chevilly-Larue |
| FCDG | Archives de la Fondation Charles de Gaulle, Paris |
| FLK | Museum Folkwang Archives, Essen |
| NARA | National Archives and Records Administration, College Park, Maryland |
| NAUK | National Archives of the United Kingdom, London |
| SHD | Service historique de la défense, Vincennes |
| SSCSC | Smith College, Sophia Smith Collection, Northampton, Massachusetts |

# Glossary

**Bataillon de marche:** Basic military unit in Free French Africa (abbreviated to B.M.).

**Carlton Gardens:** General de Gaulle's headquarters in London.

**Chicotte or Chicote:** A whip made of hippopotamus hide, widely used in the colonial era in the Belgian and French Congo.

**Corvée:** A form of statute labor imposed on colonial subjects.

**The Cross of Lorraine:** Symbol of de Gaulle's Free French and Fighting French movements.

**D.B.:** Division blindée, or armoured division.

**D.F.L.:** Division française libre, or Free French division.

**FEA:** French Equatorial Africa, a federation that included the colonies of Chad, Oubangui-Chari, Moyen-Congo, and Gabon, and whose capital was Brazzaville.

**F.F.I.:** Forces françaises de l'Intérieur. The makeshift Gaullist army born of the resistance in mainland France.

**Free France/Fighting France:** General de Gaulle's movement changed names in 1942, becoming "Fighting France" although many sources continued to speak of the "Free French."

**Maquis:** Rural guerrilla units of the Resistance in World War II France, comprised at first of men who avoided labor conscription in Germany.

**Prestations/Prestataires:** A form of statute labor imposed on colonial subjects.

**RTST:** Régiment des Tirailleurs Sénégalais du Tchad (military unit hailing from Chad, but not "Senegalese," contrary to what its name suggests).

**Tirailleur:** French term from the colonial era used to designate an African soldier.

## Place Names in the Colonial Era and Today

Fort-Archambault = modern-day Sahr, Chad
Fort-Lamy = modern-day N'Djamena, Chad
Fort-Rousset = modern-day Owando, Republic of Congo
Leopoldville = modern-day Kinshasa, Democratic Republic of Congo
Oubangui-Chari = modern-day Central African Republic (previously known also as Centrafrique)

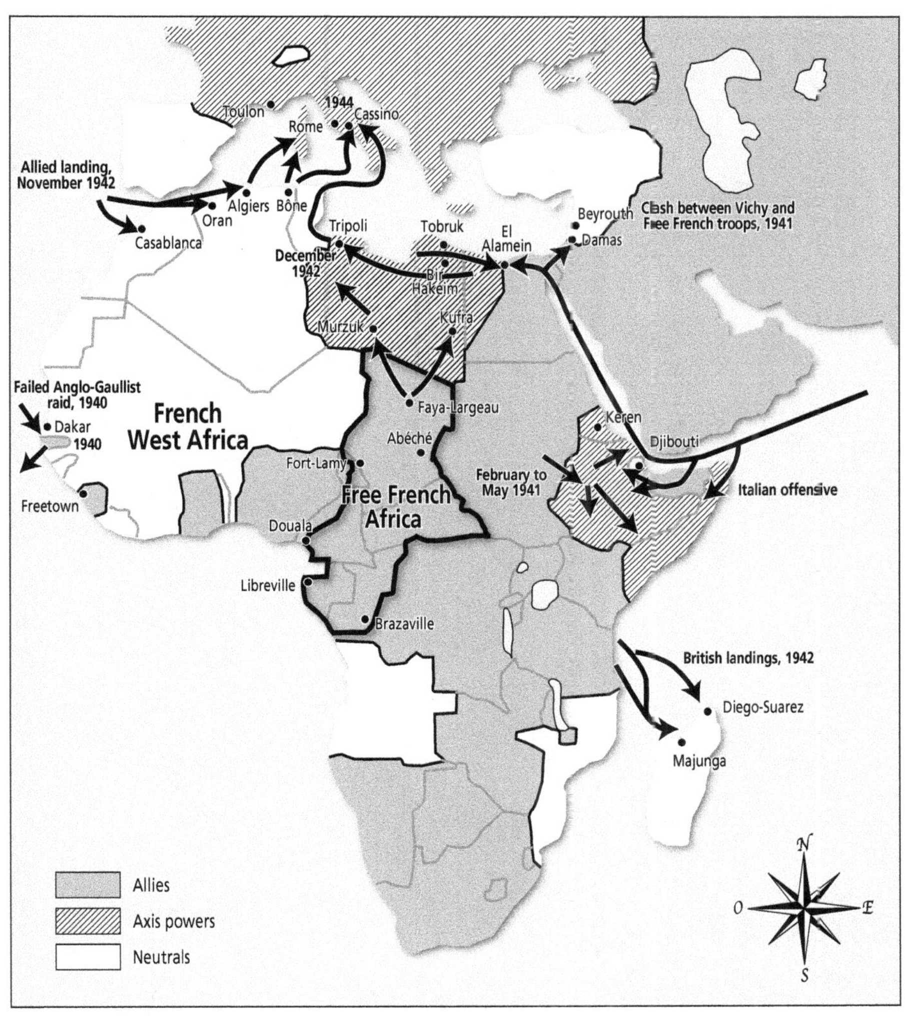


MAP 1. Free French Africa in World War II

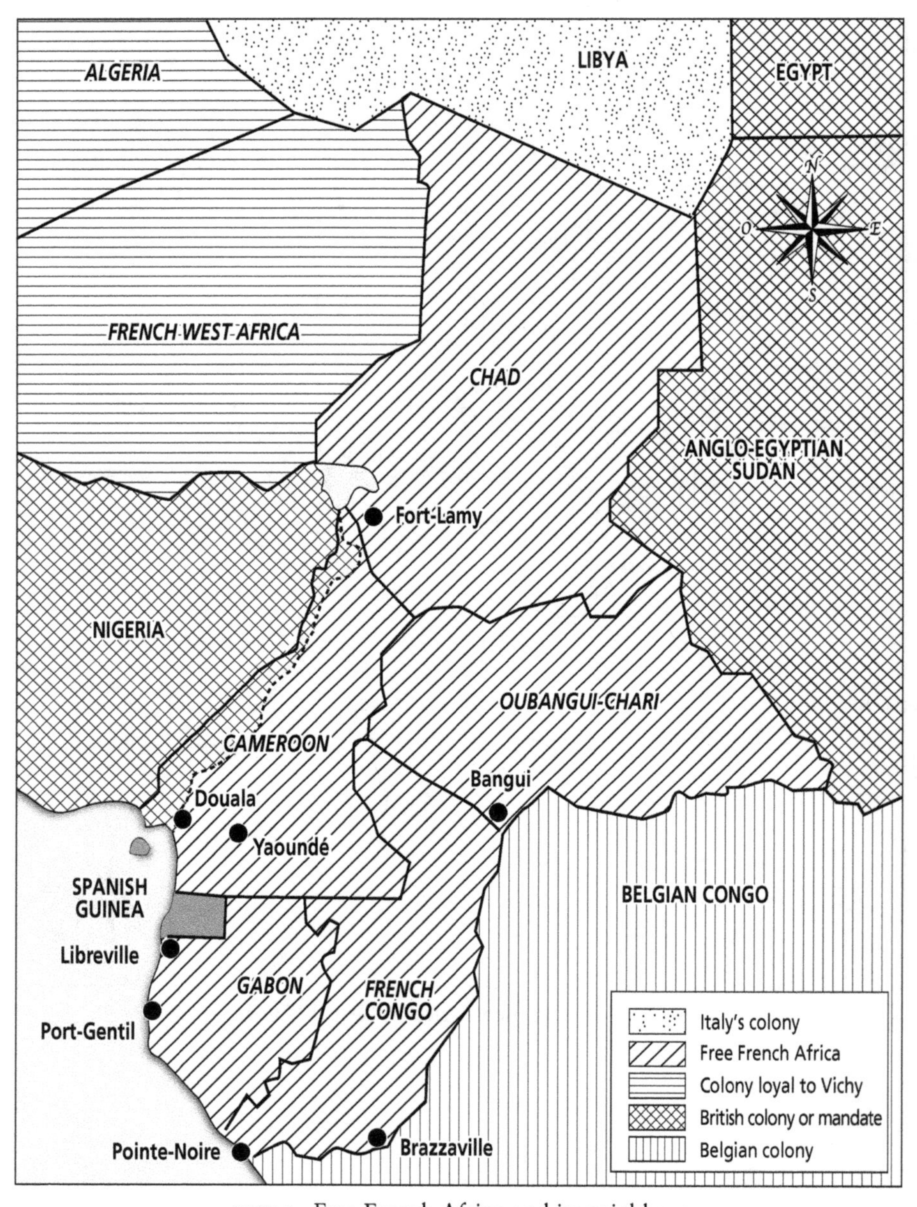


MAP 2. Free French Africa and its neighbors

# Introduction

In June 1940, France crumbled under the German blitzkrieg. The roughly forty thousand Africans[1] in French uniform during the May–June campaign fought valiantly and died in droves during the brief and tragic Battle of France. German forces infamously committed war crimes against African soldiers who had surrendered, summarily executing approximately 3,000 of them immediately after fighting ceased.[2] Nazi propaganda reels mocked African prisoners and derided the French high command for using black combatants. Captured black troops, hailing predominantly from French West Africa, would spend much of the remainder of the war in prisoner camps, guarded first by Germans, then astonishingly as of 1943, by Vichy French guards.[3]

These events are well established, recounted by historians, some of the stock images shown and re-shown in documentaries starting with *The Sorrow and the Pity*. What seems less recognized is that only months after France's defeat, another army was raised in French Africa to fight the Nazis. In late August 1940, Charles de Gaulle's Free French seized

[1] Estimates vary: Julien Fargettas advances the figure of 40,000 Africans in uniform in France in 1940, but of 200,000 troops raised by France in Africa in total (most had not yet reached France at the time of the June 1940 defeat). Myron Echenberg mentions roughly 75,000 African forces in France in 1940. Julien Fargettas, *Les Tirailleurs Sénégalais* (Paris: Tallandier, 2012), p. 20. Myron Echenberg, *Colonial Conscripts: The Tirailleurs Sénégalais in French West Africa, 1857–1960* (Portsmouth: Heinemann, 1991), p. 88.

[2] Raffael Scheck, *Hitler's African Victims: The German Army Massacres of Black French Soldiers in 1940* (Cambridge: Cambridge University Press, 2006), pp. 53, 165.

[3] Martin Thomas, "The Vichy Government and French Colonial Prisoners of War, 1940–1944," *French Historical Studies* 25:4 (Fall 2002), pp. 657–92. Armelle Mabon, *Prisonniers de guerre "indigènes"* (Paris: La Découverte, 2010).

Cameroon and French Equatorial Africa (FEA), vast territories spanning from south of the equator to the Sahara. They promptly turned them into the first hotbed of French resistance. Free French Africa lent immediate credibility, legitimacy, manpower, and revenue to de Gaulle's movement in its infancy, when it was most fragile. It is the story of this improbable French military and institutional rebirth through Central Africa that I wish to tell here.

"With what rage anti-Gaullists of both the left and the right, the Communists and the Vichyites, relentlessly propagate the myth of a London Resistance. To both sides, I counter with the truth: Free France was African."[4] So claimed prominent Free Frenchman and ethnologist Jacques Soustelle in his memoirs. Indeed, in the fall of 1940, London offered Free France neither combatants, raw materials, territory, nor sovereignty. Territorially, Free France spanned from the Libyan border with Chad to the Congo River, and to the scattered small French territories of the South Pacific and India.[5] Without the support of these colonial holdings, what credibility, what international recognition, what counterweight to Vichy's legitimacy could a maverick general in London have mustered? While we now know in detail the motivations of Félix Eboué, the black Guyanese governor who rallied Chad to de Gaulle on August 26, 1940, not to mention the exploits of the French domestic resistance, the fate of the first Gaullist bastions of FEA and Cameroon has remained curiously overlooked, save for a handful of specialized French-language studies concentrating predominantly on Gabon and Cameroon.[6]

Between August 1940 and the summer of 1943, the heart of Free France was not located in London, as standard accounts would have us believe, but rather in Free French Africa. Instead of a beret-coiffed white *maquisard* in the Alps, the archetypal early French resistance fighter between

---

[4] Jacques Soustelle, *Envers et contre tout* (Paris: Robert Laffont, 1947), p. 125.

[5] On the complicated rallying of New Caledonia and on Free France in the Pacific theater, see Kim Munholland, *Rock of Contention: Free French and Americans at War in New Caledonia, 1940–1945* (New York: Berghahn, 2005). On regime change in the rest of the French South Pacific, see Jean-Marc Regnault and Ismet Kurtovitch, "Les ralliements du Pacifique en 1940. Entre légende gaulliste, enjeux stratégiques mondiaux et rivalités Londres/Vichy," *Revue d'histoire moderne et contemporaine* 49, 4, 2002, pp. 71–90.

[6] Léon Modeste Nnang Ndong, *L'effort de guerre de l'Afrique: le Gabon dans la deuxième guerre mondiale, 1939–1947* (Paris: L'Harmattan, 2011); Eliane Ebako, "Le ralliement du Gabon à la France libre: une guerre franco-française," PhD thesis, University of Paris IV, 2004; Léonard Sah, "Le Cameroun sous mandat français dans la deuxième guerre mondiale," PhD thesis, University of Provence, 1998; Jérôme Ollandet, *Brazzaville, capitale de la France libre: histoire de la résistance française en Afrique, 1940–1944* (Brazzaville: Editions de la Savane, 1980).

1940 and 1943 was, in fact, black and hailed from Chad, Cameroon, or Oubangui-Chari (modern-day Central African Republic). Some of these early fighters volunteered; others did not. For a movement whose glory rested in part on the notion of personal and patriotic commitment, this revelation alone shifts our understanding of Free French ranks. In addition, histories of the Resistance teach us that the metropolitan French maquis only gained momentum in 1943; we also know from Jean-François Muracciole's work that between the fiasco at Dakar on September 25, 1940, and the end of 1942, Free France struggled mightily to recruit outside of its colonial holdings.[7] It is thus tempting to situate the lion's share of the first armed French resistance between the Sahara Desert and the Congo River. This of course, leads us to "rethink France from its colonies,"[8] a current historiographical trend, and already a pressing imperative of General de Gaulle's in 1940. Indeed, one of de Gaulle's first steps involved his June 1940 calls exhorting colonials to join him, if possible with their territories.

Has the story of Free French Africa really been forgotten? Aside from a few exceptions such as at the Mont Valérien memorial outside of Paris, one looks in vain for plaques or testimonials to FEA and Cameroon's contribution to the Free French cause. To be sure, recent histories have recognized the crucial role of French colonial troops in general during the twentieth century's two world wars. The topic, broadly conceived, even captured the public imagination with the release of Rachid Bouchareb's 2006 film *Indigènes,* dubiously translated into English as *Days of Glory.* A year later, Jean-François Muracciole, François Broche, and Georges Caïtucoli broke a taboo by asserting that "the majority of the Free French who saved the nation's honor in 1940 were not French citizens."[9] But even here, FEA and Cameroon's contributions remained largely underrecognized. Many a narrative, starting with Bouchareb's film, commences in 1943 with French North and West Africa's entry into the fray. This broken chronology has served to obscure another reality and memory: the tens of thousands of Chadian, Congolese, Cameroonian, Gabonese, and Central African soldiers in de Gaulle's camp since

---

7 Jean-François Muracciole, *Les Français libres: l'autre résistance* (Paris: Tallandier, 2009), pp. 135–36.

8 Frederick Cooper, *Colonialism in Question: Theory, Knowledge, History* (Berkeley: University of California Press, 2005), p. 22.

9 François Broche, Georges Caïtucoli, Jean-François Muracciole, *La France au combat: de l'appel du 18 juin à la victoire* (Paris: Perrin, 2007), p. 149.

August 1940, who managed to wage battle against the Axis from early 1941 onwards.

My research reveals the extent of FEA and Cameroon's effort starting in 1940. Between 1940 and 1944, Free France recruited 17,013 Africans in these territories. One should add to this total the troops already on location in these regions when they swung over to General de Gaulle: 16,500 men according to Jean-Louis Crémieux-Brilhac, 7,000 according to other estimates.[10] A possible overlap may exist between the two groups, for FEA and Cameroon rallied de Gaulle in August 1940. A small portion of the possible 33,513 total might therefore be counted twice. Allowing for this corrective leads me to a conservative estimate of 27,000 men in arms from FEA and Cameroon – either hailing from these territories, or already posted on them in August 1940. To be sure, this figure is lower than the number of Africans who fought in French uniform during the Battle of France in May and June 1940. But the fact remains that outside of the West Africans posted to FEA and Cameroon, West African troops found themselves out of combat between 1940 and 1943, either in prison camps in France or languishing in Vichy-controlled French West Africa. In fact, the figure of 27,000 men from FEA and Cameroon appears startlingly high when compared to Free French totals: estimates for the summer of 1943 place Free French numbers at approximately 73,000 broken into roughly 39,000 French citizens, 30,000 colonial subjects, and some 3,800 foreign nationals.[11] Given that other colonies like the French South Pacific also contributed men on top of FEA and Cameroon's 27,000 or more, the figure of 30,000 colonial troops in 1943 certainly needs to be revised upwards.

In other words, the Hollywood cliché of the average Free French soldier seems in dire need of re-writing. The actual diversity and cosmopolitanism of Free French ranks is surely more evocative than film can convey: in 1942, ethnic Sara men from Chad and Oubangui-Chari fought side by side with German Jewish and Spanish republican French foreign legionnaires in the Sahara. After traversing endless expanses of desert from their bases

[10] ANOM DSM 262, 3, table 4. The figure of 16,500 men appeared in Jean-Louis Crémieux-Brilhac, "La France Libre" in Jean-Pierre Azéma and François Bédarida, eds., *La France des années noires* (Paris: Le Seuil, 1993), p. 194. Others subsequently took it up. See Philippe Oulmont, "Le haut-commissaire de l'Afrique française libre" in Philippe Oulmont, ed., *Larminat, un fidèle hors série* (Paris: L.B.M., 2008), p. 77, as well as Jean-Christophe Notin, *Leclerc* (Paris: Perrin, 2005), p. 108.

[11] Muracciole, pp. 36–37; François Broche, Georges Caïtucoli, Jean-François Muracciole, p. 149.

in Chad, men united in their common demonization by Hitler confronted Erwin Rommel's forces head on.

This brings us to FEA's important strategic role. In 1941, then Colonel Leclerc used Chad as a base from which to attack Benito Mussolini's Libya. Free French Africa also brought de Gaulle legitimacy, territories, and subjects, making Free France not just a movement but also a government. De Gaulle readily recognized this. He wrote that in 1940, "in the vast expanses of Africa, France could rebuild its army and its sovereignty."[12]

If Free France was African, I should underscore from the outset that Africa was not free. Indeed, forced labor redoubled under Gaullist rule, coerced military recruitment as well. Gaullist Jurist René Cassin and Governor Félix Eboué clashed on the topic, the former fearing that Free France might be accused of slavery-like practices. The overriding imperative of waging war on the Axis was used to justify many a sacrifice and many a violation of Free France's own ideals.

The rallying of FEA and Cameroon in August 1940 would later be mythologized, the event earning the French revolutionary designation of "three glorious days." But at the time, the change triggered much turmoil. Prior to the war, 90 percent of FEA and Cameroon's exports had gone to continental Europe, the vast majority to France. That market was now closed. The region's economy was entirely redirected into the British imperial orbit. There too the stakes were high. The archives show that administrators and corporations never managed to overcome their differences, in the gold and timber sectors most notably. The Free French episode in Africa reveals much discord in a time of imperial reordering.

A skeptic might counter that Free France's military saga, at least, is known down to its last details. Admittedly, Free France's first victories are renowned. So too are the colorful details of Philippe Leclerc's meteoric ascension, as he added colonel's stripes to his uniform to facilitate Free France's seizure of Cameroon on August 27, 1940. Likewise in France, the "Kufra oath" remains legendary in military circles: Leclerc's pledge in the Libyan desert that he would never relent until the liberation of Strasbourg. All the more reason to reexamine this history through African and colonial lenses. For in the memoirs relating these early Free French exploits, as in histories of the Free French movement, Africans and Africa appear at once ubiquitous and invisible. Most relevant memoirs tend to specify the name of each fallen white soldier, followed by a figure,

---

[12] Charles de Gaulle, *Mémoires de Guerre* (Paris: Plon, 1954), Vol. 1, p. 89.

usually much higher, reflecting anonymous African losses. Free France's Africanness has seldom been foregrounded.

One of my objectives involves recovering African voices, actions, roles, and conditions. Not merely for soldiers, but also for truckers, miners, chiefs, porters, workers, seamstresses, orderlies, rubber collectors, all of whom played a role in Free France's African history. My goal is to measure not only how Africans contributed to the Gaullist cause, but also the ways the war and Free France mattered to Africans. How? Firstly by naming African workers, civilians, and military personnel whenever possible – a seemingly modest aim, but a significant one in light of how rarely this has been done to date. Next, by tapping into a panoply of sources to reconstitute prevailing conditions in Free French Africa. I have utilized letters, telegrams, reports, logs, journals, and memoirs, of course, but also pictures taken by titans of photography like George Rodger and Germaine Krull. Finally, whenever possible, I have attempted to recover African voices. The task proved less challenging that I first feared, for African testimonies and grievances abound in legal and military files. One must admittedly place such evidence in context and account for filters, self-censorship, and questions of transcription, literacy, intermediaries, scribes, and so on.

While I make limited use of some interviews conducted by historians in the 1980s, I have not undertaken my own oral history. Indeed, surviving African soldiers from this era are now in their nineties; non-commissioned officers (hereafter NCOs) over a hundred years old. Average life expectancy does not help: in Chad it stands at 48.9 years, in Cameroon 50.6, in the Republic of Congo 54.27, and in the Central African Republic at 46.9 years, before the current civil war.[13] The French press reported in 2011 that Joseph Djemakangar, the last surviving African combatant from the 1941 Free French victory at Kufra, had passed away.[14] What is more, even if I had arranged interviews with members of the next generation, this project's chronological sensitivity, its focus on shifts and breaks over a short four-year period, its political, social, and military focus all render pertinent, reliable, and sharp testimonies virtually impossible to gather seventy-five years on. Methodologically and intellectually I also reject the notion that oral history should

---

[13] World Bank data, available online.

[14] Marianne online, April 9, 2011 (http://www.marianne.net/blogsecretdefense/Joseph-Djemakangar-un-tirailleur-de-Koufra-s-eteint_a217.html). While the article does not explicitly state that Djemakangar was the last African survivor of the battle, I deduce this (perhaps wrongly) from Daniel Nevot's claim of being "the last survivor of Kufra."

be mandatory for conducting African history when it is patently not for other historical fields.

This is not to suggest that my approach is somehow militant or an example of what Frederick Cooper terms "doing history backwards." Instead of calling for a redress in African pensions,[15] my objective is to re-center Free France in Africa. I also have opted to focus largely on practices rather than representations. Nor am I intent on simply projecting French categories of resistance and collaboration onto Africa. Instead, it is the centrality of Africa to Free France that I attempt to reconstitute in this book. I posit the Africanness of Free France on a number of levels: the Gaullist troops engaged at Kufra (1941) and in the Fezzan (1942–43) were overwhelmingly African. Free France's territorial legitimacy stemmed almost entirely from Equatorial Africa and Cameroon; indeed, Brazzaville served as the movement's official capital from 1940 to 1943. Likewise, Fighting France's fiscal and mining assets and other natural resources were predominantly African. If General de Gaulle's regime moved its capital to Algiers in 1943, and thereafter North and West African troops did begin to play crucial roles, the fact remains that for the first three years of its existence, Free France had been tethered to sub-Saharan Africa and built on it.

I will largely steer clear from one of the best-known events held in Brazzaville late in the war, as it is mostly peripheral to the story of Free French Africa. The Brazzaville conference of 1944 has often been depicted as an attempt at colonial reform, or even a step toward decolonization. Admittedly, the event did introduce, and in some cases confirm, a significant reformist spirit. But mostly the conference looked to the postwar, and marked above all a break with the war period that concerns us here. I will therefore raise it in the epilogue while avoiding teleological temptation. Here I also break with current practice, which involves mentioning Free French Africa only at its extremities, which is to say at its inception in August 1940 and then once more at the 1944 Brazzaville conference.[16]

This book draws its sources in numerous archives including holdings in sub-Saharan Africa, long overlooked by historians of World War II. The national archives of Cameroon in Yaoundé and of the Republic of

---

[15] Cooper, *Colonialism*, p. 18. For examples of militant histories centering on the question of pensions, see Charles Onana, *La France et ses tirailleurs: Enquêtes sur les combattants de la République* (Paris: Duboiris, 2003); Bakari Kamian, *Des tranchées de Verdun à l'église Saint-Bernard* (Paris: Karthala, 2001).

[16] For an example, see Paul-Marie de la Gorce, *L'Empire écartelé, 1936–1946* (Paris: Denoël, 1988).

Congo in Brazzaville both yielded valuable material. Archival partitioning during decolonization saw France take so-called *fonds de souveraineté*, while African nations retained *fonds de gestion.* Consequently, some of the most fecund material for social history has remained on location.[17] This said, archives in France also proved crucial for this study, even shedding light on the earliest Free French period marked by a relative lack of documentation because of its high degree of improvisation. I relied especially on the extraordinarily rich collections at the French colonial archives in Aix-en-Provence. The Centre d'histoire et d'études des troupes d'outre-mer (CHETOM) in Fréjus and the military archives in Vincennes revealed much about troop conditions. Also very useful were a bevy of sources in Paris, most notably the archives of the Ordre de la Libération and those of the de Gaulle and Leclerc foundations. So too were the high commissioner to Free French Africa fonds held at the diplomatic archives in Nantes. Several collections in the United States, the United Kingdom, and Germany helped flesh out the picture. Indeed, foreign Free French volunteers like Hassoldt Davis, Germaine Krull, George Rodger, and Dudley Harmon left remarkably insightful visual and textual testimonies on Free French Africa. Together, these varied sources allowed me to weave together a study at the intersection of the histories of Africa, empire, and World War II.

Free France largely rested and depended on Africa. Africans shaped it and it affected them. Over the next three parts, I will expose the many forms of this relationship: in matters of legitimacy, with respect to military affairs, and the extraction of natural resources. Finally, in the epilogue I shall turn to questions of memory and its uses in the postwar.

---

[17] Jean-Pierre Bat, "Les archives de l'AEF," *Afrique et histoire* 7, 2009, pp. 301–11.

# PART I

# FREE FRANCE'S AFRICAN GAMBIT

# Introduction to Part I

Historians have long depicted World War II as a catalyst for national emancipation movements, or for the decolonization process, depending on one's perspective. In most narratives, the war typically takes its place as a stage en route to the end of empires. Various arguments are advanced: "the blood tax" shed by native combatants, the psychological impact of the defeat of European troops by Japanese forces in Asia, the collapse of multiple colonial motherlands, a heightened awareness of the evils of Hitlerian racism, the "awakening" of nationalisms, or the propitious opportunity provided nationalists in India, Indonesia, and Vietnam. To be sure, some have distinguished between a first wave of decolonization in Asia following closely on the heels of World War II, and a later wave in Africa several decades later. Historians like Frederick Cooper and John Darwin have also nuanced the issue, insisting on post-1945 late imperial recastings.[1] Yet even within the internal, teleological logic of World War II as a harbinger of decolonization, the moment of rupture has remained surprisingly understudied. It occurred in 1940 in the Free French case, in 1940 and again in 1942 in the Dutch East Indies, and in 1941 and 1942 for several British territories in Asia. These moments reveal imperial schisms, abrupt reorientations, and dramatic imperial reconfigurations, with former Dutch, French, and British territories colonized anew by Japan, for instance. They also concern a host of imperial contexts: to

---

[1] Frederick Cooper, *Citizenship between Empire and Nation: Remaking France and French Africa, 1945–1960* (Princeton: Princeton University Press, 2014). John Darwin, *The Empire Project: The Rise and Fall of the British World System* (Cambridge: Cambridge University Press, 2009).

the Dutch territories in the Caribbean and Oceania, one could add the Belgian and Danish colonies.

One can discern multiple scenarios, although certain patterns do emerge. The Danish monarchy remained in place in the wake of the defeat of 1940, but in April 1941 the United States signed an agreement that granted Roosevelt the authority to protect the vastest Danish colony, Greenland, from Nazi incursions. It even permitted U.S. bases on the island. Washington recognized Copenhagen's rights over Greenland, and pledged to return the territory at the war's conclusion.[2] Similarly, following the German onslaught in Norway and Denmark in 1940, the British invaded the Faroe Islands and Iceland preventatively. The vast Belgian and Dutch overseas territories remained in the British orbit because their metropoles signed no armistice involving colonies. The situation only changed in the Dutch case when the Japanese seized the Dutch East Indies (present-day Indonesia) in 1942. The Free French jurist René Cassin enviously evoked the "purely military and local"[3] nature of the Dutch 1940 capitulation, implicitly contrasting it with the French one that opened the door for collaboration and the siding of most French colonies with Vichy. Indeed, Vichy's collaboration hinged on the colonies as a bargaining chip. In the Belgian Congo, one saw a virtual repeat of the events of the previous world war, during which the vast African territory had remained on the triple entente side, while the motherland was largely occupied by Germany. During World War II, then, the French colonial nation-state bucked the international trend. The only preexisting nation to have concluded an armistice that fostered collaboration with the Third Reich, its colonies remained in the Vichy camp, with only a handful of exceptions. From Cayenne to Hanoi, by way of Saint-Pierre and Miquelon, Fort-de-France, Dakar, Conakry, Abidjan, Tananarive, the Kerguelen Islands, and Saint-Denis de la Réunion, the vast majority of "greater France" remained faithful to Marshal Philippe Pétain.

In this sense, Vichy constitutes the colonial exception, while the few colonies that rallied to General de Gaulle's Free France in 1940 followed a much more conventional path. FEA and Cameroon's exceptionality in the French colonial realm can thus be directly contrasted with their orthodoxy and exemplarity on an international scale. According to Gerhard Weinberg, this disparity can be explained by the fact that French

---

[2] Gerhard Weinberg, *A World at Arms: A Global History of World War II* (Cambridge: Cambridge University Press, 1994), p. 242.

[3] René Cassin, *Des hommes partis de rien* (Paris: Plon, 1974), p. 264.

authorities feared British designs on their colonies far more than did their Dutch and Belgian counterparts.[4] One could obviously reverse the argument: without the tragedy of Mers-el-Kébir, during which the British sank a large percentage of the French navy in port in Algeria on July 3, 1940, French apprehensions concerning British ambitions might have been dissipated.[5]

Whatever the cause, Free French authorities were clearly conscious of colonial advantages and asymmetries. The Gaullists never failed to brandish their colonies before the "club" of other defeated colonial nation-states now needing to rely mainly on the Belgian Congo, Surinam, the Dutch East Indies, and the Netherland West Indies since the occupation of the Low Countries in Europe. For instance, in August 1942 in London, Free France's Colonial Commissioner René Pleven invited the following guests to mark the rallying of FEA and Cameroon to General de Gaulle: Lord Malcolm Haily and Harold MacMillan of the British Colonial Ministry, Bernard Bourdillon, governor of Nigeria, Doctor Hubertus Van Mook, Dutch minister of the colonies, as well as his associate Dr. A. Muhlenfeld, Paul-Henri Spaak the Belgian Foreign Minister, and finally, Emile Gorlia and J. Jennen of the Belgian Colonial Ministry.[6] In the supraimperial British capital, the three untethered European empires rubbed shoulders. Nine months later, René Pleven gave a lecture in London in which he insisted on the reciprocity and cooperation between these different unbound empires. According to him, FEA and Cameroon were now in a position to replace, at least partially, the raw materials previously obtained from British Malaya and the Dutch East Indies, both of which had now fallen to the Japanese. Pleven even suggested that British support for the rallying of FEA and Cameroon in 1940 had now born fruit.[7] Thus, Free France clearly used the colonies to tilt the balance in its favor. FEA and Cameroon, which from the outset represented a vaster surface than the Belgian and Dutch colonies, now revealed themselves to be the most essential colonial territories of movements in Britain's orbit, at least according to Pleven. In the coming chapters, this importance will become clear in both the military realm and in terms of human and natural resources.

[4] Weinberg, p. 160.

[5] The question becomes intractable if one considers that in the British perspective, the Mers el-Kébir tragedy resulted from the French armistice and a French willingness to work with the German victors.

[6] ANOM Cab 48, second anniversary of the rallying of Free French Africa.

[7] ANOM Cab 48, file 282.

Beyond the question of colonial rank, the fact that FEA and Cameroon rallied to de Gaulle in August 1940 also presents strong analogies with the Dutch and Belgian colonial contexts. For contrary to what the Gaullist myth suggests, like these other Allied colonies, FEA and Cameroon entered into the British orbit, which implied a complete reorganization of their economies. From a geostrategic standpoint, once Hitler invaded the U.S.S.R. in June 1941, FEA and Cameroon allowed the Allies to establish an east-west corridor in Africa running between Nigeria and Egypt. It linked the main fronts at a time when an Axis curtain extended from Norway in the North to Libya in the South. This African corridor constituted a vital point of access to the Egyptian, Middle Eastern, and East African fronts. Between September 1940 and July 1943, more than 25,000 Allied aircraft transited through FEA, mostly across Chad.[8] Indeed, Winston Churchill mentioned the utility of this air route in his memoirs.[9] FEA and the Belgian Congo also formed a north-south cluster of colonies cooperating to liberate their metropoles. Finally, FEA and Cameroon offered the promise of legitimacy, a territorial base for a previously nomadic and expatriate movement, a reserve of men and resources, and mostly an alternative empire possessing its inherent logic, codes, legislation, and even its own colonial ambitions.

How did FEA and Cameroon join the Free French camp in 1940, and how did French West Africa conversely come to fall under Vichy's boot? No formula could have predicted it. The colonized were not consulted, colonials either for the most part. The decision hinged on startlingly little. The geographical contours of French West Africa lent it a coherency, a relative autonomy, and tactical robustness that FEA and Cameroon arguably lacked. The latter were more dependent on neighboring territories like the Belgian Congo, Nigeria, and the British Sudan. Other considerations certainly factored in. René Cassin deemed that "the Free French were well inspired to take their efforts in August 1940 to the least organized territories, furthest from the sea, rather than to Dakar." In his eyes, the British-Gaullist fiasco of September 1940 in Dakar, during which Vichy repelled Churchill and de Gaulle's seaborne assault on the African port city, was due to the fact that part of Vichy's fleet had managed to pass the Strait of Gibraltar to reach Senegal.[10] For his part, de Gaulle explained as

---

[8] ANOM DSM 262.

[9] Winston Churchill, *The Second World War*, Vol. 2, "Their Finest Hour" (Boston: Houghton Mifflin, 1949), p. 494.

[10] Cassin, pp. 189 and 197.

follows the difference of results his movement experienced in West versus Equatorial Africa in 1940: "In West Africa, authority was highly centralized, and closely linked to those in office in North Africa. West Africa boasted considerable military assets... Finally [in West Africa] Governor General Boisson, an energetic man, whose ambition was greater than his discernment, had chosen to take Vichy's cause."[11] According to the general, individual choices, starting with the decisions of high-ranking officials in Algeria and Morocco, had created a kind of imperial domino effect. Inertia did the rest.

Individual decisions and networks did indeed play determining roles in the chaos of the 1940 French military debacle, followed at a distance by disoriented colonials. Gaullist dissidents in Chad, Cameroon, and the French Congo established close links with Nigeria, with the slice of Cameroon under British mandate, as well as with sympathetic parties in the Belgian Congo. In Chad, the trio composed of Governor Félix Eboué, Henri Laurentie, and Colonel Marchand relied on British connections to withstand Vichyite Pierre Boisson's pressure on them. In FEA and Cameroon, Gaullist emissaries from without joined and soon coordinated networks within, comprised of both Europeans and Africans determined to continue the fight against the Axis. The moment chosen to rally FEA and Cameroon between August 26 and 28, 1940, also proved critical. The Gaullists in Cameroon were in the process of losing their advantage when Leclerc and his team arrived in the nick of time. In West Africa, conversely, if an opportune time ever existed, it was clearly missed. The attempt to rally the colony came from without, from a joint British-Gaullist naval expedition. The catastrophe of September 25 ensued: Vichy repelled the attack and issued jubilant propaganda depicting de Gaulle in Churchill's pay. From a Free French standpoint, the Dakar disaster of September 25, 1940, marked a major rupture. Thereafter, voluntary enrollments in the Free French movement dwindled. Over the next two years, the Free French effort would rely largely on colonial subjects.[12]

These few pages offered a brief overview of the global context. In the following three chapters, I will apply a magnifying glass to Free France's implantation in FEA and Cameroon, analyzing pitfalls, disillusions, expression of power, and sovereignty. Free France's African gambit was a delicate exercise, one that relied in large part on Africans, whose fate changed in 1940. Contrary to the Belgian Congo or the Dutch East

---

[11] De Gaulle, p. 122.
[12] Muracciole, pp. 135–36.

Indies, Free France's colonial experience was a maverick one. Other than the vast expanses of FEA and Cameroon, only the small French territories in India and the Pacific joined the Free French cause in 1940. Thereafter, colonies would have to be taken from Vichy by force, be it in Syria and Lebanon, or Saint-Pierre and Miquelon in 1941, or Madagascar in 1942. As the first sizeable areas controlled by Free France – Soustelle likened the distance between Pointe-Noire and the Tibesti Mountains to that between Toulouse and Moscow –[13] FEA and Cameroon would serve as both laboratories and guarantors of Gaullist legitimacy. According to the general's memoirs, the task involved "organizing in the center of Africa a base of action and sovereignty for the France that wished to continue the struggle."[14] The France in question was largely African.

[13] Soustelle, p. 93.
[14] De Gaulle, p. 128.

# Chapter 1

# Colonies Without Motherlands

## Regime Change

In June and early July 1940, General de Gaulle was the landless leader of a rebel movement. Professor Denis Saurat, who would soon voyage to Free French Africa, recalls the general's desperation during those long weeks: "'Give me some land,' the general kept saying, 'some land that is France. Anywhere. A French base. Somewhere to start from.'"[1] The tiny Franco-British New-Hebrides islands in the South Pacific answered his call on July 20, but this was hardly the base he had hoped for. Chad, Cameroon, Moyen-Congo, Gabon, and Oubangui-Chari became that fateful starting point in late August 1940.

Free French Africa was conceived in London, but born in Fort-Lamy (current N'Djamena), the capital of Chad, on August 26, 1940. The act of conception – de Gaulle's orders to a handful of trusted emissaries – is by far the best known of the two events. I will focus here on aspects that have been largely ignored: the broad context in which FEA and Cameroon came to join the Gaullist camp and the Free French quest for international legitimacy resting on Africa.

One of the leitmotifs in the telling and retelling of the events of August 1940 in FEA and Cameroon involves an emphasis on these territories as second-rank and counterintuitive starting points for the Free French cause. De Gaulle himself described them as "the poorest of our entire empire." Colonel René Boisseau added, "This movement of revolt that

---

[1] Denis Saurat, *Watch over Africa* (London: J. M. Dent and Sons, 1941), p. 7.

prefigured the magnificent political and military revival undertaken by France thereafter, started in FEA, which is to say the most backwards, the weakest colony." Another recurring trope involves the designation of the events of August 26, 27, and 28 as "the three glorious days." The reference to the Revolution of July 1830 in France was no accident. To Boisseau, the events in Africa like the nineteenth-century Parisian insurrection "marked the end of the divine monarchy and the coming to power of popular sovereignty." With hindsight, this seems a tenuous parallel. Although Vichy's authoritarianism leaves no doubt, Free France certainly fell short of embodying popular sovereignty, especially in Africa.[2] Moreover, the reality behind these territories shifting from Vichy to Free France was messier, less unanimous, and less predetermined than most testimonies allow. As Jean-Pierre Azéma has noted, "[the events of August 1940 in FEA and Cameroon] are more prosaic [than is usually imagined], while remaining singular, as is often the case when a small minority takes charge."[3]

From its very inception, Free France in London sought to rally colonies, but it lacked colonial experience. Battered but not beaten by the Battle of France, Captain Philippe de Hauteclocque visited the Wellcome Bureau in London on August 1, 1940, to receive vaccination against yellow fever. From there he set off to W. H. Gore and Company to be outfitted for the tropics.[4] The chrysalis process had begun. In less than a month he underwent a profound metamorphosis. He changed his name to François Leclerc so as to avoid reprisals against his family in France, and then transformed into a colonial.[5] By the time he arrived in Cameroon on August 27, he rose to the rank of colonel "as if by enchantment," noted de Gaulle whimsically.[6]

On August 6, Leclerc along with René Pleven, André Parant, and Claude Hettier de Boislambert, received the improbable mission of bringing African territories over to de Gaulle's side. Pleven boasted experience as the head of a telephone company, Parant as captain of a unit of Algerian troops during the Battle of France, and Boislambert was an avid big game

---

[2]  De Gaulle, *Mémoires de Guerre*, Vol. 1, p. 144. René Boisseau, *Les trois glorieuses de l'empire, 26–27–28 août 1940* (Paris: Office français d'édition, 1945), pp. 9–13.
[3]  Jean-Pierre Azéma, *1940, l'année terrible* (Paris: éditions du Seuil, 1990), p. 303.
[4]  AML, Leclerc 5a. Edgard de Larminat, *Chroniques irrévérencieuses* (Paris: Plon, 1962), p. 124.
[5]  Leclerc possessed some experience here, having previously served in Morocco.
[6]  Charles de Gaulle, *Mémoires de guerre*, Vol. 1, p. 120.

hunter who had served as liaison officer with the British. Of the three men, it was Boislambert who passed for a "specialist of black Africa"[7]– he who would end up a prisoner of Vichy after being captured during the failed Dakar operation of September 1940. Soon, Edgard de Larminat joined the team of conspirators. A veteran of the Battle of Verdun, this career officer possessed some colonial experience. On August 18, in Lagos, the group divvyed up their roles. A week later, from the slice of Cameroon under British mandate in the shadow of Mount Cameroon, as well as from the shores of the immense Congo River that separated Leopoldville (now Kinshasa) from Brazzaville, these Gaullist agents prepared to seize FEA and Cameroon from Vichy's clutches. They secured vital support from sympathetic Belgian and British officials. At the same time, from within, Governor Félix Eboué was poised to announce the rallying of Chad, which would mark the operation's starting point on August 26. The conspirators had established contacts within FEA, not merely with Eboué, but also with Africans who wished to continue the struggle. At this point, despite some unrest, French Congo, Cameroon, Oubangui-Chari, Chad, and Gabon had remained faithful to Pétain's Vichy regime. The ragtag team of adventurers sent from London to change this state of affairs bore code names that could have come from Hollywood: Sullivan, Douglas, and Charles. They were lightly armed. Cameroon was taken with seventeen pistols. As Jean Lacouture has observed, although the scheme succeeded, it resembled some bizarre "giant automobile rally," whose course was quite simply "outlandish."[8] I will now analyze several dimensions of the "three glorious days," which is to say the rallying of Chad on August 26, 1940, Cameroon on the 27th, and French Congo on the 28th.

## British Proximity and Support

Like the rallying of the New Hebrides and the tiny French colonies in India that same year, the "three glorious days" were largely conditioned by British aid and proximity. In fact, some historians have rejected the very term of "rallying" altogether to describe the events that concern us. Outside of Chad, they contend, all of the other territories went over to de Gaulle under external pressure, Vichy officials often having to be led

---

[7] Charles de Gaulle, *Lettres, notes et carnets*, p. 72.
[8] Jean Lacouture, *De Gaulle*, Vol. 1 (Paris: le Seuil, 1984), p. 433.

away at gunpoint.[9] I would add that the contiguity of British colonies like Nigeria proved decisive, as well as the broader 1940 geopolitical context. It bears reminding that in June 1940, Churchill and Jean Monnet had contemplated the creation of a single Franco-British citizenship, a veritable union between the two nations. In the colonial sphere, following discussions in March 1940, a permanent liaison office had been established linking the British Colonial Office and the French Ministry of the Colonies.[10] Locally in FEA and Cameroon, the very first rumblings of resistance involved just such a rapprochement with Britain. On June 22, 1940, the very day that France signed the armistice with Germany, an administrator in the Sanaga Maritime region of Cameroon reported to his superiors that "a few madcaps descended on Douala with the intention, they stated, of finding the British Consul and putting him in charge of Cameroon's destiny." The district head finally dissuaded them from this undertaking, by arguing that it risked "spreading concern among natives."[11] Sangfroid in the face of the colonized was no small matter as the motherland crumbled.

The tragic sinking of French naval vessels by the British at Mers el-Kébir Algeria on July 3, 1940, and the resulting death of 1,297 French sailors, sowed doubt in many a French official in Africa. Yet it did not scuttle a Franco-British rapprochement that was already strong in the regions that concern us. From the outside, in August 1940, British officials in Africa did their utmost to aid de Gaulle's delegates. The Secretary General in Nigeria, Miles Clifford, put Leclerc in touch with Frenchmen who had left Cameroon, relayed telegrams to him, handed him numerous maps, and provided him with a car. All of was this accompanied by attentive letters drafted in shaky French – but in French nonetheless. Clifford accomplished the task while abiding by the rules. On September 11, 1940, he asked Leclerc to kindly restitute the seventeen revolvers he had lent him in Victoria, weapons that had allowed the Free Frenchman to take Cameroon a few days prior. The Victoria police force now wished to see them returned.[12]

---

9 Muracciole, p. 207; Marc Michel, "Les ralliements à la France Libre en 1940," paper delivered at the round table "La seconde guerre mondiale et son impact en Afrique," University of Aix-en-Provence, February 11, 1996.

10 Cécile Istasse-Moussinga, "La collaboration de guerre franco-britannique en Afrique," *Guerres mondiales et conflits contemporains* 181 (January 1996), p. 7.

11 ANCMR 2AC 11190A, Edéa to Yaoundé, June 22, 1940.

12 AML, Leclerc 6a, file 1.

Meanwhile, Boislambert evoked an £80,000 loan in cash, "handed to me by our English friends, in exchange for a simple receipt" aimed at funding the rallying of FEA in August 1940.[13] Likewise, Edgard de Larminat obtained aid from the governor of Nigeria, Sir Bernard Bourdillon. The latter provided him with the aircraft he used to reach Leopoldville. Once he crossed the river into Brazzaville, Lord Hailey and Frederick Pedler of the British economic mission in the Belgian Congo supported and underwrote Larminat's efforts.[14] Pedler spent much of September scrounging for funds to keep Free French Africa afloat. This is evidenced by his September 15, 1940, diary entry that cites ongoing discussions to "provide ready money in French Equatorial Africa." Between September 23 and 24, he mentions raising 434,000 francs "for Larminat... on Hailey's personal guarantee" and visiting the bank in Brazzaville to discuss future loans. The following days saw Pedler secure several hundred thousand pounds, to be placed "at Larminat's disposal." By the end of the month, Pedler and consorts came to realize that FEA required an immediate injection of 30 million francs to pay its bills. Thereafter, both parties agreed to a monthly British contribution of £200,000.[15]

One can speak of an enduring dependency of Free French Africa on Great Britain and its American suppliers. Consider the list of supplies obtained by Leclerc's forces in Chad in 1940 and 1941, on which one can find ginger ale, Heinz sandwiches, bacon, assorted teas, and Sunlight brand soap.[16] And yet, Larminat remained adamant that Free France appear to be completely independent, and resented any overt sign of British or Belgian assistance.[17]

Chad swung over first to Free France on August 26 thanks in large part to ongoing British support. On June 27, Eboué had established contact with Theodore Adams, the Chief Commissioner of the Northern Provinces of Nigeria. Three days later, Lieutenant Reynes and Lieutenant-Colonel Marchand drew up a list of men in Chad willing to continue the fight against Germany, and prepared to cross the border into Nigeria to do so. Shortly thereafter, a proponent of Pétain, Commandant Perry, got hold of the list and ripped it to shreds. Eboué's desire to maintain the

---

[13] Claude Hettier de Boislambert, *Les fers de l'espoir* (Paris: Plon, 1978), p. 201.

[14] Philippe Oulmont, "Le haut-commissaire," p. 63; Robin Pedler. *The Free French: Beaconsfield and* Africa (Beaconsfield: self-published, 2006), p. 31.

[15] BD Mss Afr s 1814, box 18, 38/13 to 38/16 and 38/192 and box 19, Hailey to Bourdillon, September 28, 1940.

[16] AML, Leclerc 6b.

[17] BD Mss Afr s 1814, box 19, FP A2, 32–33.

alliance with Britain and continue the struggle was evidently not unanimously shared. On July 6 and 7, Adams engaged with further talks with Eboué and Marchand. On the 8th, Eboué's Secretary General Henri Laurentie embarked for Lagos where he met with the Governor Sir Bernard Bourdillon. As Eboué biographer Brian Weinstein has observed, the following weeks proved challenging for the Guyanese-born governor. He had not yet received the ironclad guarantee that he sought from Britain, yet he still had to convince recalcitrant military and administrative personnel in Chad, all the while dealing with the staunch Vichyites in Dakar and Zinder (Niger), without arousing suspicion. Henri Laurentie worked on persuading local skeptics. He contended that failing to join the British camp would spell economic isolation for FEA. This, in turn, could trigger a native revolt against the French. On July 20, Governor Pierre Boisson landed in Fort-Lamy where he tried to coax Eboué into adopting Vichy's position. The move nearly backfired on the spot. Boisson irked several of his interlocutors, one of whom even suggested that Eboué arrest him there and then.[18]

On August 4, the British issued the guarantee Eboué sought. The assurances were aimed at any and all French colonies that might rally Free France. Addressed from Churchill to de Gaulle, they read: "Until such time as an independent and constitutional authority has been re-established on free French soil we shall do everything in our power to maintain the economic stability of all French oversea territories, provided they stand by the Alliance [with Britain]."[19] Between August 2 and 5, British envoys hammered out the details of a commercial accord in Fort-Lamy.[20] While the basic principles were in place, the British government still hesitated on the details. Churchill worried that action in FEA and Cameroon might undercut an operation he considered more important: the attack on Dakar. Conversely, de Gaulle and the British War Office deemed that one operation need not interfere with the other. They managed to convince Churchill on this score.[21] Given the ongoing Franco-British uncertainty about which colony to target first, on August 6,

---

[18] Brian Weinstein, *Eboué* (New York: Oxford University Press, 1972), pp. 238–40, 243. Boislambert, p. 198. ANOM 1Affpol 891, details on FEA entry into "dissidence." ANOM DSM 262, file 3, report on the events of July and August at Fort-Lamy. The events are also recounted in BD Mss Afr s 1085.

[19] ANOM Cab 49, 288, Churchill to de Gaulle.

[20] ANOM DSM 262, 3, Report on the events of July and August at Fort-Lamy.

[21] Desmond Dinan, *The Politics of Persuasion: British Policy and French African Neutrality, 1940–1942* (Lanham: University Press of America, 1988), p. 55. On the support of the War Office for de Gaulle, also see Jean-Christophe Notin, *Leclerc* (Paris: Perrin, 2005), p. 90.

1940, de Gaulle issued modular instructions to Leclerc, René Pleven, Claude Hettier de Boislambert, and André Parant, setting the following objective: "Establish and maintain liaison with the British authorities in Gambia, Sierra-Leone, Gold Coast, and Nigeria."[22] The presence of the first three British colonies in West Africa reminds us that the Dakar card was very much in play. Yet it was Nigeria that would prove decisive in its aid, thanks to the borders it shared with both Cameroon and Chad. On August 7, London decided to assist concretely in the rallying of FEA and Cameroon, by providing naval assistance if necessary. This was no easy decision: the United Kingdom faced many other pressing concerns including the Battle of Britain, which had begun in earnest.[23]

On August 13, advanced negotiations took place between representatives of Chad and Nigeria. Governor Bourdillon in person assured the Gaullist delegation of his spirit of cooperation. Both sides then took stock of the alarming economic asphyxiation that FEA was experiencing, and of Vichy's refusal to engage in talks with the United Kingdom. This brought the Gaullist delegation to ask whether Bourdillon "was prepared to discuss the economic situation of Chad with them, a situation which General de Gaulle ardently wishes to resolve in a particularly favorable manner." The rallying of Chad depended on a proactive Gaullist stance concerning Chad's economic interests, neglected by Vichy. The French delegation offered the United Kingdom the use of Fort-Lamy's airfield and the Benue River. The British, in turn, agreed to purchase Chad's production in pounds sterling, via Nigerian banks, and to guarantee Chad's supply of oil. The two sides even settled on a currency conversion rate of 176 francs per pound. Eboué was asked to inform the United Kingdom of Chad's needs in petrol for the following two months. This very first protocol, held at the French colonial archives, marked the opening up of landlocked Chad.[24]

The alliance with the United Kingdom was once again put forward as a prime motive in the wake of Chad's official rallying to the Gaullist cause on August 26. At least this is what one recalcitrant non-commissioned officer (NCO) posted in Fort-Archambault contended following his personal refusal to join de Gaulle.[25] According to Sergeant Raymond Waag, Chad's military leader, Lieutenant-Colonel Pierre Marchand, had

---

[22] AML 5a, Charles de Gaulle, August 6, 1940.
[23] Dinan, p. 55.
[24] ANOM Cab 55.
[25] This 4,000-man-strong garrison hesitated for two days before finally declaring for de Gaulle thanks to François Ingold's impassioned speech, which left only a few dissenting in the end.

clumsily cited only economic motives to justify Chad's move to join Free France. In a speech at Fort-Archambault, Marchand apparently dwelled on the financial troubles of the Cotonfranc Corporation, Chad's main economic engine. Marchand allegedly pronounced the words "we have rallied Chad to English Nigeria" – a statement that needs to be read with caution given Vichy's propensity for amalgamating Free France with Britain. In fact, Leclerc was quick to counter such claims. In a speech in Yaoundé on August 29, he insisted on Free France's independence.[26] However, other sources do lend credence to Waag's point. Many across FEA were evoking a spirit of "joining Britain" – for better or for worse, in August 1940. Take the Spiritan missionaries in Mouyounasi, French Congo, who confided in their diary on August 28: "Cameroon, Chad, and Oubangui have rallied to England's side. Congo has not yet decided but its isolation will probably make it follow suit." Two days later, the diary evokes a "coup" in Brazzaville, and adds: "we too have now rallied to England."[27]

In British circles, the explanation for the events of August 26–28 had everything to do with British economic support. Historian G. E. Maguire cites a report from the British Treasury, likely dating from 1941, which indicates: "It is scarcely an exaggeration to say that the whole course of the Free French Movement in Africa was economic… The unanimity of popular sentiment which made possible the coups d'état at Douala and Brazzaville was very largely due to the fact that French Equatorial Africa and the French Cameroons were at that time faced with economic ruin and were, therefore, swayed by our offers of prompt economic assistance."[28]


## Upheaval

The changeover to Free French rule marked an unprecedented colonial rupture since the loss of a vast part of the French empire after the defeat of Napoleon. Free France's followers doubtlessly claimed to embody true France in 1940. Yet this did not alter the fact that the French empire

---

[26] ANOM, GGAEF 5D 187, Haag to Pétain, April 23, 1941. On the hesitation of the garrison of Fort-Archambault, see Boisseau, pp. 19–20. On Eboué, see ANOM 1Affpol 891, p. 18. On the Yaoundé declaration, see ANS, 16G 4, report on the events of Cameroon. Viewable at the ANOM on microfilm 14Miom 2284.

[27] CSE, 3J1.19b, diary entries for August 28 and 30 1940.

[28] G. E. Maguire, *Anglo-American Policy Towards the Free French* (Oxford: Macmillan Press, 1995), p. 115.

had been split and that a group of colonies and one country under mandate rule had left metropolitan France's orbit. For Free France, functioning without a metropole involved a series of risks. Territories might be chipped away by other powers (a perpetual Gaullist fear); the empire might come undone; a constitutional void resulting from the absence of a central power might sap the movement's legitimacy; the colonial or mandate relationship might be strained or even broken.[29]

If Chad rallied first, it was no doubt in part because of its leaders' convictions, but also because of the territory's strategic location. Félix Eboué's motives have been well studied. He was certainly moved in part by the discriminatory nature of the regime that was taking shape at Vichy. The fact that he was black, a freemason (admittedly not a very fervent one), and a member of the SFIO, or French Socialist party, likely weighed in. Yet Brian Weinstein is correct to suggest that none of these factors should be considered overriding. After all, he reminds us that the black Guadeloupean deputy Gratien Candace, the former freemason, and Vichy Minister Marcel Peyrouton, and the purported socialist colonial Governor Hubert Deschamps, all remained unwaveringly faithful to Vichy, never allowing internal contradictions to get in the way.[30] Let us therefore return to geostrategic explanations and set aside monocausal ones. On June 27, in Brazzaville, Pierre Boisson received the order to demilitarize the border between Chad and Mussolini's Libya. Five days after the armistice, the hour of placating both Axis powers had rung. This fueled Eboué's concerns. The governor-general dreaded the possibility of an Italian armistice commission setting foot in Chad.[31] He therefore sought to remain in the war at all cost, knowing full well that his colony lay on a potential military front line. Before taking action, however, he quite sensibly sought assurances from London, which he received.[32]

At eight o'clock on August 26, 1940, Governor Félix Eboué and Lieutenant-Colonel Pierre Marchand solemnly entered the main chamber of Fort-Lamy's city hall. The ensuing speech was read by Marchand, the more lukewarm of the two men toward Gaullism. The idea was to display complete unity. Pleven, Eboué, and Laurent-e had drafted the

---

[29] On the fear of imperial disintegration see Cassin, p. 216.

[30] Weinstein, pp. 249–50. On Eboué being a tepid freemason, see Raymond Guillaneuf's entry in the following edited volume: Josette Rivallain and Hélène d'Almeida-Topor eds., *Eboué, soixante ans après* (Paris: SFHOM, 2008), p. 45.

[31] ANOM GGAEF 5D 290, Boisson June 27, 1940. Weinstein, p. 237. Lacouture, p. 433.

[32] Larminat, pp. 128–29.

seminal declaration.[33] It began by asserting that Chad had fulfilled its responsibilities. It had initially obeyed the motherland: "the garrisons of Chad submitted in sadness but in the strictest discipline to an armistice that was reached without consulting the French empire." The fact that the colonies were never consulted was surely nothing new, but here it was utilized to justify the territory's entry into dissidence. The text went on to explain that over the last two months the "metropolitan government" placed "under the evident constraint of the enemy" had attempted to force the colonies to "multiply hostile measures towards Great Britain and to impose a policy of economic isolation on French Africa which would lead both native and European populations to ruin."[34] A thesis was being established, one that would be crystallized by the organic decision of November 16, 1940. The thesis held that the metropolitan government was not only unfree, but also illegitimate, having gone so far as to abolish the very term "republic." Furthermore, the metropolitan government now operated against colonial interests, and those of yesterday's ally. It is no doubt significant that administrator Jean Belay, who refused to be swayed by the August 26 declaration, later remembered it as having signaled "Chad's independence."[35]

In point of fact, Eboué, Laurentie, and Pleven contended that Chad now found itself without a free and responsible metropole. It was not so much that Chad had seceded, as France was no longer in a position to fulfill its proper function as a motherland. This presented an obvious contradiction. Free France insisted on maintaining what René Cassin defined as "the unity of the French empire as an international personality indivisibly linked to France"[36] – a legal point on which the great Free French legal mind insisted – while at the same time untethering FEA and Cameroon from the Vichy government, and hence from mainland France. The balancing act only really worked if one could conceive of the motherland as being portable.

The authors of the August 26 declaration decided to "proclaim the union of the territories and troops that protect them with the Free French forces of General de Gaulle" and to "immediately undertake economic planning with neighboring British colonies." They then allowed themselves a colonial barb directed at the motherland: "Chad was won to

---


[33] Weinstein, p. 246; Boisseau, p. 16.

[34] SHD, 11P 21, declaration of 26 August 1940.

[35] Jean-Louis Crémieux-Brilhac, *La France libre* (Paris: Gallimard, 1996) pp. 180–181. ANOM DSM 262, 3, Jean Belay report.

[36] Cassin, p. 217.

France despite the indifference of its central authorities; faithful to the spirit of our elders, the Chadians will keep these territories French, come what may."[37] Here we see a clear articulation of colonial *esprit de corps*. The authors predicted that salvation would come from the empire, while observing that the empire in question had been built in spite of the metropole's indifference. Here the colonial army and lobby expressed revenge against colonial skeptics. But mostly the declaration both rested on and fostered an enduring myth, according to which the French were indifferent to their empire, despite its manifest importance to France's rank and future. In this sense, Gaullism of the first hour undertook a kind of colonial self-marginalization: the Resistance was colonial, Chad forged ahead, alone if need be, in its martial tradition. De Gaulle's external resistance was draping itself in the mantle of the French army's conquest of Africa.

A few days later Colonel Leclerc pronounced Cameroon's "political and economic independence." He added, "Thanks to the agreements reached with the British government, we are bringing Cameroon assurances of economic revival." As for the origins of Cameroon's shift to Free France, Leclerc attributed it to "a response from General de Gaulle to the calls that reached him." He concluded with a resounding: "Long live France! Long live free Cameroon!"[38] No doubt he used the term "independence" to signify a break with Vichy; no doubt the expression "free Cameroon" alluded to German ambitions. Yet the words were out, pregnant with meaning, and starkly contrasting with the August 26 declaration that insisted on Chad's eternal ties to France. In many ways, August 1940 marked a moment of rupture.

A close analysis reveals many holes and contradictions in these early arguments. The colonies were breaking with the motherland so as to guarantee the rights of native and white populations, but none of these populations had been consulted. Admittedly, some individuals had called on de Gaulle to intervene. Yet could these isolated requests really be mistaken for collective will? The representatives of the colonies proclaimed themselves judges of the motherland's freedom of action, withdrawing in the process that decision from General de Gaulle, whose constitutional legitimacy in August 1940 seems equally uncertain. Cameroon's independence proclamation emanated from a maverick representative of the French army, who held the rank of captain only a few weeks before.

[37] SHD, 11P 21, August 26 declaration.
[38] AML Leclerc, 5a, poster.

None of this removes from the daring of Governor Eboué and General de Gaulle's project; on the contrary, the institutional haze derived from this audacity and vice versa.

## Local and Imperial Stakes

The regime changes in French central Africa in late August 1940 involved grafting General de Gaulle's vision in London onto a local context. In Cameroon, as elsewhere, the French community was divided in these troubled times. On June 25, the man at the helm of the mandate territory, Commissioner Richard Brunot, indicated that "Cameroon is unanimous and firm in wanting to continue the fight alongside British Nigeria." But the context was shifting rapidly, and Brunot "equivocated," notes Jean-Louis Crémieux-Brilac. According to Marc Michel, Brunot's strategy or coping mechanism involved "tacking" to and fro between different interests and imperatives. Brunot was certainly not alone in hesitating at the time. Recalling this period in FEA, future Olympic medalist René Lemoine wrote, "Gaullists and Vichyites one day had changed their mind the next. Only to shift back the day following!"[39] Bernard Bourdillon's secretary Robert Wright recalls preparing to receive Brunot with a bottle of Vichy water, then scrambling to replace it with champagne, after Brunot professed his loyalty to de Gaulle. In fairness, it should be pointed out that Brunot faced intense pressure from within and without. Even the Free French in London recognized that his position had become "very difficult" over the course of July.[40]

In a bid to stem the tide of opposition to the armistice across Cameroon, on July 5, a group of Pétain supporters distributed flyers in Yaoundé's hotels that read as follows: "The government of France, led by men like Pétain, Weygand, Darlan, and Colson, whose patriotism is unquestionable, is the legal government. The entire French empire has closed rank behind Pétain. Distance yourself from maneuvers aimed at

---

[39] ANOM GGAEF 5D 290, Yaoundé, June 25, 1940. Crémieux-Brilhac, *La France libre*, p. 143. Marc Michel, "Leclerc et l'Afrique Noire," in Christine Levisse-Touzé, ed., *Du capitaine de Hauteclocque au général de Gaulle* (Brussels: Complexe, 2000), p. 261. René Lemoine testimony, cited by par Yves Boulvert, *Bangui, 1889–1989* (Paris: Sepia, 1994), p. 188.

[40] AMC Boislambert F50 (2) Africa (1940) note on Cameroon dated July 31, 1940. On the champagne and Vichy water (an image right out of the film *Casablanca*), see BD MSS Afr. s 1085, folio 10b.

dividing Frenchmen."[41] On July 6, Brunot asked the United Kingdom for "the necessary help ... to secure the welfare of the population and to maintain the country's economic activity."[42]

In Cameroon, rumors abounded between June and August 1940. Some imagined General Francisco Franco's troops massing on the Spanish Guinean border ready to invade; others evoked the imminent arrival of a German armistice commission. Like many others, Raymond Dronne saw an invisible German hand lurking behind the Spanish Guinea border. According to him, one of the Germans present on the island of Fernando-Po "has already given himself the title of governor of Cameroon." In this extremely tense context, a brawl was narrowly avoided between pro and anti-British sides when Pétainist Admiral Charles Platon, furious at Albion since Dunkirk, visited Cameroon between July 20 and 22, 1940.[43] Platon's visit unquestionably "accelerated" what one British report termed the "deterioration of the political situation." On July 23, a slightly embarrassed Commissioner Brunot informed British official Godfrey Allen that he had received the order to prevent British planes from flying over French Cameroon.[44]

Another high-ranking Vichy official, Commissioner to French Africa Pierre Boisson, also intervened frequently. He initially called on the leaders of French territories in Africa to temporize, then, after the tragedy of Mers el-Kébir, to ignore the British siren calls.[45] Over the course of August, Boisson's messages became more explicit, his language sharper. On August 12, he warned Governor Husson in Brazzaville to be on the lookout for possible Gaullist landings, enjoining local African chiefs to alert the army if such an attack occurred. On August 20, he informed all rulers of French territories in Africa that it was henceforth illegal for French nationals to set foot in British territories.[46]

---

[41] ANS, 16G 4, Brunot, confidential information. Viewable at the ANOM on microfilm 14Miom 2284.

[42] Ibid.

[43] ANS, 16G 4, report on the dissidence in Cameroon. Viewable at the ANOM on microfilm 14Miom 2284. Raymond Dronne, *Leclerc et le serment de Koufra* (Paris: Editions du Temps, 1965), p. 47. On the rumors, also see Pascal-Henry Biwole, "Le ralliement et l'œuvre de Leclerc au Cameroun" paper for the Ecole supérieure militaire de Saint-Cyr, June 2002, p. 22.

[44] BD Mss Afr. s. 424, folio 241.

[45] Boislambert, p. 196.

[46] ANOM, 217 APOM, box 2, Telegram 73 from Boisson dated August 12; Telegram C28.

Cameroon constituted a special case. As a country under League of Nations mandate, it was governed by different rules than colonies. In the wake of World War I, Cameroon had been divided into two mandates, one British the other French. This proximity facilitated dialogue between the two allies. A former German colony prior to the Great War, Cameroon also crystallized both intense fears of a return of German influence in this part of Africa, and French paranoia concerning possible Germanophilia in some African circles.[47] Police investigations appeared to confirm Free French fears. One reported on August 24 that "the native Diboti Ekwalla, an employee at the King company in Yaoundé, publicly expressed joy at the news that Germany had defeated France."[48] Pro-German and anti-colonial sentiment merged seamlessly in French security reports. It seems safe to conclude that the fear of a German return played an important role in the events of August 1940 in Cameroon.[49]

Cameroon's unique status also conditioned the events of the "three glorious days." In the wake of the armistice, Commissioner Brunot asserted that Cameroon was henceforth under League of Nations control, given the annihilation of the metropole that had previously held tutelage over the territory in the League's name.[50] This argument became an important thread for the anti-Vichy camp on location. On July 5, Miles Clifford, the head of a British liaison mission in Cameroon, delivered an impassioned speech before Yaoundé's chamber of commerce. Seeking to minimize the damage caused by Mers el-Kébir two days prior, he evoked the spirit of Franco-British cooperation. Then he played his trump card: "There is one more important consideration, a moral question. This territory does not belong to France but to Africans. It was conferred to a democratic government representing the authority of the League of Nations, which served it well. This government is no longer free to follow the policy of the League of Nations. It has fallen under the

---

[47] In British Cameroon, the situation was arguably even more fraught, given that Germans overtly sympathetic to Hitler still controlled several sectors of the economy prior to 1940. Anthony Ndi, "The Second World War in Southern Cameroun and its impact on mission-state relations," in David Killingray and Richard Rathbone, ed., *Africa and the Second World War* (New York: Saint Martin's Press, 1986), pp. 206–10.

[48] Yaoundé was a small capital of 9,080 inhabitants. André Franqueville, *Yaoundé, Construire une capitale* (Paris: ORSTOM, 1984), p. 12. On the Ekwalla case, see: ANCMR 2AC 11190A, note to the director of political affairs, August 24, 1940.

[49] On this point, see Lacouture, p. 434.

[50] ANS, 16G 4, report on the origins of the de Gaulle movement in Cameroon. Viewable at the ANOM on microfilm 14Miom 2284.

boot of a man, a monster, who has called Africans sub-human."[51] Thus, at this critical moment, a British representative cautioned his audience in Yaoundé that France's presence in Cameroon rested on an institution despised by the Third Reich, and on France's status as a democracy. For good measure, he added a reminder of Hitler's racism toward Africans.

Everything and anything having to do with Germany assumed serious proportions. While Brunot hesitated in June and July of 1940, he transferred to the British authorities the German inmates held in French Cameroon (Germans had been interned since the declaration of war in 1939). This step contravened the orders received from France. In Yaoundé on July 20, 1940, a soldier supporting Pétain by the name of Jean Floch wrote an outraged letter underlining that in both Togo and Syria, territories presenting institutional and historical analogies with Cameroon, the French authorities had rigorously respected the clauses of the June 22 armistice; only Cameroon had opted to take a different path.[52] However, according to the testimony of Lieutenant François Denise, Commissioner Brunot soon regretted his bold decision, and was reprimanded for it by Admiral Platon during his passage in Cameroon. And yet even after issuing this admonishment, the admiral was not fully reassured by Brunot's position: he noted the presence of a British war ship, the HMS *Dragon*, in Douala's harbor, a major infraction to the line advocated by the French government since Mers el-Kébir. On July 27, he observed French and British flags flying in unison at Douala's airport. When he uttered an acerbic remark on the topic, he was harangued by the head of the public works department, Roger Mauclère. Mauclère's colleagues had elected him leader of the local Gaullist current. He evoked a past defeat of France when he proclaimed, "After the capitulation of Metz and Sedan in 1870, France continued to fight and won victories, saving its honor; and yet at the time France was alone and did not have its immense empire behind it as it does today."

That very day Mauclère contacted General de Gaulle in London, requesting instructions. On the 30th, he called for aid from Nigeria. The following day, de Gaulle telegraphed him underlining "the necessity to proclaim Cameroon's provisional autonomy for the duration of

---

[51] "Le Colonel Clifford définit l'attitude de l'Angleterre," *L'Eveil du Cameroun*, July 9, 1940, reproduced in ANS, 16G 4, viewable at the ANOM on microfilm 14Miom 2284.

[52] ANS, 16G 4, Floch to commander of police forces in Cameroon, July 30, 1940. Viewable at the ANOM on microfilm 14Miom 2284.

the war."[53] At this juncture, French military personnel were deserting in ever-growing numbers in Cameroon. Persuaded that Boisson and Platon had brought Brunot back into Pétain's orbit, these men began leaving for British Cameroon on and around July 30. All signs seemed to point to the tide now turning in favor of the Pétain camp. Starting on July 30, 1940, the main newspaper, *L'Eveil du Cameroun*, removed the remarkable running title it had been displaying for weeks on its front page: "Franco-British Empire."

In this sense, the operation conducted by the roughly forty men who toppled the Vichy presence in Cameroon on August 27, 1940, occurred at the eleventh hour, at a time when momentum had actually shifted away from the Gaullist side. The main actors of the coup de main were broken down as follows by Christian Laigret: eleven men on the inside in Douala, another seven in Yaoundé, and twenty-two men including Leclerc and Boislambert coming from Tiko in British Cameroon by pirogue under driving rain. Laigret's distinction between those on the inside and the outside is at once helpful and misleading insofar as many of the men on board the pirogues were Frenchmen from Cameroon who had left for British territories over the previous two weeks. They were therefore returning to French Cameroon, more than invading it per se.

Colonial methods prevailed during the nocturnal crossing on the evening of August 26 and the morning of August 27. The paddlers, who hailed from Calabar in Nigeria, had been given only the vaguest and misleading sense of their mission. British official Godfrey Allen had falsely depicted the expedition as comprising: "French officers who had left the French Cameroons because they did not get on with their officer commanding; as this officer had now been replaced, they wished to return with as little fuss as possible." According to Lieutenant Denise, the paddlers were deemed too slow, leading the Free French team to beat and whip them. When the paddlers expressed concern about accosting clandestinely in Douala under the cover of darkness, Adjudant Henri Drouilh threatened to throw them overboard. The Nigerians subsequently complained to the British that the Free French had behaved as "rascals."

---

53 AML, Leclerc 15, André Rogez, the de Gaulle movement in Cameroon; AML Leclerc 5a, note from Denise; ANS, 16G 4, report on the rebellion in Cameroun, viewable at the ANOM on microfilm 14Miom. 2284. Théodore Ateba Yene, *Cameroun, mémoire d'un colonisé* (Paris: l'Harmattan, 1988), p. 27. Christian Laigret, *Sur les chemins de l'union française* (Châteauroux: Editions Novelty, 1949), pp. 41, 48; Boislambert, p. 198, Adolphe Sicé, *L'AEF et le Cameroun au service de la France* (Paris: Presses universitaires de France, 1946), p. 113. Dinan, p. 54. De Gaulle, *Lettres, notes et carnets, 1940–1941*, p. 69.

Allen suggests that they only agreed to continue paddling after negotiating a pay hike. According to Lieutenant-Colonel Robert Quilichini, the members of the expedition ended up having to row themselves near the end of the crossing.

Some limited planning had been undertaken in advance: Leclerc had sent a message – again by pirogue – to known Gaullist supporters in Douala, asking for their aid, and for vehicles on his arrival. On August 28, in the capital Yaoundé, a veritable putsch unfolded in the administrative district. Gaullists burst into government buildings, brandishing revolvers, and asking officials and especially officers to answer the following question on the spot: "Do you want to join Free France in order to continue the war against the Germans and the Italians?" Those who responded negatively were instructed to leave for French West Africa, which remained under Vichy control. All told, the preparation and scale of the operation had been astonishingly modest: on August 28 a single airplane had flown over Yaoundé dropping Gaullist leaflets. Pirogues had played a more decisive role than aircraft.[54]

Local contexts profoundly shaped the regime change. As Eliane Ebako has explained, in Gabon more was at stake than simple patriotism and political conviction. Old Libreville quarrels surrounding religion, trade, and other local interests also played important roles. In French Congo, in early August 1940 a "patriotic league for freedom and honor" was formed with the goal of tipping the colony over to the Gaullist side.[55] It should be added that Brazzavillians followed international developments, via U.S. radio and Belgian information outlets. The local and the international coalesced. Thus, on August 3, 1940, the British Consul in Leopoldville, speaking on Leopoldville radio, addressed the inhabitants of French Congo directly, informing them that trade could resume again as soon as French Congo honored its commitment to the alliance with Britain.[56]

Again, preexisting tensions mattered. In February 1941, six months after the "glorious days," an official in Edgard de Larminat's office

---

[54] Laigret, pp. 51, 52, 59, 61; Larminat, p. 136; Dronne, p. 33; Quilichini, "Le ralliement du Cameroun," *Tropiques*, February 1948, p. 7. AML Leclerc 5a, note from Denise. On the pamphlets, see ANS, 16G 4, report on the dissident movement in Cameroon. Viewable at the ANOM on microfilm 14Miom 2284. The list of the twenty-two men who accompanied Leclerc and Boislambert to Douala (not counting the paddlers) can be found in AMC FL 50 (2) Africa 1940, liste nominative. For the British account on the paddlers, see BD MSS Afr. s 424, folio 293.

[55] Ebako, p. 96. Sicé, pp. 122–23.

[56] ANOM Fonds Galasus box 2, declaration of the British Consul general in Brazzaville.

explained that Louis Duplaquet, an official serving in the forestry department in Brazzaville, "asked to be relieved of his duties and to return
to France." The note added: "Yet another one who has not understood
things, and has allowed himself to be dominated by personal animosities.
Pathetic fellow."[57] In Cameroon, tensions crystallized around ongoing
economic concerns. Friction between planters and administrators over
the question of African labor reached such levels in the summer of 1940
that a representative of Edwards Spears' mission – charged with liaison between the United Kingdom and Free France – termed it a crisis.
Planters refused to offer decent wages. Under such conditions the administration grumbled about implementing forced labor. The economic question risked undoing Free France's August gains. Indeed, two months after
the "glorious days" of August, Leclerc himself deemed that if large-scale
exports did not resume promptly, Free France could be toppled much as
Vichy had been before it.[58]

Unlike Chad, whose regime change was truly impelled from within,
before the "three glorious days" leaders in FEA and Cameroon displayed
either outright hostility to Free France (as in Brazzaville) or hesitation
(as in Yaoundé). Interestingly, André Rogez suggested after the fact that
in July and August 1940, de Gaulle proponents in Cameroon tended to
occupy lower ranks. This would later lead to recriminations after the shift
to Free France, for Rogez deemed that those who had been "cowards"
in 1940 occupied more important posts than genuine Gaullists a year
later.[59] In this particular case, regrets were expressed that an early Gaullist
engagement had not translated into a spectacular ascension through the
ranks. Others expressed the opposite complaint: that some Gaullists came
to occupy high office simply by virtue of their political gamble. In other
words, the August 1940 moment was something of an earthquake that
impacted careers, networks, and families. Its aftershocks set off jealousies,
disillusions, and disappointments, even among the victors.

### Convincing Colonials

The "three glorious days" were above all an act of persuasion directed at
the handful of administrators who ran the colonies that Free France was

57  Ebako, p. 96. Sicé, pp. 122–23.
58  Martin Thomas, *The French Empire at War* (Manchester: Manchester University Press,
    1998), pp. 59–60.
59  AML, Leclerc 15, André Rogez, the de Gaulle movement in Cameroon.

targeting. In an August 20, 1940, document intended to convince those on the fence, Edgard de Larminat surveyed each side's arguments. First, he asserted, were Vichy to continue to rule over FEA and Cameroon, these territories "won at the cost of so much beautiful French blood" would be "entirely shared by the victors. There is no chance that any part of them would stay French." He then sapped Vichy's legitimacy: "Do not hesitate to disobey the orders of this government that calls itself legal. The government is not free." Then followed a more down-to-earth point: the isolation of FEA and Cameroon and the difficulty they faced in exporting their products. Finally, Larminat turned to careerist concerns: "Many of you are preoccupied by your personal situations and are persuaded that obeying Vichy constitutes a guarantee of your retirements and wages." Here Larminat did not dodge the question or hide behind values of patriotism and bravery. He retorted pragmatically: "There is something ludicrous about this illusion. France is ruined and the enemy controls nine tenths of its revenue sources."[60] Larminat clearly mastered this self-debating genre, although it may also have revealed the fragility of his own position, since it forced him to repeat Vichy's line in order better to rebut it.

In any event, real dialogue proved hard to engage. Unmoved, on August 21 Paul Louis Husson the Vichy governor-general of FEA reported proudly to his superior Pierre Boisson in Dakar (Husson had only recently replaced Boisson in Brazzaville), that he knew nothing of the contents of Larminat's messages, because he had refused to open them when he realized that they came from de Gaulle.[61] British Major J. G. C. Allen evoked an "immediate" and "hysterical" reaction on Husson's part. The latter sought to break all contacts between Brazzaville and Leopoldville. A certain Tezenas du Montcel, whom Allen describes as the *éminence grise* of the Vichy side in Brazzaville, applied intense pressure on Husson to remain steadfast.[62] Three days later, Husson warned the governors of Chad, Congo, Oubangui, and Gabon of Larminat's letters. He asserted confidently that "good Frenchmen" would reject them, for they "aim to break French unity."[63] At Fort-Lamy, Larminat's words preached to the converted.

[60] AOL, 4B 1, AEF.
[61] ANOM GGAEF 5D 290, Husson to Boisson, August 21, 1940.
[62] AOL 4B1 AEF, Allen report, January 1943.
[63] ANOM GGAEF 5D 290, Husson to colonial gouverneurs, August 24, 1940.

On August 26, Larminat applied further pressure. He dispatched a very frank note across the river to Husson, informing him that: "his days are numbered," before explaining: "we in the Gaullist camp are neither adventurers nor anarchists, but patriots and soldiers who know how to respect the bonds of discipline when they are respectable."[64] Larminat's plea constituted a remarkable balancing act. It intended to show that a movement based on the principle of disobedience was in fact bound by military values; and that a solitary Gaullist envoy, threatening French officials from the Belgian Congo, was no "adventurer." In his memoirs, Larminat light-heartedly described himself as one of five "desperados" sent by de Gaulle.[65] The poker hand of the "three glorious days" depended on speed and bluff, but also on intense pressure exerted on the rulers of Cameroon, Oubangui, Gabon, and especially French Congo. August 1940 saw a swarm of ultimatums zip across the Congo River.

This said, Gaullist emissaries were also interested in the political position of Africans. Indeed, African veterans helped impel the Gaullist movement in both Bangui and Brazzaville.[66] Over the course of the "three glorious days," Boislambert noted that he received assurances of support from Pointe-Noire's colonials but also from "a few [of the town's] African notables."[67] Free France felt the need to persuade African elites. Many were already deeply committed to the cause. A few days after the June 1940 armistice, several members of Brazzaville's Senegalese community informed Doctor Adolphe Sicé of their desire to continue the fight. One eminent member of this community, Amadou Diop, told Sicé "when one loses a round... one tries to win the second one, one does not pull out of the ring entirely" – a close paraphrase of de Gaulle's words that same month. In early September, the same Diop assured the Free French administration that he would do his utmost to "attract all of our Muslim brothers around the Free French standard." Finally, Sicé points out that Edgard de Larminat's August 1940 leaflet campaign influenced not only Brazzaville's white rulers, but also literate Africans who embraced the cause.[68]

---

64  AML Leclerc 5a, Larminat August 26, 1940. The same letter can be found in ANOM 217 APOM.
65  Larminat, p. 128.
66  ANOM 1Affpol 891 and AMC FL 50 (2) Afrique 1940 text entitled "A Brazzaville," 1942, p. 1.
67  Boislambert, p. 226.
68  Sicé, p. 86, 141; ANOM Cab 48 dossier 281, Sicé speech June 30, 1942, p. 4; and ANOM 217 APOM, box 1, telegram signed by Diop, September 11, 1940.

FIGURE I. Vichy Governor General Husson being carried away on a truck to be expelled from the colony. Brazzaville, August 28, 1940. Archives nationales d'Outre-mer, fonds Géraud de Galassus (ANOM, 217APOM) All rights reserved.

Similarly, one should not forget that the men serving under Commandant Raymond Delange, Captain Pierre Rougé, and Lieutenant Guy Baucheron de Boissoudy during the events of August 28 in Brazzaville were overwhelmingly African (see Figure 1). It was in trying to move Rougé's unit from Brazzaville that Husson "lit the tinder keg."[69] Major J. G. C. Allen recounts how the Pétainist Commandant Sacquet attempted in vain to sway these African troops. Allen then observes that several African NCOs displayed strong anti-German sentiment, which steeled their resolve. One African soldier answered Sacquet's insistent pro-Vichy admonishment by training his weapon on him. Sacquet responded with a suicide attempt. A black soldier refusing to obey the orders of a white officer against this highly charged political background created a rare and volatile situation. More was being toppled on this fateful day in the French Congo than merely Brazzaville's allegiance.[70]

Perhaps unsurprisingly, Vichyites used the argument of a loss of "white prestige" in their propaganda against Free France. On September 1, 1940, Boisson reproached those he called "dissidents" with "having made a

---

[69] Soustelle, p. 122.
[70] AOL B to 4B1 AEF, Allen report, January 1943.

spectacle in front of natives under your responsibility. You have shown them the arrest of France's official representative by a faction."[71] Both Vichy and Free French officials fretted over the possibility of native revolt at a time when wounded, amputated France faced a humiliating armistice. A small number of Africans, who take up a disproportionate amount of space in police reports, were indeed tempted to support Germany in 1940, no doubt by virtue of the adage that an enemy of an enemy might serve as a friend. This was particularly the case in Cameroon, where some pro-German voices were heard. But not only. According to a July 1940 report, in the town of Diosso in the Pointe-Noire area, individuals of the Bavilis (or Vilis) ethnicity "sang and danced to the glory of the Germans who, it was hoped, would bring abundance and riches." The police identified an employee in the colonial administration, Pierre Tchikaye, as the instigator of these songs and dances.[72] In Brazzaville in January 1941, the police accused Michel Kéké, a 24-year-old illustrator and resident of the Bacongo neighborhood, of having uttered the following words: "It would better if the Germans who have taken Paris also occupied Brazzaville, and decapitated the whites." After an expedited trial, Kéké received a sentence of three years in jail and five years of banishment from Brazzaville for endangering the security of the state. His condemnation was based entirely on two testimonies, the search of his house having yielded nothing damning. Kéké denied having uttered the phrase, and pointed out that the two witnesses were rivals who envied him.[73] In these two cases, one can question the guilt of the accused, given colonial hypersensitivity to any seditious note in this era, and the meager evidence on which the convictions were based. However, if the songs and words were in fact pronounced, they would seem to illustrate above all the psychological impact of the French defeat of June 1940. Overthrowing the colonizer suddenly became a concrete possibility in the wake of the motherland's defeat in June, and a regime change in Africa two months later.

Europeans also proved deeply divided. Contrary to what Gaullist legend would have us believe, many Pétain followers resisted the resistance in Africa. Vichy leaflets were distributed in FEA refuting Larminat's arguments: "British propaganda tells you that without England you will not be able to sell your products. In reality France buys all of our colonial

---

[71] ANOM fonds Télégrammes, 685, Platon September 1, 1940, telegram 1195.
[72] SHD, 11P 21, bulletin de renseignements up to July 20, 1940.
[73] ANC GGAEF 379, Michel Kéké file.

production, and France needs it." And further: "French soldiers, to convince you that your duty lies on England's side, the British are calling upon your sense of honor. They tell you that your duty commands you to continue fighting against Germany and Italy. Since you have been by England's side, where and whom have you fought?"[74] This last argument may have backfired, for many colonials regretted having to look on from a distance as France was invaded. Vichy also deployed less subtle arguments. Beginning in September 1940, Zinder radio (from Vichy-controlled Niger) evoked reprisals in France against the families of Free Frenchmen in Africa.[75]

Positions hardened on both sides. Edgard de Larminat issued the following unciphered telegram on September 3, 1940: "We inform all French people that chief objective of the governments of Free France in FEA and Cameroon is to keep these colonies intact so as to return them to an independent France, and to use all of their resources to help liberate the motherland." However, a clear warning followed: "We could not accept that French people who consented to the crushing armistice imposed by Germany would take up arms to force their compatriots to obey the orders of an unfree government. In the event of such an attack, we would exercise the strictest but firmest right of self-defense."[76]

One last point should be mentioned with respect to the layering of French domestic and colonial agendas. Masonic networks were quite extensive in French colonies.[77] Across the empire, freemasons and missionaries had frequently clashed since the nineteenth century, sometimes leaving the French administration caught in the middle. The Vichy regime's decision to add "secret societies" to its list of scapegoats for the defeat of June 1940 therefore presented immediate and sizeable colonial ramifications. On August 27, after Chad had already gone over to de Gaulle and Cameroon was in the process of doing so, Pétainist Governor Husson relayed the order to all of FEA to apply a new law freshly received by wire from Vichy.[78] Aimed squarely at freemasons, this was

---

[74] AOL, 4B 1, AEF.

[75] ANOM GGAEF 6B 710, Eboué September 4, 1940. On the intensification of Zinder's propaganda campaign, see Félix Eboué's September 4 telegram in ANOM 217 APOM.

[76] ANC, GGAEF 82, Larminat September 3, 1940.

[77] See Owen White, "Networking: Freemasons and the Colonial State in French West Africa, 1895–1914," *French History* 19:1, pp. 91–111.

[78] ANC GGAEF 82, Husson telegram dated August 27, 1940, relaying the text of Alibert and Marquet.

one of Vichy's very first discriminatory texts, after the one denaturalizing Jews. Fort-Lamy and Yaoundé never answered as they had already joined the Gaullist cause. In Brazzaville, the order to dissolve secret societies must still have rested on Husson's office table when Edgard de Larminat stormed into the governor's palace to seize power, backed by African troops on August 28. Free France was anything but angelic with respect to individual liberties: many of its leaders, starting with Larminat and Leclerc, shared Marshal Pétain's rigid conceptions of social hierarchies. In his memoirs, Larminat mused at how ironic it was that he would defend the cause of freemasonry. Yet the point remains that on August 28, 1940, Larminat did just that. He swiftly discarded this Vichy elixir with which Pétain promised to cure France through exclusion, repression, and discrimination.[79]

## Subterfuge

Much stealth and bluff surrounded the "three glorious days."[80] Boislambert evokes "the deception to which we resorted given what we called our insufficient ranks." Leclerc's magical transformation into a colonel constitutes a case in point. British Major L. Sealy-King explained how his wife rapidly removed a stripe from Boislambert's uniform, then transferred it to Leclerc's, to produce the lightning-fast promotion.[81] Edgard de Larminat's meteoric rise to general represents another example.[82] The feeling that Vichy possessed an overwhelming advantage in military ribbons, titles, and medals was such that one reader suggested to the *Courrier d'Afrique* that Admiral Emile Muselier and General Georges Catroux confer the rank of marshal on de Gaulle so that "their chief could hold the . . . rank necessary for him to accomplish his mission."[83]

These examples involve more shortcuts than subterfuge per se. There was no shortage of either. Edgard de Larminat claimed to be a francophone Canadian so as to pass as discretely as possible between British, Belgian, and French circles. Many Free Frenchmen in Africa adopted pseudonyms, as is revealed in a Free French telegram from November 16, 1940, that explained: "Commandant de Benschofsheim is actually

---

79 Larminat, p. 209.
80 On bluff, see Jean-Luc Barré, *Devenir de Gaulle, 1939–1943* (Paris: Perrin, 2003), p. 93.
81 BD Mss Afr. s. 424, folio 240.
82 Boislambert, p. 223; Sicé, p. 161.
83 "Une suggestion d'un Français Libre," *Le Courrier d'Afrique* (édition AEF), December 7, 1940.

Commandant Ingold. He wishes to keep his name secret so as to avoid reprisals... The Ingold family line in Alsace once bore the name of Benschofsheim." The constant goal involved throwing off Vichy and hence the Germans. On December 10, 1940, Leclerc requested that telegrams from Fort-Lamy continue to bear Félix Eboué's signature, even though he had assumed his new role as Governor-General of FEA on November 12 and was therefore in Brazzaville. Leclerc's explicitly stated goal was to "confuse Vichy's people" snooping from French West Africa.[84]

## Civil War

Regime change succeeded immediately in the three targeted territories of Chad, Cameroon, and French Congo. In Oubangui-Chari the situation proved more muddled. In much of the colony, Free France won over military leaders. However, in the capital Bangui, Commandant Cammas remained unconvinced, and even tried to persuade his men to fight Free France tooth and nail. Historian Pierre Kalck evokes the threat of a "counter-coup" against de Gaulle in Oubangui. On September 4, one alarmist message from Libengé to Brazzaville reported that the Vichyites were "winning over the undecided." Thanks to interminable negotiations and the personal intervention of Edgard de Larminat, Oubangui did end up swinging over to de Gaulle's camp over the course of September 1940. The task was anything but simple. When the dust settled on the evening of September 21, several officers tried to arrest civilians whom they deemed "lukewarm" to the Free French cause. In the rural Kemo-Gribingui province in central Oubangui, one military unit refused to fly the Free French standard bearing the cross of Lorraine until mid-October 1940.[85]

While tensions simmered in Oubangui, in Gabon they spilled over. On the evening of August 28–29, Governor Georges Pierre Masson initially decided to join Free France. However, he was almost immediately confronted by the revolt of a large part of Libreville's French population. An archival document suggests that the Gabonese schism of 1940 was shaped

---

[84] ANOM GGAEF 6B 710, telegrams dated November 16, 1940 (signed Eboué) and December 10, 1940 (signed Leclerc). Larminat, p. 122.

[85] ANOM GGAEF 5D 290, Saint-Mart, September 3, 1940. Pierre Kalck, *Histoire centrafricaine des origines à 1966* (Paris: l'Harmattan, 1992), pp. 262–63. ANOM 217 APOM, box 1 telegram 527, dated September 3, 1940; telegram from Libengé, dated September 4, 1940; report from Bangui dated September 22, 1940, signed Saint Mart and letter from Saint Mart dealing with rural Ouganbui, dated October 1940.

and conditioned by an intense rivalry between forestry magnates, overlaid onto political differences.[86] According to Eliane Ebako whose thesis deals with the Gabon crisis, the cleavage in 1940 also resulted in part from tensions between freemasons and missionaries (the lines were not rigid: several Gabonese missionaries, including Fathers Weiss, Thiébault, and Heidet, took Free France's side). Libreville's Bishop Louis Tardy, who commanded great respect at the time, became the most fervent supporter of the Pétainist camp. It was under his pressure that Gabon slipped back under Vichy rule. It promptly applied the new Vichy laws banning masonic lodges.[87]

In attacking Free France, Tardy targeted its weakest flank, which is to say its legitimacy. He dubbed the three glorious days "a military putsch reminiscent of South America."[88] On September 8, a metropolitan French delegation congratulated Gabon for having chosen the right side. The Pétainists denounced Gaullist motives as follows: "You have understood that there was more at stake than your wages, okoumé wood, flour, and wine."[89] According to local Vichyites, the Free French were rapacious adventurers, overthrowing regimes like banana republics, caring only for matters of commerce and personal gain. In early October, a funding drive was launched in Libreville to come to the aid of the victims of the recent Anglo-Gaullist "aggression" on Dakar.[90]

Gabon's Gaullists, who had been in power for roughly twenty-four hours, were now hunted, arrested, and in some cases "deported" by air to Dakar. Africans like the Catholic Jean Hilaire Aubame, who would become a close friend of Eboué's, continued to support the Gaullist cause, under cover of a seemingly apolitical cultural association (Africans were banned from creating political associations at that time).[91] In Brazzaville, Free France resolved to act. One of Vichy's staunch supporters in Gabon, René Labat, who would buck the trend of history by fleeing Gaullist Equatorial Africa for Vichy France, noted in 1941 that General de Gaulle could "scarcely accept the Gabon enclave, a loyalist island in his fiefdom of dissidence." De Gaulle uses much the same language in his *War Memoirs*: "a hostile enclave, that was hard to reduce because it gave on to the ocean, was created in the heart of our equatorial holdings." Later, de

---

[86] ANOM GGAEF 5D 290, note on the events at Libreville.

[87] Ebako, pp. 95–96.

[88] Ibid, pp. 98, 101.

[89] René Labat, *Le Gabon devant le Gaullisme* (Paris: Delmas, 1941), p. 40.

[90] ANOM GGAEF 5D 290, radio-presse officielle dated October 9, 1940.

[91] ANOM GGAEF 5D 290, note on the events at Libreville. Ebako, p. 99, and Weinstein, p. 276.

Gaulle relates having issued the order on October 12, 1940, to "liquidate the hostile pocket in Gabon."[92]

Adolphe Sicé remarked that if Gabon could "separate from FEA" then it followed that Gabon itself was no longer indivisible.[93] This was the key to the first Free French strategy utilized to deal with the unprecedented secession of Gabon. In early September, Brazzaville declared that the Gabonese region of N'Gouiné was henceforth part of Free French Congo. Then on September 14, it made the same claim regarding the Nyanga department. There followed surprise attacks by Free French forces on Mayumba and Sindara. But the capture of Lambaréné, Libreville, and Port-Gentil required heavy interventions. Those assaults involved combined air, sea, and land operations.[94]

The civil war in Gabon was far from the meaningless skirmish that some would describe after the war. Nor was it a drawn-out wholesale slaughter. The fighting left in total "dozens" of dead according to Ebako, "some twenty" according to General de Gaulle, thirty-three according to Jean-Christophe Notin, and "roughly one hundred" according to Jean-Pierre Azéma.[95]

At the time, Gabon seemed crucial to the survival of Free French Africa itself. On November 3, 1940, as Gaullist forces prepared to invest Libreville, Larminat described Gabon as the key to Gaullist success, arguing that the loss of this territory would have jeopardized "the very principle of our presence in Africa." Furthermore, the events of Gabon and Dakar in late 1940 marked the first time since the Paris Commune of 1871 that French troops received fratricidal orders.[96] In fact, some Gabonese struggled to distinguish between two armies wearing the same uniforms. Like any civil war, it exacerbated already heightened antagonisms. On November 8, Gaullist forces intercepted the following instructions from the Vichy loyalists in Libreville to their comrades in Port-Gentil: "set fire to the place so that those Gaullist pigs can't use it, assuming they get as far as Port-Gentil." Vichy forces manifestly did not stick to a half-hearted defensive show, as some have implied. There was real conviction in their

[92] De Gaulle, *Mémoires de Guerre*, Vol. 1, pp. 96, 112.

[93] Sicé, p. 168.

[94] Ebako, pp. 173–74, Larminat, p. 191.

[95] Ebako, p. 244. De Gaulle, *Mémoires de guerre*, Vol. 1, p. 147. Notin, p. 123; Azéma, p. 304. Azéma's estimate strikes me as the most probable, given that Free France lost seven men on the morning of November 9 on the Libreville airfield alone.

[96] The consequences were legion. Pierre Kalck notes that in Oubangui-Chari, "for the first time, imprisoned French officers were escorted down the Oubangui river, guarded by black soldiers." Kalck, p. 264.

anti-Gaullist stance. Consider the case of submarine Captain Bertrand de Saussine who preferred to sink with his vessel, damaged by a British ship, rather than surrender. Finally, the war triggered important population movements of African civilians, who left in numbers for Spanish Guinea, Gabon's northern neighbor.[97]

Libreville fell to Free French forces on November 10; Port-Gentil, the last Vichy bastion, four days later. Recriminations outlasted the fight. When a U.S. official visited the area unofficially in the wake of the battle, defeated Vichy General Marcel Têtu injudiciously sought to persuade him that "the U.S. Civil War was nothing" next to what had just transpired in Gabon. Accusations of perfidy flew from both sides. In Gaullist ranks, Lieutenant-Colonel Parant pointed to what he called "flagrant espionage" by missionaries secretly working for Vichy. Leclerc declared before his troops that "by entering Libreville... you have dealt a direct blow to Hitler," which seems hyperbolic in retrospect. Meanwhile, the Vichy side accused Free France of deliberately attacking Libreville's hospital and of tormenting Bishop Tardy. On November 12, Leclerc ordered that "dangerous and undesirable civilians" be detained on the *Cap de Palmes* vessel – the very same "floating prison" in which Gaullists had been interned weeks prior.[98] Finally, the Gabon crisis even strained alliances. The British had emitted serious doubts about de Gaulle's plan to crush the rebellion, although they ultimately did agree to lend naval support. Anger in London over Pétain's handshake with Hitler at Montoire on October 24 likely nudged the British in the direction of aiding Free France in Gabon.[99]

## FEA and Cameroon as "French Lands"

Once they were solidly lined up behind Free France, FEA and Cameroon brought de Gaulle both real legitimacy and a territorial base. Henri Laurentie wrote, "The empire, limited at first to the few Gaullist colonies... ensured France a political expression despite the eclipse

---

[97] AC, GGAEF 84, transcription of a conversation between Libreville and Port-Gentil. On the departures to Spanish Guinea, see ANOM GGAEF 4(1) D51, Report for Woleu Ntem, 1st semester 1943, p. 35.

[98] AC, GGAEF 84, Parant November 13 1940; Larminat, November 3rd 1940; Leclerc, telegram dispatched on 12 November 1940. AML, 5A, Gabon, November 11, 1940. ANF, 3AG 1 164, Pleven relaying Têtu's words. Larminat, pp. 202–3, 207. On the floating prison, see: ANOM GGAEF 5D 290, note on the Libreville events.

[99] Dinan, pp. 66–7, Thomas, p. 76, Crémieux-Brilhac, *La France libre*, p. 169.

caused by its defeat and capitulation."[100] The Gaullist vision of Vichy's illegality rests on the counterpoint of legality residing with Free France in Brazzaville beginning in August 1940. Without the colonies, Free France in London would have constituted a movement, even perhaps a regime, but not a government. According to Jean Lacouture, thanks to the three glorious days, "de Gaulle ceased to be squatter on the shores of the Thames." René Cassin had observed much the same: "de Gaulle was no longer simply the leader of a small military organization composed of veterans. He now possessed ... territorial authority over parts of the French empire that escaped any control by the enemy."[101] FEA and Cameroon spelled legitimacy.

As soon as they controlled African territories, Free French officials worked to establish sovereignty that served to heighten their credibility. On October 9 from Douala (which replaced Yaoundé as Cameroon's capital on October 5, 1940),[102] General de Gaulle dispatched two telegrams, one to FEA, the other to Winston Churchill. The first read: "On French land free from the enemy's control I am addressing you and the entire population of French Equatorial Africa my ardent patriotic confidence. Long live the French empire! Long live France!" The second, to the British Prime Minister, ran: "On French land free from the enemy's control, I am transmitting to you and the valiant people of the British empire the ardent confidence and faithful friendship of 14 million French citizens and subjects now united with me to pursue the war on the allied side until the final victory."[103] Despite identical introductions, the messages contained striking differences. In his letter to Churchill, de Gaulle included a misleading phrase claiming 14 million French citizens and subjects when in reality FEA and Cameroon counted 8,881 "Europeans" and 6,124,391 Africans in 1941. Consciously or not, he was clearly exaggerating the size and importance of the territories that had joined his cause. To the inhabitants of FEA, he simply expressed his patriotic confidence.[104] However, both messages did share an assertion regarding

---

[100] Henri Laurentie, *L'Empire au secours de la métropole* (Paris: Office français d'édition, 1945), p. 25.

[101] Cassin, p. 233.

[102] André-Hubert Onana Mfege, *Les Camerounais et le Général de Gaulle* (Paris: L'Harmattan, 2005), p. 35. The transfer of various administrative structures from Yaoundé to Douala over the course of the war is recorded in ANCMR NF 382/2.

[103] The first message comes from AC GGAEF 82, circulaire 33; the second from de Gaulle, *Lettres notes et carnets*, p. 136.

[104] The population numbers are drawn from ANOM, Fonds de Galasus, box 2.

FEA and Cameroon as legitimate French lands, beyond Axis control and influence.

The statement of Frenchness was especially dubious with respect to Cameroon, given its status as a League of Nations mandate under French protection since 1922. René Cassin did insist on pursuing mandate language, notifying the Society in Geneva in 1940 that General de Gaulle "has assumed the administration of the part of Cameroon placed under French mandate with all of the powers and obligations that this mandate involves."[105] But in reality, General de Gaulle named Philippe Leclerc, and then a few months later Pierre Cournarie, "governors" rather than "commissioners of the republic" in Cameroon. After all, the republic was no more. According to Richard Joseph, this change in title implied the "annexation" of Cameroon.[106]

In any event, in the fall of 1940, Gaullist legitimacy rested squarely and almost entirely on Free French Africa, a freshly invented designator that linked Cameroon to FEA more than ever. In the wake of his two telegrams on October 27, 1940, de Gaulle recycled his earlier formula, instituting the Empire Defense Council in Brazzaville "on French land."

For his part, Colonel Leclerc considered FEA and Cameroon to be laboratories for postwar France. Early experiments left him concerned. The continuation of pre-1940 quarrels and an inability to agree on the causes of the 1940 defeat constituted ominous signs for the crucial moment when the homeland would be liberated.[107] For in Leclerc's eyes, there existed a real, palpable continuity between France and its colonial realm. While to Leclerc FEA and Cameroon might not have been the jewels of the empire, they nevertheless represented a legitimate point of departure for the Free French movement. Indeed, Leclerc declared before officers and NCOs assembled in Chad on March 21, 1941:

Where are we? We are in French Equatorial Africa, which is to say the only part of France and the French empire not to have accepted submission to Berlin. We do not have a choice and must accept this colony and its sufferings. Let us be happy that this part of the French colonial empire, one of the least developed, had the strength to wave the national

---

[105] Cassin, p. 195.

[106] Marc Michel, "Leclerc et l'Afrique Noire," p. 269, note 3. Richard Joseph, *Radical Nationalism in Cameroun: Social Origins of the U.P.C. Rebellion* (Oxford: Clarendon Press, 1977), p. 46.

[107] ANOM Cab 63, Leclerc to de Gaulle, June 1, 1942.

flag. We would perhaps have had less merit "holding on" under the gentler climate of Morocco or Tunisia, but those beautiful provinces were not able to avoid the Vichy landslide. Today, Free France is French Equatorial Africa.[108]

In this vision, FEA and Cameroon brought nobility to the Gaullist cause precisely because of their underdevelopment and the "sufferings" they purportedly inflicted on the Free French. Which? The harshness of the climate, but also the state of infrastructures, the distance from the main war theaters, the fact of being expatriated so far from France, the accompanying homesickness, but mostly Africa's fundamental otherness in Leclerc's eyes. This seems enough to question whether Free France was entirely comfortable with its Africanness.

### The Genesis of Free French Africa

In FEA and Cameroon as elsewhere, the year 1940 brought fundamental change. In Gabon colonial forces fired at each other before the colonized. In Brazzaville, the governor was toppled and escorted away at gunpoint. After much debate, intimidation, and mutual accusations, many recalcitrant French people from FEA and Cameroon ended up being sent to Vichy-controlled French West Africa, at least until the war in Gabon froze positions and borders. FEA and Cameroon were proclaimed "independent" and regardless of terminology, broke with the motherland and from French West Africa materially, militarily, economically, and politically. Their economy was reoriented into a new British sphere, tied chiefly to Nigeria. The early discussions with Britain would soon yield vast formal commercial agreements linking Free French Africa to the British Empire. Finally, as we shall see, Free France endeavored to establish a constitutional continuity in Brazzaville, which became the capital of an alternative empire, closely linked also to Leopoldville and the Fighting Belgian Congo.

These developments squared poorly with a discourse that asserted the absolute Frenchness of FEA and Cameroon at a time when ties with France were broken. So too did the language of fidelity clash with the reality of the August 1940 rupture with a metropole now judged to be both irresponsible and illegitimate. Yet in spite of these contradictions and its fragile standing in Africa, Free France would succeed in mounting

---

[108] Cited by Général Vézinet, *Le Général Leclerc de Hauteclocque, Maréchal de France* (Paris: Presses de la Cité, 1974), p. 76.

an effective military machine. Over these immense territories spanning from south of the equator to the Sahel, it launched its delicate process of legitimation. It was in Africa that Free France printed money, produced a record of decrees, established institutional foundations, extracted taxes and natural resources, and governed subjects.

# Chapter 2

# Africa as Legitimacy

### Brazzaville, Capital City

From a Gaullist perspective, Brazzaville became the capital of legitimate France on August 28, 1940. According to Jacques Soustelle's memoirs:

> It was in Brazzaville, on French soil and only there, that Fighting France's provisional powers could see the light of day. Only there could they escape the mortal dangers of emigration. It was there that General de Gaulle created the Conseil de Défense de l'Empire on October 27, 1940. In an organic declaration of November 16, also published in Brazzaville, and to which a magistrate from Pointe-Noire contributed judicial input, the Council solemnly refused to admit the Vichy regime's legitimacy.[1]

It was therefore in Brazzaville that Vichy's authority was defied, in Brazzaville that the empire was defended, and from Brazzaville that the struggle was coordinated. In this vision, the capital of FEA became a guarantor of Free France's independence, at once from the Axis and from Free France's own allies. The city on the Congo served as a legitimate capital for the movement in a way that the city on the Thames never fully could. Soustelle reminds us that London evoked the legacies of Huguenot, counterrevolutionary and Second Empire emigration from France. Furthermore, de Gaulle was something of a guest at his Carlton Gardens headquarters, while at Brazzaville his government operated on sovereign French territory.

In Brazzaville, Free France endeavored to establish its legitimacy both legally and practically. Organic Act #1 literally invented the concept of

---

[1] Soustelle, p. 129.

Free French Africa. In fact, its hastily concocted governmental structure involved considerable haziness. Thus, Edgard de Larminat first held the title of delegate, before becoming high commissioner for Free French Africa. His mandate and its limits remained ill-defined vis-à-vis those of the governor-general of FEA, Félix Eboué.[2] The movement rapidly set about instituting a *Bulletin officiel de l'Afrique française libre*, a record of decrees that began in Brazzaville long before being copied in London.[3] Larminat recalls that when General de Gaulle first set eye on it, he exclaimed: "this is good, it looks serious." This was, in other words, a case of "covering legality in a Gaullist sauce," rendering legitimate a dissident movement that aspired not merely to set up a parallel regime in exile, but actually to become France's sole legitimate government.[4]

Pierre Legoux, who directed Brazzaville's mining offices, remembers, "Our first political act involved organizing public authority. Colonel Larminat drew up two organic acts.... As everyone knows, colonial legislation was undertaken by decree, in accordance with the 1854 *sénatus consulte*. We therefore began decreeing in Brazzaville."[5] This point seems essential. Free French legitimacy rested in part on the authoritarianism inherent to colonial rule. Only it could justify the recourse to emergency measures, the systematic use of decrees, even the bundling of powers in the person of General de Gaulle. Free France was not African by accident: the colonial context offered a kind of institutional reprieve to a movement exposed to criticism for its lack of democracy. Against such accusations, Free France could use colonial continuity as both a shield and a mantle.

In practice, of course, such continuity was fragile at best. As a capital Brazzaville resembled neither London, nor Paris, nor Algiers. In 1943, Brazzaville counted 47,500 inhabitants, 1,439 of them Europeans.[6] Like other colonial cities, it featured a white administrative quarter and two so-called native districts, those of Poto-Poto and Bacongo. Europeans socialized at the club (*cercle*), which offered theme-based events such as Corsican and Breton soirées. The administrative district dominated the rest of the town from the "plateau." Since 1934, Brazzaville had taken

---

[2]  Oulmont, "Le haut-commissaire," p. 75.
[3]  Cassin, p. 236.
[4]  Larminat, pp. 167–68.
[5]  AOL, 4B1, Legoux file.
[6]  ADN 116PO/1/95, political report, Pool, March 27, 1943.

on new importance thanks to the completion of the Congo-Océan rail line that linked the capital to the Atlantic.[7]

Susan Travers is known as the only woman to have ever officially served in the French Foreign Legion. Prior to that, however, the young Briton had volunteered to practice as a nurse in Brazzaville in late 1940 and early 1941, before moving to the front and taking part in the battle of Bir Hakeim. Travers depicted the capital of FEA at the time in the following unflattering light:

> Brazzaville was a depressing town on a plateau.... All the *colons* living in the old French Quarter seemed to dislike one another and. divided into rigid social cliques, were mainly pro-Vichy and anti-English. There were three restaurants and no shops except a native market.[8]

Might Travers have exaggerated Vichy's popularity in these early days of Free French rule in FEA? What seems certain is that the city, like the rest of the vast territory now under Free French rule, threw itself rapidly into the war effort.

Seemingly overnight, a martial fever consumed Brazzaville. Three thousand Africans were hired and trained to confect uniforms for the newly created *bataillons de marche*. They toiled in vast workshops that were hastily constructed "from scratch" in 1940. They made buttons, jackets, belts, pants – full uniforms in fact – but also tents, tarps, and other military necessities. A journalist observed patronizingly: "The output of the best trained native workers even matches that of an average worker in Europe." A short distance away, a distillery transformed spoiled wine, of which FEA possessed vast quantities, into medical grade disinfectant, which the Free French desperately needed.[9] Free French Africa now produced finished goods that had previously come from the motherland. The need to propel and support a military campaign, and the resourcefulness that accompanied it, had ushered in a new era.

The Colonna d'Ornano military camp was founded in late 1940. It trained Free France's officer and NCO corps. Its newspaper *La Catapulte* aligned itself with the Allied cause. It reported on lectures pertaining to

---

7 Blanche Ackermann Athanassiades, *France libre capitale: Brazzaville* (Paris: Editions La Bruyère, 1989), p. 74. Phyllis Martin, *Leisure and Society in Colonial Brazzaville* (Cambridge: Cambridge University Press, 2002), p. 51; Weinstein, p. 260.

8 Susan Travers, *Tomorrow to be Brave* (London: Transworld Publishers, 2000), p. 56.

9 Athanassiades, p. 59, and Jean Saigne, "Comment l'intendance de Brazzaville a résolu quelques problèmes en apparence insolubles," *AEF*, June 19, 1943, pp. 3–4.

Great Britain and its colonies. In August 1941, the newspaper offered a large V for Victory as an insert, which readers were asked to post in full view. Perusing it reveals a Brazzavillian emanation of the Gaullist principle according to which FEA constituted and embodied true France. Consider the following announcement: "July 14, 1941: mass at the plateau church, followed by absolution for Free French soldiers fallen on the field of glory. In peaceful contemplation, this July 14 takes on deep significance. All of France stands behind us in this church, true France, the beautiful France of Joan of Arc, which we serve with pride." Even some lighter-hearted columns attest to a local and global positioning, a view on the world shaped by its Brazzavillian standpoint. Thus, *La Catapulte*'s September 1941 issue featured a series of puns in a humorous piece entitled "The Pool stock market." It included references to the "Laval-Kiri cheese company" in which funds could only be invested in deutsch marks. It followed the fictitious climb of "Corned Beef Ltd." and vaunted the sturdy stock of one of Brazzaville's imposing trees. It mentioned tourism futures in Cape Town.[10] Through such puns and many more that defy translation, a universe re-emerges riddled with allusions to Vichy's collaboration, colonial monotony, local languages, British foodstuffs streaming into FEA, Brazzavillian landmarks, and the many furloughs organized for Free Frenchmen to holiday in British South Africa or in the highlands of the Belgian Congo.

The Free French press also had to be forged *ex nihilo*. By January 1941, Brazzaville produced *France d'abord*, a bi-monthly review aimed primarily for external consumption. Subsequently, a weekly publication was created, entitled *AEF* (FEA) that mainly targeted a local audience. According to a U.S. report, the latter was established in 1943, and was initially printed like the former on a press in Leopoldville. It then crossed the Congo River for distribution in Brazzaville. Free France later acquired a press in Luanda, Angola, by means of the Bank of England in Portugal. The U.S. consul, commenting on the publication, remarked that given the degree of censorship the government exerted over it, it could be considered the official mouthpiece of Free France in Africa.[11]

In theory, Radio Brazzaville constituted one of Free France's main sources and guarantees of legitimacy. There can be no doubt that

---

[10] *La Catapulte*, 7, August 1941, pp. 1 and 3, and issue 8, September 1941, p. 4.

[11] NARA, RG 84, U.S. Consulate Brazzaville, classified general records, box 2, publication of a newspaper in Brazzaville. On the Portuguese connection, see: ANC, GGAEF 82, AFL, délégation des services financiers, Brazzaville, August 26, 1942.

General de Gaulle could "say things on Radio Brazzaville that he could not in London."[12] Opened in December 1940, the station conveyed the unfettered and unadulterated voice of the Gaullist movement.[13] However, according to cosmopolitan avant-garde photographer Germaine Krull, who directed the photographic branch of the Free French Information Services in Brazzaville, the station's creation and development had proven laborious. Military authorities had relegated the project to the back burner, judging no doubt logically that it should receive lower priority than armed action. Indeed, the Desjardin brothers, who directed the Information Services, expressed satisfaction when their bureaucratic chain was shifted from military to civilian command.[14] But the archives also reveal deep discord, even chaos, in-house. Thus Warrant Officer Pierre Madeleine deplored the turmoil and disarray in the ranks of the editorial staff. American volunteer Dudley Harmon complained of not being consulted on issues relating to the United States. She also evoked tyrannical labor practices. Finally, a ranting and anonymous 1942 letter denounced a purported Jewish conspiracy at the station, enumerating the handful of "Aryan" staff members (which did earn a red exclamation mark in the document's margins, from a reader at the high commission).[15] In many ways, Radio Brazzaville served as a mirror to Free France itself: admittedly ambitious, it was torn apart by multiple priorities and sapped by a host of internal conflicts. In this sense, it can be likened to a broken utopia.[16]

Radio Brazzaville emerges from archival files as a hornet's nest. It faced threats from both within and without. The idea of establishing a high-powered, short-wave radio emissions post on the shores of the Congo initially preoccupied the Belgian authorities. The latter complained "of seeing two large posts within a few kilometers of each other."[17] To make matters worse, essential matériel was repeatedly delayed. And yet, after much perseverance, a new building opened. On September 24, 1942, General de Gaulle inspected the information services' new headquarters,

---

[12] Hector Marie Tchemo, *La francophonie dans le sang. 1940: aperçu sur l'effort de guerre en Afrique centrale* (Yaoundé: Editions CLE, 2004), p. 49.
[13] FCDG, F11 Desjardins papers, decision dated November 27, 1940.
[14] FLK, Germaine Krull, manuscript "Hallo, hallo Brazzaville vous parle," pp. 26–27.
[15] ANOM, Cab 49, file on Radio Brazzaville.
[16] On the concept of a failed Free French utopia, see: Guillaume Lachenal "Le médecin qui voulut être roi: Médecine coloniale et utopie au Cameroun," *Annales, Histoire, Sciences Sociales*, January-February 2010, 1, pp. 121–56.
[17] ANOM, Cab 49, dossier Radio Brazzaville.

as well as the emitting post. He claimed to be struck by the "modern conception of the installations" and "congratulated the conceivers of a project realized in the heart of Africa despite many difficulties."[18] In the end, however, the powerful emissions equipment only arrived in 1943. If one takes the example of a typical day in June 1943, Radio Brazzaville's programming included music, messages to families, and French-language news reports from Canada and London, as well as Portuguese-language news from Brazil and Spanish-language news from Argentina.[19] A records purchase in October 1941 reveals an emphasis on classical music, even though Ray Ventura, Lucienne Boyer, and Charles Trenet all appear. The accompanying note strictly forbade German language lyrics, although interestingly not Italian ones. Feedback from listeners proved to be generally positive, be it from metropolitan France, the U.S.A., and Canada, or even Invercargill in New Zealand, where one listener congratulated Radio Brazzaville for having reached the world's southernmost city. Letters from France were signed "a listener who wishes to remain in a Free France" and "a group of Frenchmen who refuse to be defeated."[20] Radio Brazzaville news reports generally eschewed simple repetition of press agency statements, and were painstakingly assembled in-house.[21] In this sense, despite the many conflicts that sapped it from within, Radio Brazzaville fulfilled its role of propagating an unfettered Gaullist message.

General de Gaulle quickly imagined a grand capital for Free France in Africa. In late 1940, he decided to have a monument erected in memory of the city's namesake, Pierre Savorgnan de Brazza. In so doing, he was not only reviving a never-realized 1937 project, but also inscribing his regime into a form of colonialism he judged to be especially humane (Brazza was seen by many at the time as an austere colonial hero). A special stamp was conceived to fund the project, yet it languished. By January 1942, only the statue's base was in place. The bust of Brazza and an obelisk remained to be built. They were still missing in 1944 when de Gaulle inaugurated the monument during the Brazzaville conference. In the end, the monument was only completed in 1952, when it was covered by bas-reliefs signed by Barroux. But even this was a scaled-down product, without a bust or an obelisk. Dominating the Bacongo promontory, overlooking the impressive Congo River, set beside the French Ambassador's residence

---

[18] ANF, 3AG1 167, telegram dated September 24, 1942.
[19] "Radio Brazzaville du 18 juin 1943," *AEF*, June 19, 1943, p. 5.
[20] FCDG, F11 Desjardins, note concerning the purchase of records.
[21] Dudley Harmon, "Brazzaville's Radio Sounds a Happier Note," *Christian Science Monitor*, no date, in FCDG, F11, Desjardins.

(the former Case de Gaulle, itself from the Free French era), there remains only a massive concrete skeleton of this ensemble today. The bunker-like stub is known as the "lighthouse" and presently seems to serve mostly as a resting place for passers-by.[22] In 2006, a jarring neoclassical behemoth opened in the heart of Brazzaville. It was intended to replace and even outshine the lighthouse, for it serves as an actual mausoleum containing Brazza's remains.[23] This twenty-first-century temple to the glory of a colonial explorer understandably elicited popular opposition. It, in turn, led the President of the Republic of Congo Sassou Nguesso to erect purportedly more Congolese-inspired statues out of compensation. It is to this chain of events that we owe Brazzaville's shining new black statue of liberty, improbably built in North Korea.[24]

Like its unfinished monument, wartime Brazzaville itself was not without critics. According to Félix Eboué, the city desperately lacked a high-end hotel.[25] Indeed, Free France's makeshift capital quickly encountered a housing crunch. It had never been intended to accommodate an entire regime, with its cohorts of radio personnel, consuls, jurists, inspectors, military leaders, and other functionaries. The housing shortage grew so dire that in October 1941, the high commissioner suggested to the governor-general grouping unwed officials by two or three per dwelling. In April 1942, Eboué went so far as to expel the colony's lead medical official Dr. Jeansotte from his home, so as to make room for the newly named U.S. Consul to Brazzaville.[26] No wonder American Journalist Dudley Harmon quipped that lodging in Brazzaville "is even more difficult to find than in the American capital."

---

[22] ANOM, GGAEF 3B 1091, letter from Sicé dated March 17, 1941, and the file on the Brazza monument in ANOM GGAEF 2Y 12. On the 1937 project, see: "Hommage à Savorgnan de Brazza," *France Outre-mer*, October 28, 1938, in ANOM Agefom 357. On the fate of the monument since 1944, see http://historiensducongo.unblog.fr/histoire-contemporaine/ and Stephen Smith, *Voyage en postcolonie: le nouveau monde franco-africain* (Paris: Grasset, 2010), p. 262.

[23] See Nicolas Martin-Granel, "Abracadabrazza, ou le roman du mémorial Pierre Savorgnan de Brazza," *Cahiers d'études africaines*, 197 (2010), p. 306; and Edward Berenson, *Heroes of Empire: Five Charismatic Men and the Conquest of Africa* (Berkeley: University of California Press, 2012), epilogue.

[24] Marien Ngapili, "Érection des monuments à Brazzaville: réécrire autrement l'histoire du Congo," *Congo Ya Sika*, January 7, 2010, pp. 1–3. On the influence of New York's Statue of Liberty on Brazzaville's, see: "La délégation congolaise du FESPAM visite la Statue de la Liberté à New York," *Les Dépêches de Brazzaville*, May 23, 2009.

[25] ANOM GGAEF 3B 1090, Eboué, February 23, 1941.

[26] ANC GGAEF 138, October 1, 1941. On Jeansotte, see: ANOM GGAEF 3B 1104, Eboué April 8, 1942.

Harmon quit the *Washington Post* in September 1941 to join FEA as a volunteer in the Free French Information Services. She has left an ambivalent portrait of Brazzaville in this era. Her articles on the "Free French Capital in Africa" published in the influential *Christian Science Monitor* in January 1942, sang the praises of the place. Conversely, her personal notes, conserved at Smith College, Massachusetts, complained of a litany of miseries. In her January 7 article, no doubt aimed at improving the image of the Gaullist movement in the United States, Harmon depicted Brazzaville as a "little Paris of Free France...as much in the war as London or Moscow." However, in her own correspondence and notes, her stay in FEA's capital more closely resembled a long-suffering. She complained of the "conversational desert," of Leclerc's refusal to be interviewed because of his contempt for journalists, of inedible food, of interminable hours worked at Radio Brazzaville in a windowless room, of the Information Services' refusal to play to her strengths, and of the sexism of Free French authorities incredulous at the idea of a woman pursuing a career. She vowed never again to complain of Washington.[27] Having crossed the Atlantic to trumpet the success of Free France only to return to the United States miraculously surviving the torpedoing of her vessel by a U-boat, this extraordinary woman betrayed less enthusiasm in private for the Gaullist movement in Africa than she suggested in her public writings.

## Spreading the Word Among Africans

Dudley Harmon's role was clearly to proselytize for Free France across the English-speaking world. But the Gaullist gospel also had to be preached in Africa itself. Prior to June 1940, General de Gaulle's name was perfectly unknown to the vast majority of French people, let alone Africans. Free French efforts in Africa first targeted the lettered elites. The task was not without pitfalls. In Yaoundé, an initial version of the world's very first street panel bearing de Gaulle's name featured only one "l." A second one was squeezed in subsequently and somewhat awkwardly within the angle of the first. The hand-painted tricolor panel in question is now held at the Museum of the Order of Liberation in Paris (see Figure 2). Soon, de Gaulle streets, avenues, and squares proliferated throughout FEA, starting with the capital Brazzaville. There on February 5, 1941, the municipal council decided to name an avenue after the general, and

---

[27] SSCSC, Dudley Harmon papers, box 2, file 18, and box 2, file 15.

FIGURE 2. The first ever de Gaulle street plate, from Yaoundé, Cameroon, 1940. Reproduced with the permission of the Musée de l'Ordre de la Libération in Paris, where it is housed.

another after Colonel Colonna d'Ornano, the camel-mounted officer who had fallen a month prior at Murzuk during a Free French raid in Libya.[28]

Should Africans even be implicated in internal French quarrels, asked an August 1942 note forwarded to the head of police in Brazzaville? The note pondered a theater script that had been presented to the censors for inspection: "It might not be the best idea to allow natives to criticize white leaders, be they Governor Boisson or General Husson."[29] And yet, in the heat of battle, at a time when FEA and Cameroon were experiencing full mobilization, when the war effort required many sacrifices including production increases, when Vichy and Italian inmates languished in prisons throughout the region, African involvement was inevitable. The thought nevertheless bothered this European official. He no doubt saw in the challenge to Husson and Boisson a threat to a tacit colonial pact that in theory upheld the unity, the prestige, and the power of colonial domination. Such seemed to be the price of FEA joining Free France in 1940.

---

[28] ANOM, GGAEF 5D 291, Brazzaville's municipal commission.
[29] ANC GGAEF 126, note signed Clap, Brazzaville, August 11, 1942.

In fact, a large propaganda effort was being directed toward Africans, one couched in colonial methods. According to his memoirs, Joseph Freitag utilized a form of broken French sometimes called *Français du tirailleur* to exhort the African men in his unit to rally to de Gaulle on August 28, 1940: "General Husson no longer command. There be new General. What his name? His name be General de Gaulle. This good!"[30] Freitag evidently did not share Romain Gary's attitude toward *Français du tirailleur*, despite the two men being Free French companions in arms. One of Gary's characters in his award-winning novel *Les Racines du Ciel* contends that this form of speech "constitutes one of France's greatest disgraces in Africa."[31] The episode recounted by Freitag nevertheless reminds us that the very first Free French propaganda campaign in Africa rested on paternalistic word of mouth. The few posters placarded by Leclerc's men in Cameroon were rather rudimentary even by the standards of the day.

The legitimation process also involved sapping Vichy's credibility and insisting on the importance of defeating Germany. In Africa, this implied an obvious emphasis on Hitler's racial theories. Thus on January 7, 1941, Commandant René Genin delivered a speech at Brazzaville's club (*cercle*) entitled unambiguously, "The German hatred of the black race." He cited as evidence the German massacres of colonial troops during the Battle of France in May and June 1940, and the destruction of statues to the glory of Charles Mangin (who had hatched the idea of a French "black army") in Paris and to African troops in Reims. Genin's speech was broadcast over the radio and relayed in the press. One can deduce that it was directed as much to French West Africa under Vichy rule as it was to an internal audience. Genin insisted, "The Nazi press represents blacks as brutes, raised to ranks to which they should have no right by ill-considered French policies."[32] Genin would perish five months later in Syria, felled by Vichy bullets. His words evidently ring true, although their impact remains unclear. What is certain is that he was not alone to play on this theme. Raphaël Onana remembers a veritable "indoctrination" campaign about the evils of Nazi racism aimed at young Cameroonian recruits in Free French ranks, himself included.[33]

---

[30] Joseph Freitag, *Histoires vécues* (Paris: Bernard Neyrolles, 1977), p. 52.

[31] Romain Gary, *Les Racines du Ciel* (Paris: Gallimard, 1956), p. 20.

[32] "La haine des Allemands envers la race noire," *Le Courrier d'Afrique* (FEA edition), January 13, 1941.

[33] Raphaël Onana, *Un homme blindé à Bir-Hakeim, récit d'un sous-officier camerounais qui a fait la guerre de 39–45* (Paris: l'Harmattan, 1996), p. 184.

One should not neglect the important symbolic dimension of the Gaullist accession in Africa. Careful staging marked the occasion of General de Gaulle's first visit to Ati, Chad, in October 1940. The general reviewed troops, greeted European officials then veterans before engaging in head-to-head discussions with Chadian chiefs. The latter addressed him as "the grand sultan of the French," perhaps on the advice of colonial officials. Over the course of their discussions, they assured de Gaulle "of their attachment to France, whose rapid victory they ardently desire."[34] The legitimation process, the argument according to which Vichy represented an illegal parenthesis and that real France was embodied by General de Gaulle, were all being elaborated in the Sahel in October 1940, four years before they reemerged as the official narrative in France.

Fidelity oaths and other sermons were fairly routine in colonial settings. Yet they assumed new meanings once the colony was severed from the motherland. Thus a range of new ceremonies and holidays provided opportunities to prove loyalty not just to the metropole, but also to the Gaullist movement. They included June 18, the day of de Gaulle's foundational radio message, and a set of other significant dates. On June 25, 1941, Governor Pierre-Olivier Lapie transmitted the following message to London to mark the anniversary of de Gaulle's June 26, 1940, memorandum to Churchill: "Mohamad Ourada, Sultan of Ouaddaï, one of the oldest states in black Africa, Mustapha Sultan of Sila, Mohamet Abba, Sultan of Fitri all address for themselves and on behalf of the native population a renewal of their attachment to General de Gaulle and their loyalty and absolute faith in our armies and in the liberation of France on the occasion of this anniversary of the creation of Free France."[35]

In 1941, an anonymous African sergeant from the Mayombe region of Congo told Denis Saurat, a professor at the University of London and director of the French Institute in London, of something Saurat named "the black legend on de Gaulle." The professor described it thus:

De Gaulle was a corporal, and had been dead five years. In a negro village, a corporal is man of very high rank: a mere *tirailleur* already wields considerable power. Being dead is also advantageous: a dead person can accomplish things that a living one cannot. So from the bottom of his grave, General de Gaulle heard that a German corporal whose name was unknown to him,

---

34 ANC GGAEF 138, Lieutenant Ponton to governor of Tchad, Ati, October 18, 1940.
35 ANF, 3AG 165, Lapie to London, June 25, 1941.

had taken Paris. In a surge of indignation, corporal de Gaulle rose from his grave and stated: "now I am a general. Watch out! War is about to begin."[36]

A product of an African oral culture, this story demonstrates at once the degree of penetration of the Gaullist myth in Africa and its modes of appropriation. Some allusions may betray the influence of French propaganda, like the mention of de Gaulle's refusal to give up the fight on June 18, 1940, or the reference to Hitler as the "little corporal" of World War I. But there are also African readings, perspectives, and signifiers at work. The redoubling of de Gaulle's strength from beyond the grave, his surpassing Hitler in rank, and even the key place of ancestry all serve to make this an African story. In an intriguing inversion, in this rendition it was Hitler and not de Gaulle, who had been unknown prior to 1940. As for the final sentence of the passage, it can possibly be explained as follows: to many inhabitants of these territories, the war only really began in earnest with de Gaulle's involvement and Eboué's answering his call in late August 1940. The war effort then took on an intensity never before witnessed in these parts of Africa.

Phyllis Martin has recorded other African readings of this sort, dating from the postwar. Some suggested that de Gaulle could transform himself into a beautiful woman to entrance the enemy; others believed that his words were understood immediately in a wide range of vernacular languages. Raphaël Onana recalls a rumor in Cameroon in 1940, according to which "chased by German aircraft and tanks, de Gaulle suddenly made himself invisible and . . . appeared instantaneously in London, without anyone being able to explain how he had crossed the Channel."[37]

One registers numerous African appropriations of the figure of General de Gaulle. It was incorporated into the kébé-kébé (or kyébé-kyébé) dance in Congo, including in the Poto-Poto and Bacongo districts of Brazzaville.[38] A de Gaulle dance also emerged among the Fang people of Gabon. Elongated-faced de Gaulle masks and rituals appeared in several parts of Gabon. According to Julien Bonhomme, the phenomenon was tied in part to "a multiplication of anti-witchcraft movements at the Gabon-Congo border region." Rites known as Ngol – a phonetic

---

[36] Denis Saurat, "Attention au Tchad," *La France libre*, June 20, 1941. The episode is also recounted in Saurat's book *Watch over Africa* on pp. 83–84, but with a few modifications.

[37] Phyllis Martin, *Leisure*, p. 49; Onana, p. 167.

[38] Phyllis Martin, *Leisure*, p. 49.

adaptation of "de Gaulle" – seem to have mostly expanded after 1945. No doubt these various appropriations stemmed in part from the perceived utility of de Gaulle's image and power. Sometimes however, the Ngol rite could involve subtly subversive objectives, or according to Florence Bernault, it could reflect "a desire to cancel out everyday oppression, at least symbolically."[39] Bonhomme goes further still, suggesting that the de Gaulle dance among the Fang resembled "a parody of colonial order," involving an evocation of the rallying of FEA to the Free French side. Indeed, these dances probably featured echoes of the highly formalized and abundant Free French fidelity ceremonies and oaths to de Gaulle.

Free French officials were on the lookout to ensure that their leader's image was not tarnished. This proved challenging at the height of the war effort, because of the many sacrifices demanded of local populations. Governor Jacques Rogué of Chad was left apoplectic after receiving a 1943 report from Captain Jean Basset, the head of the Bokrou-Ennedi-Tibesti region in northern Chad, which read:

> Here, high quality products are reputed to be "pre-de Gaulle." Poor quality or newer goods are dubbed "de Gaulle" and are held in contempt. The Bank of West Africa five franc bill was replaced by a de Gaulle bill. Although the latter is worth twenty-five francs, it is still deemed inferior to the five franc note. De Gaulle sugar is likewise considered less desirable than British sugar. De Gaulle textiles are more expensive than older ones, but serve different ends.... These value judgments are made clear from conversations with and observations by natives, who remain insensitive to the Free French spirit of heroism and sacrifice.[40]

Here was terrible news for a movement whose legitimacy was based so squarely on its leader. Yet how could things be otherwise when in much of Free French Africa, the standard of living had fallen since 1940?

Already in December 1940, missionaries in French Congo had noted that "prices have almost doubled since the onset of war."[41] The trend only worsened over time. In the Lower M'Bomou department of Oubangui in 1942, an official reported "the return to old modes of dress that had disappeared many years ago; cork outfits are being used once again."

---

[39] Julien Bonhomme, "Masque Chirac et danse de Gaulle: Images rituelles du blanc au Gabon," *Gradhiva* 11, 2010, pp. 81–99. Florence Bernault, *Démocraties ambiguës, Congo-Brazzaville, Gabon: 1940–1965* (Paris: Karthala, 1996), pp. 187–95 (quote on p. 189), and ANOM GGAEF 4(1) D54 August 1946.

[40] ANOM, GGAEF 4(4) D53, Borkou, Ennedi, Tibesti political report, first semester 1943.

[41] CSE, 3J1.19b, journal de communauté, December 4, 1940.

He added, "How could the native purchase trade textiles with the few hundred francs he makes from the sale of cotton? After having paid his taxes, his marriage debts and a little salt, he is left with very little."[42] At Bongolo in Southern Gabon in September 1942, Pastor Donald Fairley of the Christian and Missionary Alliance reported an uninterrupted climb in the cost of living. Vegetable oil had doubled in price in the span of one year, and dried fish had become too costly for most households.[43] Also in Gabon, a report from the Ogooué maritime district in 1942 observed that fish in particular now cost fourteen to fifteen times more than before the war. In the margins, an official at the governor-general's office could only acknowledge: "This complaint is on everyone's lips: it's the price of the war."[44] While some rural areas suffered greatly, they were not alone in bearing the brunt of war. Towns also registered new economic hardships. So suggests an intercepted letter penned by Etienne N'Kom in Douala in September 1941. It reads, "Life in Douala is increasingly unaffordable, impossible in fact for those with small wages."[45] The reality on the ground was a far cry from the promises of economic boom expressed by de Gaulle's champions during the regime change of August 1940.

With so-called de Gaulle products denigrated and the cost of living skyrocketing, some went so far as to question the very meaning of the Free French effort. In his 1942 report on the Ogooué maritime region of Gabon, an administrator observed, "The rather paradoxical situation of a French colony wanting to do something for France against the wishes of metropolitan authorities." This state of affairs, he continued, "has troubled the spirits of the indigenous elites who hold great influence over the less advanced rural elements that come to work in the towns and villages."[46] Setting aside the official's set of hierarchies, it seems worth highlighting the observation, that it was hard to justify Gabon's involvement in the war at a time when the French from Corsica to Lille stood idly by.

[42]  ANOM GGAEF 4(3) D53, Bas-M'Bomou, political report, second semester 1942.

[43]  CMA, RG 820 Gabon, letter dated September 3, 1942, to Reverend Snead. On the history of food and food supply in Gabon, see Jeremy Rich, *A Workman is Worthy of his Meat: Food and Colonialism in the Gabon Estuary* (Lincoln: University of Nebraska Press, 2007).

[44]  ANOM GGAEF 4(1) D50.

[45]  ANOM GGAEF 5D 295. For Douala, Achille Mbembe notes the hike in the cost of a key foodstuff, macabo in the first half of the 1940s. Achille Mbembe, *La naissance du maquis dans le Sud-Cameroun, 1920–1960* (Paris: Karthala, 1996), p. 196.

[46]  ANOM GGAEF 4(1) D50.

### African Tribute

Free France's struggles were not initially limited to matters of legitimacy; they extended to the economic realm. Africa contributed greatly to the movement's fortunes, through natural resources, taxes, and a range of other fund-raising efforts. Although voluntary in theory, fund-raising drives often involved tacit or explicit pressure. They also reached the remotest villages. According to one oral testimony, in Cameroon "the administration posted large images resembling children's drawings. They featured an aircraft and read, 'Here is the airplane that you must buy for General de Gaulle.'"[47] Indeed, the purchase of Spitfires was long considered a prime contribution to the Free French cause. In the Chadian region of Salamat in 1941, one official interpreted the donations organized by the "Salamat chief" Ali Fadel on the one hand, and the "Arab" Cheikh Choa on the other hand, "as a proof of their attachment to our cause." In this corner of Chad neighboring Darfur, the official highlighted the dual origin of the contributions. He explained that after troubles spilled over from Darfur in 1937, the French colonial solution had involved "splitting populations into racially divided villages," a rupture he was now thinking of reversing.[48] In the official's eyes, it was therefore significant and revealing that several ethnic and religious groups had undertaken this identical and virtually feudal act of allegiance.

African chiefs were not the only ones targeted by donation campaigns. Félix Eboué urged officials to give generously. In some cases, African organizations were called on, as was the case of the cooperative of indigenous planters of robusta coffee at Bafang in Cameroon. On November 4, 1941, its president Ngassa handed the authorities 82,420 francs in cash "for the purchase of weapons and munitions in view of delivering the motherland from the invader, and to crush the Germans, so that never again will we be subject to the influence of this enemy."[49] Coming from Cameroon, which had been a German colony until 1916, such claims took on special meaning. Edgard de Larminat was no doubt correct when he observed that many Africans considered the Nazis to be an enemy of Africa "as

---

[47] Testimony cited by Engelbert Mveng, "L'œuvre de Leclerc au Cameroun et la contribution des Camerounais à l'effort de guerre" in Fondation Maréchal Leclerc de Hauteclocque, *Le général Leclerc et l'Afrique française libre, 1940–1942* (Paris: Fondation Leclerc, 1989), pp. 67–68.

[48] ANOM GGAEF 4(4) D 51, report from Salamat, 1941.

[49] ANOM GGAEF 2Y12, Bafang, November 4, 1941.

much if not more than an enemy of the motherland."[50] Yet this point should not obscure the highly ritualized ceremonies of allegiance staged in Free French Africa at this time, ceremonies that frequently involved a rejection of a past German presence on the continent.

One finds similar attitudes expressed in the Legone region of Chad that had been occupied much more briefly by the German Kaiserreich between 1911 and 1916.[51] According to a 1941 report:

> The very day the call went out for voluntary contributions aimed at offering a Chad-Kufra named aircraft to General de Gaulle, two great Noundou chiefs pitched in 10,000 francs apiece. Other chiefs immediately followed their example. Everywhere, the rationale is the same. "We suffered during the period of German domination... and we do not want the Germans to return to this land."[52]

In his book *Mes tournées au Tchad*, Governor Pierre-Olivier Lapie drew up the list of Chadian benefactors to the Spitfire campaign. In every one of the cases he cited, the offering was specifically cast as a donation aimed at defeating Germany. "The Germans killed my father," reads one. Another states: "The Germans always shot at us." However, officials were left with a quandary. In 1941, the Free French were taking aim at Italian, not German forces in East Africa and Libya. Administrator François Pierret in Legone proposed a solution. He simplified the message to Africans as follows: "Germans and Italians were one and the same."[53]

It also bears noting that contributions were systematically personalized, thereby promoting the image and reputation of the new French leader Charles de Gaulle. This was the case in the Baguirmi department of Chad, where the fund-raising drive was presented as follows to local populations: "The Governor of Chad wishes to purchase General de Gaulle a gift on your behalf. This gift is a Spitfire fighter plane."[54]

The funding drive presented multiple symbolic layers. Besides the fact that allegiance was now paid to an individual rather than to the republic, there was also the matter of explicitly or implicitly comparing French

---

[50] Larminat, p. 95.

[51] The region had been ceded by France in 1911, as part of the so-called Caillaux treaty. It also included parts of Oubangui, Moyen-Congo, and even Gabon. Germany took control of these areas – known as Neukamerun – in exchange for recognizing French rights over Morocco. They returned to France during the Great War.

[52] ANOM GGAEF 4(4) D 51, Logone department, first semester 1941.

[53] P. O. Lapie, *Mes tournées au Tchad* (Algiers: Office français d'éditions, 1945), pp. 80–81; ANOM 27 PA1, Pierret testimony.

[54] ANOM GGAEF 4(4) D 51, Baguirmi department, first semester 1941.

colonization to Germany's. In this way, the local past experience of German rule was inscribed into the larger context of the world war. When indigenous populations failed to express this notion themselves, colonial officials did it on their behalf. Thus, Governor Pierre de Saint-Mart of Oubangui-Chari announced by telegram on May 17, 1941: "I am addressing you five thousand francs... for the voluntary contribution fund. This fourth set of donations brings Oubangui's total to 2.5 million francs. I would be pleased if this second plane could bear the name of Ouham-Pende, the region once subject to German domination, which has spontaneously donated 700,000 francs."[55] Such practices differed little from those of Vichy in French West Africa. Indeed, Marshal Philippe Pétain's regime solicited donations from all colonial populations to rebuild French towns that lay in ruins.[56]

Any fund-raising campaign of this sort runs the risk of abuses. In a November 1941 report on the region of Kribi in Southern coastal Cameroon, Jean Brette noted the "dishonest negligence of the superior Fang chief in failing to reimburse contributions made by villagers for a Spitfire, which had been collected after the funding drive had officially terminated."[57] In the hamlets of Bissing and Bidou, Brette insisted on being present to oversee the restitution to villagers, although one can speculate that the donations might well have found their way right back to the chiefs after his departure. The outsourcing of contributions in itself raises questions over the methods used to extract important sums of money from local populations.

Confusion also reigned at the point of arrival. A telegram from General de Gaulle in London dated November 25, 1941, suggests that the Spitfire campaign had encountered a series of hurdles:

> Four aircraft in the French unit that has just been created in Great Britain will bear the names of Chad, Kufra, Oubangui, Ouham-Pendé and Cameroon. For practical reasons, the British Air Ministry prefers to maintain legal property of these airplanes. This presents the advantage of allowing us to replace them immediately if they are destroyed or damaged. In view of this,

---

55 ANOM GGAEF 5D 300, TO Saint-Mart to Eboué.

56 Eric Jennings, *Vichy in the Tropics* (Stanford: Stanford University Press, 2001), pp. 109–10, and Vincent Bonnecase, "Quand le Niger aidait la France: le parrainage de Rosières-en-Santerre par la colonie du Niger (1942–1952)," *Afrique & histoire* 2009: 1 (vol. 7), pp. 131–52. The practice continued after the Liberation; in November 1944, Bangui raised funds to reconstruct a French village. "Bangui reconstruira un village de France," *Bulletin hebdomadaire d'Information du Ministère des Colonies*, November 27, 1944.

57 ANCMR, APA 10092, rapport de tournée, November 1941.

the English government believes that we should not cash the funds earmarked for Spitfires, given that the wishes of donors will be fully respected since we will always have four aircraft bearing the names of the contributing colonies within the unit. I agree with the British Treasury that we should instead direct these funds intended for aircraft towards our general military action. This would serve to diminish the need to borrow from our allies.[58]

This passage reveals at least one conflation: Kufra was actually chosen as a name because of Leclerc's March 1941 victory, and not because the inhabitants of the oasis had contributed to the campaign. Next, it betrays the relative satisfaction of the head of the Free French at seeing these aircraft remain under British control, insofar as this solution promised to ease the movement's cash flow problem. In the end, reasoned de Gaulle, the funding drive in Africa contributed to Free France's overall military effort, thereby reducing its dependency on Britain.

The Spitfire campaign was not isolated. In 1943, a subscription aiming to aid "the patriots fighting in France" swept FEA and Cameroon. The metaphor was clear: the elder external French resistance was shouldering the younger interior one. In Middle-Chari, Chad, a colonial official named Filoche stressed that he did not exert any pressure on the inhabitants to raise funds for this drive named "Valmy" in honor of the French victory of 1792. He admitted only to making a speech in which he "explained the suffering of France and the reasons why General de Gaulle sought a 'voluntary' contribution from all of France's sons, be they white or black." The official seems to have missed some of colonial implications of naming the campaign after a French revolutionary battle against despotism. He also took care to place the word "voluntary" in quotes in his report. Like most of his peers, he extrapolated from the amount raised that "the political climate here is very healthy."[59] In the eyes of authorities, donations served as indices of stability, fidelity, and engagement.

## A Free French Currency

A legitimate power typically prints money. According to Edgard de Larminat, despite its abundant timber, FEA and Cameroon did not produce paper. Furthermore, Governor Eboué and High Commissioner Larminat inherited a very precarious currency situation from the Third Republic. The territories under their control already experienced shortages of French West African bills at the time when FEA and Cameroon sided with

[58] ANOM GGAEF 2Y12, de Gaulle to Haut-Commissaire, November 25, 1941.
[59] ANOM GGAEF 4(4) D 53, political report for Moyen-Chari, 1943.

de Gaulle in August 1940. In addition, Larminat explained that West African bills were not the only legal tender before 1940: many regions in FEA utilized the *Neptune* as their de facto currency – an invention of the Haut-Ogooué corporation, which exchanged them for trade goods. For these reasons, as well as to stamp their legitimacy, Free French officials were eager to create a unique currency for Free French Africa. The decision also reflected the break with Vichy-controlled West Africa, and lent new coherence to the union of Cameroon with FEA. It contributed, moreover, to what Philippe Oulmont has called a Free French strategy of "monetary, and if possible, financial independence."[60] For his part, Larminat described the exercise with his usual sarcasm:

> [The new bills] were printed on beautiful butcher's paper, off-white, thick and overly crisp. But we made up for texture with size – these were big bills. The 1,000 franc bill had as its watermark (if one can use the term) a robust African pirogue-paddler against a pinkish background. For the 5,000 franc bill we had a charming and curvaceous young African woman, soberly donning a glass necklace and a narrow belt confected with seashells. She jiggled in seeming ecstasy against a green background. Here, as in other realms, we were pioneers – this time in the pin-up girl genre.[61]

Beyond this passage's curious blend of sexism and self-disparagement, it bears mentioning that the use of female national allegories of this sort possessed both a long history internationally (Marianne, Germania, Britannia), but also a rich future in Africa.[62] One can only speculate as to the impact of this iconography on conceptions of territoriality and federalism within the new FEA-Cameroonian ensemble. Marking a rupture with French West Africa, these bills in many ways foreshadowed the C.F.A. Franc of 1945,[63] and hence the current central African monetary union. But might they also have materialized the common experiences of the only French territories at war in Africa, or even a federalist ideal in the making? Might they, in this sense, have foreshadowed the project of a United States of Latin Africa championed by Central African President Barthélémy Boganda in the 1950s? It is difficult to move beyond speculation, because the sources at our disposal fail to shed light on a collective or individual experience of Free French federalism in Africa.

---

[60] Philippe Oulmont, *Pierre Denis, Free Frenchman and Citizen of the World* (Paris: Nouveau monde, 2013), p. 202.

[61] Larminat, pp. 168–170 (quote on p. 170).

[62] Odile Goerg, "Couper la Guinée en quatre ou comment la colonisation a imaginé l'Afrique" *Vingtième Siècle*, 111 (2011), p. 85.

[63] First called Franc des Colonies françaises d'Afrique.

Other local considerations also conditioned how the change of currency took place in FEA. On April 13, 1941, Henri Laurentie wrote General de Gaulle to "insist that the new bills bear a distinctive sign beyond the simple mention of 'Free French Africa.'" According to him, "the natives are overwhelmingly illiterate and would fail to recognize the new bills if the only difference resided in those words. Moreover... the changeover operation would be extremely complicated if the old bills resembled the new, and there were no reason to prefer one figure over another." Lastly, Laurentie wished to avoid as much as possible the infiltration or the trafficking of B.A.O. (West African) bills in the border regions of Chad, where West African currency entered via Niger.[64] All of these factors help to explain the decision to create the new bills described by Larminat.

Philippe Oulmont has shown that the first run of Free French African bills was financed with gold extracted from Free French Cameroon and Congo.[65] The exchange of B.A.O. bills for this new Free French currency took place on a large scale. Initially, both currencies served as legal tender, between the formal acceptance of the new bills on February 3, 1942, and the withdrawal of the old ones in the fall of that same year.[66] Rivers and roads teemed with convoys of cash.[67] Finally, an expiration date of October 1, 1942, was imposed on the old B.A.O. bills. The operation encountered some difficulties. In June 1942, for instance, the governor of Chad began changing bills before receiving formal authorization to do so. On November 23, 1942, well after the formal expiration date of the B.A.O. bills, Yves Digo, the financial officer at the High Commissioner's office in Brazzaville, granted a further extension to certain regions. He noted that "the delays in the exchange have been caused not by the state of the roads, but by a shortage of new bills."[68]

In the second semester of 1942, the head of the department of Likouala-Mossaka (Moyen-Congo) reported that the currency changeover had offered a welcome opportunity to "gauge the fortunes and savings of natives. For our department the exchange totaled over four million francs." This "fortune" was of course relative. The overall savings of

---

[64] ANOM GGAEF 3B 2381, Laurentie to de Gaulle, April 13, 1941; and ANOM GGAEF 5B 712, Laurentie to Fort-Lamy, January 20, 1942.

[65] Philippe Oulmont, *Pierre Denis*, p. 201.

[66] ANOM GGAEF 5B 712, Brazzaville, February 7, 1942.

[67] ANOM GGAEF 5B 712, Eboué to Libreville, May 13, 1942.

[68] On the October expiration date, see: NARA, RG 84, U.S. Consulate Brazzaville, classified general records, box 1, Norman Horner's report, p. 2. Digo's telegram is in: ANOM GGAEF 6B 718, Douala, November 23, 1942.

the inhabitants of this area amounted to only four times the taxes they had paid in 1942.[69]

## Materializing Legitimacy

On March 31, 1941, Free France's Commissioner to the Colonies René Pleven congratulated the wife of General Serres in Brazzaville for the ivory crosses of Lorraine that she had left with him in London. Commenting on the "great success" that these symbols of Free France's Africanness enjoyed in the British capital, he asked her to send at least twenty more in order to "show our friends, and those who deserve them, how you have been able to trace such a beautiful image of the cross of Lorraine in French Equatorial Africa."[70] The word "those" originally appeared in the masculine; Pleven then changed his mind, crossed the word out, and replaced it with the feminine. These crosses of Lorraine evidently fulfilled multiple purposes: they served as medals specifically reserved for Free French women (the Free French stood out for having so many women in their ranks), fashion symbols, and markers of both Free French Africa and a kind of African mystique. They conveyed faith, colonialism (as the spoils of hunting in Africa), and an attachment to the Free French cause. The crosses also brought out the lyrical side of General François Ingold, who waxed poetic: "In the clearings of the vast equatorial forest where villages made of bamboo and banana leaves slumber, Africans are polishing the ivory of Lorraine crosses."[71] No doubt the general intended to contrast what he considered the ephemeral nature of African building materials on the one hand, with the splendid firmness of the Free French cause on the other hand. But he seems to have betrayed something else in the process: the fact that the movement's reliance on an African base of operations often sat uncomfortably with some Free Frenchmen. Finally, this ivory extracted from central Africa is evocative in its own right. Like the opulent collection of ivory that Henri Laurentie proudly displayed to his dinner guest Germaine Krull, these trophies constituted the flip side the allegory of Gaullism as conservationism. Romain Gary articulated the latter in his famous novel *Les racines du ciel*.[72]

---

[69] ANOM GGAEF 4(2) D 76, political report for the department of Likouala-Mossaka, second semester 1942; and G. Fortuné's response, dated June 11, 1943.

[70] ANOM Cab 55, Carlton Gardens to Mrs Serres, March 31, 1941.

[71] François Ingold, *L'Epopée Leclerc au Sahara* (Paris: Berger-Levrault, 1945), p. 42.

[72] See Anne Simonin's innovative reading of the elephant metaphor, in which she contends that it reflects "an idealized Free France." Anne Simonin, "L'Eléphant français libre:

An uncommon book appeared in Brazzaville in 1943. Only a few copies of the first edition seem to have survived. Entitled *Gutenberg in the Bush*, it contains African folktales presented by Bela Sara (an ethnonym, Bela hailed from Chad). Pierre Romain-Desfossés coordinated the project and would subsequently go on to found the influential Academy of Popular Art in Elisabethville. The precise division of labor between Romain-Desfossés, Bela Sara, and other African artists within the pages of *Gutenberg in the Bush* remains unfortunately nebulous. The preface announces that the book is composed in the style of La Fontaine but in "tirailleur" French. It further explains that the remarkable woodcuts that illustrate the text "are all done by knife, on wood, by natives of FEA,"[73] with profits from the volume earmarked for the war effort. The book's frontispiece crystallizes the act of allegiance at the heart of this project. It features two Africans wielding lances. They are shown surrounding, protecting, and perhaps even appropriating a cross of Lorraine, thereby both exalting and rooting the Gaullist cause in Africa (see Figure 3).

Displays of fidelity to the new regime abounded, whether forced, encouraged, or staged. In November 1940, an African worker at Armand Vigoureux's mine in the French Congo stumbled on a gold nugget weighing 552 grams. It bore a remarkable resemblance to the contours of the African continent, save for the fact that it was missing the Horn of Africa – a happy coincidence given that it was partly under Italian control at the time. According to one testimony, the worker found the nugget in an area that Vigoureux had ruled out as unpromising. We shall see in a subsequent chapter that Vigoureux experienced frequent run-ins with the administration over his labor methods. No doubt he was trying to gain favor by offering it to de Gaulle. At Brazzaville on April 24, 1941, engineer Pierre Legoux, director of mining across Free French Africa, issued the following speech before solemnly handing the nugget to the leader of Free France:

> In a spontaneous gesture, FEA has decided to place half of its gold at the disposal of the Free French forces. Here is an expression of its fighting spirit. Gold, which so often stirs the basest appetites, which often fuels the vilest sentiments, this evil metal whose mirage causes madness, gold is today assuming a noble role; it is now an instrument of war. The golden calf is being transformed into tanks and fighter aircraft.... That is the message of this nugget. Let us listen to the lesson: among the thankless tasks of the

Babar, Romain Gary et la France libre," *Vingtième Siècle. Revue d'histoire*, 112, 2011, pp. 70–82.

73 *Gutemberg dans la brousse*, Brazzaville, 1943, preamble. Thanks to Naomi Greani for sharing her findings about Bela.

FIGURE 3. Frontispiece to *Gutenberg dans la brousse* (Brazzaville, 1943). Artist unknown. Author's copy and photo.

home front, gold production may be less glorious and intoxicating than direct action at the front. It is nonetheless a form of warfare.[74]

While the speech succeeded in underscoring that half of FEA's gold streamed straight into Free France's coffers, and in stressing the role of FEA as a productive Free French "home front," it also contained important silences. Completely absent were the African laborers, whose weekends Vigoureux had abolished, and who experienced humiliating body searches on leaving the mine. The spontaneous nature of the African sacrifice described by Legoux can therefore be called into question. The episode, nevertheless, reveals Free France's dependency on an Africa that was literally figured in the gold it brought to de Gaulle's movement.

[74] AOL, box B, 4B, 4B1, Legoux file.

The Africa nugget would experience interesting and rich afterlives. Without referencing his version of events, Albert M'Paka recounts that General de Gaulle immediately handed the nugget to Governor Eboué, declaring: "A golden Africa! That belongs to you, Mr. governor general!"[75] Meanwhile, Free Frenchman Jacques Bauche, who fought in Gabon, Eritrea, Syria, and Provence, relates that "a gold digger in Congo handed General de Gaulle an enormous nugget in the shape of France, which the treasurer of Carlton Gardens immediately used to fill the movement's coffers."[76] Were country and continent-shaped nuggets emerging in such abundance from the soil of the French Congo? A more likely explanation would be that Bauche allowed his imagination to transform the Africa nugget into a French one – an interesting slippage. Finally, after Congolese independence, the actual Africa nugget ended up in the confines of the French embassy in Brazzaville. References to it resurfaced periodically, most notably during the diamond scandal involving Jean-Bedel Bokassa and Valéry Giscard d'Estaing.[77] Nowadays, the nugget on display at the magnificent Case de Gaulle – as the French ambassador's residence in the Republic of Congo is known to this day – is but a copy of the original.[78]

## Preparing for War

All this symbolism rested on a reality: Free French Africa was plunged into war upon its creation. Militarization took place rapidly. As of October 24, 1940, the governor-general of FEA ordered that African children holding a certificat d'études, as well as children attending the Edouard Renard school in Brazzaville, be subject to military training.[79] In a note dated November 6, 1940, Adolphe Sicé explained that he wished to apply to Fort-Lamy in Chad the same measures that had been undertaken in Brazzaville. These involved introducing "basic military training" in schools, with the goal of "training future native N.C.O.s and soldiers." Next on

---

[75] Albert M'Paka, *Félix Eboué, Gouverneur général de l'Afrique équatoriale française, premier Résistant de l'Empire* (Paris: L'Harmattan, 2009), p. 115.

[76] Jacques Bauche, "L'histoire financière de la France libre," *Revue de la France libre* 232, 1980, available online at www.france-libre.net/temoignages-documents/temoignages/histoire-financiere-fl.php.

[77] AOL, carton B, 4B, 4B1, Legoux papers.

[78] R. Césaire, "L'Afrique centrale au cœur des cérémonies du 70ème anniversaire de la France libre," *AROM* 22 (November-December 2010), p. 9.

[79] ANOM GGAEF 5D 290, note dated October 31, 1940.

FIGURE 4. George Rodger. Original caption reads: "Camerocn, Douala. Children play at soldiers with the Free French flag, 1941." ROG 1940010W00010/25. © George Rodger, Magnum Photos.

the list of priorities was the objective of "giving rudimentary knowledge of military terms in French" to African volunteers "while at the same time providing basic military training." All of this was to be accomplished in a period of six months, "everywhere where there are native trainers." An expert in military pedagogy by the name of Lieutenant Louis Marand was charged with spearheading these activities, and then extending them to Bangui and Pointe-Noire.[80] African youngsters were marching in rank under the banner of the cross of Lorraine as of the fall of 1940.

In Douala in July 1941, British photographer George Rodger, famous for his work in *Life Magazine*, trained his camera on a scene he titled "children playing soldier" (see Figure 4). These young Cameroonians marched with wooden guns on their shoulders. Their leader, a few years older than the rest, waved the Free French flag featuring the cross of Lorraine. His expression seems somewhat less carefree than his younger comrades in toy arms. Were these children simply imitating what they saw at school or in town? Several signs suggest that Rodger had actually captured a formal school activity like those introduced by Marand. The

---

[80] ANOM GGAEF 5D 290, note dated November 6, 1940. Also see in the same file: "application des directives du Gouverneur général de l'AEF," November 6, 1940.

sameness of the youngsters' hats as well as their white uniforms all point in this direction. The fact that they were barefoot in no way detracts from this hypothesis, for as we shall see, African troops usually trained in these conditions.

## An African Gaullist Phoenix

While the rallying of FEA and Cameroon in August 1940 afforded instantaneous capital and recognition to the Free French movement, there followed a period of growing pains. It involved a civil war in Gabon, an uphill battle aimed at instilling a new cult of de Gaulle, the creation of an alternative imperial capital, new iconography, currency, statutes and statues, the laborious inception of an international radio transmissions center, and the quest for African tribute. Such offerings are admirably encapsulated by the Africa-shaped gold nugget, extracted from the Congolese earth by an African miner, before being presented to de Gaulle by his white employer in the name of the African continent.

Africans obviously reacted in a range of ways to the new political norm. Many chiefs learned new political registers and idioms. The fear of German influence or even of a German return remained strong, but was also manipulated by a host of actors. In many regions, populations elaborated resourceful strategies to compensate for a spectacular drop in the standard of living. Young people faced incorporation into a new military machine that extended its tentacles as far as the school system. For various motives, some Africans aligned themselves with the Gaullist phoenix raised from the ashes of defeat. Others sought to profit from the new regime, be it by channeling its powers or by embezzling donations aimed at purchasing a Spitfire for a distant general.

# Chapter 3

## Dysfunction in Gaullist Africa

From the outset, Free France faced monumental difficulties in Africa: chronic shortages of legitimacy, matériel (i.e., military hardware), and numbers. Soon, it engineered the exploitation of resources and populations in regions that colonial stereotypes had consistently depicted as the most backwards of the empire. One needs to add another item to this list of hurdles. In many ways, Free French Africa proved to be dysfunctional. Indeed, the movement soon experienced both internal and external dissonance. Administrators who arrived with utopian reform schemes found themselves digging through avalanches of conflicts and having to forestall their grand projects until the postwar. The proximity of Vichy-controlled French West Africa, as well as the presence of pro-Pétain elements in Free French Africa, further fueled tensions. These cleavages were anything but trivial. Through them, one can gauge the weight and reach of institutions, networks, ideologies, and colonial structures, as well as the impact of the massive shifts brought about by the three glorious days of 1940.

As reflected in the work of many novelists such as Marguerite Duras, Louis-Ferdinand Céline, Georges Simenon, Jean Paulhan, and André Gide, the colonial universe bore a reputation for rivalry, pettiness, and dysfunction. FEA and Cameroon were no exception. Thus, in the midst of the Phony War, on March 18, 1940, Corporal Charles Priem who served in a motorized unit in Mbalmayo, Cameroon, wrote back to his family in Mérignac near Bordeaux:

> It's best not to mention the colony's everyday life. It's purely colonial: administrative and military chaos, favoritism, negligence. etc. It would be

astonishing to win a war in such a fog. Lost colonial products, men kept in uniform for no apparent reason, absence of rules.[1]

Indeed, this war, or rather the Battle of France that took place within months of this verdict, would be lost so quickly and calamitously that it would shake France's very foundations. The "colonial fog" evoked here was obviously not its cause, although Priem's testimony seems symptomatic of the kind of disarray described by Marc Bloch in his famous *Strange Defeat*. A few months later, as Free France established a foothold in FEA and Cameroon, de Gaulle's representatives inherited these deep and ancient fissures. They would try to bridge them as best they could. To further complicate matters, new disagreements emerged from within and without, some of them intractable.

### Relations with Pétainist West Africa

The greatest divide of all was naturally the one that separated Pétainists and Gaullists. Winston Churchill wrote in his memoirs that the three glorious days had managed to stem the spread of the "Vichy virus" in Africa.[2] What was its degree of virulence in continental sub-Saharan Africa in the second half of 1940?

On November 10, 1940, following a long inspection tour of "loyal" North and West Africa, Vichy's delegate general in Africa, Maxime Weygand, reported the prevailing attitudes he had encountered as follows: "In the souls of most French people, both civilians and military, the dismay and the pain of the defeat and the armistice persist. For them, Germany remains the enemy and England is perceived favorably despite Mers el-Kébir and Dakar." He estimated the proportion holding such opinions at "all French civilians . . . and more than half of officers and administrative officials." As for Africans, he deemed that they too "preferred to be ruled by the English than by the Germans." Obviously concerned, Weygand warned that Vichy was also losing the radio war: "The B.B.C.'s lies remain unanswered because we do not have the resources to counter them."[3] Weygand identified other problems. Mined by what he saw as freemasonry's insidious influence, colonial personnel on location needed

---

[1] ANOM Togo-Cameroun 29, file 256, excerpt from a March 18, 1940, letter intercepted by postal censors.
[2] Churchill, Vol. 2, p. 494.
[3] Weygand to Pétain, November 10, 1940, in *Documents diplomatiques français 1940* (Vol. 2), (Brussels: Peter Lang, 2009), pp. 851–53.

replacing. While this was only one man's opinion, it was that of Pétain's personal representative in Africa, a convinced Vichyite who had no reason to make the situation appear bleaker or rosier than it actually was.

Despite this anti-German and pro-British attitude, and even though Britain did indeed hold an imperial radio advantage in 1940, Weygand and his acolytes like Pierre Boisson prevailed. They managed to keep the vast territories of French West and North Africa under Vichy control. Several factors can help explain this, starting with Weygand's own very effective actions. He spared no energy explaining to West Africa's inhabitants that the "Anglo-Saxons" were responsible for the war and the 1940 defeat. At the same time, he labeled the Free French "traitors who have taken up arms against their fatherland."[4] Moreover, from Dakar, Governor Boisson orchestrated a coordinated repression of Gaullist dissidence, with the help of instruments both old and new.[5] Boisson had recently served as governor of FEA, which only reinforced the fratricidal nature of the conflict that pitted him against Eboué and de Gaulle. The latter provided another, extremely compelling explanation for why West Africa remained faithful to Vichy: Pétain's "National Revolution, which relied on notables, increased the power of administration, featured veterans parades, and showcased anti-Semitism; all of this answered the desires of many."[6] In other words, Vichy ideology appealed to many colonials and in particular to those at the helm in Dakar.

Finally, Boisson and his men showed resolve. When another opportunity for switching to the Allies presented itself in late November and early December 1942 following the Anglo-American landings in North Africa, Boisson initially tried playing the Admiral François Darlan card. Then, after the admiral's assassination, he turned to the Henri Giraud option. In his November 25, 1942, speech announcing his support of Darlan, Boisson let out an enthusiastic "Long live the Marshal! Long live France!" Only timidly and gradually were Vichy's most odious measures reversed during the Giraud phase in West Africa from January to July 1943. Thus, remaining political prisoners were released on February 26, 1943. On March 14, the laws against Jews and freemasons were finally repealed, although the specifics of these abrogations were still being debated in Dakar on April 6.

---

[4] Ibid, p. 852. On Weygand's role, see Jacques Cantier, *L'Algérie sous le régime de Vichy* (Paris: Odile Jacob, 2002), pp. 57, 94.

[5] William Hitchcock, "Pierre Boisson, French West Africa and the postwar épuration: a case from the Aix files," *French Historical Studies*, 24:2 (2001), pp. 322–24.

[6] De Gaulle, *Mémoires de Guerre*, Vol. 1, p. 115.

The crucial point is that French West Africa remained on the sidelines of Free France's war effort so long as Boisson remained in power. Boisson was only toppled on June 23, 1943. A protest involving some thousand Africans and five hundred colonials finally forced his hand from within. Around the same time, from without, de Gaulle was gaining an upper hand over Giraud in Algiers. Fighting France's governor of West Africa, Pierre Cournarie, only took control of the territory on July 17, 1943.[7]

While FEA and Cameroon were in overdrive for the war effort, invading Mussolini's Libya through Chad, between August 1940 and July 1943, French West Africa had been cloistered. Its leaders had remained deaf to countless Gaullist and British overtures. There were in fact no official contacts between Vichy and Free French Africa. Accidents offered the occasional insight into what was happening on the other side of the Chad-Niger border. This occurred in 1941 when two Gaullist dissidents in West Africa, Raby and Journeux, were dispatched by ship to France to be judged, only to have their vessel intercepted by the Royal Navy. Freed by the British, sent to Freetown, they finally ended up in Free French Africa. There they were probably mined for information by the Gaullist secret services.[8] They no doubt chronicled the purges they themselves had experienced.[9] In addition to these revocations, many West Africans were profoundly shocked by the accrued racism they suffered under Vichy, with for instance the creation of an "all white" beach in Dakar under Boisson.[10]

In these conditions, one can easily understand why Fighting France put Boisson on trial. However, it bears mentioning that Free France's native policy was generally no more enlightened than Vichy's. Indeed, as both Frederick Cooper and Jean Suret-Canale have noted, Félix Eboué's approach in many ways mirrored that of his former superior Pierre Boisson. They shared an essentialist vision of the African peasantry, both of

---

[7] Boisson faced charges drawn up by the commission d'épuration of the Committee for National Liberation on November 13, 1943, as Giraud lost out. Tony Chafer, *The End of Empire in French West Africa: France's successful decolonization?* (Oxford: Berg, 2002), pp. 41–42; Hitchcock, pp. 332–35. On the April 6 date, see ANS 17G 169, letter from the Director of Political Affairs, April 6, 1943, viewable at the ANOM on microfilm 14 Miom 2324 reel 241.

[8] The Journeux and Raby saga is recounted in ANOM GGAEF 3B 192 (Eboué to de Gaulle, July 25, 1941).

[9] On purges in Vichy West Africa, see Catherine Akpo-Vaché, *L'AOF et la seconde guerre mondiale* (Paris: Karthala, 1996), pp. 67–68; 138.

[10] Ruth Ginio, *French Colonialism Unmasked: The Vichy Years in French West Africa* (Lincoln: University of Nebraska Press, 2006), pp. 107–10.

them seeking to avoid its "uprooting" at all cost. "The African peasant resembles the French one; he may move around but he is attached to his village, his tribe, his land and beliefs; outside of his village he loses his soul," wrote Boisson in 1942, in a sentence that could equally have been penned by Eboué. While in theory both men contemplated abolishing forced labor, in reality the practice redoubled on their clocks. In the name of wartime productivity, both ended up facilitating the recruitment of African workers, to the benefit of banana planters in Guinea and that of gold miners in French Congo. If one were to identify a break in labor policy, it would not be tributary of the Vichy-Gaullist divide but would instead have to do with the postwar advent of African trade unions.[11] In point of fact, Free France like Vichy imposed harsh labor conditions, aggravated in the West African case by a British naval embargo. In West Africa, forced labor's zenith came in 1943–44 after Fighting France's advent to power, and not before.[12] It should come as no surprise then that one of the characters in Guy Menga's novel *Case de Gaulle* would accuse Félix Eboué of being "Boisson's twin brother."[13]

On August 13, 1943, less than a month after Fighting France came to power in West Africa, scientist Théodore Monod forwarded to René Pleven an anonymous letter from Côte d'Ivoire, dated July 25, 1943. Deploring the paltry wages of African workers, the letter also denounced the attitude of big planters who felt the need to whip workers with the notorious hippopotamus-hide chicote to obtain what they termed "normal outputs." The letter added, "This coterie misses Vichy, whose neoracism seemed to open fine perspectives of forced labor for blacks." In the note accompanying the letter, Monod wrote candidly: "I cannot help but think that these are the same methods that we are blaming the Germans for in France, and which we employ elsewhere to the vanquished." Here was a remarkable association of Nazi and colonial methods, articulated seven years before Aimé Césaire would do so in his famous *Discourse on colonialism*. Monod's outcry seems not to have altered

---

[11] Jean Suret-Canale, *Afrique noire occidentale et centrale* Vol. 1 (Paris: Editions sociales, 1964), p. 574; Hubert Deschamps, *Méthodes et doctrines coloniales de la France* (Paris: Armand Colin, 1953), pp. 177–78; Frederick Cooper, *Decolonization and African Society: the Labor Question in French and British Africa* (New York: Cambridge University Press, 1996), pp. 144–49; 156–59. The Boisson quote is from ANOM 1Affpol 883, 10, "Directives pour un programme d'équipement administratif et économique," p. 2.

[12] Nancy Lawler, "Reform and Repression under the Free French: Economic and Political Transformation in the Côte d'Ivoire, 1942-1945," *Journal of the International African Institute*, 60: 1 (1990), pp. 88–110.

[13] Guy Menga, *Case de Gaulle* (Paris: Karthala, 1984), p. 48.

much in West Africa. The war effort continued to be used to justify output under Fighting France. The advent of Free France left many disillusioned.[14]

Despite the similarities between Vichy and Free France's outlooks on Africans, the fact remains that in West Africa, as elsewhere, Vichy fought the Gaullist movement tooth and nail between 1940 and 1942. It follows, therefore, that West Africa's incorporation into Fighting French ranks in 1943 was anything but seamless and harmonious. Already on June 19, 1943, during Boisson's last days in office, René Pleven had announced his intention of reestablishing "republican legality" in West Africa, much as had been done with considerable difficulty on Réunion Island. A few weeks later, Pleven admitted that the challenges were daunting. From a "legislative point of view," he took stock of "confusion" resulting from three nondemocratic regimes that West Africa had experienced, namely the Vichyite, Darlanist, and Giraudist phases. As a result, he instructed that all laws and decrees from these three eras be individually combed over.[15] The legal transition to Free France was one matter, managing the change on the ground quite another. Starting in July 1943, grievances piled up on Dakar desks. In one of them a pastor complained of the harassment and internment he and his fellow missionaries of the U.S. Christian and Missionary Alliance suffered in Ntoroso over the previous three years. Whites evoked intimidation, blacks the use of the chicote.[16]

Tensions endured, as is suggested by an incident that unfolded at Dakar on January 9, 1944. In broad daylight, a French merchant tore up an image of King George VI from the hands of an African newspaper salesman. The salesman reported the matter to nearby British agents, shredded evidence in tow. The incident quickly became diplomatic.[17]

Georges Chaffard and Jean Suret-Canale have provided other examples of the strained atmosphere in post-Vichy West Africa. Some Pétainist military personnel defiantly displayed their medals to arriving Free French

---

[14]  AOL, Pleven correspondence. Monod, August 13, 1943, and the accompanying letter dated from July 1943.

[15]  ANS 17G 169, Pleven, Alger June 19, 1943, and Pleven to the Governor of West Africa, August 7, 1943, viewable at the ANOM on microfilm 14 Miom 2324 reel 241. On the slow and delicate reestablishment of republican rule on Réunion Island, see Eric Jennings, "Les anciennes colonies: laboratoires pour la France libre?" in Anne Simonin, Jean Quellien, Bernard Garnier and Jean-Luc Leleu eds., *Pourquoi Résister, Résister pour quoi faire?* (Caen: Editions du Mémorial de Caen, 2006), pp. 227–236.

[16]  ANS 17G 11, letter from Pastor Mabille, February 14, 1944, viewable at the ANOM on microfilm 14 MIOM 2289.

[17]  ANS 17G 14, viewable at the ANOM on microfilm 14 MIOM 2289.

officials, medals won for having fought Gaullist forces in Syria and Lebanon. On D-Day, and even on the day of Paris' liberation in August 1944, some Abidjan missionaries refused to raise the tricolor flag. Some of these zealots were the same men and women who had insisted on leaving FEA and Cameroon when they swung over to de Gaulle in August 1940. In those cases, the Free French cause was being rejected a second time.[18] Similarly, a letter intercepted in French Soudan (Mali) on January 9, 1944, explained that a large percentage of military personnel wished to see de Gaulle's Fighting French overturned just as Vichy had been in FEA and Cameroon four years prior. These elements clamored mostly for the "end of democratic rule." Democracy was a paper tiger at best in most of French Africa, but that technicality seemed to matter little to staunch authoritarians.

Finally, on January 6, 1944, a ship captain was judged and condemned in Dakar for having ostentatiously displayed a portrait of Marshal Pétain on board his vessel. The accused claimed to have no knowledge of the October 12, 1943, law banning all images of Pétain and other Vichy dignitaries in public places. On learning of the light sentence he incurred, an anonymous source noted: "Enough accommodating! Whoever would have displayed a portrait of de Gaulle before November 1942 would have been condemned to death, or at least to forced labor."[19] The remark was more or less accurate, and underlines how French West Africa's incorporation on the Free French side proved laborious and contested. These examples also tend to belie Weygand's 1940 opinion: it would seem that Vichy counted quite a few ardent supporters in West Africa.

The Vichy pill proved no easier to swallow over time. In November 1944, the representative of the Cross of Lorraine organization in French West Africa complained that the wave of administrative reinforcements that had finally arrived from France and from North Africa included: "some scandalous arrivals like S.O.L.,[20] notorious collaborators, etc."[21] West Africa relived its painful 1943 switchover time and again. In this instance, it was the liberation and purges in France that produced echoes

---

[18] Georges Chaffard, *Les carnets secrets de la decolonisation* (Paris: Calmann-Lévy, 1965), pp. 31–32. Suret-Canale, pp. 582–83.

[19] All of these incidents are reported in ANS 17G 14, viewable at the ANOM on microfilm 14 MIOM 2289.

[20] The Service d'Ordre légionnaire (S.O.L.) was Pétain's vanguard that became the core of the notorious Milice in 1943.

[21] ANS 17G 14, Croix de Lorraine association, Dakar, November 9, 1944, viewable at the ANOM on microfilm 14 MIOM 2289.

of French West Africa's. Shock waves and reverberations bounced back between metropole and colony.

As elsewhere, in French West Africa the purge failed to satisfy all parties concerned. In a sense, the rapid succession of Pétain, Darlan, and Giraud phases, as well as the absence of Germans, rendered the situation hazier and more confusing than in the metropole. After all, in France retribution occurred after the extreme radicalization of Vichy and in the wake of the nation's descent into civil war. Tony Chafer and Nancy Lawler conclude that the purge process in French West Africa was timid and largely unfinished, mostly out of pragmatism. Indeed, due to a lack of qualified personnel, some governors from the Vichy era, like those in Niger and Mauritania, remained in office. Pierre Boisson's own trial got bogged down. He perished before sentencing and even managed to garner some sympathy by invoking both his purported Germanophobia and his desire to keep the empire French.[22]

The interminable intrigues in Algiers and Dakar in 1942 and 1943 proved a source of both frustration and pride in Free French Africa. Thus, on November 17, 1942, the head of the Free French delegation in Cameroon transmitted the following message to the authorities:

> Yaoundé's whole population asks you to telegraph General de Gaulle to tell him our indignation at seeing Fighting France cast aside in North Africa, to the benefit of military traitors, degenerate politicians and incompetent functionaries who, after having prepared France's defeat through carelessness have only soiled its honor through lowly conduct with the enemy. This is an insult to the dead of Gabon, Kufra and Murzuk, of Syria and Bir Hakeim. We Free French of the first hour remain resolutely behind our leader who was the only one to cry out revolt and hope on June 1940 to galvanize the nation. Only he has always shown the clairvoyance and energy needed to save the country, while the likes of Darlan, Flandin, Pucheu and their consorts were useless traitors in the past and will remain so in the future.[23]

The message betrayed firstly the positioning of the Free French in Cameroon as the earliest and hence the most legitimate resistors. They buttressed this assertion with the battles Free French Africa had waged against Vichy, Italy, and Germany. Secondly, the text elaborated a Gaullist argument revolving not only around a precocious engagement, but also around their leader. Thirdly, the passage revealed the contempt

---

[22] Chafer, p. 43. Hitchcock; Lawler, p. 91. On the governor of Niger, Jean Toby, see Camille Lefebvre, "Territoires et frontières: du Soudan central à la République du Niger, 1800–1964," PhD thesis, University of Paris I, 2008, p. 375.

[23] ANCMR 2AC 11190A, Yaoundé, November 17, 1942.

Cameroonian Gaullists heaped on converted former Vichyites in North Africa, like Darlan. They considered them unredeemable, their initial treason precluding any subsequent rehabilitation. Finally, the message contained no reference to democracy or to the republic. In fact, it conflated Vichyites and politicians as sources of dishonor. Instead, these Gaullists rooted their legitimacy in military victories. Battle-hardened and defiant, these first Free French could scarcely tolerate to see their leader contested in either Algiers or Dakar. This was perhaps what unified them the most.

### Refractory Vichyites

To the external Vichy threat, one should add an internal one. Initially, in the wake of the three glorious days, Gaullist authorities allowed recalcitrant individuals to leave Free French Africa for Vichy-controlled West Africa. But Gabon's secession and the ensuing tensions at the Niger-Chad border fundamentally altered the situation, as did the treatment that Vichy meted out to Gaullist sympathizers. In an October 16, 1940, telegram to all regions of FEA and Cameroon, Larminat announced a harsher policy: "I have decided as of today to grant no further request for repatriation on the grounds that individuals are refusing to join the Free French cause. Those wishing to return to France in spite of this will be considered to have resigned their positions."[24]

Repatriation to France on ideological grounds was henceforth prohibited. But what of the lukewarm and the fence-sitters? On December 8, 1941, René Pleven reported the National Committee's recommendations to this very question: such individuals should be maintained at their posts, regardless of their lack of enthusiasm. Indeed, the committee deemed that "it is not opportune to pronounce judgments if they cannot be acted upon." The hour of justice was merely being delayed, the committee insisted. Finally, Pleven noted that "it was best to leave Vichy with the monopoly of odious behavior and sanctions like those they have taken against the Free French." On paper, then, freedom of opinion reigned in magnanimous Free French Africa.[25]

In reality, despite the nobility of such sentiments, the Franco-French schism was creating an untenable atmosphere. On April 12, 1941, Pierre-Olivier Lapie informed Brazzaville of "the problem of sending a Vichyite here given the tense conditions." Rightly or wrongly suspected of being

---

[24] ANC GGAEF 82, Larminat October 16, 1940.
[25] ANOM Cab 55, Pleven to the High Commissioner, December 6, 1941.

pro-Pétain, the magistrate in question was greeted at Fort-Lamy's club to chants of "throw the Vichyites into the Chari River!" The threat was less innocuous than it might sound, for at the time hippopotami still basked on its shores in central Fort-Lamy. A few days earlier, the governor of Chad had alerted his superior in Brazzaville of the suspicious behavior of one administrator's wife. She had allegedly undertaken "skillful propaganda, giving the impression that France was not too unhappy, and that the Vichy government was effectively managing France's interests." Lapie therefore asked Eboué to transfer the administrator outside of Chad and to place the couple under "honorable surveillance." He added that "this transfer is to seem on the surface like a promotion."[26] Such an outcome could only stoke conspiracy theories or at least resentment.

Although other regions certainly experienced considerable rancor and strife, Gabon proved especially chaotic. The civil war of 1940 long remained an open sore. In a telegram addressed to Félix Eboué dated April 1941, Edgard de Larminat held the Gabon Police Chief Redon responsible for the "persistence of tensions," accusing him of "several baseless arrests."[27] Larminat obtained assurances from a few Vichy prisoners that they would act honorably if released. But Eboué opposed the idea of conditional liberation, as it "put him in an impossible situation." Indeed, their liberation coincided with the arrival of Colonel André Parant's mortal remains, he who had lanced the Vichy abscess in Gabon. The measure came at the worst possible time, Eboué contended, for the limited purges had "begun to appease public opinion" in Gabon.[28] Governor-general and high commissioner clashed once more. Eboué was bombarded with grievances from Gabon. One of them, from April 1941, argued that officials in Brazzaville had bungled the psychological dimension of the Gabon crisis. Scandals in the wood sector grafted themselves onto the question of Vichy internees, which in turn fueled "resentment against administrative inertia."[29] The complainant warned, "The situation is serious." Europeans were not the only ones drafting grievances. In March 1942, Henri Laurentie worried of rumors in Gabon suggesting that Free France was to blame for food shortages. But he seemed persuaded that the rumors emanated initially from "Europeans who only joined our movement grudgingly, and who are seizing the opportunity to

<hr>

[26] ANOM GGAEF 6B 710, Lapie to Eboué, April 7 and 12, 1941.
[27] ANOM GGAEF 5D 291, Larminat to Eboué, April 5, 1941.
[28] ANOM GGAEF 5D 291, Eboué to Larminat, April 4, 1941.
[29] ANOM GGAEF 5D 294, letter from Port-Gentil, April 14, 1941.

foment discontent among the natives."[30] In this sense, the fallout of the Gabon civil war was aggravated by shortages and economic troubles that arguably affected Gabon more than other parts of FEA.

The attitude of Bishop Louis Tardy, Vichy's *éminence grise* in Libreville, served to forestall any rapid resolution of the Gabon crisis. On March 19, 1941, Edgard de Larminat took the matter to Giovanni Dellepiane, the apostolic delegate in Leopoldville. Larminat hinted that it would have been logical for Free France to ask for the Vatican's pure and simple support, "for our raison d'être is to fight Nazism, an ideology that was solemnly condemned by the Holy Father as Christianity's greatest enemy." Out of diplomatic sensitivity, wrote Larminat, Free France did not request such a concordat. But, he insisted, Tardy's attitude in Gabon was so intolerable that the Church had to take action. The bishop continued to preach that "the Free French are not French in either their origin or their hearts." He persisted in seeing Vichy as France's legitimate government. Larminat, who could scarcely be accused of anticlericalism, concluded sharply: "Our men are fighting and dying for the most disinterested of causes, that of Christian civilization...It is scandalous to many to note that eminent representatives of the Catholic religion seem blinded by partisan politics to the point of losing sight of this essential fact."[31]

The Tardy splinter was not easily dislodged. It should be added that in his 1941 book *La seule France*, Charles Maurras had made the Libreville prelate a key weapon against the Gaullists.[32] It therefore became counterproductive to mistreat him. In point of fact, Tardy remained as divisive as ever in 1944. At this date, Gabon's governor reported that the ceremonies in memory of Colonel Parant, victor over Vichy in Gabon, and of Captain Charles N'Tchoréré, Gabonese war hero summarily executed by the Germans in 1940, had been partly ruined by the presence of Tardy. Indeed, much of Libreville boycotted the religious ceremony led by Tardy. The governor threw his hands up in despair, with an admission that he was giving up on attempts to mend fences.[33]

The matter soon reached the floor of the provisional Assembly in Paris. In February 1945, Pierre Guillery denounced Tardy before Lucie Aubrac, Vincent Auriol, Pierre-Olivier Lapie, Claude Hettier de Boislambert, and

---

[30] ANOM GGAEF 3B 2382, Laurentie to the Governor of Gabon, March 7, 1942.

[31] ANOM GGAEF 5D 291, Larminat to Dellepiane, March 19, 1941.

[32] Charles Maurras, *La seule France, chronique des jours d'épreuve* (Lyon: H. Lardanchet, 1941), pp. 129 and 305 (note 1).

[33] ANOM GGAEF 5D 290, Libreville to Brazzaville, November 5, 1944.

many other delegates. After having summarized Tardy's actions in 1940 and noted that the bishop remained "in place" in Libreville, he demanded the prelate's expulsion from Africa. Roundly applauded by his colleagues, Guillery went so far as to press for Tardy to be banned from ever again setting foot in the colonies.[34] The very presence of the bishop had become intolerable at a time when a myth was being forged, according to which all of FEA had spontaneously closed ranks behind General de Gaulle in 1940. The existence of a refractory bishop in Gabon, who remained steadfastly loyal to Vichy in the heart of Free French Africa, challenged the myth head on.

### Prisoners, Deserters, and Spies

Vichy zealots, be they officials openly favorable to Pétain or prisoners of war from the Gabon campaign, represented an ongoing preoccupation to Free French officials.[35] They were placed in different detention centers that proliferated throughout FEA and Cameroon. Pro-Vichy elements were not the only possible fifth column over which to fret. In October 1940, the Spiritan missionaries in Congo registered popular discontent over the fact that some Italian civilians had been freed; two weeks later they reported their re-internment, this time alongside Vichy prisoners as well.[36]

Who were these men? Among the Italians, one should distinguish between the fifty-one civilians interned in FEA in June 1940 when Italy declared war on France, and the far more numerous prisoners of war. The latter were taken at Kufra and over the course of the much longer Fezzan campaign. They were detained mostly in Chad and at the Berbérati camp in Oubangui, where they worked on several public works projects.[37]

Vichy prisoners were individuals who refused to abjure. In September 1941, Belgian authorities reported that some of these detainees transiting through the Belgian Congo had destroyed a portrait of General de Gaulle

---

[34] Debates of the Assemblée consultative provisoire, *Journal officiel*, dated February 22, 1945. Tardy died in January 1947 at his mission's headquarters in Chevilly-Larue. Many of his fellow missionaries had taken the other side, and enlisted in the Free French forces in FEA.

[35] ANCMR APA 11230, Larminat to Yaoundé, February 7, 1941.

[36] CSE 3J1.19B, October 1940.

[37] Colette Dubois, "Internés et prisonniers de guerre italiens dans les camps de l'empire français de 1940 à 1945," *Guerre mondiales et conflits contemporains*, 156 (October 1989), pp. 53–71.

on board their vessel.[38] As of March 1941, more than two hundred Vichy prisoners remained detained in Free French Africa. Ten months later, Vichy still counted 210 of its faithful imprisoned in Free French Africa, the vast majority of them men who had fought in Gabon in 1940. Cameroon alone detained 140 Pétainists, of whom roughly one hundred had been sailors on board the *Bougainville* in Gabon.[39] Detention conditions varied. The most diehard, like a couple that attempted to escape, were sent to regions unfamiliar to them, or to isolated camps like that of Batschenga in Cameroon.[40]

Vichy propaganda never failed to instrumentalize the fate of these prisoners. The Red Cross, the United States, Portugal, and the Vatican all attempted to broker prisoner exchanges between Vichy and Free France in Africa. Rumors spread rapidly. Free France's precarious diplomatic position, rendered all the more fragile by the Dakar, Gabon, Syria, and Saint-Pierre and Miquelon affairs, offered it little leeway. Even the most outrageous charges therefore needed to be rebutted. In 1941, the high commissioner denounced Pétainist propaganda that referred to Gaullist "concentration camps" in FEA. The propaganda alleged that prisoners were allowed no contact with their families, that they suffered worse conditions than Germans or Italians, and were guarded by "natives." The high commissioner retorted that prisoners experienced the very same health conditions as other Europeans, that Free Frenchmen in Africa were likewise cut off from their families in France, and that there was no shame in being guarded by "our African troops who participated in all of our colonial campaigns as well as the war against Germany and of whom we are not ashamed and shall never be."[41]

For various reasons, including good behavior or illness, some prisoners benefitted from extra-carceral conditions in either religious missions or hospitals. They nonetheless remained on the administration's radar screen. Thus, on December 10, 1941, the governor of Gabon asked Eboué to ensure that the two Pétainist lieutenants leaving Albert Schweitzer's hospital in Lambaréné be "urgently dispatched to an internment center in another colony."[42] Gabon manifestly failed to offer the appropriate conditions for their return. In other cases, prisoners languished in a state of semi-liberty. In 1945, the U.S. evangelical missionaries of the Christian

---

[38] ADN 116PO1/115, Belgian Congo, 1936–45.
[39] ANOM 1Affpol 891.
[40] ANOM GGAEF 5B 713, Laurentie to the "Governor" of Cameroun, July 24, 1942.
[41] ANF 3AG1 165, telegrams dated June 11 and July 21, 1941.
[42] ANOM GGAEF 6B 710 Valentin-Smith to Eboué, December 10, 1941.

and Missionary Alliance in Bongolo, Gabon, exulted at having converted a "white prisoner of war." Already in 1942, the same mission had hosted several "political prisoners" for roughly six months.[43] These probably constituted two quite different cases, a German or Italian prisoner of war in one instance, and a recidivist Vichyite in the other. Furthermore, some prisoners who were deemed useful, like Italian doctors, were initially recruited to serve locally, colonial health services having been depleted by the departure of medics enlisted with the *bataillons de marche*. In 1941, one of these Italian doctors was assigned to Bangui, another to the district of Salamat. However, High Commissioner Sicé soon brought an end to the practice, and reassigned them to a prison camp.[44]

Free French opinion in Africa was particularly fractured, most notably on the question of Vichy inmates. Yet clemency seemed to dominate in 1942 when the administrative council examined a proposal for liberating Pétainist prisoners, put forward by Monseigneur Paul Biéchy, the apostolic vicar of Brazzaville. Some considered that "detention runs contrary to the nobility of our policies and we would be truer to ourselves if we were more generous than strict." This wave of generosity was all the more remarkable given that at the very time Vichy was denaturalizing, confiscating property, and sentencing Free Frenchmen to death in absentia. Félix Eboué also sided with Biéchy's proposal, though his motives appear to have been pragmatic. The governor feared a fifth column.[45] General de Gaulle too supported the proposal, although in passing he attributed the failure of numerous other negotiation attempts to Vichy.[46]

Meanwhile, the Free French kept proselytizing among Vichy prisoners. Their efforts proved largely vain. On April 29, 1942, for instance, Eboué ordered that all internees should receive a printed version of Pierre Laval's recent pronouncement.[47] In this April 20, 1942, speech Laval had announced a sincere collaboration with the Third Reich, while castigating Britain. By distributing it to inmates, Eboué no doubt wished to convince even the most skeptical of Vichy's unconditional support for Hitler. Yet few prisoners seem to have been moved. The prison camps were finally closed in March 1943. At this juncture, refractory Vichyites were asked

---

[43] CMA RG 820 box 1, report from January to May 1945 as well as for the following year.

[44] ANOM 6B 717, Bangui, May 18, 1941.

[45] ANOM GGAEF 3B 192, Eboué to Pleven, May 6, 1942. The same letter can be found in ANOM Cab 55.

[46] ANOM GGAEF 6B 712, de Gaulle to Eboué and Leclerc, June 17, 1942.

[47] ANOM GGAEF 5B 712, Eboué to the Governor of Oubangui, April 29, 1942.

to choose between returning to France or Algeria, or joining Fighting France. General Marcel Têtu, who had fought Free France in Gabon in 1940, opted for Giraud-controlled Algeria.[48]

Free French Africa also experienced its share of desertions. For instance, a lieutenant in the colonial infantry by the name of Pargny, who doubled as the head of the Pargny and Carmagnac mining company, fled Cameroon for Spanish Guinea in September 1941. Two others followed suit over the ensuing days, at the very time British intelligence warned Free France of espionage by Spanish Guinea. The matter came to a head on September 8, 1941, when the high commissioner dispatched a scathing telegram to Pierre Cournarie, the "governor" of Cameroon. He instructed that Cournarie "immediately take the measures necessary to prevent future border breaches." He added that "it was necessary to take energetic steps to bring an end to pro-Nazi propaganda in Cameroon . . . Merciless repression must be exerted."[49] However, securing a border situated at least partly in a dense rain forest proved easier said than done.

Finally, as this last document suggests, the fear of Nazi spies ran at a fever pitch. On February 26, 1941, Pierre Ryckmans, the governor the Belgian Congo, warned Félix Eboué that the Gestapo intended to send agents into his region.[50] Sometimes, spy-mania bordered on the ridiculous. In December 1941, Belgian authorities reported rumors allegedly circulated by certain "Brazzaville ladies." According to this hearsay, Brazzaville maintained suspiciously "frequent contacts" with Vichy. Laurentie was obliged to respond that the contacts in question were limited to the sending and reception of radiograms announcing deaths to families, via the Red Cross.[51]

## A Cornucopia of Colonial Conflicts

The civil war between proponents of Pétain and de Gaulle rattled and deflated morale across Free French Africa, although one can always debate its precise psychological reach. One point seems certain: far from bringing about a "sacred union," the state of war stoked preexisting antagonisms in Free French Africa. For example, the chronic shortage of

---

[48] ANOM GGAEF 6B 721.
[49] ANCMR APA 11230 telegrams dated March 21, 1943.
[50] ANOM GGAEF 3B 2381, Eboué to Ryckmans, March 2, 1941.
[51] ANOM GGAEF 3B 2381 Laurentie, December 19, 1941.

fuel led the head of Fort-Rousset in Congo to fulminate in his diary in April 1941:

> It seems to me that the health department is going a bit too far with its excursions. You can see that it's the administration that pays to fill their tanks. A little modesty and restraint, my god, we are at war and the gas comes from America. On paper, no doubt, all of these trips will be listed as visits to dispensaries, and morality will emerge unscathed.[52]

Other disputes possessed deeper roots. Dissension between colony and metropole is no doubt as old as colonialism itself, with Greeks, Phoenicians, and Romans paving the way. But the 1940 break with the metropole increased this friction and lent it new features. New rifts appeared rapidly between London and Brazzaville. On February 7, 1941, the head of military forces in Free French Africa, Edgard de Larminat, enjoined military personnel to show greater camaraderie. According to him, "It is often observed that Free French soldiers sent from England to Africa display little taste for colonial life, and express uncordial sentiments towards their colonial comrades in arms." And yet, Larminat wrote: "Free France is entirely composed of colonial lands." Exhorting his companions to steer clear from "pettiness" he concluded: "Soldiers of Free France, never forget that internal division constituted the main cause of our [1940] defeat, and that we can only revive France through union and confidence."[53]

Another equally ancient source of friction involved antagonisms between colonial capitals and remote rural outposts. It too was aggravated by the war. In July 1941, the head of the post at Fort-Rousset transcribed his colleague's observations on returning from Brazzaville: "Only the capital counts." He added, "Everybody wages their own personal intrigues, always at the expense of the outback. While rural areas lack European personnel, Brazzaville is chalk-full of little cherubs whose main occupation involves lounging around a glass with their comrades or driving around the capital."[54] Governor Eboué was sensitive to this image problem. In a January 1941 letter to the high commissioner, he wrote that "rural areas are on the lookout for what the capital shows off to others, which has led to disappointments that I wish to undo. I cannot abolish all Brazzavillian abuses (of which cars are the most visible) but I will do my

[52]  ANOM GGAEF 5Y5, entry for April 4, 1941.
[53]  ANCMR, AC 6332, Larminat, February 7, 1941.
[54]  ANOM GGAEF 5Y5, entry for July 13, 1941.

utmost to bring calm back to offices, rigor back to accounting, and general order to the administration."[55] The threat was not idle. On receiving a denunciation tip from a chauffeur, on June 10, 1941, Eboué instructed an official that for the common good, he must henceforth walk between the Plateau and M'Pila, which is to say from the administrative district to the shores of the Congo River.[56] One can imagine, however, that this kind of reprimand, while saving on fuel, ultimately led to grumblings.

Intense military recruitment in Free French Africa between 1940 and 1943 also exacerbated preexisting antagonisms between military and civil administrations. Thus on April 18, 1941, the governor of Chad Pierre-Olivier Lapie sought the backing of General de Gaulle in person. He complained that the zones controlled by the military over a large stretch of Northern Chad generally failed to provide tax revenue. "How can an administrator who neglects to collect taxes care for the everyday running of the native administration?" he asked. This was a poor omen for judicial and economic matters, he predicted, before coming to his main point. Whereas in 1931 twelve European teachers practiced in Chad, ten years later only three remained. And yet, Mr. Lacarreux, a primary school teacher who had left Vichy West Africa to join the Free French in Chad, was never transferred to civilian command. Lacarreux had volunteered to fight. But he was instead assigned to a desk job in Leclerc's service, and was frustrated at not being able to wage war. Why not, under the circumstances, send him back to his teaching post in schools that lacked even the basic necessities like chalkboards, tables, seats, and books? The teacher agreed: if he were not going to fight, he would rather return to the classroom than serve as a military typist. Leclerc proved utterly intransigent, responding to Lapie: "I won't give you a single person." Lapie justified going straight to de Gaulle with the matter because he worried that the military effort was undercutting colonialism. "We are not fulfilling our responsibilities to the natives," he concluded alarmingly.[57]

The shortage of functionaries was also felt in other areas. In FEA, likely the French colonial holding outside of the Sahara with the smallest ratio of administrators per square kilometer, the end of furloughs to France and of new arrivals from the metropole triggered profound effects. The rat cage had closed. In 1942, Bangui was literally paralyzed by a conflict between officials. It blocked the asphalting of the riverside boulevard,

[55] ANOM GGAEF 5D 291, Eboué to the High Commissioner, January 1941.
[56] ANOM GGAEF 3B 1094, Eboué to the Director of Finances, June 10, 1941.
[57] ANOM Cab 55, Lapie to de Gaulle, April 18, 1941.

which exasperated residents ended up paying to pave from their own wallets.[58]

Other sources of demoralization can be imputed to this overdose of colonial intimacy and enmity. In a sealed colonial atmosphere, some affairs of the heart took on an especially demoralizing tone in wartime. Thus on June 18, 1941, an important anniversary for the Free French cause, the military command in Cameroon was reduced to distributing an internal note regarding "letters... addressed to our military personnel at the front, which suggest rightly or wrongly that the conduct of their wives back here in Africa leaves much to be desired." Lieutenant-Colonel Tournadre took the matter seriously: "Soldiers on campaign, who are experiencing difficult conditions, who need to maintain morale, should not be receiving such letters, even were the information they contain true."[59] The matter can seem trivial, but it should be added to countless other headaches that made Free French Africa a veritable viper's nest of recriminations and dissension in the eyes of its leading officials.

## A Latent Ideological Schism

Like many resistance and liberation movements, Free France featured a set of internal political divisions. Jean-Luc Barré has shown the contrasting attitudes of different Free French clans with respect to the person of Marshal Pétain. Jean-François Muracciole has illustrated the heterogeneous nature of Free French ranks. And Jean-Louis Crémieux-Brilhac has identified shifts in Gaullist politics: de Gaulle's use of French revolutionary discourse starting in the fall of 1941, his adopting a republican credo beginning in 1942. For while de Gaulle finally expressed a "democratic commitment" in the spring of 1942, Gaullism still presented a "double face." It claimed on the one hand a revolutionary and republican lineage "infused with social-democratic reformism," while on the other hand wanting to banish a Third Republic deemed too weak, and envisioning a more "robust" model with which to replace it.[60] The topic can seem moot given that neither republics nor democracy abounded in Africa at

---

[58] ANOM GGAEF 6B 714, Laurentie to Eboué, July 23, 1942.
[59] ANCMR APA 11230, Lieutenant-Colonel Tournadre's note, June 18, 1941.
[60] Barré, p. 129; Muracciole, p. 361; Crémieux-Brilhac, *La France libre*, pp. 487–501 and 604.

this point. Yet it betrays multiple and revealing positionings projected from the colonies onto postwar France.

I will focus on the first phase during which Free French ideology was being forged in Africa – or rather ideologies, for the movement's driving principles remained hazy, contested, and plural. Even though the official line between 1940 and 1942 involved waiting until victory to reform France,[61] political wrangling surfaced regularly.

Two currents can be discerned. One, embodied by Larminat, Sicé, and Leclerc, imagined liberated France as something other than a republic. For them, the republic and its political parties stood largely responsible for the calamitous 1940 defeat. In their eyes, it was crucial to avoid repeating past errors. Hence, in February 1941 Larminat took umbrage at the journal *Free France*'s use of the French revolutionary slogan 'Liberty, Equality and Fraternity,' which he deemed to have "an absolutely deplorable effect."[62] It bears reminding that de Gaulle himself had initially substituted the slogan with: 'Honor and Nation.'[63] For his part, in response to a questionnaire circulated by de Gaulle to his closest associates in January 1941 inquiring as to how they might react were Vichy to agree to join the fight in Africa, Leclerc revealed his vision of the future. In it, "all political parties [we]re eliminated" and "Pétain's useful measures would be kept, in particular those reinforcing central authority and those favoring the family."[64] Leclerc, whose legendary temper and authoritarianism led his men in Chad to call him a "Führer" – though never to his face – [65] was evidently won over by many aspects of Pétain's National Revolution. He simply intended to wait until the end of the war to implement such measures.[66]

Conversely, other Free French were attached to democratic values, even though they often differed on specifics. Among them, one can cite René Cassin, Félix Eboué, Henri Laurentie, and Georges Boris.[67] In Africa, in any event, Eboué, Laurentie, and Cassin represented the standard-bearers

---

[61] Contrary to Vichy that sought explicitly to build immediately on the ashes of defeat.

[62] FCDG, FAA 11, personnalités (correspondance), Larminat to de Gaulle, February 21, 1941. On Larminat's politics, see Philippe Oulmont, "Le haut-commissaire," p. 103.

[63] Barré, p. 82.

[64] ANOM GGAEF 2Y 15, Leclerc to de Gaulle, February 13, 1941 Also see Barré, p. 129.

[65] NAUK, FO 859, d. 3, Paul Pazery to Enid McLeod, January 14, 1942.

[66] Notin, pp. 172–73.

[67] In a 1993 interview, Emile Delavenay, the Assistant Director of European Intelligence at the BBC, insisted on the roles of Cassin and Boris in leading de Gaulle to adopt "a democratic line." Martyn Cornick, interview of the Delavenays, May 24–25, 1993, published in *French History*, 8:3, September 1994, p. 342.

of republican continuity. Thus, the consul general of the United Kingdom in Brazzaville reported to London on August 25, 1942, that the Free French high commissioner's letterhead finally bore the heading "French Republic," a header that Governor Eboué had never ceased using on his correspondence.[68] In 1941, Cassin briefly considered creating an assembly representing all the Free French, which would have gathered in Brazzaville. The project was ultimately abandoned because of the challenges posed by distance and transportation.[69]

Individually, some Free French of the first hour embraced a nostalgic, distinctly prerevolutionary vision of their epic adventure. Captain François Garbit of the B.M. 3 penned one especially evocative example. He chronicled Free France's battles in Chad and Eritrea in 1941 in the manner of medieval author Jean Froissart. "French knights" waged battle on "the Germanick (sic.) emperor." Although the tone was obviously lighthearted, with Mussolini appearing as the Duke of Macaroni, the fact remains that the plot revolved around the "King of France," "valorous French knights," "Crusaders," and "Mahometans" as well as a "Kingdom of Chad."[70] The medieval register might be a mere coincidence, but it seems more likely revelatory of a general trend to seek France's salvation in its distant, prerevolutionary past.

While this last example remains open to interpretation, cleavages between democrats and their detractors were neither abstract nor anachronistic projections onto the past. Consider for example the altercation around René Cassin's visit to Africa. In May 1942, Leclerc dispatched a curt telegram to Carlton Gardens, before the law professor's visit to FEA. The colonel had heard from several officers that Cassin had once supported disarmament between the wars, and that he had "protested in Paris with his fist clenched" in the 1930s. Learning of Cassin's visit, an officer apparently announced that he was quitting Free France on the spot, before Leclerc persuaded him to stay, promising that de Gaulle "would not lose sight of France's national revival."[71] Cassin, the future drafter of the universal declaration of the rights of man was persona non grata in

---

[68] NAUK FO 859, 4.

[69] Marc Agi, *René Cassin, 1887–1976* (Paris: Perrin, 1998), p. 140. Cassin, pp. 252–53.

[70] AOL, box B, la France libre, "Honorificques chroniques de l'ost du pays du Tchad en la guerre de Érythrée." A note in pencil attributes the text to François Garbit, who died at Damas in December 1941.

[71] ANOM Cab 63. Leclerc to de Gaulle, June 26, 1942. Leclerc also seemed vaguely apologetic for an "unwise telegram" that he had sent to the general about Cassin.

Free French African military circles. As Crémieux-Brilhac has observed, "Overseas, the placid Cassin was taken for the henchman of the Popular Front."[72]

Divergences extended to the realm of native policy. Particularly divisive was Eboué's creation of a "notable évolué" status. For all of its paternalism and elitism, the policy sought in theory to support the emergence of a Francophile elite within African society. In the end, only some 103 Africans obtained the status in 1943, 218 in 1944. In a related matter, in December 1941, Eboué issued instructions to the head prosecutor in Brazzaville to stay the application of a September 1941 decree prohibiting the sale of alcohol to Africans in FEA. According to the governor-general, "one should... take into account the fact that an évolué class has, like many Europeans, taken the habit of drinking wine with meals, in moderation." Eboué "saw no reason to ban these natives from drinking a beverage that can only be considered dangerous if one abuses it." He added that a ban might prove counterproductive, "pushing natives towards locally produced alcohol... often absorbed in large quantities."[73] Ten days later, Eboué's stay drew the ire of Adolphe Sicé, the former doctor, now high commissioner to Free French Africa. He fumed, "The reign of the bistro and its influence on elections, paved the way to France's decadence." He then added, "Concerned about the ravages of alcoholism, General de Gaulle wishes to do for Africans what the Vichy government has done for France. He has decided to allow the use of hygienic and fermented drinks containing moderate percentages of alcohol, while banning distilled alcohol."[74] Sicé closed his harangue by invoking his twenty-five years of experience as a doctor in Africa. But his main point lay elsewhere. He was persuaded that the 1940 defeat, national decline, and electoral decadence, all stemmed from the republic's alcohol problem. He even cited Vichy as an example on the path to moralization. Eboué conversely wished to avoid infantilizing a tiny slice of African society. He lined his arguments in favor of this social category with the language of rights. Behind this very old debate over the alleged ravages of alcohol in Africa, lurked two competing conceptions of postwar France.

---

[72] Crémieux-Brilhac, *La France libre*, p. 489.
[73] ANOM GGAEF 3B 1100, Eboué to the head prosecutor, December 11, 1941.
[74] ANC GGAEF 138, Sicé to Eboué, December 21, 1941. On the numbers of Africans holding évolué status, see Suret-Canale, p. 587.

### Peter versus Paul

Cumulatively, these divergences created a fairly somber picture. Leclerc depicted nothing short of discord in a letter from Fort-Lamy to General de Gaulle in London on July 2, 1942:

> The dominant impression when one lives amongst different circles in Free French Africa and has the time to observe them, is division. I will spare you the reports, letters, requests established by Peter against Paul, often addressed directly to you. You have better things to do than read such papers. I can summarize them as follows: administrators, settlers, merchants, mining operators, workers, all mutually accuse each other of the worst crimes, asking for punishment to be meted out. They see injustice everywhere, as well as plots and perceived fifth columns. Clans, groups, sects are gathering steam. In short, we are turning back the clock to the ancient Gauls, whose inability to get along some 2,000 years ago became a constant leitmotif in our history.

Leclerc then proceeded to point to consequences of these quarrels. First of all, officials could never satisfy all parties. Next, the discord "left an unfortunate impression on foreigners." He who had left Cameroon for the front shortly after the three glorious days took stock of what had transpired in Free French Africa in the nearly two years that had elapsed: "The interior situation is clearly poorer than it was at the end of 1940 at the time of our August operation. My impression must be accurate, for in the far reaches of the Chadian desert, I had really left this land for a year and a half, and can now observe it impartially." For according to Leclerc, after a short honeymoon phase during which "the freemason collaborated with the bishop, the planter with the administration," the hour of recriminations had rung. Whereupon, the victor of Kufra took his distance, zooming out to a planetary scale:

> You might retort that this is a secondary matter. If the Russians defeat the Boches, if the American army arrives, in a year or two the quarrels of Brazzaville and Douala will matter little. The only reason why I am taking the liberty of reporting on all of this is that I often wonder if what is happening here could portend what will transpire tomorrow in France.

Lastly, Leclerc put forward several causes for the disarray he reported. Beyond the central explanation of Gaulish bellicosity, he pointed out that he was partly responsible, having recruited "the best elements" from the administration and transferred them to the military. Next, he imputed the strife to moral turpitude resulting from partisanship, old habits, the press, foreign radio, and last but not least: "unfortunate readings."[75]

Whatever the cause, the archives reveal a conflict-ridden Free French Africa. If not Africa itself, then certainly its colonials. In a political report on the Sangha region (Moyen-Congo) dated 1943, an official lamented: "the thirty or so Europeans who reside in the region have given me more grief than the 30,000 natives." He hazarded the following by way of explanation: "between those drained by a long colonial stay, by the absence of news from France, by homesickness, by an often difficult climate, rumors run rampant, and disputes are legion."[76]

Quarrels reached their zenith at the top of the administrative pyramid. The undeclared war between Governor-General Eboué and the two High Commissioners Edgard de Larminat (from August 1940 to July 1941) and Adolphe Sicé (July 1941 to June 1942) created such a tempest that General de Gaulle ended up abolishing the position of high commissioner altogether in June 1942. No doubt all parties concerned were correct in arguing that the ill-defined two-headed system involving both a governor-general and a high commissioner lent itself to conflict. Yet it seems to me that such conflict cannot be dissociated from the many strata of resentment we have just reviewed. The animosity between governor and high commissioner bore the marks of profound institutional and ideological differences, as well as those of older grievances linked to the local context.

There was another psychological dimension to the question. As Martin Shipway has indicated, Eboué repeatedly enjoined his right-hand man Henri Laurentie to show greater tact in his administrative interactions. This singular character, at once Dadaist poet and fervent Catholic, firmly believed that he belonged to a tiny circle of a "dozen" men imbued with an enlightened colonial philosophy. He would say as much to de Gaulle in person in 1944.[77] Such extreme confidence verging on self-righteousness stemmed from what one could term the Fort-Lamy syndrome. The handful of individuals who propelled the rallying of FEA in 1940 subsequently claimed a monopoly of virtue in matters of native policy, much to the

---

[75] ANOM Cab 63, Leclerc to de Gaulle, July 2, 1942.

[76] ANOM GGAEF 4(2) D 76 Political report, Sangha department, 1943.

[77] Martin Shipway, "Thinking like an Empire: Governor Henri Laurentie and Postwar Plans for the Late Colonial French 'Empire State'" in Martin Thomas, ed., *The French Colonial Mind*, Vol. 1 (Lincoln: University of Nebraska Press, 2011), pp. 226, 244, 246 note 20. To complete the portrait of Laurentie, see Maurice Martin du Gard, *La carte impériale: histoire de la France outre-mer, 1940–1945* (Paris: André Bonne, 1949), p. 53.

chagrin of military and other authorities, entrepreneurs, settlers, and high commissioners.

Furious over a reorganization of the public works inspection system, in June 1941 Larminat invoked what he termed "a systematic bias" on the part of Governor Eboué's office, "aiming to undermine a decision taken by the head of the Free French." Eboué retorted by asserting his place as "head of the colony" and berating his detractors for "cruelly accusing him." Governor Eboué reminded his correspondent of the precocity of his engagement for de Gaulle on July 7, 1940, and his role in Chad the following month.[78] Here was a first salvo. In July 1941, Eboué reported the ambient cacophony to General de Gaulle, asserting that "the governor general's office and that of the high commissioners are operating at cross-purposes."[79] Then, on September 23, 1941, Laurentie informed Eboué, who was visiting the Oyem sector, that High Commissioner Sicé was repeating Larminat's unacceptable ways. Laurentie evoked "a military dictatorship contrary to the present and future interests of FEA and of France itself." He elaborated: "I think you must put an end to this immediately and I have had enough."[80] In the colonial sphere, the military-civilian chasm was as ancient as it was impassable, reminiscent of fin-de-siècle tensions in Madagascar and Indochina. Four days later, Eboué followed suit, chastising Sicé for employing "unfortunate expressions" while overstepping his bounds. Eboué did conclude on a conciliatory note, mentioning Sicé's "magnificent role" in bringing the Congo to Free France "in late August 1940 when we shared a common position."[81] Being early Gaullists in Africa, it seemed, constituted their only common ground.

Despite this nostalgic reminder of the three glorious days, relations soured once more. Countless files fanned the flames, including recriminations over the wood sector in Gabon, and the resulting dismissal of Gabon's Governor Victor Valentin-Smith. The pettiest points turned into fodder. In September 1942, although already removed from his post, Adolphe Sicé complained to London that Eboué was having a lavish palace erected for himself overlooking the Congo River. Eboué had the perfect answer in store. The construction was not a governor's palace but rather the "headquarters of General de Gaulle" – what would become

---

78  ANOM GGAEF 5D 301, letters from Eboué and Larminat.
79  Quoted in Philippe Oulmont, "Le haut-commissaire," p. 92.
80  ANC GGAEF 138, Laurentie to Eboué, September 23, 1941.
81  ANC GGAEF 138, Eboué to Sicé, September 27, 1941.

the famous Case de Gaulle. Today, this handsome structure houses the residence of the ambassador of France in the Republic of Congo. Eboué's answer appears to have disarmed his critic, leading Eboué to exult: "all of Sicé's protests cannot transform a lie into the truth."[82]

De Gaulle's abolishing the position of high commissioner in June 1942 thus appeared as one of his few remaining options for ending a war of attrition. The straw that broke the camel's back involved Sicé entering into negotiations with the United States over the use of Pointe-Noire's naval base. This initiative earned him de Gaulle's ire, for the general had warned that any such international negotiations required his approval.[83] Interestingly, the abolition of the high commissioner's post also triggered a deluge of grievances. Thus, on June 28, 1942, Leclerc sent a detailed missive to de Gaulle imploring him to reverse his decision. He contended that "the fighting I waged in Fezzan was made possible by the energetic intervention of Sicé, who, as high commissioner, forced the local civilian authorities to requisition vehicles without which the operation could not have been launched."[84] Fractures were not healed nor arguably could they be. Like Larminat and Sicé, General Leclerc considered Free French Africa to be a military machine. Eboué and Laurentie for their part seemed to be chiefly and rather paternalistically concerned with the moral and social fiber of Free French Africa itself. Seldom did the two parties see eye to eye, except on the need to liberate France.[85]

## Bewildered Allies

Precisely as Leclerc worried, these many schisms were exposed to dumbstruck foreigners present in FEA and Cameroon. Americans and Britons crisscrossed the roads and rivers of Free French Africa by virtue of the trade agreements reached between Free France and the United Kingdom. They seldom failed to report discontent and registered even low-grade grumblings. Truculent and sometimes off-color U.S. Colonel Harry F. Cunningham reported on his many conversations in Bangui in 1942. He specified to the U.S. consul in Brazzaville that his interlocutors had freely volunteered all of the information he was relaying. First, a high official

---

[82] ANC GGAEF 128, file on de Gaulle's residence.
[83] Munholland, p. 185. For de Gaulle's warning, see Jean-Pierre Guéno, Gérard Lhéritier, *Les messages secrets du général de Gaulle, Londres, 1940–1942* (Paris: Gallimard, 2011), p. 226, de Gaulle to Eboué and Leclerc, June 10, 1942.
[84] ANOM Cab 63, Leclerc to de Gaulle, Brazzaville, June 28, 1942.
[85] Oulmont, "Le haut-commissaire," p. 89.

in the government at Bangui allegedly expressed frustration over the fact
that rubber was being sold to the British for 14.5 francs a kilo, when the
United States was offering twice that. A businessman in Oubangui likewise shared his mind, suggesting that the British monopoly could only be
explained by René Pleven's corruption. The rumor was as vile as it was
unfounded. The rubber was of course fueling the Allied war effort, and as
we will see the British monopoly had been imposed on Free France. The
official then pointed out that Oubangui could produce more rubber, but
that Eboué opposed such an increase because he wished to protect local
populations. All of this was expressed in a disapproving tone. Another
Oubangui official hinted to Cunningham that hostility toward Eboué and
Laurentie was such that he would not be surprised if the two were chased
from power, much like Vichy's officials had been two years prior. He
added revealingly, "We do not wish to be governed by a worn-out black
man and his clever mentor who have sold out to the British and refuse
to allow us to trade with whom we will." In short, the military effort,
the need to support Britain, which remained Free France's most steadfast
supporter, all appear lost to noxious squabbles and personal gain. And
of course the previous passage reveals pronounced racism toward Félix
Eboué, which other historians have already underscored.[86]

The British portrait was scarcely more flattering. In October 1942,
his majesty's consul in Brazzaville reported to London: "In regard to
the Cameroons under French mandate...I consider that the European
population has no clear insight of the war or of its effects upon the world.
What has tried the French Europeans most is that they are cut off from
their people and that they cannot return home for their leave. They only
very dimly realize the tremendous issues at stake and the sufferings of the
people who are taking a direct part in the war, or are under the heel of
the Nazis."[87]

Partly based on intercepted messages from American missionaries in
Cameroon, the O.S.S. (precursor to the CIA) had drawn similar conclusions a month prior. French officials were at the end of their rope,
suggested the intercepts. Most were exhausted by an inordinately long
colonial stay. Generally, the O.S.S. added, the French in Cameroon were

---

[86] NARA RG 84, Classified general records 1942–1944, box 1 (UD 2519), Cunningham
to Taylor, August 18, 1942. On racism toward Eboué, see Weinstein, pp. 253, 262,
281, and Oulmont, "Le haut-commissaire," p. 93. Oulmont mentions the hatred of
Oubangui's main treasurer toward Eboué. Might this be Cunningham's anonymous
source?

[87] NAUK FO 859, 5, Douala, October 3, 1942.

not solidly behind de Gaulle. Many seemed more or less "pro-Vichy" without daring to say so overtly. Some even contemplated leaving Free French Africa for neighboring Vichy territories, undertaking the reverse course of the fictional Captain Renault in the film *Casablanca*. Only their salary, pensions, and other pragmatic considerations prevented them from making the jump, the O.S.S. observed. On a brighter note, material conditions seemed acceptable. For instance, French wine had been adequately replaced by South African vintages. What is one to make of these reports? They appear tendentious in some respects; U.S. missionaries might well have been attune to particularly disaffected elements. Yet overall, the O.S.S. seemed well informed. For example, the same report rightly noted the massing of Free French troops near the Spanish Guinea border at this same time. Mostly then, such reports tend to confirm Leclerc and other's testimonies, depicting a Free French Africa torn by discord.[88]

It would naturally be absurd to think that Franklin D. Roosevelt read such reports personally. But on the basis of this testimony, U.S. officials in Brazzaville were in no position to counter the State Department and the president's already tepid attitude toward the Free French cause (on the military side, Colonel Cunningham's erratic and sometimes recklessly personal reports did not help either). To summarize prevailing U.S. attitudes, one could say that until August 1943, the U.S. administration considered the Free French cause to be one of Winston Churchill's pet projects, resting on a motley and checkered group with uncertain legitimacy and credentials. To be sure, the U.S. administration was not monolithic. For instance, the War Department and the State Department did not see eye to eye on the Free French movement.[89]

However, individual American citizens who volunteered in the movement trumpeted a much more positive image of the Free French cause in Africa. This may have at least partly offset the dimmer official view. Among the Americans in question, I should cite Hassoldt Davis, Dudley Harmon, and Ben Lucien Burman. The latter heaped praise on the Gaullists, writing that "the heart of France" had migrated from the shores of the Seine to those of the Congo. For his American readers,

---

[88] NARA RG 84, Classified general records 1942–1944, box 1 (UD 2519), Report on French Cameroons, September 23, 1942.

[89] Munholland, p. 189. On the importance of the August 1943 recognition and on internal divisions in Washington on the question of the Free French, see Maguire, p. 88. On Cunningham's turbulent and ill-defined mission to FEA, see Dorothy Shipley White, *Seeds of Discord: De Gaulle, Free France and the Allies* (New York: Syracuse University Press, 1964), pp. 270–271.

he added not so subtly that de Gaulle's "rebel" army reminded him of George Washington's at Valley Forge.[90]

## African Mobilization and the Colonial Context

Africans often became involved in Free France's power struggles. In his largely autobiographical book *Promise at Dawn*, Romain Gary recalls having helped foment an African protest aimed at sending him into battle. Gary and his fellow war pilots were languishing on the ground in Bangui. He describes "a protest of black citizens bearing banners that read: 'Bangui's civilians want the aviators at the front.'" This testimony should be taken with some caution, because as Gary's biographer suggests, the famed Free French novelist tended to distort some of his African experiences.[91] In this same town, in 1942 six Africans signed a petition calling for the release of an alleged pro-Pétain prisoner, a certain Mr. Viellard-Baron. They called for his liberation on the grounds that "he was an old colonial liked by all" and had shown real sympathy for Africans.[92]

In other cases, it was the inequality and stratification of colonial society that served as a source of tension. We have seen how Félix Eboué sought to foster an elite "évolué" status. Paradoxically, after the advent of Free France, Africans wishing to become French citizens were asked to delay their request, and to accept "évolué" rank as a kind of consolation prize. Free France did not naturalize any Africans, at least not between August 1940 and February 1943. Only on March 3, 1943, did the National Committee accept to "reopen access to French citizenship for natives" of FEA and Cameroon.[93]

The new category of "notable évolué" was just the latest in a litany of colonial special ranks. In many ways the colonies functioned on a regime

---

90  Ben Lucien Burman, *Miracle on the Congo: report from the Free French Front* (New York: John Day Co.), 1942, pp. 13, 24.

91  Myriam Anissimov, *Romain Gary, le caméléon* (Paris: Denoël, 2004), p. 164.

92  ANOM GGAEF 5D 205, petition in favor of M. Viellard-Baron.

93  ANOM 1Affpol 873, file on the "naturalization of natives" telegram dated March 3, 1943. For a file rejected on these grounds, see that of Bobindza in ANOM GGAEF 1D 120, Brazzaville, February 12, 1941. On June 10, 1943, Eboué clarified the relationship between the two statuses as follows: "while conditions for attaining the local citizenship represented by the evolved notable status are not as demanding as those required for French citizenship, they are nevertheless of a similar nature and should be examined in the same spirit." ANOM GGAEF 3B 2383, Eboué, June 10, 1943.

of exception. An elite in their own right, the métis were often perceived as an intermediate category that could further colonial causes, but they had also long blurred and sometimes threatened colonial boundaries. In October 1942, a crime committed by a métis man soon consumed Brazzaville.

On October 20, 1942, a serviceman by the name of Aristide Léon Mattey killed Marcel Ngandou, the driver of Brazzaville's apostolic vicar. The perpetrator was métis, the victim African, described in official reports as being of Balali ethnicity. Mattey's motives remained murky. His sentence proved surprisingly light: two years in prison for manslaughter. Turmoil erupted as soon as the verdict was announced. Apostolic Vicar Paul Biéchy took up his late driver's cause. Deploring "an unjust and revolting sentence," he vowed to stir unrest among his flock unless the case was retried. On October 21, Biéchy wrote to Governor Eboué in person to denounce "this flagrant injustice towards an industrious and honest native, to the benefit of a métis bastard."[94] As the historians who have studied the status of the métis have suggested, paternal nonrecognition constituted a recurring source of colonial anxiety, tension, and introspection in many a colonial setting.[95]

What is so striking about Biéchy's involvement is his threat to light the powder keg himself if necessary. Clearly the knives were out between the Vatican's representative and the colonial justice system. I could easily have added to the list of conflicts in Free French Africa the one that raged between the secular and the temporal, had space permitted.[96] In his missive to the governor, Biéchy pursued: "I protest against this verdict that will revive old racial hatreds. The natives are on alert, and the responsibility rests with you." Roughly a month later, on November 28, on learning that Mattey was serving his sentence in Brazzaville proper, working for the street maintenance department, Biéchy exploded: "Basic decency dictates that the guilty party purge his light sentence elsewhere than under the eyes of stunned natives. This second affront seems to

---

[94] ANOM GGAEF 5D 205, Mattey file.

[95] See Owen White, *Children of the French Empire: Miscegenation and Colonial Society in French West Africa, 1895–1960* (Oxford: Oxford University Press, 1999) and Emmanuelle Saada, *Empire's Children: Race, Filiation and Citizenship in the French Colonies* (Chicago: University of Chicago Press, 2012).

[96] Consider the case of Capuchin missionaries in Doba who protested bitterly in 1943 of not being invited to the ceremony marking the anniversary of the three glorious days. AFCF, Berbérati, 3R2, dossier 43, letter from Father Arthur, August 30, 1943.

constitute a deliberate challenge to the black population. I will defend it against this métis bastard, and ask that the murderer be at the very least distanced from Brazzaville." The incident was rapidly turning into a scandal. Its proportions speak to some of the tensions in Brazzaville. Biéchy now indicted all métis on the basis of this one case. And over the course of just a few exchanges, the correspondence itself seemed to get out of hand. The mayor of Brazzaville next asked Biéchy to explain why he would use the seemingly out-of-place phrase "thou shall not covet thy neighbor's wife," to frame his complaint to the mayor about the Mattey scandal.

More seriously, the authorities reported a general indignation in African circles surrounding the Mattey sentence. Although the sentence led to more outrage than violence, a gendarme posted to the Bacongo quarter nevertheless registered "a certain discontent." He chronicled how a writer for the finance department in Brazzaville named Laurent Mampouya presided two meetings at his house on the aptly named Voltaire Street. Some thirty Congolese met there: orderlies, translators, writers like Robert Nato employed at the government press, and André Bayounga, who worked at Brazzaville's city hall. The passionately engaged Mampouya attended the reading of the verdict then promptly set about mobilizing opinion against it. In Poto-Poto, it was Alphonse Samba who took the lead. According to one gendarmerie report, Samba was none other than Mampouya's representative: he too set about organizing a movement to decry the unjust sentence, deftly circulating between different social classes and circles. By night, he discretely ran informal polls, and collected funds to support Ngandou's family.[97] The French administration almost systematically read the affair through an ethnic or racial lens. But to Mampouya, it mostly bore the mark of a great miscarriage of justice like the Dreyfus affair on a local scale. It led, in any event, to a moment of acute consciousness and organizing among urban African professionals – precisely the lettered elite that Free France hoped to rely on in Central Africa. Undoubtedly, colonial categories, regimes of exception, and profound stratification also played important roles in the scandal.

In 1942, the so-called amicalistes of Brazzaville were outraged by the death of their founder André Matsoua Grenard in one of FEA's jails. A veteran of the French army, in the 1920s Matsoua had protested

---

97 ANOM GGAEF 5D 205, Mattey affair file.

against the injustice of the indigénat legal code, and established an influential "amicale" or friendship organization of Equatorial Africans present in Paris. It served as an engine of colonial reform. As Martial Sinda has underscored, Matsoua was profoundly attached to the principle of racial equality. Florence Bernault describes the amicale as "the first organized political movement, structured around protonationalist demands." Already in February 1941, the amicale had assumed such stature that Félix Eboué decided to remove from schools "children of the Bassoundi and Balali ethnicity." The parents of the students in question signed a petition to persuade Eboué to reverse his decision, claiming to have been duped by Matsoua's adepts. The episode exerted enough of an impact to be recounted subsequently by Congolese author Guy Menga in his novel *Case de Gaulle*.[98]

Matsoua died behind bars in 1942 after having been condemned to a life sentence of forced labor a year prior by the Free French justice system. In the postwar, the late Matsoua's popularity continued to rise, so much so that he won several electoral contests from the grave. His followers soon created a religious order around him.[99] In the short term, Félix Eboué was held responsible for Matsoua's death. Moreover, the Free French administration mounted a concerted repression of Matsoua's followers, precisely as they were transforming into a messianic movement. Once more, colonial officials read the phenomenon through the prism of ethnicity, seeing in it yet another "Balali Affair." While Free French Africa was not consumed by internal violence per se, signs of trouble and of malaise clearly surfaced in regions under the shadow of the Cross of Lorraine. The Matsoua and Ngandou-Mattey cases seem in this sense symptomatic of a vaster underlying crisis.

### "All Is Well in Free French Africa?"

On January 6, 1941, General de Gaulle confidently asserted in private correspondence that: "in Africa, all is going very well in our little piece of empire."[100] Although his foundations in Free French Africa were sturdier than anywhere else, the opinion seems optimistic at the very least. This

---

[98] ANC GGAEF 126, February 1941 petition. Menga, p. 48.
[99] Bernault, pp. 72–74; Martial Sinda, *André Matsoua, fondateur du mouvement de libération du Congo* (Paris: ABC, 1977).
[100] De Gaulle, *Lettres, notes et carnets, juin 1940-juillet 1941*, p. 219.

said, sturdy does not necessarily imply unshakable or united. Scenarios varied across space and time. Those FEA territories that experienced a Vichy relapse, like Gabon, or a long Vichy period like French West Africa, presented lasting scars. Here was perhaps the main fault line: the one separating Central Africans of the first hour against North and West Africans.

However, even within Free French ranks of the first hour, fractures abounded: between rural and urban areas, between rival administrative branches, between civilians and military, and between advocates of democracy and proponents of alternative political forms. Leclerc pointed to discord across the board. Even if one accounts for the fact that problem areas tend to generate more of an archival trail than serene ones, the mass of testimonies and documents cited earlier does point to an especially divided Free French Africa.

English photojournalist Paul Pazery toured FEA in 1941. He witnessed a quarrel between Free Frenchmen over Pétain, and registered several cases of Free Frenchmen approaching him to enlist in the British army. Taking stock of his experiences, he reached the following bitter verdict: "Internal strife, dishonesty among many officers, boundless pride . . . and in general lack of leadership have reduced the vitality of Free France . . . The regeneration of France will come – if it does at all in the near future – not from the Free French but from those who lived under German rule."[101]

What can one draw from such a harsh judgment? Many underground movements experienced greater schisms still, like the Greek, Yugoslav, or Polish resistance. But Free France's colonial fog appears to have been especially dense. Waging battle against Vichy on the inside, and the Axis on the outside, the Free French struggled to find common ground beyond these two causes. They turned on one another on topics as varied as the position to take vis-à-vis Pétain, the allocation of fuel reserves, the right of Africans to consume wine, the future constitution of France, the price of rubber, and the distribution of trucks between military and civilian sectors.

The question can also be inverted. How did territories where such discord reigned manage to function militarily in a relatively efficient and coherent way? How did they succeed in undertaking the remarkable south to north advance we are about to follow? For Free French Africa not only

---

[101] NAUK, FO 859, 3, Paul Pazery to Enid McLeod, January 14, 1942.

fought in Libya, Tunisia, then Italy, and beyond, it also triumphed. And yet, the very recognition on de Gaulle's part that a conference dedicated to colonial reform must be organized in Brazzaville in 1944 suggests that he too realized that all was not for the best in the best of all possible worlds.

PART II

THE WAR

# Introduction to Part II

The following chapters do not aspire to cover the totality of military operations involving FEA and Cameroonian forces. Several narratives penned by both historians and participants have already traced the main battles in question.[1] In addition, I have chosen explicitly to privilege African and colonial dimensions. This has proven challenging, for the archives rarely distinguish troops from the territories in question from other colonial forces. While some bataillons de marche, the basic military unit in Free French Africa, hailed from Oubangui-Chari, Chad, Cameroon, and Congo, the constant retooling of units in 1940 and then again in 1943 renders it nearly impossible to isolate FEA and Cameroonian elements in Free French ranks.[2] Far from simplifying the task, labels typically prove misleading. Thus, the famous B.M. 2, known as the Oubangui battalion, included many Cameroonians and Chadians, and was probably comprised of roughly 50 percent ethnic Saras.[3] The régiment des tirailleurs sénégalais du Tchad counted more Chadians than Senegalese. In fact, the latter was a term most often used at the time to designate all African troops.

---

[1] See the work of Jean-Noël Vincent, Jean-Louis Crémieux-Brilhac, François Broche, Georges Caïtucoli, and Jean-François Muracciole, as well as memoirs like those of François Ingold.

[2] Jean-Noël Vincent, *Les forces françaises libres en Afrique, 1940–1943* (Vincennes: Services historique de l'armée de terre, 1983), p. 50.

[3] Bernard Lanne, "Le Tchad pendant la guerre (1939–1945)," in Charles-Robert Ageron, éd., *Les chemins de la décolonisation de l'empire français, 1936–1956* (Paris: CNRS, 1986), p. 444.

Calculating totals for Free French forces has proven equally delicate, all the more so for African troops for which much less individual information is available (consider the records for Africans in the prestigious Ordre de la Libération whose files are incommensurably thinner than those of their European peers). To further complicate matters, sub-Saharan African soldiers do not systematically appear on Free French databases, like the one drawn up by Free French veteran Henri Ecochard. Jean-François Muracciole has rightly suggested that while Ecochard's document is reliable for European volunteers, it is far less exhaustive for colonial recruits. This is due in large part to the ways in which the latter were recruited and the resulting absence of a paper trail.[4]

The question of sources is crucial here, all the more so because so few African officers and NCOs – and even fewer soldiers – have left memoirs. Sergeant Rapahël Onana constitutes an interesting exception. His rich account reveals a certainty, ingrained by his mother, that he was "armored" at birth in rural Cameroon in 1919 against a premature death. No doubt this confidence came in handy during the three campaigns in which Onana fought: in Gabon in 1941, the Middle East in 1941, and at the battle of Bir Hakeim against Rommel's forces in 1942.[5] Unfortunately, testimonies of this type are extremely rare – a point rendered all the more glaring by the contrasting profusion of autobiographies by metropolitan French resistors of all stripes. Among the many explanations for this disparity, one counts an imbalance in the economy of memory, conditioned by North–South relations since decolonization, as well as radically different access to the written word and to editors. As a result, there is scant material with which to reconstitute individual trajectories: a few reports, unit diaries, lacunar personnel files, sparse oral testimonies from now aged veterans, and photos, such as ones showing two different clusters of NCOs in the legendary B.M. 2: whites on one side and blacks on the other.[6]

And yet the archives yield remarkable riches on other counts. They reveal ongoing debates among Free French authorities over the use of African troops, the role of truck drivers and other African auxiliaries during the desert war, the experiences of African soldiers and NCOs, the

---

[4] Muracciole, p. 37. The Ecochard database can be accessed at: http://www.charles-de-gaulle.org/pages/la-memoire/accueil/organismes/liste-des-volontaires-des-forces-francaises-libres.php.

[5] Onana.

[6] The photo appears without a page number in R. Soriano, *Historique du bataillon de March 2 de l'Oubangui-Chari* (Beirut: Imprimerie catholique, 1942).

conditions in which they were recruited, trained, fed, and treated, their family relations as well as the discriminations and other challenges they faced. One can also decipher and extrapolate their intentions, fears, and hopes, sometimes even their revolt. Chapters 4 and 5 adopt a documentary-inspired approach that privileges these sources. They zoom in on facts and themes revealing at once African contributions to Free France, African soldiers' experiences, and prevailing attitudes toward these earliest Free French forces.

# Chapter 4

## The Empire Strikes Back

After rallying to General de Gaulle in August 1940, FEA and Cameroon focused initially on defensive preparedness. On September 1, 1940, Leclerc requested immediate reinforcements with which to protect Cameroon's vulnerable coastline. Five days later, he announced on Cameroon radio:

> Fighting does not mean throwing oneself headlong against an imaginary adversary. Fighting means entering into the struggle with all of one's assets fully prepared to combat for the civilized world against the barbarians. This implies…reinforcing the country's defenses immediately. The process is already underway, and I wish to thank those of you who have been working on this task for the past ten days. It also implies a rapid growth of our military forces. This has already begun, first with the opening of a European recruitment office, next with the creation of the French volunteers from Cameroon. Finally, as of next week, I shall begin recruiting natives.[1]

De Gaulle's man found himself in a delicate position because of Cameroon's unique status as a mandate territory. The League of Nations' rules clearly forbade any recruitment of Cameroonians beyond police work and self-defense.[2] This did not dissuade Leclerc, who concluded his speech with a flourish: "Mangin's African troops ended up standing guard at Mayen, Cameroonian forces will do the same."[3] Leclerc deliberately conjured up the legacy of France's post-1918 occupation of Germany by

---

[1] AML, Leclerc 5A.
[2] Sah, p. 328.
[3] AML, Leclerc 5A.

African forces, imagining that this time troops from formerly German Cameroon would lead the way.

Aside from those troops already present on Cameroonian and FEA soil in 1940, the region's remarkable military accomplishments would occur in virtual autarky. Recruits were raised and trained on location, in areas like Cameroon that had been German only twenty-four years earlier. To Free French officials, Leclerc's ambitious decision to enroll Africans must have seemed all the more risky given how marginal or extraneous these regions had been to France's recruitment efforts in the Great War, and how fragile and contingent Cameroonian allegiance to France might prove.

Yet very quickly, prudence gave way to effervescence. In the first two months after the rallying of FEA and Cameroon, bricolage, resourcefulness, and urgency were the order of the day. One source evoked "a kind of general impatience"[4] to erase the defeat of June 1940. The *Eveil du Cameroon* newspaper betrays those heady days: the September 1940 issue includes a decree dated September 7, 1940, on the Free French emblem as well as an article on sizeable nighttime and daytime exercises at Douala. Free French officials were on the lookout: in September 1940 in Pointe-Noire, Congo, thirty-two Africans were rapidly trained to serve as stretcher-bearers in the event of an enemy attack. In Cameroon, another measure dated September 3, 1940, folded all militiamen into the colonial army.[5] Among them was Raphaël Onana, who would subsequently be seriously wounded at Bir Hakeim in 1942.[6] In other words, Cameroon's police force was being revamped into a front-guard military unit.

Massive shifts were under way, while seemingly insurmountable obstacles loomed. Equipment was in short supply – especially transport aircraft, trucks, anti-aircraft material, and anti-tank weapons.[7] A December 1942 report underlines that "Free France's military inheritance in Africa on August 28, 1940, was at once heavy and slim." Firstly, in the "disorganized" demobilization of June 1940, "many natives had been

---

[4] Ingold, *L'Epopée*, p. 69.

[5] *L'Eveil du Cameroun*, September 18, 1940. ANOM, GGAEF 3B 1085, Larminat, Pointe-Noire, November 5, 1940. ANCMR 2AC 11190A, excerpt from a report dated October 5, 1940.

[6] Onana, pp. 146–48.

[7] On anti-tank weapons, see Vincent, p. 48. On trucks and anti-aircraft weapons, see the letter of General de Gaulle to General Ismay, dated November 26, 1940, in de Gaulle's *Lettres, notes et carnets, juin 1940-juillet 1941*, p. 171.

sent back to their homes." Secondly, the report evokes the volatility and fickleness of the three glorious days. In particular, the document underscores the impact of the tragic civil war in Gabon, but also the enduring loyalty to Vichy "of nearly all of the officers in Oubangui-Chari who stayed faithful to the promises of their leader, Commandant [Henri] Cammas, General Huntziger's protégé [Pétain's minister of war] preferring this personal stance over the common good." Meanwhile, transport vehicles were cruelly lacking. In short, "everything needed to be rebuilt."

And yet, by the end of 1940, in a mere four months' time, four bataillons de marche would be raised in Cameroon and FEA. The report proceeds to describe "intense activity on many fronts. [Free France] has been able to adapt to this poor land and draw the most from it to create a fine military instrument of which France can be proud." Before adding: "When admiring this undertaking, one can only regret with bitterness the criminal deafness of other colonial governors to General de Gaulle, in our much richer colonies in North Africa, West Africa and Madagascar."[8]

This last point seems critical. Before the war, FEA and Cameroon were widely considered to be some of the most neglected lands of the French colonial empire. Military stereotypes placed the quality of the region's soldiers well beneath that of combatants from West Africa and Morocco. Its communication lines, infrastructures, resources, and urban centers were all perceived to lag behind those of French West Africa. From a tactical standpoint, neither FEA nor Cameroon constituted ideal sites from which to launch a movement aimed at liberating the motherland. And yet, the Free French had no alternative. It was from this "colonial Cinderella" that the bulk of the resources and much of the manpower of this first Free French military effort would come.

The argument should not be overstretched. Jean-François Muracciole has shown how both the number of forces involved, as well as their casualty rates, were considerably lower in this first phase than in the second one, when the Fighting French would wage battle in Italy and France between 1943 and 1945. Martin Thomas and Anthony Clayton have likewise taken stock of the modest scale of these first Free French forces, adding that the significance of the early African campaigns rests primarily in their propaganda value.[9]

---

[8] SHD 11P 21, the military effort of Fighting French Africa, December 17, 1942.

[9] Muracciole, p. 273; Anthony Clayton, *Histoire de l'armée française en Afrique, 1830–1962* (Paris: Albin Michel, 1994), p. 173; Thomas, *The French Empire at War*, p. 85.

However, beyond the question of scale, in my opinion the first Free French military effort in Africa is genuinely significant for several reasons. It offered the movement victories over the Axis, and not simply against Vichy troops as the tragically divisive Gabon campaign had done. It consequently conferred the movement a key stamp of legitimacy. Free France's High Commissioner to Africa Edgard de Larminat stated as much in a speech he pronounced at Brazzaville on April 5, 1941: "We proved...to the world that France was not vanquished, for we have armed forces that are fighting and are indeed capable of achieving victories."[10] At the time, this assertion rested essentially on the triumph at Kufra. Others would follow. What seems certain is that without Kufra, the Fezzan, and Bir Hakeim, General de Gaulle would have found himself in a far weaker bargaining position during his Algiers negotiations with Giraud. Without these military accomplishments, would the United States and Great Britain have consented to equip two Fighting French divisions in the summer of 1943? This is essentially what famed Free Frenchman Maurice Schuman recognized in 1988: "Without the Kufra oath, there would have been no Leclerc division and the future Marshal Leclerc would not have carved the name of Kufra into history, had he not departed from Brazzaville, the capital of Free France."[11]

## On the Attack

The Free French had little chance to regroup after the rallying of Equatorial Africa and Cameroon to their side in August 1940. At Douala, on October 21, 1940, less than two months after Chad joined de Gaulle, and at the very time when Gabon was entering into resistance versus de Gaulle's resistance, the general drafted a "note relating to our military action plan." It was intended for General de Larminat and Colonel Leclerc. In this note, the leader of Free France articulated three priorities: "1) to take part, directly in operations against the enemy...2) to hold the territories that have rallied to the Free French. 3) To utilize every opportunity to trigger the rallying of other French territories in Africa."[12] Defense had made way to a more offensive mindset.

---

[10] CHETOM, 18H 138.

[11] Maurice Schuman, preface to Ackermann Athanassiades, *France libre, capitale Brazzaville* (Paris: la Bruyère, 1989), p. 8.

[12] AML, Leclerc 5A, note signed Charles de Gaulle.

What is more, this document clearly shows that Free France's fate hung in the balance in Africa in 1940. Only one enemy appeared within reach from FEA, if one excepts Vichy forces in Niger: Mussolini's Libya. The document therefore went on to recommend the following plan of attack: "direct action against the enemy shall be undertaken as soon as possible: in Italian territory in Libya in the areas of Kufra and Murzouk. These actions are to be launched against Italian positions in close liaison with air forces and specialized troops in Chad."[13]

A mere two months later, de Gaulle issued Order 632. This December 28, 1940, document reads: "The first bataillons de marche, formed in Free French Africa, are now on their way to battlegrounds where they will take part in Italy's defeat. Others are being trained and will join them shortly. The past four months of patient reorganization have born fruit. The time of action has come. In August, the French of FEA and Cameroon expressed their will to take part in the fight. They are honoring their word. They will prove to be merciless towards the Italians; they will avenge the treason of June [Mussolini's declaration of war on France]; they will speed up the clock of national liberation."[14] In a mere four months, Free France had shifted to conquest.

In addition to the obvious motivation of wishing to attack an enemy that had ignominiously declared war on France on June 10, 1940, as it was already crumbling, and to boost morale after the debacle of 1940, another Free French consideration emerges from the colonial archives. This was a time of internal French tensions. Vichy reached Chad by radio (having tested a new powerful radio broadcasting post in Niger in October 1940), and did not hesitate to pillory the Gaullists. Vichy even considered infiltrating printed propaganda into Chad by way of African notables and covert African soldiers. Against this backdrop, on November 11, 1940, Félix Eboué focused on an encounter between Vichy and Gaullist emissaries near the Chad–Niger border, which had suddenly become an international frontier, indeed the only land point at which Free and Vichy France met. Eboué's men reported an initial impression that "Vichy wants to bring us back to reason through force." As for the project of attacking Libya, raised by the Gaullist emissary, his Vichy interlocutor, Lieutenant Michaud, responded: "in [Vichy] Niger, the idea of attacking Libya from Chad is considered to be folly, given the means available . . . [However] the undertaking could bring to [the Free French] about half of the forces

---

[13] Ibid.
[14] Cited by Sicé, p. 189.

in Niger."[15] In other words, here was an opportunity to kill two birds with one stone: return into the world war by opening a Saharan front and exposing Libya's vulnerable underbelly, while at the same time rallying Vichyites who could not be won over so long as Free France was fighting Vichy forces, rather than Axis ones.

In April 1941, such hope still lingered, at least in British circles. British Captain de Paula reported that several posts in Vichy territory, including the one at Madama in northeastern Niger, were ready to provide valuable information to Free French forces entering Libyan territory. Another Vichy post seemed prepared to join the struggle outright, according to this same report.[16] Similarly, in January 1942, Vichy officials in Bilma, Niger, turned a blind eye when Leclerc's forces passed through their territory. Yet such cases remained exceptions that proved the rule. The abiding hope of swinging supporters of Pétain to the Free French cause was not absurd in and of itself. Yet it clearly failed to take into account the cumulative impact of Dunkirk, Mers-el-Kébir, Dakar, and Gabon – in other words the depth of the Vichy-Free French chasm. It also failed to consider the widespread and deep fidelity that many colonials continued to feel toward Marshal Pétain.[17]

## Kufra and Its Lessons

The victory at Kufra has become legendary as an improbable feat achieved by Colonel Leclerc's men. Crossing the Sahara, from south to north, with very limited supplies and weapons, then taking a powerful Italian fortress was, according to many, an impossible task.[18] In fact, the attackers themselves seem not to have liked their odds. This can be deduced from a telegram from General de Larminat to London on January 18, 1941, announcing that "our limited means, the enemy forces, as well as the difficult terrain do not permit us to hope to take Kufra, unless extraordinarily favorable circumstances develop." Yet Kufra fell, and marked the first victory by troops under Free French command, departing from

---

[15] Akpo-Vaché, p. 39. On the new, powerful radio emissions post at Zinder, see ANOM GGAEF, 6B 710, Fort Lamy, October 27, 1940. The discussion between Vichy and Free French emissaries is related in: ANOM GGAEF 5D 29c, Eboué, Fort-Lamy, November 11, 1940, telegram 751.

[16] PRO WO 178, d. 5, No 20 Military Mission, War diary, April 29, 1941.

[17] Inaction favored Vichy. On these choices, see Jennings, *Vichy in the Tropics*. On the matter of Bilma, see Lefebvre, p. 374.

[18] Admittedly, early projects for such a raid had already been formulated in 1939.

Free French soil. After the victory, Leclerc famously uttered the Kufra "oath" of which several variants exist, for it was not transcribed at the time. What seems clear is that he vowed, with his men – from Bangui, Fort-Lamy, Yaoundé, and Douala – not to put down their arms until Strasbourg had been liberated.

The expedition presented innumerable challenges. The fortress in question lay "almost exactly in the mathematical heart of the Libyan desert."[19] This led one Free Frenchman to the following truism: "In order to attack Kufra, one first needs to get there."[20] Leclerc's troops had to cross some 800 kilometers of desert from their point of departure at Faya-Largeau in Chad to reach the oasis fortress. Timing was crucial: Free French Captain Girard remarked laconically, "In Chad, war is seasonal, much like hunting in Europe." In addition to conquering the desert, the expedition needed to beat the rainy season in Chad. And yet the mission set off late. On Christmas day 1940, Edgard de Larminat telegraphed de Gaulle: "If contacts are favorable, a joint camel and motorized action will be launched on Kufra, with considerable planning involved. Aerial bombardments planned on Kufra have been delayed because we have had to stash bombs and fuel en route, and because of the need to mobilize trucks for troop transport."[21] Improvisation was in full tilt.

The story of the Kufra raid is fairly well known, having been recounted by many of its participants.[22] What has been less well established is the campaign's multiple colonial dimensions, and African participation in it. Black troops made up the bulk of the Free French forces sent to Kufra. According to a report signed by Leclerc in person, the expedition included 295 African troops – not counting drivers – and 101 European servicemen, as well as six civilians. Out of the four who perished on the Free French side, three were African; we know the surnames of two of them: N'Donon and Digueal. Out of the twenty-two wounded, ten were. The African proportion of combatants in the ensuing Fezzan

---

[19] The phrase was coined by the geographer Gauthier, cited by Vézinet, p. 64. It is then taken up by François Ingold in, *L'Epopée*, p. 14. The Larminat quote is from ANF 3AG1, 169, January 18, 1941.

[20] The phrase appeared for the first time in "L'Affaire de Koufra," *Le Cameroun libre*, May 30, 1941.

[21] AML, Leclerc 5A, Girard's text entitled "La Genèse." ANF, 3AG1 164, de Larminat to de Gaulle, December 25, 1940. A draft dated December 23, 1940, is held at the National Archives of the Republic of Congo, under GGAEF 84.

[22] Dronne, pp. 91–130; Lapie, pp. 241–51; Roger Ceccaldi's testimony in *Actes du colloque international le général Leclerc et l'Afrique française libre*, pp. 423–42. François Ingold, *L'Epopée*, pp. 85–118. Romain H. Rainero, *Le "Serment de Koufra": regards italiens sur la campagne saharienne de Leclerc* (Paris: Publisud, 2010), pp. 89–142.

campaign of 1942–43 would be more spectacular still: 2,700 Africans for 550 Europeans.[23]

And yet, among the surrender terms of the Tag Fort at Kufra on March 1, 1941, clause number three stipulates: "Upon signature, a French unit composed strictly of Europeans will take possession of the fort."[24] Leclerc's report specifies that "the Italian officers insisted that only Europeans initially occupy the fort, excluding the Senegalese (sic)."[25] In other words, those surrendering had allegedly insisted on the clause. How can one explain this demand and Leclerc's willingness to accept it? According to Governor Pierre-Olivier Lapie, and British photographer George Rodger, it was Leclerc who summarily dictated the surrender terms to the Italians, who in turn accepted them wholesale.[26] Similarly, according to Italian historian Romain Rainero, Leclerc drew up the conditions in person without the Italians having the slightest input.[27] For his part, Jean-Noël Vincent suggests that the Italians might have proposed the clause "no doubt for fear of looting and resentment from the native troops."[28] This appears to be pure conjecture. It seems far more likely that colonial power relations precluded Africans from taking the reputedly invincible fort, itself a symbol of Italy's colonial ambitions. Consequently, the surrender terms appear to constitute an avowal that African forces taking the Tag Fort would have been tantamount to a dishonor. This is precisely what one former Free Frenchman Charles Béné concludes. He describes the surrender terms as having been "honest and humane," "devoid of humiliating conditions."[29] All of this said, Leclerc's cumulative disadvantages at Kufra (in terms of air support, firepower, and numbers), and the virtual miracle of the Italian surrender, not to mention the extreme fatigue of his troops having crossed the Sahara, may have led the colonel to deem this kind of accommodation a small inconvenience for him to

[23] CHETOM, 15H 156, Kufra operation. Another estimate has 200 participating in the operation of whom 150 were African. SHD 11P 21, Leclerc's conquest of the Fezzan. Jean-François Muracciole's figure is very close to the one I am presenting here. Muracciole, p. 273. For the Fezzan totals of 2,700 and 550 men, see Crémieux-Brilhac, *La France libre*, p. 641. For the names of the two African soldiers, see Rainero, p. 307.

[24] SHD 11P 21, Conditions of surrender at Kufra, March 1, 1941.

[25] CHETOM, 15H 156, Kufra operation, p. 9, report signed Leclerc.

[26] Lapie, p. 248; George Rodger, *Voyage au désert* (Paris: La Colombe, 1956), pp. 54–55.

[27] Lapie, p. 248; Rodger, pp. 54–55. Rainero, p. 124; Dominique Lormier, *C'est nous les Africains: l'épopée de l'armée française d'Afrique, 1940–1945* (Paris: Calmann-Lévy, 2006), p. 109.

[28] Vincent, p. 270.

[29] Charles Béné, *Carnets de route d'un 'Rat du Désert' Alsacien de la France libre*, vol. 1 (Raon-L'Etape: 1991), p. 220.

pay for the first Free French victory. Still, it comes in stunning contrast to Jean Moulin's willingness to die rather than sign a document wrongly incriminating black French troops in 1940.[30]

Kufra revealed both the weakness of the Italian defense and the extreme fragility of Leclerc's supply line, weaponry, and equipment. But it also betrayed Leclerc's low opinion of African troops. As early as December 1940, he indicated to General de Gaulle that "an African force can only be worth something if one averages one European per ten natives."[31] With General de Larminant he was even blunter: "We are literally being flooded by native recruits, and have 1,672 too many African soldiers...On the other hand, there is a real shortage of officers and N.C.O.s." Leclerc added that General François Ingold shared these concerns, having found "one deaf-mute and one idiot" among the latest African recruits. He then concluded: "Given our shortage of low-ranking officers, recruiting more African troops would be not only useless but actually harmful."[32]

The Kufra operation did not change Leclerc's mind. Troops from FEA, he railed, "are unfortunately not fit for this modern form of warfare" that was the desert war. He rekindled stereotypes according to which troops from FEA "do not have the sense or the taste for war of other native races. Any initiative is beyond them. A slow and difficult training can get them to learn some basic combat reflexes."[33] Some African soldiers clearly got wind of this low opinion. In a 1987 interview, Cameroonian veteran Womondje Barnabé stated, "Leclerc was bad for Cameroonians....He declared that no matter what a black man's abilities, he could not advance past the rank of chief warrant officer."[34] In 1942, Leclerc admitted to U.S. Free French volunteer Hassoldt Davis that Free France could have certainly used North Africa's "superb combatants."[35] Yet this would not be an option for him until the year following. In the meantime, despite all of his reticence, Leclerc made widespread use of troops from FEA and Cameroon.

Leclerc also invoked material liabilities. He wrote in March 1941: "The natural slowness of the tirailleur is only aggravated by equipment

---

30 Jean-Pierre Azéma, *Jean Moulin* (Paris: Perrin, 2003), pp. 106–107.

31 Cited by Jean-Louis Crémieux-Brilhac, *La France libre*, p. 638.

32 AML, 6A, Leclerc to Larminat, December 19, 1940.

33 SHD 12 P 259, Report concerning Free French forces from Chad from January to February 1941. Reproduced in Vincent, p. 356.

34 Cited by Sah, p. 304.

35 Hassoldt Davis, *Feu d'Afrique* (Paris: Fayard, 1945), p. 67.

FIGURE 5. George Rodger. Free French troops training barefoot in Bouar, 1941. ROG 1940010W00008/16. © George Rodger, Magnum Photos.

and arms that are dated: the ammunition belt, the 86 gun, the shoulder bag, the bayonet remove all flexibility from the tirailleur." He continued, "then there is the problem of shoes. After a few days of combat on rocky ground, most of the African troops and even some of the Europeans had bloodied feet."[36] Footwear clearly posed a special problem. According to a long-held colonial tradition, African soldiers and police forces in French Equatorial Africa were barefoot on maneuvers and outside of combat situations, unlike European troops.[37] This explains a photograph taken by *Life Magazine*'s George Rodger showing barefoot African troops training at Bouar in 1941 (see Figure 5). What is more, in the desert campaign, even when one had shoes, they tended not to hold up for long. During the Fezzan campaign of 1942, Hassoldt Davis described "heat so intense that helmets and shoes shriveled until they were unusable."[38] It was only in February 1943 when Fighting France's L

[36] SHD 12 P 259, Report concerning Free French forces from Chad from January to February 1941.

[37] Phyllis M. Martin, "Contesting clothes in colonial Brazzaville," *Journal of African History*, 35, 1994, p. 408.

[38] Davis, p. 85.

Force received British equipment that African troops were finally systematically provided with footwear. "They were elated," testified Raymond Dronne.[39]

More generally, Kufra exposed a series of problems that the Free French then promptly took to their allies. This is in substance what the high commissioner to Free French Africa explained to General de Gaulle on March 19, 1941, specifying that Leclerc had especially lacked anti-aircraft equipment.[40] Other needs surfaced. On February 28, 1941, the Spears mission demanded aircraft from the British air ministry in order to repatriate the wounded at Kufra, adding "scarcity of transport planes is tragic." Fortuitously, the Kufra expedition resolved a few shortages in and of itself. The Free French column returned loaded with enemy matériel. An ice-making machine was greeted with wild cheers in Chad, but even more useful were four 20mm guns, three 12,7 machine guns, 18 heavy machine guns, and 32 Fiat 1935 model machine guns, not to mention more than a million rounds of ammunition for machine guns and light weaponry, as well as 14 vehicles (see Figure 6).[41] With the exception of the ice-making machine, all of this loot would be used during the 1942 Fezzan campaign.[42] African drivers who had taken the troops to Kufra in the first place were the ones who hauled this booty back to Faya-Largeau, whence the raid on Kufra had begun.

### African Drivers

African drivers played a crucial role for Free France during the desert war. The archives reveal their key function during the Kufra and Fezzan campaigns, hauling men and supplies across vast distances in the Sahara (see Figure 7). Yet the Free French suffered from a shortage of trucks as well. Indeed, in 1941, 150 of them were requisitioned in Oubangui-Chari, a colony that desperately needed them for the cotton harvest. With resources stretched, this kind of measure exacerbated preexisting tensions between civilian and military authorities. The archives reveal new efforts by the army in 1943 to commandeer 400 trucks in Oubangui-Chari and in

[39] Dronne, p. 263.

[40] ANF, 3AG1 169, High Commissioner, March 19, 1941.

[41] See Vincent, p. 270 for the general figures, Rodger, p. 56 for the figure on ammunition. For the ice-making machine see Ingold, *L'Epopée*, p. 55. Hassoldt Davis remarks on how the Free French of Faya-Largeau enjoyed the ice-maker. Davis, p. 86.

[42] AML, Leclerc 15, folder 6, and Davis, p. 91.

FIGURE 6. George Rodger. RTST Free French troops loading war booty onto trucks at Kufra, 1941. ROG 1940010W00022/02. © George Rodger, Magnum Photos.

FIGURE 7. Slow progression of a Free French vehicle in the Sahara. CHETOM. Plate entitled "Les forces françaises libres" 95, photo 97121. Printed with permission.

Chad, this time to bring the B.M. 12 and 13 to North Africa.[43] Truckers were not alone in playing such vital roles. One should not overlook the navigators who ferried supplies up the Oubangui River, or the columns of men on camels who placed fuel canisters at regular intervals on the path to Kufra.[44]

For truckers, conditions sometimes proved infernal. On March 15, 1941, for instance, ill-adapted tires and overloaded trucks led to a "catastrophe" in the Sahara.[45] At Kufra, Chevrolet trucks were rigged with machine guns, while some thirty Ford trucks and twenty-five Bedfords brought water, munitions, fuel, and food, all essential for desert missions. The task proved all the more challenging because the tires on the Fords were ill-suited for the desert. Far too thin, they got stuck in the sand. Around Kufra, sheet metal was slipped under the wheels whenever a vehicle became ensnared in the dunes.[46]

---

[43] ANOM GGAEF 6B 710, Bangui, December 8, 1941, and ANOM Cab. 63, Alger, January 8, 1943.

[44] See Béné, p. 179.

[45] AML, Leclerc 6B Largeau to Fort-Lamy, March 15, 1941.

[46] CHETOM, 15H 156, Kufra operation, French forces. Béné, p. 212.

The archives hold scant information about the truckers themselves. One witness states that among the drivers at Kufra "Cameroon was well represented. Some drivers as well as workers, were wounded, one of them twice." Charles Béné observes that Cameroonians were "requisitioned" as civilians, at the point of entry of the trucks in Africa, which is to say Douala. He adds that many of them were Catholics.[47] We also know that Free France recruited the following numbers of drivers in Cameroon: 849 in 1941, 1,186 in 1942, and 368 in 1943.[48] The concentrated nature of the recruitment was such that it impacted local demographics. As the process was in full tilt, Douala registered a sizeable shrinking of its population, going from 41,400 inhabitants in 1941 to 34,326 the year following (this would account not only for those enlisted, but also for those who fled ahead of the recruiters).[49] Sometimes the thankless task of desert driving was noticed and appreciated. After the Kufra raid and the Fezzan campaign in April 1942, Leclerc requested a 30,000-franc allocation to "reward the Cameroonian drivers and soldiers wounded during the last military operations."[50]

The motivations of these truckers are equally difficult to reconstitute, inasmuch as they even had a choice to join the Free French. Gaullist censorship files reveal that in some cases patriotism and anti-Nazism served as catalysts. In September 1941, an anonymous Cameroonian from Douala wrote to his friend, a trucker now posted in Largeau, Chad. He asked if any of their three common friends were with him in Chad. Evidently, recruitment had been so swift and intense that many of the letter-writer's contacts and neighbors seemed to have vanished from the streets of Douala. He closed his message with the following patriotic exhortation: "The day will come when we reunite to rejoice after the victory of Free France and its British allies."[51] The thought seems relatively sincere, although perhaps slightly contrived. Indeed, correspondents tended to know that censors opened their letters. They may therefore have written with such an audience in mind.

[47] SHD 12 P 259, the Kufra affair. Béné, pp. 246, 248, and 252.

[48] ANOM DSM 262, file 3, table 4.

[49] Mbembe, p. 226. Catherine Coquery-Vidrovitch in Charles-Robert Ageron, ed., "Emeutes urbaines, grèves générales et décolonisation en Afrique française," *Les Chemins de la décolonisation de l'empire colonial français* (Paris: CNRS, 1986), p. 494.

[50] ANC GGAEF 84, Leclerc to the High Commissioner, April 18, 1942 (Tel 974).

[51] ANOM GGAEF, 5D 295, Contrôle postal du Cameroun, first half of September 1941. Douala, September 4, 1941.

## A Colony for the Colony

The Free French victory at Kufra is sometimes described as having been more symbolic than useful. The impact on morale was certainly immediate. A report on Northern Chad in 1941 reads, "The taking of Kufra by the French has produced an excellent impression on the natives: it showed them our strength and greatly enhanced our prestige that had been somewhat shaken by Italian bluster that had been relayed by Toubou people, crossing the border."[52] Within Free French ranks as well, the effect was striking. On March 11, 1941, a George, probably George Rodger, reported to the Spears mission that among Free French forces in Chad the "success" of Kufra "has certainly helped to sweeten the bad taste left in the mouth after Dakar."[53] It is in fact difficult to overstate the importance of Free France defeating an Axis power so soon after France's complete collapse. Little wonder that Free French postage stamps in Equatorial Africa featured a phoenix rising from the ashes.

This said, Kufra also possessed real strategic importance. Free France had gained a foothold on the other side of the Sahara, and had demonstrated an ability to penetrate Italian Libya from the south. The Gaullist movement now occupied enemy territory, albeit a territory with long-standing ties with northern Chad. Indeed, Chadian interests, especially those of Libyans who had taken refuge from Mussolini in northern Chad, now grafted themselves onto Free French ones. Free France, which so often found itself on the defensive vis-à-vis purported Vichy, U.S., or British colonial ambitions, now reinvented itself as an occupier.

Before setting off for Kufra, Leclerc had issued specific instructions governing relations with the population of the Kufra oasis. Firstly, "indigenous civilians are to be spared as much as possible." Secondly, "native soldiers will be released immediately, and charged with forming a fifth column." Leclerc was able to utilize elements of the sizeable Cyrenian and Fezzanese population that had taken refuge in Chad after Mussolini's conquest of the Libyan Sahara. Prior to 1940, this population, estimated at roughly 2,000 individuals in all of FEA, had been banned from living within a 300-kilometer radius of the Libyan border. Their knowledge of both sides of the border seemed then to constitute both an asset and a liability. Yet the Free French now recruited easily in these circles because the refugees were intent on revenge against Mussolini's Italy. As early as

<hr>

[52] ANOM GGAEF 4(4) D51, Borkou- Tibesti, 1941, report on the political situation.
[53] PRO WO 178, d. 5, George from Fort-Lamy, March 11, 1941.

November 1940, when the very first Free French raid on Murzuk was being planned, Captain Jacques Massu asked that Toubou and Fezzanese refugees in Chad be recruited to serve as informants. Members of these different exiled communities even handed Leclerc a letter of introduction to the population of Kufra.[54] Once he arrived in the oasis, Leclerc read the text to a village chief, who was left somewhat perplexed by the Frenchman's accent – Leclerc having learned some Arabic in Morocco during the Rif campaign. Theatrics aside, Leclerc sought not so much to be treated as a liberator in Libya, but rather to tap into whatever source might help him capture and hold Italian positions. On February 23, 1941, in the midst of the siege of the Tag Fort, Leclerc requested quite specific and surprising supplies from Brazzaville: "Very important from a political standpoint: send us a great deal of tea and sugar for the natives." The "natives" were those of the oasis, and not French colonial troops, as is evidenced in a following telegram from February 27 that specified, "in view of distributing it to the natives of Kufra, Colonel Leclerc requests sugar and tea."[55]

Initially, the scale of success at Kufra – taking the fortress when initial hope had been to destroy a few aircraft – placed Free France in an awkward position. In a telegram to London, Larminat, Eboué, and Doctor Adolphe Sicé agreed (for once) to state, "It would be best to keep the question of Kufra's attribution hazy, and to avoid at all cost to awaken British colonial distrust over our ambitions at the time when we most need British support. Kufra is a pile of rocks without interest to us." They added, with no less clarity: "Kufra is practically inaccessible from French Africa. The proof is that we need to ask the British to evacuate our small detachment at Kufra via Egypt. Tying Kufra to Chad would be as unviable as linking the Southern Algerian oases to Timbuktu." Finally, according to Larminat, Leclerc had allegedly pledged to hand Kufra to the British if by some feat he managed to take it. Conversely, he contended, the Fezzan could well interest Free France over the *longue durée*.[56] On March 14, de Gaulle responded by telegram that "now is not the time to make commitments about Kufra when we do not yet know the British position about the Fezzan, should it come up one day." He also made

54 Jacques Frémeaux, *La Sahara et la France* (Paris: Soteca, 2010), pp. 162–63. AML, Leclerc 6A, Massu, November 13, 1940. Béné, p. 186.

55 Colonel de Guillebon, "Les débuts au Sahara," *Tropiques*, February 1948. AML, Leclerc 6B, Colonel Leclerc to Le Nuz, Koufra, February 23, 1941, and in the same folder, Largeau, February 27, 1941.

56 ANF, 3AG1 169, Larminat to London, March 2, 1941.

clear that the decision was his, not his representatives' in Africa: "Agreements of this sort are general matters that need to be referred to me."[57] Thus, Gaullist authority and sovereignty over Kufra and the Fezzan were tightly linked already in March 1941. All of this rather prematurely wrote Italy out of the equation long before the Free French forces invested and conquered the Fezzan in 1942–43.

Meanwhile, Kufra's status remained unresolved. According to one source, its inhabitants took the initiative, "requesting," for example, "a French school" as early as March 1941. They were actors in this small-scale diplomatic tug of war. Whereupon Emir Idris As-Senussi (the future Libyan king who would one day be toppled by a certain Gaddafi) exiled since the Italian conquest of Kufra, contacted de Gaulle to formulate requests. These included the restoration of traditions and the restitution of powers and properties to the Senussi religious order. In short, he sought to erase the Italian colonial presence while gaining autonomy and a new impetus for his Muslim brotherhood. The Senussis had once harassed French forces on the Chad's confines. The irony certainly did not escape General de Gaulle who remained suspicious of their future intentions. Indeed, Idris Senussi's nationalist ambitions were well known. Yet, his brother Mohammed Al Abid was one of the many Libyans to have fled the fascist invasion, finding refuge in Chad prior to 1940. He now served as a go-between for Free France in its negotiations over southern Libya.[58]

In spite of this temporary rapprochement, many problems remained. They hinged on the fundamental rupture that Leclerc's forces had just undertaken, breaking Kufra from Libya and the Mediterranean coast. No sooner had Kufra fallen than local merchants asked the Free French what would become of their cattle that had remained north of the desert. Captain Fernand Barboteu, temporarily entrusted with the Kufra military zone, attempted in vain to compensate for this lost trade by stimulating links with Chad.[59] Between imperatives of legitimacy and the everyday headache of managing occupied territories, doubts began to grow among the Free French ranks. In April 1941, Larminat and Eboué concurred that it was "premature" to remove the label of "enemy national" from the

---

[57] ANOM, GGAEF, 5D 291 telegram 352, sent on March 14, 1941.
[58] ANOM GGAEF 2Y 14, Mohammad Idris As Senoussi to general de Gaulle, April 5, 1941. On the family ties see Frémeaux, p. 163.
[59] AML, Leclerc 6B Koufra, March 14, 1941. Ingold, *L'Epopée*, p. 108.

inhabitants of Kufra, even though doing so would have released frozen Kufra funds and other assets.[60]

The Free French debate over whether or not to extend the occupation of Kufra was sensitive enough for two reports to be devoted to the topic, one in London, the other in Brazzaville. Each reviewed the international treaties that might be used to justify French control over Kufra and its environs (the agreements of 1899 signed in the wake of the Fashoda crisis, as well as those of 1919 and 1925). The reports converged in concluding that Kufra lay well beyond both French and British claims.[61] The idea of Free France colonizing Southern Libya was not ruled out, by any stretch.

On March 23, 1941, de Gaulle ordered that a Free French detachment be maintained at all times at Kufra. The general further demanded that "France's colors fly above the fort." On April 3, 1941, de Gaulle finally accepted that British Colonel Ralph Bagnold serve as commander of the Kufra area, so long as a French liaison officer be posted with him. Yet, Free France was so short of men that in June 1941, de Gaulle began to complain to General Archibald Wavell of the amount of time that British troops were taking to relieve French ones at Kufra. Indeed, 350 Free French men were still occupying the position, while de Gaulle wanted only a "symbolic unit" there. He needed those forces elsewhere. More than ever, Free France was caught between its expansionist ambitions, its expression of sovereignty, its desire to wage war, and the difficult reality of depending so mightily on Great Britain. Leclerc's reluctance to utilize colonial troops only compounded the manpower problem.

In fact, the French flag would continue to float over the fort for the rest of the war, even though Kufra's air base would mainly serve the R.A.F., because of its position near Egypt. Lapie remarked in 1943 that the conquest of this oasis by Leclerc's men had achieved "a long-term political result." Indeed, London recognized the merit of a Free French offensive that essentially carved out a zone of French influence over a part of the Sahara in which France had previously been excluded.

Kufra offered a foreshadowing of the colonial project that Free France embarked on in the Fezzan. In February 1942, the Gaullist movement launched its first intrusion into the Fezzan, followed by a second, far more

[60]  ANOM GGAEF 2Y 14, de Larminat to Eboué, April 26, 1941, and ANOM GGAEF 3B 1092, Eboué to Larminat, April 24, 1941.
[61]  ANOM GGAEF 2Y 14, note on Kufra, April 14, 1941.

successful wave, between September 1942 and January 1943. Here too the task proved arduous: the Tibesti massif rose some 3,000 meters (nearly ten thousand feet) above sea level and created a natural border between Free French Chad and Mussolini's Fezzan.[62] Mirroring Leclerc's instructions for Kufra, in the Fezzan, Lieutenant-Colonel Louis Dio explained to his compatriots that "the natives of the Fezzan are our future subjects, and we will rely upon them for supplies." Consequently, he instructed, "Natives of the Fezzan are to be respected, both their property and their persons." Lastly, Free French forces should "repeat at every opportunity to the natives that we are waging war on the Italians and the Italians alone."[63]

The conquest of the Fezzan triggered much more serious diplomatic repercussions for the Free French. As early as November 1942, the British openly worried about Free French ambitions in the Fezzan. On November 30, Richard Casey, the British minister in charge of Middle Eastern affairs, evoked possible Free French aspirations over the area. There followed a vigorous debate between de Gaulle and the British over a British scheme to have Leclerc accompanied by UK officers. On the British side, in December 1942, strong reservations were expressed about the possibility that the French franc might become the Fezzan's currency.[64]

In response, Leclerc rebuffed schemes to impose the pound sterling over the area, and de Gaulle issued a terse statement to the Foreign Office proclaiming, "The Fezzan will be France's part for the battle of Africa."[65] De Gaulle won this set, in large part thanks to Anthony Eden and his Foreign Office. The latter persuaded the War Office that the Fezzan was not worth another quarrel with General de Gaulle. Eden added that tying the Fezzan to Chad struck him as equally logical as linking it to Libya. He further contended that the Fezzan's populations were largely Touareg and not Arab, thereby he thought, enhancing de Gaulle's case. In point of fact, the speed with which the Fezzan fell in late 1942 left little option to British planners, short of pulling the rug out from under de Gaulle's movement. However, even the question of the Fezzan's borders would eventually cause friction between French and British authorities.[66]

---

[62] FCDG, Fonds Eboué, F22, 18, note on the Fezzan and its conquest by Leclerc's forces.

[63] AML, Leclerc 5A, conduct toward indigenous civilians of the Fezzan.

[64] Saul Kelly, "Ce fruit savoureux du désert: Britain, France and the Fezzan, 1941–1956," *The Maghreb Review* 26: 1 (2001), pp. 3–4.

[65] Cited by Crémieux-Brilhac, p. 647.

[66] Kelly, pp. 7; 10–12.

Free France had launched its own colonial adventure, outside the boundaries of France's prewar empire. In January 1943, Pierre Lami, the right-hand man of Colonel Raymond Delange in the Fezzan, set about elaborating legislation for the "military territory of Fezzan," along with a native policy for good measure. He observed in a postcard to Governor-General Félix Eboué, "It's as if it were our turn to play the role of occupier, before landing in Europe."[67] Leclerc made no mistake either, telegraphing Eboué on January 9, 1943, that "our occupation regime begins today." In October 1943, Charles de Gaulle distinguished semantically between the nature of the battles his movement had waged up until then: "In Eritrea, in Ethiopia, in Libya, Free France fought. In the Fezzan, it conquered." In his memoirs, de Gaulle proved candid about his Libyan ambitions: "The conquest of the Fezzan," he wrote, "would place into our hands a chip over the future destiny of Libya." Like the occupation of Kufra, this one rested once more on the critical role played by Libyan refugees who returned to their country on the coattails of Free French forces. They include Ahmed Bey Seif-en-Naceur, whom Colonel Maurice Sarazac named native governor of the Fezzan (Delange held the post of French governor).[68]

In February 1943, specifically designed Free French bills and stamps were adopted in the Fezzan. Initially, General Leclerc had attempted to introduce French Equatorial African currency in the region. No doubt he thereby intended to mark the doubly colonial nature of the campaign: the Fezzan, occupied by troops from FEA, was to adopt the currency of that colony. Only the shortage of small bills in FEA seems to have prevented the scheme from being carried out. The compromise involved utilizing West African bills marked with a "Fezzan" surcharge. It backfired, and recalcitrant caravan traders had to be forced to use this new currency for their inter-colonial commerce. A March 1943 telegram reveals the extent of the problem: "The surcharged Fezzan bills are avoided in all neighboring territories and even by Allied armies." On April 5, 1943, the governor and military leader of the Fezzan, Raymond Delange, wrote René Pleven in person about precisely these issues: "The introduction to the Fezzan of a local currency (French West African bank notes surcharged 'Fezzan' and carrying a fictitious value of 176 francs 50 per British pound), a measure I opposed from the start, has been a dismal failure. Everything

---

[67] FCDG, Fonds Eboué, F22, 18, Pierre Lami to Félix Eboué, January 13, 1943.
[68] Leclerc cited by Ingold, *L'Epopée*, p. 208. Charles de Gaulle, preface to Ingold's p. x. Frémeaux, p. 215. Charles de Gaulle, *Mémoires de Guerre*, tome 1, p. 250.

is paralyzed." He added, "This currency is refused everywhere, starting with our own Free French cashiers in Chad . . . Chadian merchants who accompanied our forces are ruined . . . French and African soldiers paid in this currency can do nothing with it, and cannot send money home, etc. This farce of a situation has completely ridiculed us vis-à-vis the Algerians and the British." On May 24, 1943, the situation remained unchanged, with trade between Chad and Fezzan having become virtually "impossible." This was precisely the reverse of what some Free French were trying to achieve by tethering their holdings in Libya to Chad. Free France may have conquered swiftly; occupation proved more challenging. In fact, Raymond Delange so detested his mission as to implore René Pleven, "This is an SOS: do not bury me in the central Sahara; the Fezzan is but a mirage."[69]

Despite Delange's plea that the Fezzan be linked with Algeria, in January 1943 the occupied region was financially connected to FEA. In April 1943, the Fezzan took on a new designation of "occupied enemy territory under military administration by Fighting French forces."[70] Some Free French now fancied themselves not simply occupiers, but actual colonizers, assuming the same Roman mantle long used as a foundational trope in French North Africa. Thus Colonel Boisseau compared the conquering Free French to "the proconsuls of ancient Rome." Like the ancients, he wrote, the Gaullists "never failed to organize on a solid and lasting basis those territories that fall under their hands."[71] To Boisseau, it was the French, and not Mussolini's Italians, who could rightfully trace their ancestry to Pompey or perhaps even Cesar.

However, Félix Eboué remained deeply skeptical of the incorporation of these freshly conquered lands into FEA's dominion. In September 1943, he drafted a note to Pleven in which he insisted that neither Kufra nor the Fezzan "are of any interest to FEA, either from an economic or a political standpoint." He honed his argument further. "They should rightfully be controlled by those who hold the Mediterranean coast."[72]

---

[69] On Leclerc, see ANC GGAEF 82, Brazzaville to the Commissaire national aux Finances, London, January 12, 1943. On the caravans, see: ANOM GGAEF 6B 723, telegram from Lamy, sent on April 9, 1943. On neighboring territories, see telegram 425 from Lamy in this same file. Delange's moving letter, dated April 5, 1943, can be found in AOL, Pleven papers. On the impossibility of changing currency in 1943, see in the same file the telegram received from Sebha, May 24, 1943.

[70] ANOM GGAEF 6B 723, Delange, April 21, 1943.

[71] Boisseau, p. 51.

[72] ANOM GGAEF 3B 2383, Eboué to the Commissaire of the Colonies, Brazzaville, September 22, 1943.

Similarly, in April 1943 Delange deemed that Algiers should be given authority over the Fezzan "because the region is part of North Africa."[73] Eboué was willing to accept the partial redrawing of Libya's southern border so as to incorporate the so-called Sara Well within Chad – but this minor compromise he conceded for purely military reasons. The governor-general seems mostly to have wanted to spare FEA's budget any additional costs involved in managing the Fezzan and Kufra. While recognizing the region's importance, even asserting that it should remain French, he too advocated integrating it into southern Algeria. This would eventually occur.[74] Thus, Eboué's reservations seem to have been essentially financial, in keeping with his concern for FEA's coffers. On balance, the Free French were intent on making the most of these lands seized from Italy, and to have them remain French in the postwar.

In this conquered land, the Free French did not hesitate to contrast their native policy with that of Fascist Italy. A Free French report from 1943 evoked "the end of a cruel domination of peace-loving people, who will finally, after having reunited with their traditional chiefs, resume a normal life."[75] For as they had at Kufra, the Free French brought along with them a number of Fezzanese expatriates who had previously sought asylum in Chad. Some French sources evoked a litany of Italian colonial abuses, holding the Italians responsible, in fact, for the departure of some 35.000 Fezzanese for neighboring Chad and Sudan between 1925 and 1940.[76] These were the very people now returning to Libya with the Free French. In this sense, the conquest and occupation of the Fezzan constituted a fresh episode in a far older pattern of trans-Saharan migrations resulting from regional geopolitical shifts.

## Threats and Shortages

The victories in southern Libya should not conceal the many military shortcomings of Free France in Africa between 1940 and 1942. Especially glaring at the time were the paucity of mechanized assets and the vulnerability of home-front defenses. If de Gaulle ordered his troops to go on the offensive in late 1940, it was no doubt because he deemed that there was no impending attack to be feared along Chad's exposed

[73] ANOM GGAEF 6B 723, Delange, April 21, 1943.
[74] ANOM GGAEF 3B 2383, Eboué to the Commissaire of the Colonies, Brazzaville, September 22, 1943.
[75] FCDG, Fonds Eboué, F22, 18, note on the Fezzan and its conquest by Leclerc.
[76] Jacques Lorraine, preface to Paul Moynet, *L'épopée du Fezzan* (Algiers, 1944), p. 9.

western border. But this assessment was temporary, and concerns over enemy incursions into FEA resurfaced regularly until late 1942 – be they by Vichy, Spain, Italy, or Germany. Free French fears reached their zenith in May 1941, when Rommel's Afrikakorps threatened Egypt. A month later, de Gaulle relayed to Larminat credible evidence suggesting that a Vichy attack from Niger on Chad was imminent.[77] Such concerns were no mere fantasy. British intercepts of German signals in August 1942 point to planned (albeit hotly debated) German "ground reconnaissance expeditions against French Equatorial Africa"[78] to supplement existing air reconnaissance sorties. Furthermore, British command fully realized that with so many of its troops involved in the Sahara, Free France left a vulnerable flank exposed in Chad. Thus, in February 1942, UK intelligence services informed London that with the B.M. 5 having departed Cameroon, the territory was bereft of defenses. Only a single company in Douala, another training in Yaoundé, and an anti-aircraft unit at Douala's airport remained to hold down Cameroon.[79]

The war had certainly reached Free French Africa's doorstep. On January 22, 1942, a German Heinkel 111 bombarded Fort-Lamy, destroying fuel reserves. Free French anti-aircraft units happened to be training at the time, but were only able to fire dummy shells at the enemy aircraft.[80] Fort-Lamy's civilians scrambled for cover. The war also raged offshore. A profoundly moved Félix Eboué reported on November 9, 1942: "Several merchant marine vessels have been sunk near us. Torpedoes hit a British destroyer just off of Pointe-Noire. The ship lost eighty men before being able to regain port. There is nothing else. We are at war."[81] From August 5–6, 1941, an inter-Allied conference met in the suburbs of Accra to discuss the protection of Allied Africa. At that point, with the USSR so far removed from the picture in Africa, inter-Allied signified Belgium, Free France, and Great Britain. The participants examined the main threats hovering over the continent: Spanish and Portuguese colonies proved a particular source of anxiety, as was the possibility of

---

[77] Jean-Pierre Guéno, Gérard Lhéritier, *Les messages secrets du général de Gaulle, Londres*, de Gaulle to Larminat, December 24, 1940, p. 24; de Gaulle to Pleven, May 10, 1941, p. 56; and de Gaulle to Larminat, June 13, 1941, p. 70.

[78] NAUK, HW 13/52, p. 11.

[79] NAUK FO 859, dossier 6, Douala intelligence report 25, February 10, 1942.

[80] CAOM GGAEF 5B 712, Parr to Binge, January 28, 1942. Also see Rainero, p. 139. Other witnesses place the raid on January 21. See: http:////www.france-libre.net/temoignages-documents/temoignages/fort-lamy-bombarde.php.

[81] ANOM, GGAEF 5B 715, Eboué, November 9, 1942.

Axis use of Vichy territories. The United Kingdom raised the point that it could no longer afford to bring naval support to FEA and Cameroon. With the emphasis so clearly on protecting Allied Africa, Free France's representatives oscillated between offensive and defensive imperatives. Knowing that Free French forces were stretched across the Middle East, the Horn of Africa, and the Sahara, leaving the home front exposed, Commandant Clapot passed along the following assessment from his superiors: "General de Gaulle and General de Larminat still believe that Chad could be exposed to attack, but there is little likelihood that such an attack would take place soon." This balancing act aimed in part to persuade the British to equip Free France with transport planes. Indeed, as head of Free French Africa's military cabinet, Clapot transmitted Chad's desperate pleas for aircraft. After having insisted on Chad's importance for the Allied cause, he put forward another deeply revealing argument tied to France's colonial prestige: "If no [French] aircraft were present in Chad native moral would drop, which . . . would lend credence to German propaganda about the weakness of the French and British."[82]

Neither argument carried the day. On December 29, 1942, Leclerc's office brought the catastrophic scarcity of aircraft directly to the attention of the U.S. consul in Brazzaville. Among the transport aircraft loaned to FEA over the course of the war, two were out of order, another had to be returned very shortly to the R.A.F. One more was about to leave for Madagascar. The Free French had sent two airplanes to the front. Consequently, "there is only one aircraft available in all of Fighting French Africa, a situation that compromises our everyday operations." That very day, U.S. Consul Laurence Taylor agreed to support Leclerc's request. The American diplomat remarked that two of the five planes available under Lend-Lease could easily be earmarked for FEA. He added in his report to the State Department that this decision would avoid the Free French from having to bring back their wounded on camel back.[83] While Taylor may have slightly bleakened the picture in his report, the basic point can leave no doubt. We know, thanks to Kim Munholland's work, just how delicate a matter Leclerc's deal with Taylor proved to be. The State Department insisted that the aircraft be delivered indirectly, transiting through Britain's Lend-Lease program so as to avoid any official

[82] FCDG, Fonds Eboué, F22, 18, Clapot report, August 14, 1941.
[83] NARA, RG 84, U.S. Consulate, Brazzaville, Classified General Records, 1942–44, box 1, letter to the U.S. Consul, December 29, 1942. And in the same file, Taylor to the Secretary of State, December 29, 1942.

American recognition of Free France.[84] On February 1, 1943, two American planes finally arrived. Free France took possession of them at Accra, before flying them to Fort-Lamy. Two more were slated to follow, fresh off of Lockheed's assembly lines.

Leclerc might have added another cause to Free France's air shortages: planes had been dropping out of the sky in FEA. Lieutenant-Colonel André Parant, governor of Gabon, died in the hospital following a terrible plane crash that occurred in February 1941. En route to Fort-Lamy in 1940, General de Gaulle's own airplane was forced to crash-land in a swamp. Free French pilot Romain Gary, still known as Roman Kacew at the time, recounted his own experiences as follows: "Every time I took off, the sky rejected me resoundingly... I crashed with astonishing regularity." He added that in the eyes of Free France's British allies, "matériel was rare and precious, far more precious than the lives of these clumsy Frenchmen." In fact, Free French officials did, on occasion, invoke these numerous accidents to obtain new aircraft from Great Britain.[85]

One can only concur with Jean-Louis Crémieux-Brilhac's assessment: until 1943, Free France suffered terribly from matériel shortages, from a lack of spare parts and indeed a generalized dearth of equipment, especially for a military force already engaged on several fronts.[86] The problem reached chronic proportions. On August 27, 1942, the military addressed an urgent message to Cameroon's inhabitants, asking them to hand over their hunting binoculars; the military desperately needed them on board its tanks. So as to encourage donations, Governor Cournarie invoked the heroism of Free French forces at Bir Hakeim.[87]


## A Balance Sheet

Notwithstanding the obsession with its vulnerable flank, Free France conquered in Africa, in a startling south to north sweep. Originally a marginal dissident movement, it could now genuinely claim expansionist goals, even donning the mantle of Ancient Rome in the process. African

---

[84] Munholland, pp. 26–27.

[85] Romain Gary, *La promesse de l'aube* (Paris: Gallimard, 1980), p. 353 and 355. ANOM, Cab 63, dossier 437, anonymous to Sir Arthur Street, April 10, 1942. De Gaulle, *Mémoires de guerre*, Vol. 1, p. 142.

[86] Crémieux-Brilhac, *La France libre*, pp. 639–40. On truck parts, see ANOM GGAEF 2Y 15, January 25, 1942.

[87] ANCMR 2AC 6324.

troops became unwitting agents, or perhaps auxiliaries of this Gaullist imperialism. This first "politicized army" in modern French history, to borrow Crémieux-Brilhac's phrase, was now forging its own Saharan empire, which overstepped the bounds of the one it had inherited in 1940. After the war, General Ingold would ask French leaders to continue to watch over the Fezzan. His words were heeded, at least for the time being. France continued to control the region until Libyan independence in 1951. French officials sought to make it a buffer zone to be sure, but they also kept a keen eye on some of its resources, against a backdrop of growing international petroleum competition.[88]

Free France managed these feats despite serious shortcomings in the realm of legitimacy, of equipment, and of transport, most notably. Philippe Leclerc seemed persuaded that troops hailing from FEA and Cameroon should be added to the list of liabilities. But in reality, he had little choice: FEA and Cameroon being the territorial and military basis of his movement, they formed along with the French islands in the Pacific, the core of Fighting French combatants until 1943. Beyond the truckers whom I have already discussed, soldiers, officers, and NCOs were being trained at new centers in Bangui, in Brazzaville, and beyond. Free French Africa was consumed by martial fever.

[88] Crémieux-Brilhac, *La France libre*, p. 653; Ingold, *L'Epopée*, p. 247; Kelly, p. 17; Frémeaux, pp. 232–23.

# Chapter 5

## Free French Africa in Arms

### Recruitment and Its Consequences

"The founding core of Free French forces hailed from Equatorial Africa," asserted the early Free Frenchman Claude Hettier de Boislambert.[1] Indeed, it is no exaggeration to state that from September 1940 to July 1943, the first Free French military effort rested in large part on the contributions of FEA and Cameroon.

While Free French blood and ink poured over conquered territories like the Fezzan, a martial fever consumed the home front of Cameroon and FEA. In spite of Leclerc's professed reservations about the combat preparedness of recruits from these territories, the main priority between September 1940 and July 1943 involved recruitment and training. Tables I and II, drawn from the French colonial archives, demonstrate how military recruitment reached its zenith in FEA in 1940–41, and in Cameroon in 1942.[2] Within the confines of Free French Africa, Chad, Oubangui-Chari, and Cameroon provided the most troops. In total, 17,013 men were enrolled into Free French ranks Fighting French Africa 1940 and 1944 (note that these totals do not include the men already present on FEA and Cameroon soil when these colonies went over to the Free French in late August 1940). There remains considerable uncertainty about the total number of Free French troops for the period between 1940 and 1943. Based on my research, I would hazard the following estimates: to the 17,013 Africans recruited between 1940 and 1943, we should add

[1] Boislambert, p. 229.
[2] ANOM DSM 262, file 3, table 4.

140

TABLE I. *Africans enrolled in FEA between 1940 and 1944*

| Year | Chad and Oubangui | Moyen-Congo | Gabon | Total |
|------|-------------------|-------------|-------|-------|
| 1940 | 4,160 | 349 | 761 | 5,270 |
| 1941 | 1,971 | 184 | 361 | 2,516 |
| 1942 | 1,131 | 119 | 134 | 1,384 |
| 1943 | 297 | 12 | 207 | 516 |

the roughly 10,000 soldiers, at the very least,[3] already on location in 1940, for a total of some 27,000 men. This figure is corroborated by a statement from the high commissioner in Brazzaville in February 1941, which lists 17,300 men in arms in FEA and Cameroon. Several *bataillons de marche* had just left for the front at that time, and Table I shows that another 10,000 men would be recruited between the writing of this letter and 1944.[4] This brings us to the virtually identical estimate of more than 27,000 combatants from FEA and Cameroon.

Naturally, these figures can seem low in comparison with other Allied contributions. Australia recruited 681,000 men and 35,800 women over the course of the war, and Canada roughly a million men and women, to give but two British imperial examples. However, on the scale of the Free French effort, the African figures appear significant indeed, because historians place the total number of Free French combatants somewhere between 54,000 and 73,330 in 1943.[5] This means that either Free French estimates need to be recalculated or that between half and one third of all Free Frenchmen between 1940 and 1943 hailed from FEA and Cameroon or had been posted there in 1940.

Another consideration jumps out from Table I: the euphemism employed to describe Cameroonian recruits, all termed "volunteers."[6] This sleight of hand was used to circumvent the rules of the League of Nations, which explicitly precluded the raising of troops in Cameroon, save for defensive or policing purposes. Finally, we should note a marked

---

[3] Historians have put forward figures that range from 7,000 to 16,000 men in Cameroon and FEA in August 1940. The first figure strikes me as too low, insofar as the garrison at Fort-Archambault alone counted some 4,000 men in 1940. Boisseau, pp. 19–20; Vital Ferry, *Croix de Lorraine et Croix du Sud, 1940–1942* (Paris: Editions du Gerfaut, 2005), p. 94.

[4] ANOM Cab 55, Haut-Commissariat, letter 726 dated February 7, 1941. Out of this figure 2,300 were "Europeans."

[5] Jean-François Muracciole, *Les Français libres*, p. 36.

[6] On this point, see Deltombe et al., p. 35.

TABLE 11. *Cameroonians who "volunteered" in the Free French forces*

| Year | Soldiers | Drivers | Auxiliary Workers | Total |
| --- | --- | --- | --- | --- |
| 1940 | 1,321 | | | 1,321 |
| 1941 | 846 | 849 | 349 | 2,202 |
| 1942 | 1,382 | 1,186 | 303 | 2,904 |
| 1943 | 334 | 368 | 36 | 761 |
| 1944 | 139 | | | 139 |

drop in recruitment in the summer of 1943. This coincided with the entry of troops from French West Africa, North Africa, and Madagascar into the fray at long last.

As military historian Jean-Noël Vincent has observed, recruitment followed the trend of previous decades. It involved "the designation of a contingent of recruits by the administration to the traditional African chiefs or elected African officials."[7] Methods used in the buildup to the Great War resurfaced, although acts of rebellion proved generally rarer. This should not be mistaken for resignation. Many men fled ahead of the roll call, or deserted thereafter, some leaving Free French ranks for British ones.[8] Finally, such methods were in no way limited to Free French territories. Confronted with a paucity of volunteers, the British practiced conscription in West Africa as of 1941 for soldiers, drivers, and other auxiliaries, and as David Killingray has shown, they too experienced high desertion rates.[9]

The Free French recruitment of auxiliaries like porters often proved as unceremonious as it was haphazard. To take one example, during the brief civil war in Gabon pitting Vichy against Free French forces in November 1940, the latter plucked Africans from their villages. In the Gabonese town of Sindara, a certain Jean Malonga declared having been "caught" in "his home" and abducted by the Free French forces, before being made into a porter by them. Shortly thereafter, on his way toward Lambaréné, a locale held by loyalist troops, Malonga was strafed by a Vichy aircraft. He spent six months in hospital with a wounded arm. It was there that he drafted an indemnity request to Governor Félix Eboué.[10]

---

[7] Vincent, p. 21.

[8] Fargettas, pp. 42 and 48. Muracciole, *Les Français libres*, pp. 62–64.

[9] David Killingray, "Labour mobilization in British colonial Africa" in David Killingray and Richard Rathbone, *Africa and the Second World War*, pp. 77–78.

[10] ANC GGAEF 379, Malonga to Eboué, May 25, 1943.

Although military recruitment usually involved some form of formal enrollment process, it did not necessarily involve consent in the true sense of the term. In Cameroon on October 27, 1942, "Governor" Pierre Cournarie announced that: "an important recruitment of indigenous troops will be undertaken in 1943." Consequently, he instructed all of his regional officials to "relay, as soon as possible, availability of men based on tribe, as well as the most favorable dates for recruitment operations."[11] Nothing was left to chance. On location, district officials were supposed to keep a number of parameters in mind, including the time of year (the rainy season was to be avoided if possible), as well as the migration of populations due to agriculture and mining. But the chief selection criterion remained ethnic, as is revealed by the response of the district head Etcheber, from Ngaoundéré in December 1942:

> I have the honor of reporting that the region of Adamaoua can provide another contingent of roughly a hundred men. Thanks to the action of the region's head, one hundred healthy volunteers were raised over the course of 1942, and formed into a goum. This figure will certainly not be surpassed in 1943, as the region's capacity for providing healthy, fit men capable of becoming soldiers is limited. The experience of past recruitments undertaken between 1940 and 1942 proves that the Foulbé people, comprised of herdsmen or cattle salesmen, can only provide a very limited number of volunteers. It is in the servant milieu, as well as among the Mboum, Tikar, Kaka and other groups that subdivision chiefs will once again recruit the most actively.... I am intentionally not planning any recruiting in the subdivision of Meiganga. The Baya have certain qualities, but there are only five thousand adults aged 18 to 45, out of whom a thousand are already occupied in mining and public works. The remainder is in charge of crops ... the subdivision constitutes a veritable bread-basket for the entire region.[12]

Considerations of class, of regional balance, of essential sectors, and of food supply were thus grafted onto clichés of military aptitude to combat based on ethnicity, which the British had long ago distilled into the concept of "martial races."

On March 4, 1943, Lieutenant Grollemund, commanding the fourteenth recruiting company of Cameroon, received the order to step up the pace. In hindsight, we now know that this marked the last vast recruitment campaign in the area, for a few months later, the incorporation of North African troops would bring enlisting in FEA and Cameroon to a halt. Daily logs show that recruiting units themselves counted many

---



[11] ANCMR 2AC 5871.
[12] ANCMR 2AC 5871.

"indigenous cadres."[13] The orders Grollemund received also contain interesting details. Lieutenant-Colonel Louis Marie Lanusse, the military commander of Cameroon, advised Grollemund to be selective: "Given that mountain people generally adapt better to Saharan and Mediterranean combat, the lieutenant commanding the 14th company should try to recruit as many of them as possible." In this instance, selection was conditioned by bioclimatic determinism – a factor that would subsequently be invoked to exclude some colonial troops from combat in Europe. And yet, when and where the need for troops proved particularly pressing, as in Chad in 1942 for instance, old habits of recruiting so-called warrior races or those supposedly predisposed to certain theaters of battle were periodically abandoned. In their place, a form of comprehensive recruitment was implemented spanning all ethnic groups, by means of a quota system.[14]

On the ground, even recruiters who by definition tended to be rather upbeat in their reports were recognizing by 1942 that their task had become arduous. On April 1, 1942, Léon Salasc, the head of the North Cameroon region, reported to the governor-general: "The 1943 recruitment campaign can only happen if military service is made mandatory – a measure that could prove dangerous for the future of North Cameroon, and which we should only apply if it were absolutely essential to do so."[15] Not only would the measure have been dangerous, it would also have been illegal in Cameroon, because it violated the statutes of the League of Nations. The difficulties faced by recruiters are all the more striking when one considers the means of persuasion at their disposal: in North Cameroon in 1942, Free French recruiting agents handed each "tirailleur candidate" a 50-franc signing bonus.[16]

The enrollment campaign was in full tilt. So much so that even German intelligence took notice. An October 1942 British summary of German intercepts cites a German report evoking "general mobilization" in Free French Africa.[17] Friendlier foreign sources reached similar conclusions. In May 1943, shortly before the merger of the Free French forces from

---

13  ANCMR, APA 10209, information in Lieutenant Grollemund's March 25, 1942, letter. CHETOM, 15H 156, journal de marche du CDCC (Compagnie de découverte et de combat du Cameroun), December 20, 1941.

14  ANCMR, APA 10209. Pierre-Olivier Lapie, *Le Tchad fait la guerre* (Algiers: Office français d'édition, 1943), p. 13.

15  ANCMR, APA 10209, Salasc to the governor, April 1, 1942.

16  ANCMR, APA 10209.

17  NAU.K. HW 13/52 "The German Watch on the Sahara," p. 1.

FEA and Cameroon with those of the "Armée d'Afrique," as the troops once loyal to Vichy in North Africa were known, the consul general of the United States in FEA took stock of the same fever-pitched recruitment. He noted: "General Leclerc assembled all the available troops in the colony at Fort-Lamy and went with them through Libia (sic) to join forces with the British Eighth Army. Replacement troops are being hastily assembled. The native villages are being searched for men and a large number are being pressed into service."[18] Consul Laurence Taylor was witnessing the last spasm of Free French recruitment in FEA.

In this frenetic setting, enthusiasm soon led down the slippery slope to abuses, sometimes committed by recruiters themselves, sometimes by middlemen. On March 26, 1942, an outraged Henri Laurentie learned that a corporal and sergeant from Cameroon had strayed into the Mayo-Kebbi district of Chad to recruit thirty-five tirailleurs in the villages of Tiken and Fianga. Laurentie demanded that the "governor" of Cameroon intervene, "to have the recruited natives returned to their villages and to ban such ways of operating."[19] Laurentie thus watched to ensure that recruiters did not cross the line, at least the threshold separating FEA and Cameroon.

And yet, dubious practices became commonplace. Leonard Sah observes that half of the Cameroonian Free French veterans he interviewed in the 1980s evoked some kind of coercion at the time they enlisted. Pierre Minko Oyono from the Akonolinga region, remembers being "enrolled then chained to two hundred other persons. This is how I arrived at the Ornano Camp near Nachtigal where a military outfit was assembled before setting off to war." Valentin Tsala recounts that his mother implored the village chief to intercede "so as to bring back her only son taken by the whites."[20] Léon Modeste Nnang Ndong has obtained corroborating testimony from Gabonese veterans. They too evoke forms of coercion. One veteran in Mitzic relates that at age eighteen he was "forced" to enroll, "the village chief having given our names." He adds that he would have deserted were it not for the fear of reprisals against his family.[21] Meanwhile, in the French Congo, Jérôme Ollandet has shown how a village chief was responsible for supplying the administration with

---

[18] NARA, RG 84, U.S. Consulate, Brazzaville, Classified General Records, 1942–44, box 2, Brazzaville, May 7, 1943, the application of Lend-Lease in French Equatorial Africa, p. 3.

[19] ANOM, 5B 712, Laurentie to the governor of Cameroon, March 26, 1942.

[20] Sah, pp. 335, 338.

[21] Nnang Ndong, p. 67.

a list of young men considered suitable for military service. In practice, the chief "mostly listed the young people who posed problems to him." Furthermore, he waited until militiamen arrived before reading out the list of those selected. Then, after a "general sob erupted" the chief slipped away, "fearing for his safety."[22]

In French Congo, inhabitants turned to local remedies to ward off recruiters. The latter were given unflattering titles like mbulu-mbulu, or jackals. In Gabon, rumors spread concerning the massacre of the class of 1939 over the course of the Battle of France in May–June 1940.[23] Many Africans voted with their feet, much as they had done in French West Africa during the Great War.[24] Thus, the head of the Gabonese department of Ogooué-Ivindo observed in 1943 that local populations "considered the recruitment of soldiers to be a public calamity." He added that "as soon as recruiters are spotted, entire villages empty of their young people, and for a long time afterwards, white strangers who might be confused with military officials…are greeted with suspicion, if not outright hostility."[25] Serving as intermediaries between recruiters and the population at large, African chiefs sometimes manifested their hostility to a role that led them to be perceived as "traitors" by their subjects. In protest, in 1942 several Gabonese chiefs from Woleu-Ntem handed over women in lieu of men to the military authorities.[26]

Enrolled under dubious circumstances, to say the least, many new recruits fled at the earliest opportunity. After the war, an inquiry was launched into the "very numerous" desertions in the ranks of the 14th company of the Régiment des Tirailleurs Camerounais in 1942. The deputy-chief of the North Cameroon region Raymond Doudet told investigators that the deserters in question had been "forcibly led to their unit." He added that nearly all of the desertions occurred within two weeks of enrollment, "some even before the incorporation had taken place." This lends credence to the theory of forcible recruitment or at least of enlistment without full knowledge of the commitment being undertaken. Doudet concluded: "the deserters in question were very simple-minded, recruited among backwards populations; at the time of their enrolment

[22] Ollandet, p. 90.

[23] Phyllis Martin, *Leisure and Society*, p. 49. Nnang Ndong, p. 51.

[24] Myron Echenberg, "Les migrations militaires en Afrique occidentale française, 1900–1945," *Canadian Journal of African Studies*, 1980, 14: 3, pp. 429–50.

[25] ANOM GGAEF 4(1) D51, report from Ogooué-Ivindo first semester of 1943, p. 8.

[26] Nnang Ndong, p. 60.

they probably had not comprehended what was expected of them."[27] One can speculate that they may not have understood expectations because the transaction was conducted in a foreign tongue, or on unfamiliar terms. Regardless, Doudet appealed for an outright pardon. He reasoned:

> Today we see faithful tirailleurs returning, decked with medals, bringing home from their military campaigns endless stories that they weave over long evenings in the bush in front of raptured crowds. Those unfortunate ones who lacked the confidence [to join the army] are now humiliated, and scorned by women. Ridicule kills. This maxim is as true in black Africa as it is in the rest of the world, and personally, I consider it to be sufficient punishment.[28]

This line of reasoning rests on and betrays at once the special status of African veterans[29] and gender considerations (African women supposedly scornful of noncombatants), as well as questions of social status, honor, and rumor. These in turn are wrapped in a series of reductionist clichés of African oral cultures and campfires conducive to tall tales. Yet the passage is also shrouded in universalism: ridicule can prove devastating everywhere. One can, of course, question the idea that military experiences were universally positive. Beyond the physical and mental toll on combatants, many Cameroonian soldiers actually complained that their wives did not want them to serve in the army given the lengthy absences that this line of work entailed.[30]

In other instances, the very first contact with the military drove new recruits away, a sign that they were not advised of what would follow their enlistment. A 1942 report from Northern Cameroon reads: "The Toupouri tirailleurs... undergo mandatory injections as soon as they arrive to camp, a measure which they do not appreciate one way or another, rightly or wrongly." Then, suggests the colonial official, these fresh recruits deserted in the same way they had enrolled: "out of camaraderie and imitation."[31] Although such colonial reports need to be examined critically, they nevertheless highlight two important aspects of resistance to recruitment: the widespread concern over syringes, injections, and bloodwork frequently associated with a kind of colonial

---

[27] ANCMR, APA 10209, Doudet, December 4, 1945.

[28] Ibid.

[29] The status of African veterans is a complex issue, which Gregory Mann has expertly analyzed in *Native Sons: West African Veterans and France in the Twentieth Century* (Durham: Duke University Press, 2006), most notably pp. 86–98.

[30] Sah, p. 430. Mann, p. 153.

[31] ANCMR APA 10209.

vampirism[32] and the idea that deserters could find some kind of strength in numbers.

Not all were forcibly recruited. One can discern a host of motivating factors among volunteers. Elikia M'Bokolo has rightly underscored the massive nature of these voluntary enlistments, and Jérôme Ollandet has suggested that coercion was less often employed in urban settings.[33] Some preferred the army to forced labor. Others made the leap out of patriotism, anti-Nazism, or to keep or perfect a profession like that of truck driver, for instance.[34] Remuneration and a desire for social ascension certainly account for some choices: as early as October 1940, recruiters in FEA's schools vaunted "the advantages reserved to military recruits." In Bousso, Chad, in February 1943, officials took stock of the large-scale disappointment of volunteers who had been turned away.[35] Other enrollments reveal a clear understanding of hierarchies. On December 20, 1940, the young Jacques Eoné Eoné, son of the superior chief Oscar Eoné Eoné of the Sanaga Maritime region, asked to be admitted to Colonel Leclerc's regiment. But he added as a caveat, "in the French troops, not the black ones."[36] The testimony of Cameroonian Free French volunteer Raphaël Onana also suggests that volunteers enjoyed certain perks, or at least greater prestige. He mentions the "EV" or volunteer (*engagé volontaire*) label that stuck to them.[37]

Volunteers and forced recruits found themselves side by side at their mandatory medical exam. In Middle-Chari, Chad, in 1941, 1,447 candidates showed up at the medical exam to answer a call for 336 positions in the air force. In such instances where supply largely outpaced demand, volunteering became the main selection criterion. In the case under consideration, this brought the number of candidates down to 484. The 963 forcible recruits who were not ultimately chosen had been raised in each

---


[32] Luise White, *Speaking with Vampires: Rumor and History in Colonial Africa* (Berkeley: University of California Press, 2000), pp. 89–121.

[33] Elikia M'Bokolo, "Brazzaville" in Claire Andrieu, Philippe Braud, and Guillaume Piketty, *Dictionnaire de Gaulle* (Paris: Robert Laffont, 2006), p. 148. Ollandet, p. 90.

[34] In her study of the Mbam region of Cameroon, Crécence Memoli-Aubry notes the rumors of future Nazi crimes against African children. She suggests that these rumors contributed to "propelling the voluntary recruitment of Africans." Crécence Memoli-Aubry, "Le Mbam dans la Seconde Guerre Mondiale: contribution d'une région administrative du Cameroun à l'effort de guerre français," *Outre-mers, revue d'histoire*, 2009, p. 263.

[35] Sah, pp. 329–33. ANOM GGAEF 5D 290, programme type d'une séance en salle. ANOM GGAEF 4 (4) D 53, political report Baguirmi, first semester, 1943.

[36] AML, Leclerc 6A, letter to Colonel Leclerc.

[37] Onana, p. 150.

subdivision of the department. Even though they were not selected, an administrator noted: "this year, we forced the people of Kyabe to furnish a contingent."[38] Regional quota sweeps and volunteering could therefore go hand in hand.

In their own way, Free French officials measured the impact of recruitment on African populations. Haunted by fears of degeneration and national decadence that had been rehashed for half a century, they projected these anxieties onto the African continent. In his June 1945 report, Doctor Marie-Etienne Farinaud gauged as follows the consequences of military recruitment in Cameroon, combined with the departure of men gone to collect rubber in the forest for the war effort:

> Already stripped of an important part of its male population, deprived by military recruitment of its most solid and robust men, and hence its best reproducers, the village is shrinking, its number of children dwindling.... Abandoned women no longer conceive; to satisfy nature's call, they throw themselves at men other than their husbands, often contracting venereal diseases. If they become pregnant, they have abortions. The family cell is destroyed. Young women, who cannot marry, have no option but to wed the weakly and the feeble, left behind by the recruiters. Removed from the authority of the family leader, they slide towards prostitution for gifts or for money, give themselves to truck drivers or to the white man's servant who passes by. Soon they are afflicted with syphilis and gonorrhea, and are no longer able to procreate.[39]

The military recruiter plays the role of natural selector in this somber Darwinian tale, which owes more to the doctor's own conception of power, family, gender, and sexual relations than it does to any local observation. Farinaud's impressions are also the reflection of what Guillaume Lachenal has studied in Free French Cameroon: the "demographic imperative" of French colonial doctors persuaded that they were invested with the mission of "saving the black race."[40] Finally, it bears noting that Free French officials in Cameroon seemed conscious of having overturned an equilibrium deemed to be eternal and natural within African villages. In their eyes, victory had a social cost in Africa.

## Discrimination

Be it a cause or a consequence of the recruitment process, African Free French troops were enduringly classified along ethnic lines. Charles Béné,

---

[38] ANOM GGAEF 4(4) D51, political report for Moyen Chari, first semester 1941.
[39] ANCMR, APA 11324B, Farinaud report, June 16, 1945.
[40] Lachenal, pp. 134, 139.

a Free French radio expert who asked to join a camel-mounted unit, remembers a set of designated specializations. Within his troop, he recalls: "The soldiers and their black officers all hailed from Chad, but from two different races." These two groups were the Saras from the Fort-Archambault area (modern-day Sahr) and the Hadjeraïs from the region east of Lake Chad. Béné describes an incident during which a Sara soldier murdered his Hadjeraï warrant officer. Then came the Goumiers-guides, "civilian auxiliaries conscripted in Northern Chad" who were believed to know the trails and the lay of the land. Finally, "Goranes from the Borkou area" – nomads from Northern Chad – were used to tend to the camels. Being nonmilitary, they were not allowed to carry weapons, which earned them the scorn of the other men, still according to Béné. On a larger scale, the Free French high command accepted and indeed endorsed this ethnic specialization. A 1943 document stated that its logic "has been confirmed by experience and has therefore become doctrine."[41] The resulting ethnolinguistic diversity also tended to reinforce the use of the French language within Free French African ranks. Captain Yves Marzin recalls that in his anti-aircraft unit at Fort-Lamy in early 1942, "my men were comprised of 25 blacks, from 15 different races, who could only understand each other in French."[42]

While differences in living conditions were striking among Africans, the main fault line separated Africans and Europeans. Béné explains for instance that a Sara soldier was put at his disposal as a servant, whose job included "preparing my bed and my meals" and "tending to" a Goranne adolescent whose services as a "female companion" had been negotiated for him, "the white man."[43]

Similarly, sartorial distinctions between Africans and Europeans (pants and ranger shoes for the Europeans, narrow leg bands and red fez hats for Africans) constituted one of the most enduring memories of the war for Cameroonian artilleryman Gaston Mvondo. It is no doubt significant that Mvondo attributed the subsequent elimination of this clothing difference to the intervention of a British officer.[44]

Contrary to what Pierre Messmer has suggested, one of the most flagrant disparities in the treatment of white and black Free French troops

---

[41]  Béné, pp. 117 and 124. ANOM, Cab. 64, dossier 447, note on the use of colonial forces, Algiers June 14, 1943.
[42]  http://jeanclaude.hyrien.free.fr/Histos/BarakaFFL.php?chap=8, consulted in 2012.
[43]  Béné, pp. 119, 207, and 256.
[44]  Sah, p. 734, interview by Sah, 1991.

concerned food.[45] Besides the fact that meals were taken separately, rations themselves were radically different, save for some rare exceptions like after the fall of Kufra. There in 1941, Leclerc offered all of his troops, Africans included, macaroni with parmesan seized from the Italians.[46] For Europeans, officials usually sought replacements for classic tin can military meats, asking for instance the Raphaely and Son Co. in Capetown to elaborate a canned beef "seasoned in the way of the French army," whereas manioc and millet was being secured for Africans. On November 6, 1940, the governor-general ordered Pointe-Noire to ensure that "troops be provided with regular supplies of native goods (manioc, tobacco, etc.) as well as European ones (chickens)." Fifteen months later, the civilian population surrounding Pointe-Noire would experience a scarcity of manioc, which had been distributed to the army.[47]

Food supply presented frequent complications. At Mindouli in French Congo, a shortage of manioc in June 1941 led to a dispute between civilian and military authorities over dividing scarce supplies. The military recommended requisitioning the root, even closing the train station to ensure that it remain on location. In Cameroon, where similar issues arose, oral testimony suggests that military authorities condemned chiefs to forced labor in cases where villages could not adequately supply Free French troops posted in their vicinity.[48]

Unevenly fed, subjected to long marches, African forces sometimes fell ill. Within the ranks of the Compagnie de découverte et de combat du Cameroun, corporal Ndouma Nanga and several of his comrades were felled by meningitis as they advanced from Cameroon toward the front in Chad between January 26 and the end of February 1942.[49]

---

[45] Pierre Messmer, *Les blancs s'en vont: récits de décolonisation* (Paris: Albin Michel, 1998), p. 17.

[46] On dietary discrimination and on eating meals separately, see Fargettas, p. 72, and Jean-François Muracciole, p. 239. On the macaronis at Koufra, see Moynet, p. 28. The same dish was served to the American Ben Lucien Burman. See Burman, pp. 83–84.

[47] On these beef preserves (commonly called "singe" in the French army), see ANC GGAEF 502, Souques to the governor, November 20, 1940. For the quotation on European vs. African foods, see: ANOM GGAEF 3B 1085, Brazzaville to Douala, November 6, 1940. On the shortage of manioc: ANOM GGAEF 3B 1102, Laurentie to Moyen-Congo, February 28, 1942.

[48] ANC GGAEF 502, de Larminat to Eboué, June 10, 1941. On Cameroon see the testimony cited by Engelbert Mveng, "L'œuvre de Leclerc au Cameroun et la contribution des Camerounais à l'effort de guerre" in Fondation Maréchal Leclerc de Hauteclocque, *Le général Leclerc et l'Afrique française libre, 1940–1942* (Paris: Fondation Leclerc, 1989), p. 70.

[49] CHETOM, 15H 156, journaux de marche of January 26 and February 22, 1942.

Beyond nutrition, inequalities in pay proved particularly flagrant. Even the signing bonus, the tobacco supplement, and a daily bonus for Africans holding a driver's license could not bridge the fundamental gap. Léon Modeste Nnang Ndong estimates that in 1940 a second-class European soldier with no specialization earned at least 1,223.2 francs a month, whereas his African peer with three years' experience received a paltry 145.5 monthly wage.[50]

The homesickness of white Free French troops constituted a source of constant preoccupation, even anguish within official correspondence. Authorities went so far as to dispatch Europeans to the more clement climes of the Kivu mountains of Belgian Congo, to South Africa, or to the fast-expanding hill station of Dschang in Cameroon so as to re-immerse them in the weather and atmosphere of the motherland. Yet African troops also suffered from long absences away from their loved ones.

Some wed before leaving for the front, others en route to it. Such was the case of 233 Sara soldiers at Fort-Achambault in 1941. Before leaving for battle, these men sought to register their married status with the colonial authorities, so that their wives might "collect the allowances to families in need." By rule, such allowances were only granted to the families of soldiers sent outside of the colony. The figure of 233 men only counts marriages validated by certificates: roughly a hundred additional men sought to regularize preexisting relationships before their departure. The colonial administration then conducted detailed detective work to confirm the authenticity of these marriages. The official at the helm of the subdivision of Fort-Archambault reported that "most of the single tirailleurs sought a wife among the women who loiter in Fort-Archambault. I noticed that the same women presented themselves twice accompanied by a new pretender as soon as the first one had left town."[51]

In the subdivision of Koumra, in the Middle-Chari of Chad in 1943, an administrator leveled an astonishing critique at the system of family allowances for African Free French troops. Commandant Wetterwald asserted that in this region, it was the women "who through their work manage to feed both husbands and children." Consequently, he reasoned, the enrollment of a husband in the military was tantamount to "lightening the burden" for his wife. Thanks to his departure, the children would have three to four times more millet during the dry season, he

---

[50] Nnang Ndong, p. 100.
[51] ANOM GGAEF 4(4) D51, Département du Moyen Chari, second semester 1941, Etat civil indigène.

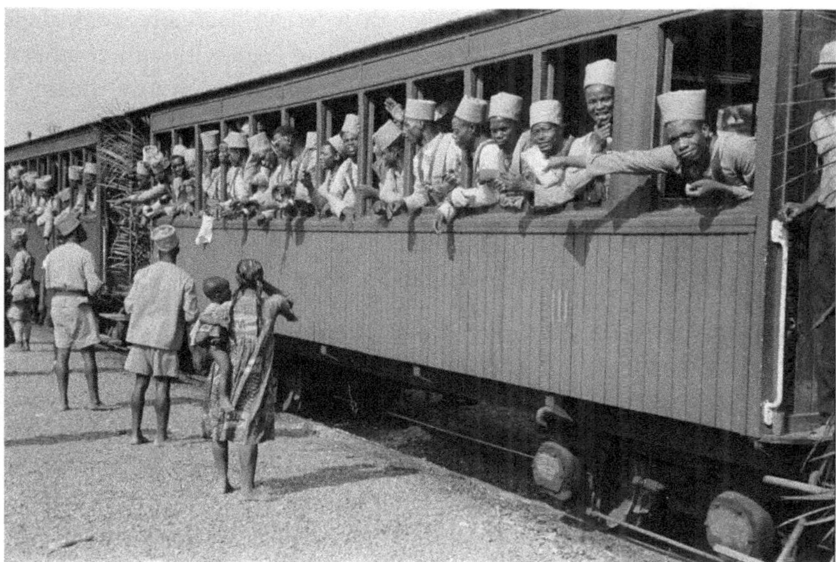

FIGURE 8. George Rodger. Free French troops leaving for the front, Douala 1941. Note the farewell to wife and child. ROG1940010W00006/34. © George Rodger, Magnum Photos.

contended. In Wetterwald's eyes, this facet of the welfare state, or at least of the modern state at war, was simply not transposable to Africa. Wetterwald also pointed to injustices inherent in the system: while "such and such an 18-year-old girl was lucky enough to marry a soldier from the B.M. 1 or B.M. 3 during his last furlough and is therefore eligible for an allowance," conversely long-married women whose husbands could not present the necessary document, be it because their husbands were prisoners or actively engaged at the front, were ineligible for allowances. Another subdistrict head complained of not being kept abreast of the soldiers posted outside of the colony, and of being consequently unable to ascertain which wives could receive allowances.[52]

Having left behind wife and child in FEA or Cameroon (see Figure 8), Free French African soldiers were often dispatched to distant theaters of war, in the Horn of Africa, in Syria, or Lebanon. From Beirut on September 1, 1941, Commandant Raymond Delange solicited Félix Eboué's help to improve the mail service between Sara soldiers under his command and

[52] ANOM GGAEF 4(4) D 53, political report for Moyen-Chari, 1943, pp. 8–9, as well as the report on the Moissala subdivision.

their families in Chad. He asked that their letters "actually reach their intended destinations" adding that his men had been without news from their families since March.[53] Postal glitches such as these were a source of constant complaint from African soldiers.[54] Indeed, many of them grew increasingly wary of postal mandates and other methods of transferring funds to their loved ones, developing informal networks in their place.[55]

## Brawls and Disorder

Troops stationed on the home front often experienced long inactive spells. As sometimes happens under such circumstances, fights broke out between soldiers and surrounding populations. On July 16, 1942, Colonel Claude Chandon reported one such quarrel in Ebolowa, between Yaoundé and the coast, which ended with the killing of a civilian. Eight days later, the same observer reported another brawl, this one involving African troops and police forces in Yaoundé, which also led to a fatality.[56]

Sometimes the authorities reported veritable raids undertaken by troops on leave, which went well beyond the limited and seemingly spontaneous fist fights just described. At Fort-Archambault in Chad, in late March 1941, some fifty servicemen sacked the Bouna district. Two women were raped. Shopkeepers and other inhabitants who tried to defend themselves were severely beaten. Several dwellings were burned. The instigators left with chickens, horses, peanuts, millet, and jewels.[57] An investigation concluded that the guilty parties were new recruits, having joined the army only a few weeks prior to the attacks. However, months later, in May 1941, more seasoned soldiers committed eerily similar crimes in the same area. Yet again, troop "inactivity" was blamed for the tragedy. But a report narrows down the cause, clearly specifying that this second incident stemmed from rising tensions after a soldier refused to accept the rejection of a woman in the Baguirmien district of Fort-Archambault.[58]

---

[53] ANOM GGAEF 5D 303, FFL, B.M. 1 to Beyrouth. Delange to Eboué, September 1, 1941.

[54] Fargettas, pp. 123–24.

[55] Mann, 156.

[56] AML, Leclerc 5A, Colonel Chandon's records for July 16 and 24, 1942.

[57] ANOM GGAEF 5D 303, F. Casamatta to the head of the Moyen-Chari, March 28, 1941.

[58] ANOM GGAEF 5D 303, Casamatta to Lapie, March 10, 1941. In the same file Casmatta to the head of Moyen-Chari, May 21, 1941, as well as the police reports.

In other cases, like in Chad's Batha region in 1942, colonial officials complained of the behavior of soldiers returning on furlough. The local administration concluded that their brazenness to fight and pillage must stem from matters of legal jurisdiction. Indeed, by rule, they were subject to a military tribunal in Brazzaville, rather than a local court. Incredibly, in the heart of Chad, court-martials could appear lenient compared to more expeditious colonial civilian courts.[59] The department head of Likouala-Mossaka in Congo in 1943 reported that soldiers on furlough had undertaken "raids." He added that rumors were circulating according to which tirailleurs on leave "were inciting the population to disobey, especially with respect to war production."[60]

In some instances, like at M'Pouya and other villages bordering the Congo River in December 1941, brawls were ascribed to poor provisioning for troops. Local official Robert Maisonnier recognized that if military planners had arranged for sufficient foodstuffs for the soldiers on board the *Olga* steamer, the men in uniform would not have threatened villagers along the river in a bid to get hold of their bananas, poultry, and manioc.[61] In October 1941 in Pointe-Noire, functionaries reported nearly daily brawls between soldiers and civilians. Food lay once again at the root of these tensions. Many of the quarrels involved fishermen, tired of seeing their catch stolen on the beach. This said, an inquiry suggested that such incidents sometimes provided an excuse for fishermen to hoard their fish. In sum, in this time of shortages, tensions were legion between the military and civilians in matters of provisioning.[62]

Such tensions preoccupied the administration, which devoted considerable time to resolving them. In June 1943, Félix Eboué's attention was drawn to the town of N'Djolé in Gabon. There, administrator Paul Butel had been obliged to settle countless differences between residents and military passers-by. Eboué explained that "it sometimes happens that tirailleurs pass through N'Djolé without being escorted by European officers." In such cases, the governor-general contended, African soldiers "cannot understand that a civilian, even a high-ranking one, could arbitrate and in some instances impose a penalty on them." Consequently, Eboué recommended transferring Butel from his rank of sub-lieutenant

---

[59] ANOM GGAEF 4(4) D51, Batha report for the second trimester 1942.

[60] ANOM GGAEF 4(2) D 76, political report for the Likouala-Mossaka department, 1943.

[61] ANOM GGAEF 5D 302, Maisonnier to the governor of Moyen-Congo, December 22, 1941.

[62] ANOM GGAEF 3B 2381, Pointe-Noire; Eboué's letter dated November 1, 1941. The military report is from ANC GGAEF 379, letter from Plochet, September 22, 1942.

in the air force reserve, to active status in the colonial infantry.[63] If rank obviously lay at the heart of military affairs, it was also at the core of this colonial situation.

Indeed, colonial dynamics endured in the army. In many cases, colonial microcosms were quite simply transposed to the front. Edgard de Larminat highlighted the fact that white officers and black soldiers of the B.M. 2 who fought Rommel's forces at Bir Hakeim in 1942 all hailed from Oubangui. Thus Africans found themselves under the orders of the same "professional hunters, settlers, loggers, gold-seekers and so on, all of them rough fellows" – for whom they had once been employed as domestics or in agricultural work. They were once again at the mercy of the very men for whom they had previously performed compulsory labor services.

## Revolt?

Mutinies are by definition exceptional acts. Most testimonies concerning soldiers from FEA and Cameroon report complete, even impressive discipline. Consider the letters of young sergeant Raymond Sautot to his father Henri.[64] On February 15, 1942, in the midst of the Fezzan campaign, Raymond Sautot left his cushy administrative post in Brazzaville to join the B.M. 6 (or bataillon du Pool). He boasted to his father of the "discipline of the tirailleurs" in his unit, adding: "it is true that they have undergone a stringent selection process."[65]

And yet one can identify numerous acts of revolt, mutinies, and insubordination as well as multiples causes for them. Jean-Noël Vincent mentions that the "troubles" in the ranks of B.M. 4 resulted from the fact that it had languished in Ethiopia without any clear objective. However, on closer inspection, the single cause of boredom does not withstand scrutiny. Many of the tensions in question seem to have involved men from French West Africa. While some were on FEA and Cameroonian soil in 1940 and therefore embraced the cause early on, others had first served with Vichy's units in the Middle East before joining the B.M. 4 after Vichy's defeat in Syria-Lebanon in 1941.[66] West African troops, like

---

[63] ANC GGAEF 502, Eboué to the head of military forces in Free French Africa.

[64] On July 22, 1940, Henri Sautot had led the rallying of the tiny New-Hebrides islands to General de Gaulle. Then, as of July 30, 1942, he served as governor of Oubangui-Chari. On the composition of the B.M. 2, see Larminat, p. 179.

[65] ANOM, Cab. 55, dossier 353, Raymond to Henri Sautot.

[66] Vincent, pp. 21, 45–46; Ruth Ginio, "French Colonial Reading of Ethnographic Research, the case of the 'desertion' of the Abron King and its aftermath," *Cahiers d'Etudes africaines* 166 (2002), pp. 337–57.

French foreign legionnaires, had been involved in fratricidal fighting in the Middle East in 1941. Within Free French ranks, one can imagine that yesterday's enemy was not always received with open arms.

The B.M. 4's diary shows that already on January 31, 1942, the unit's command had purged "undesirable elements" dispatching them to other sectors. At the end of February, the group mourned the death of soldier Mohamed Omar, who had fallen victim to a scorpion sting. Morale could not have been high at this juncture. Then on March 6, the log reports "troubles caused from within by a group of Senegalese tirailleurs." The situation seems to have only stabilized by mid-month, at which point the "leaders" were tracked down. Twenty-five soldiers were arrested on March 16, and three more on March 20. The unit's officers advanced two hypotheses to explain the sudden unrest: some West African soldiers had been exposed to "Italian elements" and others might have been encouraged by "Vichyite Somalis coming from Djibouti."[67] We know from the work of Sarah Zimmerman that Chadian men of the B.M. 4 complained bitterly of harassment and hostility on the part of their West African comrades.[68] These internal tensions, superimposed on the divisions over the Vichy past of some elements, seem more plausible causes in retrospect than the idea of enemy infiltration per se.

We should also not lose track of material conditions in Free French ranks. As with the rebellions of African forces in the British army, Free French African mutinies usually presented very specific objectives.[69] In many instances, Free French forces complained bitterly of their diet; some protested that the signing bonus they had been promised never materialized. Joseph Freitag, a metropolitan Free French officer who put down the mutiny of the B.M. 1 in Syria in 1941, explained, "Wages were at stake, as well as the exchange of Syrian bills, that had been refused." Another Free French African mutiny in Lebanon in 1942 was provoked when troops demanded a transfer to British command.[70]

Not all trouble took place near the front. In March 1943, several Cameroonian soldiers came home after being dismissed for "moral ineptitude." The French administration in Cameroon was warned of the arrival of these men. First of all, it worried of "the state of mind they might have

---

[67] CHETOM, 15H 153, journal de marche of the B.M. 4.

[68] Sarah J. Zimmerman, "Living beyond Boundaries: West African Servicemen in French Colonial Conflicts, 1908–1962," PhD thesis in History, University of California Berkeley, 2011, p. 88.

[69] David Killingray, *Fighting for Britain: African Soldiers in the Second World War* (London: James Currey, 2010), p. 125.

[70] Zimmerman, pp. 87–88. Freitag, p. 134.

acquired during their time in the Levant" – an old fear toward colonial subjects having gained experience elsewhere, including in metropolitan France. Secondly, it fretted over the discovery of troubling signs uncovered on their arrival in Yaoundé. A luggage search had yielded "copper insignia featuring the German eagle and a swastika" as well as "pornographic cards and photographs on which the soldiers appear in company of white women." On the podium of colonial anxieties, breaking the colonial taboo of interracial sexual relations evidently ranked on par with suspected pro-Nazi sentiment (in point of fact, the swastika and eagle could well have been war trophies).[71]

A tragedy occurred in Bangui on October 12, 1942, involving the African soldier Sambegaz.[72] In an act he would later describe as one of revenge, this serviceman stabbed to death Sergeant Chaligne and a Greek merchant by the name of Revithis, as well as wounding Warrant-Officer Le Meur, Sergeant Bidart, and another man. Contrary to what the first report suggested, it would seem that the perpetrator did not use his machete (the mythical *coupe-coupe* was associated with African ferocity in the colonial imagination), but rather a dagger. Under questioning, the accused spoke of resenting a punishment imposed on him by his superiors. He also told of never forgetting the day Revithis had uttered a terrible racial slur toward him. The very evening of the murders "a group of over-excited Europeans," leaving empty bottles in their wake, vowed to exact revenge on the accused. With the incident threatening to turn into a "race riot," the military commander sternly turned back this white lynch mob.[73]

According to the then mayor of Bangui Charles René Louvel, Sambegaz's actions could be directly attributed to the lack of resolve the Free French army had displayed in putting down the mutinies in Syria – this in spite of the fact that Sambegaz had never served outside of FEA. Louvel continued: "If we want to avoid violent incidents, which could go as far as arson being committed on the natives of the same race as that of the murderer, and the subsequent retaliation of other natives, a judgment needs to be handed out in Bangui itself. It must end in capital punishment."[74] The jittery tone speaks to ambient tensions, as well as a desire to dissuade General Charles de Gaulle from considering a pardon.

---

[71] ANCMR 2AC 5868.

[72] There is considerable orthographic variation in the rendering of his name.

[73] ANOM GGAEF 5D 301, report of police official Gangui on the incidents of October 12, 1942. And in the same file: Bangui to Brazzaville, October 12 and 13, 1942.

[74] ANOM GGAEF 5D 301, Louvel to the governor of Oubangui, October 13, 1942.

More remarkable still is Louvel's revelation that a "punitive expedition" had already been plotted against Sambegaz's entire ethnic group. Hastily condemned, Sambegaz was executed by firing squad on December 18, 1942.[75] This revealing tragedy reflects the fragility of colonial order in FEA at the time, as well as powerful underlying tensions, ready to erupt at the slightest spark. In many ways, the context, the threats, the lynching instinct, not to mention the racist taunting, all call to mind the context of the U.S. South at the time.

## Racism in the Ranks

Initially, Free France seemed reluctant to promote African soldiers to the rank of NCO. In December 1940, Edgard de Larminat informed London of "an imperious and urgent necessity to send us European officers, especially non-commissioned officers and corporals. We can train officers among the proven NCOs and aspiring candidates, but what is missing is recruitment from below. All of our native troops are suffering cruelly from a lack of European petty officers. Their combat-readiness is diminished because of it." Such an implicit refusal to consider raising African NCOs from the ranks is all the more surprising in light of the paucity of Free French officers across the board.[76]

However, this first approach made way to a more pragmatic one. As of 1942, growing numbers of Africans were achieving NCO status. Take the following lines from a battalion diary dated January 1, 1943: "By order of Battalion 9, the following are named to the rank of indigenous sergeant: corporals Mouna (fourth company), Bembeya (third), Koumba (first), Gangaza (fourth), N'Doumbe (second), Linguedoum (second). Promoted to the rank of indigenous corporal: soldiers Baidoum (second company), Abakar (secnd), N'Zarafaso (first), Yambingue (third), Yadilembaye (fourth)."[77] It bears mentioning that only two of these surnames (Mouna and N'Doumbe) appear on Ecochard's database of Free French men and women.

However, it is not because Africans were being promoted that racism receded. In a document dated June 1943, Governor Félix Eboué drew up a list of incidents within Free French ranks, all of which he was personally

---

[75] ANOM GGAEF 6B 715, telegram dated December 18, 1942.
[76] ANF, 3AG1, 164, Larminat Brazzaville to de Gaulle, December 1940. On the shortage of low-ranking officers, see Muracciole, *Les Français libres*, p. 128.
[77] SHD 12P 268, journal de marche, January 1943.

willing to certify as accurate. Like Eboué, many of the complainants hailed from France's so-called old colonies of Guiana, Réunion, Martinique, and Guadeloupe. This might be because Eboué's networks rendered him more likely to learn of these grievances, or because the victims in question, as full French citizens (contrary to the inhabitants of FEA who were French subjects) proved more likely to express grievances in the first place. However, other cases involved men from FEA and Cameroon. One hinged precisely on the question of promotion. According to Eboué, "a [black] NCO, after having taken the necessary courses, was not presented on the candidate-list, even though his grades met the requirements." According to the governor-general, "In some garrisons, newcomers are warned not to fraternize with colored officers and N.C.O.s." Seeking to shame his colleagues into taking action, Eboué then suggested that even the Vichy regime did not openly discriminate against blacks in mainland France. He concluded, "It is vain to evoke restoring French grandeur without showing perfect solidarity with the empire."[78]

In some ways, Idrisse Doursan's trajectory is a textbook one for Africans in the Free French forces. Born in 1914 in the town of Mayaye in Southern Chad near the Cameroonian border, he volunteered in 1933. He first served in the Régiment des Tirailleurs Sénégalais du Tchad (R.T.S.T.) where he was promoted to sergeant on July 1, 1940. In August of that year, his R.T.S.T. rallied to Free France, a decision that proved decisive for the Gaullist movement. Doursan was then transferred to the B.M. 3. In its ranks, he participated in the Eritrean campaign (see Figure 9). General de Gaulle decorated him with the Cross of the Liberation on May 26, 1941, for his bravery at the battle of Kub-Kub four months prior. After confronting the Italians, Doursan went on to fight Vichy forces in Syria in June and July 1941. He was promoted to sergeant-in-chief on September 1, 1941. He was captured by the Germans during the terrible

---

[78] ANOM, GGAEF 3B 2383, Eboué, Brazzaville, June 28, 1943. Regarding Vichy's attitude toward blacks, Eboué cites the example of Robert Delavignette, the director of the Ecole coloniale, who apparently protested vehemently against a decision blocking entrance to the school to people from the French Caribbean. On the issue of discrimination against blacks in metropolitan France under Vichy, see Eric Jennings, "Vichy fut-il aussi anti-Noir?" in Eric Jennings and Jacques Cantier, eds., *L'Empire colonial sous Vichy* (Paris: Odile Jacob, 2004); Dominique Chathuant, "Gratien Candace: une figure de la vie politique française, 2ème partie: de Vichy à la Quatrième République," *Bulletin de la Société d'Histoire de la Guadeloupe*, 149, January–April 2008, pp. 61–63; and Dominique Chathuant, "L'émergence d'une élite politique noire dans la France du premier 20ᵉ siècle?" *Vingtième Siècle, revue d'histoire*, 2009, 101, p. 142.

FIGURE 9. George Rodger. Free French troops parading at El Fasher, Darfur, before their departure for Eritrea, 1941. ROG 1940010W00032/21 © George Rodger, Magnum Photos.

fighting at Bir Hakeim in June 1942, but was fortunate to be rescued the next day. In 1948, Doursan reached the rank of warrant-officer.[79]

In many ways, Doursan's career was exceptional. He was one of only eleven Africans named compagnons de la libération, received the médaille militaire and the Croix de Guerre, some of the highest French military honors, and was decorated chevalier de la légion d'honneur. Yet still, his trajectory speaks to a glass ceiling facing Free Frenchmen from FEA and Cameroon more broadly. Deeply involved in the first phase of Free France's war effort (Eritrea, Syria, North Africa), he did not participate in the fighting in Europe. Named NCO before the advent of General de Gaulle's Free French movement, he never rose to the rank of officer. As Jacques Frémeaux and David Killingray have shown, at the time there were very few black officers serving in the French army, even fewer in the British forces (none in the South-African army, a handful in the R.A.F.).[80]

To be sure, one can find a handful of exceptions that prove the rule. Another compagnon de la libération, Georges Koudoukou, was promoted to the rank of second lieutenant on December 27, 1941, thus becoming the first officer hailing from Oubangui-Chari. He is credited with having "taken with him the native forces of the garrison" during the so-called three glorious days of late August 1940. As an officer in the famed B.M. 2, he participated in the desert war. At the battle of Bir Hakeim that helped stall Rommel's advance toward Egypt, between June 8 and June 10, 1942, Koudoukou "held a rallying point that broke several Germano-Italian infantry advances supported by tanks." Between June 2 and June 10, Free French positions at Bir Hakeim underwent sustained Axis shelling. On June 10, a volley seriously wounded Koudoukou. His leg was amputated on the spot. The B.M. 2 suffered disproportionately at Bir Hakeim, for it formed a rear guard responsible for covering the retreat that eventually took place. Gravely wounded, second lieutenant Koudoukou was successfully evacuated from the battlefield on June 10, during the extraordinary Free French escape from Rommel's encirclement. Susan Travers, who drove General Koenig's vehicle that night, recalled the plaintive wailing of the wounded being evacuated by ambulance as the vehicles negotiated the terribly bumpy terrain in the middle of the night. A few days later, Koudoukou passed away from his wounds at an Egyptian hospital.[81]

---


[79] AOL, Compagnons files.

[80] AOL, Compagnons files. On the British case, see Jacques Frémeaux, "Les contingents impériaux au cœur de la guerre," *Histoire, Economie et Société*, 23: 2 (2004), p. 225, and Killingray, *Fighting for Britain*, pp. 85–88.

[81] AOL, Compagnons files. Travers, pp. 188 and 190.

## The First "Whitening"

In his "personal and secret instructions" dated September 22, 1942, General de Gaulle shared with Leclerc his appraisal of Free France's military positions and objectives. Although he recognized that the Axis could still strike Free French Africa, he hurried to add, "We must now prepare Free French Africa for offensive action above all else. In this regard, I am planning three operations (corresponding to how events might unfold) which I will list by order of priority." These were "the rallying of Niger, with Zinder as our first goal." Next: "an offensive into Southern Libya in view of occupying the Fezzan region with an eye to future advances towards either Tripoli or Ghadames." Lastly, the general raised the possibility of a Free French participation in "Allied operations on metropolitan French territory."[82] Indeed, at the time, all signs seemed to suggest that the soldiers from FEA and Cameroon, who had been in the thick of battle at Kufra, Kub-Kub, and Bir Hakeim, would disembark on the beaches of Europe.

With a continental European campaign looming on the horizon in 1943 came a major and unexpected upheaval affecting FEA and Cameroonian forces. The "whitening" (blanchiment) of Fighting French forces in France in 1944 – involving the purging of African elements on climatic pretexts – has been well documented by Gilles Aubagnac most notably.[83] A similar decision taken on a large scale a year earlier is less widely known, but has been rightly described by Jean-François Muracciole as a "first wave" of "blanchiment."[84] On the surface, this 1943 upheaval involved making room for the forces formerly loyal to Vichy in North Africa.

In Algiers on August 2, 1943, General Leclerc urged de Gaulle to incorporate elements of the Armée d'Afrique, formerly loyal to Pétain, then Darlan and Giraud. Thus retooled, the so-called L Force metamorphosed into the second armored division (2ème DB).[85] At the core of the transformation lay the unit's mechanization: the 2ème DB obtained U.S.

---

[82] SHD 11P 21 Personal and secret instructions, Brazzaville, September 22, 1942. This message is partly reprinted by Crémieux-Brilhac, p. 631.

[83] He called into question the motivations of this "whitening," contending that the climatic reasons invoked were little more than a pretext. Gilles Aubagnac, "Le retrait des troupes noires de la première Armée à l'automne de 1944" *Revue historique des armées* 2 (1993), pp. 34–46; Muracciole, p. 61; and Frémeaux, "Les contingents impériaux," p. 223.

[84] Muracciole, p. 31.

[85] SHD 11P 21, Leclerc to de Gaulle, August 2, 1943. On the merger also see Vincent, pp. 60.

equipment, whereas the First Free French Division (1ère DFL) was out-fitted with British matériel.[86] But the move also involved a clear request from Leclerc: "White reinforcements are destined to replace black forces that are ill-adapted to war in Europe: they will be replaced by 1,500 Frenchmen including 190 officers, and 2,370 native North-Africans."[87] The second DB that emerged from this metamorphosis was therefore more Maghrebi and French than sub-Saharan African. Conversely, troops from FEA and Cameroon continued to play important roles in the other Fighting French units, primarily within the 1ère DFL. Some units thus survived the whitening purges of 1943.

More often than not, the *blanchiments* were framed climatically. Thus, after drawing admiration at Bir Hakeim, the B.M. 2 was first assigned to Madagascar in February 1943 (after peace had returned to that island) then repatriated to Bangui under climes deemed more natural for African troops. Only in January 1945 would the unit see combat again, mopping up the last German pockets on France's Atlantic coastline.[88]

The departure of Free French African forces of the first hour pro-foundly scarred units as they were being recast from the L Force into the 2ème DB. Such was the case of the anti-tank company number 5, formerly known as the CDCC (Compagnie de Découverte et de Combat du Cameroun). The author of the unit's diary, perhaps Lieutenant Pierre Schrimpf who would die in Normandy in August 1944, noted with deep emotion on September 13, 1943:

> Departure of the 99 native men of the company, transferred to the First Free French division. It is painful for us officers to see those who once formed the unit's nucleus leave ... These tirailleurs were very disciplined, a proud and distinguished group, and their reaction under fire showed that they could honorably figure in our Free French ranks of the first hour. We then accompany these last representatives of the old CDCC to their ship and receive their last salute.[89]

The author of these lines must no doubt have been thinking of Sergeant Manga Fabien, who perished at the hands of the Germans at the battle of Ksar Rhilane on March 10, 1943, and of the fighting spirit of the soldier Abdoulaye Amaselbé who was named to the division's honor roll after this same battle.[90] Raymond Dronne has depicted Manga Fabien

---

[86]   AML, Leclerc 5A, de Larminat au Major Steele, Alger le 10 juillet 1943.
[87]   SHD 11P 21, Leclerc to de Gaulle, August 2, 1943.
[88]   CHETOM, 15 H 156, B.M. 2.
[89]   CHETOM, 15 H 156, journal de marche B.M. 15 (2ème DB), Septembre 13, 1943.
[90]   CHETOM, 15 H 156, journal de marche B.M. 15 (2ème DB), March 10–12, 1943.

as follows: "a young Cameroonian intellectual, who previously worked as a bureaucrat for the rail service in Douala, a remarkable young man with a bright future, who had volunteered to fight to defend blacks and France.'"[91]

Ksar Rhilane, where Fabien fell, had proven a decisive turning point in Tunisia. Over the course of the battle, Free French forces repelled an assault from the ninetieth Panzergranadier division. Without the help of a single tank, these Free French troops, aided by their Greek allies and by British air support, endured lengthy aerial bombardment from the Luftwaffe, before repelling some fifty panzers and finally carrying the day.[92] There was, it should be mentioned in passing, a remarkably cosmopolitan quality to the Allied effort in the desert, where Free French forces from Chad and Central Africa rubbed shoulders with Norwegians, Maltese, New Zealanders, Ethiopian patriots and Libyan partisans, Sikhs, Greeks, Mauritians, White Russians, German Jews, Australians, and Britons, to name but a sample.[93]

## The B.M. 4 and B.M. 5: From the Desert War to the Liberation of Europe

The B.M. 4 and 5 stand out among the early Free French units hailing from FEA and Cameroon that managed to escape reshuffling in 1943. The former was founded on December 28, 1940, out of Cameroonian elements blended with West African troops (especially Ivorian) who had assembled in British Gold Coast before being redirected to Douala. It then put down roots in Cameroon for training.[94] The battalion initially counted 506 African and 21 European enlisted personnel, 51 African and 43 European NCOs, and finally fourteen officers and one chaplain, all European. On February 1, 1943, the B.M. 4 was folded into the First Free French division.

Like so many Free French units, the B.M. 4 was by definition heterogeneous. Admittedly, Cameroonians made up its original core, along with the West Africans who had come via Gold Coast in 1940. When subsequent transfers occurred, the high command often ensured that

---

[91] Dronne, p. 275.

[92] Crémieux-Brilhac, *La France libre*, pp. 648–49; Notin, pp. 251–52; General Vezinet, "Le Maréchal Leclerc de Hauteclocque," short work published by the Fondation Leclerc; and General Ingold, *Ceux de Leclerc en Tunisie* (Algiers: Office français d'édition, 1945).

[93] Raoul Aglion, *War in the Desert* (New York: Henry Holt, 1941), pp. 227–33.

[94] CHETOM, 15H 153, journal de marche B.M. 4; and Sah, pp. 412–14.

Cameroonians were selected. Thus in late February 1943, 26 soldiers from the B.M. 5, also largely Cameroonian, were redirected into the B.M. 4. Nevertheless, in early March 1943 a new infusion took place, this time comprised of former Vichy forces posted in Djibouti. I have already suggested that this incorporation must have ruffled feathers. After all, in 1943 the B.M. 4 had fought the Italians in Ethiopia and Eritrea while Vichy forces in Djibouti had stood idly by. In turn, the men posted at Djibouti reproached the British for having blockaded them in 1941 and 1942. It also seems safe to deduce that the Cameroonian and Ivoirian men enrolled under the cross of Loraine since 1940 must have had some difficulty accepting being suddenly placed under the leadership of officers previously loyal to Vichy, a regime which in Africa at least, had reserved its bullets for strictly Free French, British, and American targets.

As of April 18, 1943, the B.M. 4 counted 490 African soldiers and 66 African NCOs, as well as an African officer. On May 6, 1943, the unit took up a position on the southwest flank of the Takrouna Djebel in Tunisia. Over the course of the fierce fighting that followed against both Germans and Italians, the B.M. 4 lost fourteen African men as well as one European. Contrary to the list of the dead, that of the wounded featured places of residence. It is therefore possible to establish that of the 31 Africans wounded over the course of this battle, 22 came from French West Africa, the vast majority from Côte d'Ivoire. However, on November 7, 1943, 55 West Africans who had once formed the "nucleus" of the battalion, were transferred from the B.M. 4 and replaced by Cameroonians.

After landing in Italy in April 1944, the unit took part in the battle of Pontecorvo the following month. German artillery inflicted serious losses on the battalion.[95] On June 11, the B.M. 4 again fell under heavy fire, this time on the road between Montefiascone and Bolsena.[96] On August 17, 1944, the B.M. 4 landed in Provence before giving chase to German units in the direction of Avignon, then up the Rhône toward Burgundy. In the village of Lyoffans in the Vosges, in late September 1944, the B.M. 4 waged house-to-house combat against an SS unit. The second "whitening" occurred shortly thereafter. As happened elsewhere, unseasoned F.F.L. (resistance) fighters came to replace the Cameroonians and Ivoirians who had constituted the unit for four years.[97]

---

[95] CHETOM, 15H 153, journal de marche, B.M. 4.
[96] Sah, p. 415, and http://www.1dfl.fr/decouvrez-ses-unites/bataillon-de-marche-n-4/.
[97] http://www.1dfl.fr/decouvrez-ses-unites/bataillon-de-marche-n-4/. Much the same thing occurred in the ranks of the B.M. 11.

Similarly, the B.M. 5 was largely Cameroonian. In fact, on August 27, 1942, in the heart of the Egyptian desert, Battalion Chief Roger Gardet made a point of marking the second anniversary of Cameroon's rallying to General de Gaulle. He declared it "a holiday for the B.M. 5." Before adding that "those in colonies that did not budge [in August 1940] will long bear the stigma of their pusillanimous inaction, for if the entire empire had stood together, the boches would already be defeated." Although Gardet no doubt got carried away in his assessment, it nevertheless seems significant that he asserted the primacy of Cameroon and FEA by virtue of their precocious commitment to the Gaullist cause. The unit's emblem conveyed much the same message, as it featured an elephant superimposed with the cross of Lorraine with the date 1940 figuring prominently.[98]

Between October and November 1942, the B.M. 5 participated in the campaign against Rommel's forces around El Alamein. Then in May 1943, following fierce combat, the unit savored the victory of Takrouna in Tunisia. The battalion's diary reports "the delirious joy of African soldiers: dancing and songs," as thousands of German and Italian prisoners were ushered past. Soon the B.M. 5 crossed the Mediterranean, and was thrown into the Italian campaign.[99]

First-class soldier Dangsalla was born at Lokoro in the far north of Cameroon in 1919. He joined the military in December 1940, at a time when Free France was recruiting very intensely. A member of the B.M. 5, he was killed in the region between Parma and Modena on June 12, 1944. After having advanced steadily a day prior, the B.M. 5 encountered a fierce German counterattack. The fighting on hill 562 of the Bagno-Reggio area involved tanks as well as infantry. The unit's diary attributes its first setbacks to the element of surprise, but also to the fact that African troops were implicated. It reads: "The tirailleurs were surprised by this sudden attack. They are not apt at close combat in covered terrain, where even Europeans find the going difficult." Over the ensuring hours and firefights, the B.M. 5 managed to hold hill 562 as well as the surrounding plateau. This time, the unit's diary did not call into question its African soldiers, far from it. According to this same source, Dangsalla "contributed with his adjusted shooting to stem an enemy infiltration along the northern slope of hill 562." His citation, with the *Croix de Guerre*, specifies that he served as "a sharpshooter." He perished from "a burst of enemy machine

---

[98] CHETOM, 15H 153, journal de marche, B.M. 5.
[99] CHETOM, 15H 153, journal de marche, B.M. 5.

gun fire from close range" as he was trying to save a gravely wounded comrade.[100]

Cameroonian Free French soldiers in Europe experienced combat against German units that was incommensurate in its intensity and lethalness from the early skirmishes Leclerc's men had known in the Sahara against Italian forces in 1941. After Italy, the B.M. 5 participated in the landings of Provence, and in the liberation of Toulon, taking Mount Redon to the northeast of the port city.

## Last German Bastions, 1945

While large parts of France were rebuilding in 1945, troops from Free French Africa were tasked with cleaning out the last German pockets on the Atlantic coast. Near the Pointe de Grave in April 1945, the FEA and Somali regiment met steadfast German resistance from hardened soldiers with their backs to the sea, obeying Adolf Hitler's stubborn orders not to surrender. The "AEF/Somali" regiment included the B.M. 14 and 15, as well as the bataillon de marche Somali (B.M.S.). The first two were largely comprised of men from Chad and Cameroon.[101] On the evening of April 15, 1945, several African troops perished after the Germans broke a truce in the village of Croix, near Talais. In all, the regiment lost 22 men that day, most of them from the colonies (18 of the 22 to be precise). By sunset the following day, on the outskirts of Talais, ten more Fighting French men had perished, eight of them colonials. During the April 17 assault on Talais itself, large numbers of Germans surrendered; the B.M. 15 alone took 193 prisoners that day. Yet the Germans continued to inflict serious losses on their assailants. In the ranks of the B.M. 15, seven Africans and two Europeans died that day. On April 18, 1945, "violent street fighting" took place in the center of Soulac-sur-Mer a small Atlantic resort town. French troops advanced behind their tanks. The Germans clung to a bunker and to whatever smoldering ruins remained. Free French forces were obliged to fight in a swamp outside of Soulac, mired in deep mud for more than four hours. While the various units comprising the AEF–Somali regiment took 410 prisoners that day, twelve Africans perished

---

[100] CHETOM, 15H 153, journal de marche, B.M. 5. The information on Dangsalla comes from this source as well as from his dossier at the Centre des archives du personnel militaire in Pau. Numéro de classement 1049, numéro de matricule E.39.996.9464.

[101] *Héros Méconnus, Mémorial des combattants d'Afrique noire et de Madagascar* (Paris: Association française Frères d'Armes, 1990), p. 278.

for "zero Europeans" according to French military records.[102] This last Fighting French effort, like the first one, rested largely on the shoulders of African forces.

In nearby Royan at the same time (April 14 to 16), the B.M. 2 from Oubangui-Chari threw 528 African soldiers and 70 African NCOs into battle alongside 116 European NCOs and 125 white soldiers.[103] The B.M. 2 was supported by the bataillon de marche Antillais number 5 and by tanks from the 2ème DB. Facing them were some 13,000 Germans ready to fight to the bitter end. "Waves of flying fortresses succeeding one another without interruption" had completely leveled the town of Royan in advance of the Fighting French attack. Other aircraft had dive-bombed to drop "incendiary liquids." At the operation's conclusion, there remained of Royan "consumed by flames" only "a chaotic pile of calcinated rocks."[104]

In the ranks of the B.M. 2, the operation cost the lives of fifteen Africans and seven Europeans, as well as wounding 52 Africans and 34 Europeans. In his report on the mission, the commandant remarked that "these last combats represent the crowning achievement of the B.M. 2's long path, marked by the blood of our men, European and natives alike, blended in a common sacrifice, along this road followed since 1940, across battlefields in Africa and Europe."[105] However, behind this language of common sacrifice lay some fundamental differences in perception. Indeed, the unit diaries and reports of the fighting in these Atlantic pockets offer far more details on the European dead and wounded than on "native" ones.

Also exposed during the battle for the Atlantic pockets were the tense relations between experienced African troops on the one hand, and the F.F.I. (the Forces françaises de l'Intérieur, born on the resistance) on the other hand. In relating the operation of Pointe de Grave, the commandant wrote of "F.F.I. herds" that threw themselves into battle "in rather spectacular disorder." In contrast, reports depict colonial troops as "fine combatants."[106] At Didonne, near Royan, a war crime further stoked this discord. On April 15, some twenty Germans who had already

---

[102] CHETOM, 15H 158, Régiment d'AEF-S, Journal de Marche, opérations de la Pointe de Grave.

[103] CHETOM, 15H 158, Participation des unités coloniales à la libération des points d'appui allemands de Royan-Pointe de Grave.

[104] CHETOM, 15H 158, Jean Perrisson's testimony, Royan, April 14, 1945.

[105] CHETOM, 15H 158, Participation des unités coloniales à la libération des points d'appui allemands de Royan-Pointe de Grave.

[106] CHETOM, 15H 158, Old Soulac headquarters, April 22, 1945.

surrendered were machine-gunned "at point-blank range by a soldier in the Bigorre regiment: 3 Germans were killed, 7 seriously wounded." A witness recorded with bitter irony, "In a wave of alcohol-induced hate, all of the F.F.I. present screamed with joy and admiration for such a heroic act."[107] Here, the officers of an African army engaged in battle since 1940 heaped scorn on a soldier of the Bigorre regiment, a unit born of the French resistance. The many rifts and recriminations between the internal resistance and the Free French are well known. Let me insist here on two dimensions that arose on the Atlantic coast in 1945. Firstly, it was the colonials who led by example, the metropolitan resistance that needed to be reined in. Secondly, these same colonials implicitly claimed a far deeper commitment to the Gaullist cause. The army from FEA and Cameroon, at war since the battle of Kufra, clearly considered the metropolitan resistance – a latecomer to the stage – to be amateurs at best.

The incident was certainly not isolated. Similar ones led the head of the Bataillon de Marche Somali to deduce: "it is desirable that all contact with F.F.I. hoards like the Blayais unit be halted as soon as possible, because the tirailleurs cannot understand why they should be prevented from killing prisoners, pilfering corpses, and pillaging homes when they witness such acts of savagery being committed by the F.F.I."[108] Here we find a remarkable inversion of the colonial equation, in which the F.F.I. play the role of "savages." Yet it also bears mentioning that this officer seems to have feared that African troops might regress into what he considered a state of natural savagery, precisely because of the F.F.I.'s deplorable example.

On a vaster scale, Edgard de Larminat claims to have used the partly African First Free French division to "round up the F.F.I." Such inversions, and their profound consequences, were witnessed all over France during the liberation process. The former high commissioner to Free French Africa recounts how he tried to reel in the F.F.I. during the liberation of Poitiers. The only thing stopping him, he wrote, was "that I only received a battalion of motorized Tunisian forces. They were of good quality and would have been perfect for use against the enemy, but as they were composed of Tunisians I could not employ them for a police action against the Maquis without risking not so much a civil war, but a racial war or even a religious one."[109] Once in charge of raising a black

---

[107] CHETOM, 15H 158, Jean Perrisson's testimony, Royan, April 14, 1945.
[108] CHETOM, 15H 158, Old Soulac headquarters, April 22, 1945.
[109] Larminat, p. 240 and 246.

army with which to free France, and thereby wage a civil war against Vichy, Larminat now balked at using colonial troops to put down not collaborationists or Nazis, but rather his companions in the maquis.

## From FEA to Royan

On balance, FEA and Cameroon contributed enormously to the Free French effort. From the very beginning they provided soldiers, NCOs, drivers, supplies, and logistics. Like other troops, those from Free French Africa occasionally mutinied, deserted, and experienced tensions with civilians near their bases. Yet overall their contribution to Free France was as decisive as it was essential.

One can therefore assert without exaggeration that the first phase of the Free French war effort – the real one so to speak, since in 1942 the movement changed its title to Fighting France – was largely African. This certainly overturns clichés, given how rarely these black soldiers of the first hour are represented in film, fiction, and history. The movie *Indigènes* (*Days of Glory*) no doubt reminded audiences that many Fighting Frenchmen hailed from the colonies, but it also obfuscated the fact that North and West Africa, whose soldiers are at the heart of the plot, joined the fray three long years after FEA and Cameroon. This is all the more jarring because seniority mattered profoundly within Gaullist ranks. If France found its way to the victors' table in 1945, it was no doubt due to General de Gaulle's pugnacity, but also largely thanks to five years of efforts from Chad, Cameroon, Oubangui-Chari, French Congo, and Gabon.[110]

Yet behind this reality of an African Free France, ambiguities, contradictions, and inequalities abound. The attitude of Leclerc toward African troops offers one example of this. Others can be found in cases of racism in the ranks spelled out by Félix Eboué, not to mention forced military enrollments in FEA and Cameroon, and the "whitening" of Free French forces in 1943. Nor should we lose track of the very limited means at the disposal of the Free French, especially prior to 1943. FEA and Cameroonian troops that achieved victories in the desert did so with virtually no transport aircraft, with largely useless tires, sometimes even without adequate footwear and tank binoculars.

---

[110] Jacques Frémeaux has written, "The devotion of overseas troops, too often neglected, powerfully contributed to the restoration of an international role for France. It was colonial territories that allowed the rebirth of a military whose eventual 'crusade in Europe' contributed to having France admitted to the concert of victors." Jacques Frémeaux, "Les contingents impériaux," p. 220.

The first large territory to take up arms after the armistice of June 1940, Free French Africa also proved to be the last one fighting the Nazis on French soil, symbolically closing the circle on the Pointe de Grave and Royan in 1945.[111] In an episode that sums up the ambivalence of Fighting France toward its African troops, Gaullist officers accused the F.F.I. of savagery, adding that said savagery was sure to set a poor example for black soldiers who had been banned from such conduct. Barbarism had rarely seemed so subjective, so mutable and prone to shifting sides.

[111] On July 22, 1940, the tiny New-Hebrides actually rallied before FEA and Cameroon.

PART III

# RESOURCE EXTRACTION, WARTIME ABUSES, AND AFRICAN EXPERIENCES

# Introduction to Part III

The mobilization of resources constitutes a crucial dimension of World War II. It is well established, for instance, that Nazi Germany's prodigious war effort suffered from two major shortages in oil and rubber.[1] Like Germany and Japan, the Allies undertook a frenetic quest for raw materials. It soon encompassed Free France's colonial holdings. British and American experts prospected widely in FEA and Cameroon in search of rubber and rutile, a mineral containing titanium dioxide, used in the armament sector. The U.S. consul in Brazzaville relayed every new lead he could to Washington: rumors of oil deposits off Gabon's shores, the discovery of molybdenite in Cameroon, and so on. In the last case, he even enclosed samples.[2] Rarely had diplomatic bags weighed so much.

FEA and Cameroon's rallying Free France in August 1940 ushered in profound economic transformations. The territories "had to turn unexpectedly towards an allied market that was also global," noted a 1944 report. It added, "Up until then they had lived in the metropole's orbit and their economies had moved in sync with the motherland's. Their economies were radically different from those of English-speaking lands and the abrupt shift from one to the other presented grave dangers."[3]

Two Franco-British agreements sealed this new state of affairs. One dated May 20, 1941, concerned FEA. The other, ratified on January 21,

[1] Adam Tooze, *The Wages of Destruction: the Making and Breaking of the Nazi Economy* (New York: Viking, 2006), p. 443.

[2] NARA RG 84, Classified general records, 1942–44, U.S. Consulate Brazzaville, UD 2519, box 1, telegrams dated November 7 and 10, 1942.

[3] ANOM Cab 55, "dispositions prises par la Grande Bretagne en 1940–1941–1942 en ce qui concerne les récoltes des Colonies immédiatement passées à la dissidence."

1941, involved Cameroon. The original agreement for FEA guaranteed that the British would purchase Free French cotton (20,000 tons), rubber (1,000 tons), as well as wax, copal, nut and palm oil, peanuts, and lumber. For its part, Great Britain agreed to supply FEA in finished goods. The agreement for Cameroon featured special clauses concerning timber, bananas, and coffee.[4] Beyond these agreements, the British did not hesitate to formulate additional requests to Free French authorities, to obtain lead, wax, tin, palm oil, antelope skins, and logs chosen to meet the specific dimensions set by the British admiralty.

Following this first phase, Free France resisted the temptation of even greater integration into the Allied economic sphere. In 1942, American and British officials suggested to the Free French a tripartite scheme based on the one recently implemented in the Belgian Congo. In such an arrangement, the Allies would swap finished goods directly in exchange for the colony's "strategic materials."[5] The joint U.S.–British mission to the Belgian Congo even took the time to cross the river into Brazzaville to inquire about Free French Africa's needs. At the very same time, General de Gaulle was on the cusp of signing an agreement allowing the United States to use Pointe-Noire's naval and air bases.[6] Yet Pleven and his team deemed Free France's existing agreements already "too rigid" and de Gaulle consequently rejected the proposed tripartite agreement against a backdrop of increased inter-Allied tension.[7] Would it have benefited FEA and Cameroon's populations had it been adopted? It seems doubtful given that in January 1943, overwhelmed U.S. authorities suspended shipments of manufactured goods to the Belgian Congo. In order to temper the decision's psychological impact, the U.S. consul in Leopoldville suggested that Washington arrange the screening of films and the distribution of documents in the Belgian Congo showing average Americans experiencing rationing. To save face, however, he added, "We don't want a picture of America suffering but cheerfully sacrificing."[8]

---

4 ANOM 1Affpol 2557.
5 NARA RG 84, Classified general records, 1942–44, U.S. Consulate Brazzaville, UD 2519, box 1, Cordell Hull, note 131 from Washington received in Brazzaville on September 5, 1942.
6 AC GGAEF 84, Eboué Brazzaville, September 30, 1942, and ANF 3AG 167, telegram from Brazzaville and Douala, August 30, 1942. On the Pointe-Noire negotiations, see ANOM GGAEF 5D 301, file on the U.S. agreement.
7 ANOM Cab 55, "dispositions prises par la Grande Bretagne en 1940–1941–1942 en ce qui concerne les récoltes des Colonies immédiatement passées à la dissidence."
8 NARA RG 84, Classified general records, 1942–44, U.S. Consulate Brazzaville, UD 2519, box 2, Taylor to Washington, January 8, 1943.

In fact, Free French authorities rejected the tripartite project for a number of reasons. The sense of urgency that had prevailed in 1940 had now dissipated: "The necessities that had imposed the agreements of 1940 and 1941 had vanished. [By 1942], FEA and Cameroon had aligned their prices on global lines, commercial movement had been launched and maintained, the machine was in order and could now run smoothly on a bigger stage."[9] Starting in October 1942, with the exception of rubber and gold, Free France now privileged individual contracts with Allied ministries and firms over any new general agreement.[10] One can thus discern successive phases in Free French Africa's economy: the earthquake of August 1940 and its aftershocks were followed by a period of British monopoly during which FEA and Cameroon aligned their prices on those of the British Empire. Starting in October 1942, the two territories entered into a competitive global market for the first time before the French imperial circuit was reactivated at the Liberation of France in 1944.

Cameroon's export data reflect these transformations. Before the war, the main importers of Cameroonian products had been France, followed by the Netherlands, Germany, Belgium, and the United States. As of August 27, 1940, Cameroon abruptly halted shipments to its four main prewar continental European markets. Henceforth, Great Britain occupied by far the first rank (60% in 1941), followed by the United States (17%), then Nigeria and the Union of South Africa.[11] Only in 1944, with the reopening of the French and French colonial markets to Cameroonian goods, did this situation shift once more.

While the British dominated trade relations with Free French Africa, the United States came in second place, despite Roosevelt's reticence to recognize de Gaulle. As early as August 1941, at a time when the United States had not yet entered the war, and Britain theoretically possessed a monopoly over Free French production, the British ambassador in Washington informed Free French authorities that the United States would gladly purchase copal, vanilla, and especially rutile from Free French

---

[9] ANOM Cab 55, "dispositions prises par la Grande Bretagne en 1940–1941–1942 en ce qui concerne les récoltes des Colonies immédiatement passées à la dissidence."

[10] Ibid.

[11] Ministère des Colonies, *Bulletin hebdomadaire d'information*, 45, October 1, 1945, pp. 11–12. The percentages are drawn from a British report found in NAUK: FO 859, file 6, memorandum by W. W. Lawson on conditions prevailing in the French Cameroons.

Africa.[12] The following month, the United States issued more specific requests prioritizing rutile, tin, cobalt, and cobalt concentrate.[13] Although FEA responded that it possessed none of these materials in sufficient quantities, Cameroon conversely jumped into action. French Cameroon possessed rutile deposits and soon shipped the war material to the United States.[14] The Mayo-Darlé mine in northern Cameroon experienced rapid expansion. Cameroon went from producing 150 tons of rutile in 1939 to 2,400 tons in 1942, and 3,300 tons in 1944.[15]

Even though the tripartite agreement was never ratified, American goods soon streamed into Free French Africa: machines and other heavy equipment via the Lend-Lease agreements, smaller articles by way of the Red Cross. U.S. tractors, toothbrushes, and distinctively yellow American school buses all made their appearance in FEA. The influx of new consumer goods captured imaginations and opened some unexpected capitalist stakes. For instance, the U.S. consul in Brazzaville advised Washington in March 1943 to reconsider the plan to export textiles to Free French Africa that featured warplanes, stars and stripes, and other Americana. The British had attempted to sell their fabrics bearing Union Jack and the image of the royal family, but the operation had failed, he explained. He added for good measure that the plan seemed akin to the French sending "agents to the United States to pin French flags on the American Indians." In other words, he saw little point in targeting indigenous hearts and minds. If effective propaganda was the goal, then Consul Taylor recommended exporting high-quality textiles bearing simply the words, "Made in U.S.A." in French. The consul opined that African women displayed a "canny sense of value" and that this would serve the American cause far better than ostentatious eagles, flying fortresses, or stars and stripes that would only alienate colonials without winning over Africans.[16]

What was the cost of these many changes to the inhabitants of Cameroon and FEA, and how did they experience their sudden entry into a globalized market? How did Gaullist authorities set about increasing production so as to answer pressing Allied demand in selected sectors? Were prewar colonial practices transformed or cast aside? These are the questions that will guide the next two chapters.

---

[12] ANF 3AG1 165, Pleven to Larminat, August 16, 1941.

[13] ANOM GGAEF 3B 1098, Félix Eboué's response dated October 4, 1941.

[14] ANOM GGAEF 6B 721, telegram from the U.S. consul, Douala, May 1, 1943.

[15] Memoli-Aubry, p. 246.

[16] NARA RG 84, Classified general records, 1942–44, U.S. Consulate Brazzaville, UD 2519, box 2, suggestions for propaganda in French Equatorial Africa, March 12, 1943.

# Chapter 6

# Rubber, Gold, and the Battle for Resources

A 1947 documentary entitled *Autour de Brazzaville*, filmed partly by avant-garde photographer Germaine Krull, sets about informing the French public about what "Equatorial Africa brought Free France" during World War II. While the film exalts the troops from these territories and chronicles the rallying of the colonies in question in August 1940, not to mention the heroism of doctors and the development of infrastructures under Gaullist rule, it nonetheless depicts the region's chief contribution to the Allied cause as resource-based. FEA had "offered" massive amounts of rubber, gold, and to a lesser extent, wood. Indeed, a 1943 order outlining Krull's mission describes plainly "a film about the production of gold, rubber and timber."[1] It is precisely this focus on extraction that constitutes the most captivating aspect of the film today, more than its perhaps predictable civilizing discourse and condescending tone ("A hundred years earlier FEA had been in the stone age," trumpets the boisterous narrator). Frame upon frame focuses on Free French Africa's contribution of natural resources. One is left thinking that FEA and Cameroon must have been bled dry in the span of four years.[2]

Rubber is closely linked to the brutality for which the Congo Free State and the Belgian Congo became so notorious in the late nineteenth and early twentieth century.[3] The regions that would subsequently be known as FEA proved little different in this respect. In the 1890s, rubber was collected in lieu of taxes. Concessionary companies dealing in wood

---

[1] ANOM Affpol 873, Colonies Algiers to Governor Douala, September 22, 1943.

[2] *Autour de Brazzaville* 1947, viewed at: http://www.ina.fr (in 2012).

[3] See Adam Hochschild, *King Leopold's Ghost* (Boston: Houghton Mifflin, 1999).

and rubber carved up the area. Gabonese like Vincent de Paul Nyonda, Valère Mourigou, and Pototu Mbumb reported acts of sadistic cruelty linked to rubber production: rapes, forced incest, and other sexual crimes committed on those unfortunate enough to have brought rubber that the authorities deemed to be of insufficient or inferior quality.[4]

This first rubber fever peaked in 1917. In the wake of the Great War, the commodity's price collapsed. Thereafter, wild rubber collection dropped considerably across Africa, including in FEA and Cameroon, even though a British scheme to limit production in the 1920s briefly caused rubber demand to rebound.[5] This is when André Gide and Albert Londres, among others, denounced terrible abuses in the rubber trade in their broad condemnations of colonialism in Central Africa. With the Depression, production tapered off once more in the 1930s. Thus, after having produced 3,000 tons of rubber at its zenith in 1917, FEA only generated 522 tons in 1934. According to Catherine Coquery-Vidrovitch, rubber's future in the region seemed "condemned" by 1921.[6] The same observation holds true for Cameroon under French mandate, which exported 945 tons of rubber in 1922, yet only produced 20 tons nine years later.[7]

In 1939, British Malaya and the Netherland Indies (modern-day Indonesia) held by far the top two global spots in rubber output. Their production rested on hevea trees tapped for their sap on vast plantations. Wild rubber, extracted from roots, vines, grasses, and forest sap, had largely fallen out of favor at this point, because of its less even quality. Farmed heveas provided greater, more reliable, and rational yields. The hevea tree's superiority came with only one caveat: one could not produce rubber from it instantly. Saplings took years before achieving maturity.

The war triggered a scramble to secure latex reserves. Great Britain and the United States possessed relatively limited stockpiles, and scurried to find alternatives to tropical rubber in the form of both synthetic materials and rubbery substances derived from temperate plants. Although synthetic rubber production was stepped up, it failed to compensate entirely

---

4  Testimonies cited by Christopher J. Gray, *Colonial Rule and Crisis in Equatorial Africa: Southern Gabon ca. 1850–1940* (Rochester: University of Rochester Press, 2002), p. 157.

5  Howard and Ralph Wolf, *Rubber, a History of Glory and Greed* (New York: Covici-Friede, 1936), p. 142.

6  Catherine Coquery-Vidrovitch, *Le Congo au temps des grandes compagnies concession-naires, 1898–1930* (Paris: Mouton, 1972), p. 168.

7  Mbembe, pp. 169–72.

for natural rubber, most notably in the production of large tires essential for the military.[8]

On the eve of war, most French rubber came from Indochina. Up to Pearl Harbor and the ensuing U.S. involvement in the war in December 1941, the Vichy authorities in Indochina continued to export rubber to America. Thereafter, shipments ceased abruptly. The Japanese occupiers in Indochina found themselves awash in rubber.[9] Meanwhile, in France, the Germans gradually seized local stockpiles, first by way of the armistice commission, then through negotiations undertaken one by one with French companies, and finally within the framework of a European rubber union that Nazi Germany tried to establish in Heidelberg in April 1942.[10] It is as tragic as it is revealing of Vichy's actions that the inhabitants of FEA and Cameroon were forced into forests to dig up rubbery roots when thousands of tons of rubber rotted in hangers throughout French Indochina. At the same time Nazi Germany got its hands on thousands more tons of rubber stored on French soil, and even ordered ordinary French citizens to register their tires.[11] Through a kind of global butterfly effect, FEA and Cameroon found themselves answering a desperate plea for rubber.

## Allied Demand

Indeed, the course of the war dictated that FEA and Cameroon suddenly attracted considerable Anglo-American attention in 1942. The rapid fall of British Malaya (January 1942) then Singapore (February 1942) and the Dutch East Indies (March 1942) to the Japanese sent London and Washington calling. Those territories combined had accounted for 77 percent of the world's rubber supply up to then, which does not include

---

[8] William G. Clarence-Smith, review of John Andrew Tully, *The Devil's Milk: A Social History of Rubber* in *The International Review of Social History*, 56 (December 2011), p. 542.

[9] William G. Clarence-Smith, "La SOCFIN (groupe Rivaud) entre l'Axe et les Alliés" in Hubert Bonin, Christophe Bouneau, and Hervé Joly, eds., *Les entreprises et l'outremer français pendant la seconde guerre mondiale* (Bordeaux: Maison des Sciences de l'Homme d'Aquitaine, 2010), p. 104.

[10] Francis Koerner, "Le contrôle de l'industrie française du caoutchouc par l'Allemagne nazie (1940–1944)," *Guerres mondiales et conflits contemporains*, 240, 4, 2010, pp. 43–61.

[11] Tire registration even comes up in Vercors' famous resistance novel *The Silence of the Sea*. Vercors, *Le Silence de la Mer* (Paris: Albin Michel, 1951), p. 59.

French Indochina, now also under de facto Japanese economic control.[12] Between 1941 and 1943, Asian rubber exports to the United States collapsed, dropping from 1,007,600 tons to a mere 20,100 tons. Pierre Ryckmans, the governor of the Belgian Congo, set the tone in a radio broadcast on March 10, 1942: "This breach in the allied front in Equatorial Asia can only be filled by Equatorial Africa. The world is counting on us to restore the balance of resources that the Japanese advance tilted in the enemy's favor."[13]

FEA and Cameroon had not even appeared on global rubber-producing rankings prior to the war. By 1943, they found themselves practically tied with the Belgian Congo as the sixth Allied rubber producer. Indeed, Cameroon and FEA provided some 7,000 tons of latex in 1943 and 1944, then another 8,000 tons in 1945. Admittedly, this placed the territory's output far behind Ceylon's (present-day Sri Lanka: 98,000 tons in 1943), India's (17,000 tons in 1943), and Liberia's (15,000 tons in 1943), but right on the heels of Brazil's and Nigeria's.[14] By 1943, the latex streaming from formerly Vichy West Africa mingled with that of FEA and Cameroon. Adding French West and Equatorial Africa's totals for 1943–44 vaults Fighting French Africa's production into fifth position for the Allies for that year.

Placing oneself in the context of 1942, one should recall that after the unexpected collapse of Singapore in February of that year, many Allied experts worried that Ceylon might fall next. It was therefore all the more urgent to stimulate production in Allied sub-Saharan Africa. According to one contemporaneous estimation, "The total annual production for the year 1941 of the areas remaining [in 1942] to the United Nations in Africa, South America, and Mexico amounted to less than two weeks' current consumption for the United States alone."[15] To be sure, the global wartime economy was less binary than is sometimes allowed: the British Dunlop tire corporation continued producing for the Germans

---

[12] On the impact of the fall of Southeast Asia and the quest for rubber from temperate climes, see William G. Clarence-Smith, "The Battle for Rubber in the Second World War: cooperation and resistance" Commodities of Empire working paper #14. The figure of 77% is drawn from John Andrew Tully, *The Devil's Milk: A Social History of Rubber* (New York: Monthly Review Press, 2011), p. 294.

[13] Pierre Ryckmans, *Messages de guerre* (Brussels: Ferdinand Larcier, 1945), pp. 88–89.

[14] For the data output figures outside of Free French Africa, see B. R. Mitchell, ed., *International Historical Statistics: Africa, Asia and Oceania, 1750–2000* (London: Palgrave, 2003), pp. 258–59. Also see *Flight*, January 7, 1943, p. 18.

[15] Paul Wendt, "The Control of Rubber in World War II," *Southern Economic Journal*, January 1947, p. 204.

throughout much of the war.[16] Yet, with the rubber balance having tilted so far in the Axis' favor in 1942, Free French Africa's latex definitely contributed to increasing the region's importance in the eyes of British and U.S. authorities.

In point of fact, British territories in Africa were the first to feel the brunt of the fall of Southeast Asia. By 1942, they were being urged to increase their resource output, most notably by means of conscription, which is to say forced labor. Now that tin could no longer be imported from Southeast Asia, it was extracted with due "urgency" from Nigeria. This involved the rapid enrollment of 100,000 Nigerians for this sector alone. Free French labor practices in Central Africa tended to mirror those of the British. Mauritian sugar-cane harvesters, Kenyan farmers, and Rhodesian mine-workers were being enrolled and kept in certain industries by force, according to new draconian laws passed at Westminster by invoking the war effort.[17] In this regard, Free French Africa followed the path set by the British war economy.

The catastrophic fall of Southeast Asia to the Japanese left far too little rubber for the Allies and posed the question of how scant quantities would be divided. Indeed, in addition to the British and American war efforts, there were the Soviets to consider. Negotiations held in March 1942 led to an agreement whereby 12,000 tons of Ceylon's rubber production would head to the USSR, the remainder to the United States. The Americans also retained Liberian rubber through the Firestone Corporation. Soon, the United States was receiving 60 percent of Ceylon's production.[18] In other words, because so much of its colonial rubber was funneled to its own allies, Great Britain relied considerably on Belgian and Free French contributions. The United Kingdom dispatched several rubber emissaries to Free French Africa in 1942. The main scheme involved selling the entire rubber output of FEA and Cameroon to the British, in a bid to avoid competition among British, Americans, and South Africans and to avert the "astronomic rise" of rubber prices.[19]

The Free French initially balked at the idea of a British monopoly, so important were FEA rubber shipments in providing the Gaullist movement with U.S. dollars.[20] FEA risked losing its previous U.S. market

---

[16] Tooze, p. 133.

[17] Killingray and Rathbone, pp. 70–90.

[18] Wendt, pp. 204 and 208.

[19] NARA RG 84, Classified general records, 1942–44, U.S. Consulate Brazzaville, UD 2519, box 1, March 3, 1942.

[20] AOL 4B2, Haut-Commissaire Brazzaville, March 24, 1942.

and especially what it had received from the United States in exchange: "finished goods and foodstuffs."[21] Ultimately, Great Britain issued an assurance to the Fighting French that they could trade pounds for dollars directly if the need arose.[22] The resulting agreements stipulated unambiguously: "All rubber exported from Fighting French Africa shall be at the disposal of the United Nations. It has been agreed that purchases shall be effected by the United Kingdom Ministry of Supply."[23] This veritable British monopoly would hold until September 1944, at which time FEA and Cameroon's rubber was entirely redirected to the U.S. war effort.[24]

In 1942, the UK also expressed assurances that FEA would receive a fair rate, and that prices would follow those of Liberia and Belgian Congo should they rise.[25] The Free French, in turn, agreed to operate through accredited intermediaries: starting in March 1942, all FEA rubber would run through four export companies approved by the United Kingdom.[26] In an August 1942 telegram to the Free French representative in Washington, Free French colonial commissaire to the colonies René Pleven signaled that FEA alone would increase its exports from 1,500 tons in 1941 to 5,000 tons in 1942.[27] This proved an inflated estimate: FEA proper would produce roughly 2,000 tons in 1942, and Cameroon would export 1,055 tons in 1942, and some 3,000 tons the year following.[28]

Pleven did express some bitterness, however, that the United States was attempting to foster the creation of massive rubber plantations in FEA and Cameroon. He saw this "uprooting workers," when in point of fact it had been U.S. "lack of foresight" that had caused the Americans to abruptly lose their supply, leaving them without any backup source. The stakes were high, and the Free French honed their argument as follows: "We are currently ahead of the Belgians and the British in terms of the rubber war in Africa, and we cannot accept that the State Department

---

[21]  AOL 4B2, Haut-Commissaire Brazzaville, March 27, 1942.

[22]  ANOM GGAEF, 5D 299, London to Brazzaville, January 6, 1943.

[23]  AOL 4B2, Memorandum of agreement regarding rubber purchases from Fighting French Africa.

[24]  ADN 378PO/C/2/172 telegram from Algiers received on September 6, 1944.

[25]  AOL 4B2, Gouverneur Douala, April 2, 1942.

[26]  ANOM GGAEF, 5B 356, Laurentie, March 31, 1942.

[27]  AOL 4B2, Pleven to Washington, August 29, 1942.

[28]  The figures on Cameroon come from AOL, Douala, January 14, 1944, and the *Annuaire statistique du Cameroun*, Vol. 1, 1938–45, p. 63. The figures from FEA are drawn from AOL, Gouverneur Général Brazzaville to Pleven, February 2, 1943.

impose a native policy on us. The policy in question is one of big concessions; it runs contrary to the entire French colonial mission."[29] To this bitterness, Pleven added a dose of caution: he suspected the State Department and the British Supply Council of plotting to impose a policy of large concessions, without consulting the Free French.[30] Rubber had become a matter of Gaullist sovereignty. In the end, these large concession schemes were definitely shelved. Admittedly, the pace of production on preexisting hevea plantations, like that of Dizangué in Cameroon, rose markedly. Yet Gaullist trepidation over the question of new plantations carried the day. The *New York Times* reported tactfully on May 29, 1942, that while the Belgian Congo was testing new techniques and establishing new plantations, "Free French Africa also is pushing on with plans for swelling rubber production and existing plantations in the Cameroons are making a useful contribution."[31] Instead of the ambitious Allied plans involving the Belgian Robert Hallet and the SOCFIN corporation, the Free French clearly preferred increasing production where it already existed, and mostly stepping up wild rubber collection. This too would come at a considerable social cost, as we shall see.[32]

These debates should not obscure the fact that FEA and Cameroon swung full-tilt toward rubber production so as to answer Allied demand. In the words of Eboué, beginning in 1942 the rubber crop had become "the natural resource for which our war effort has an imperious demand."[33] In July of that year, Laurentie ordered all rubber companies to account for their stocks immediately.[34] In the span of a few months, rubber became the staple in areas where it had languished behind wood, palm oil, or cotton for years. According to the calculations of the governor-general's office in Brazzaville, rubber production in the second half of 1942 climbed 54 percent over the first half.[35] This confirms the responsiveness of FEA officials toward the UK agreements, but it also suggests that the plight and number of Africans involved in the rubber sector had radically changed in a short span.

[29] AOL 4B2, Pleven to Washington, August 29, 1942.
[30] AOL, Pleven papers, Pleven to Bourdillon, August 12, 1942.
[31] "Rubber Production Intensified in Africa," *The New York Times*, May 29, 1942, p. 10.
[32] On Hallet and SOCFIN during the war see William G. Clarence-Smith, "La SOCFIN," pp. 110–11.
[33] AFDG, F22, 17, Brazzaville to Bangui, October 23, 1942.
[34] ANC, GGAEF 84, Brazzaville to Bangui and Libreville, July 20, 1942.
[35] AOL 4B2, Eboué to Pleven, February 2, 1943.

Pressure from London was unrelenting. On January 9, 1942, Eboué cabled the governor of Oubangui:

The decree of January 5 concerning rubber processing calls for the exporting of this resource under two forms. Firstly native-style rubber called standard rubber. Secondly, plantation rubber prepared in the form of crêpes. In view of satisfying the demand of the British government, I bid you to inform me: firstly how far we can push Oubangui's rubber output upwards without compromising public health and by using pre-existing plantations if possible; secondly, how long it would take to achieve maximum tonnage; thirdly your suggestions for the price we would pay natives for the wild rubber they collect.[36]

Clearly, wild rather than plantation rubber continued to constitute the main focus in FEA, in keeping with Gaullist priorities. A document dated July 1943 itemized the purchases made by the British Rubber Control Board in FEA: 120,595 kilos of plantation rubber for the year running between July 1942 and June 1943, versus 2,393,044 kilos of wild rubber.[37] Conversely, in Cameroon, plantation rubber narrowly outpaced wild rubber collection. In 1942, French Cameroon produced 1,602 tons of hevea latex; in 1943, the region's plantations would yield 1,718 tons.[38]

In a March 1943 telegram aimed at congratulating recruiters, buyers, and plantation owners, Pleven mentioned that FEA would need to maintain rubber production "at the highest possible level" at least until "Indochina has been retaken."[39] This reminds us that in Free French eyes FEA had abruptly come to replace Vichy- and Japanese-controlled Indochina as a source of rubber, while in British eyes, it had become a stand-in for Malaya. In other words, the expectations placed on FEA and Cameroon were completely out of touch with past practice. In April 1943, Eboué began to temper Allied and even Free French demands. He especially opposed a project aimed at transforming more of Oubangui's cotton growers into rubber collectors. Eboué knew the region well, having served there during the First World War. He contended that the proposal risked undoing decades of work by dismantling the cotton sector; all of this, he complained, for a mere 1,500 possible extra tons of rubber.[40]

The British Ministry of Supply dispatched several representatives to FEA and Cameroon, and established a branch of the Rubber Control


[36] ANOM GGAEF 5B 712, Brazzaville (Affaires économiques) to Bangui, January 9, 1942.
[37] ANOM GGAEF 5B 720, Brazzaville (Affaires économiques), July 8, 1943.
[38] *Annuaire statistique du Cameroun*, Vol. 1, 1938–45, p. 65.
[39] AOL 4B2, Pleven to Eboué, March 15, 1943.
[40] AOL, Eboué to Pleven, April 30, 1943.

Board on location. Its agents recruited Africans. They were paid between 150 and 200 francs a month in 1943, "which is a lot," sighed a Free French official fearing upward pressure on wages.[41] In 1942, a Rubber Control Board official named Mackenzie approached Laurentie with numerous requests. He outlined Britain's desperate rubber situation, adding that his country was on the verge of exhausting its stock. He offered a cash advance to the Free French government, proposed to contribute per diems for administrators involved in the rubber sector, and demanded that whole trains be reserved for rubber. He even solicited Laurentie's permission to show films on the sacred substance, which would be projected by mobile cinema units. These productions, targeting both Africans and Europeans, were explicitly intended to "stimulate rubber production." Without rejecting the idea flatly, Laurentie expressed some skepticism about its effectiveness.[42]

British requests sometimes went too far. On April 11, 1943, a visibly upset Félix Eboué wrote Free French headquarters in London to accuse the British Rubber Board of intolerable behavior: "Kitts...the local rubber purchaser, tells everyone as loudly as possible that my administration lacks the energy the British require for rubber production. Rubber, he tells anyone who will listen, is the only reason FEA matters at all in British eyes." Eboué added that Kitts "put forward the idea of having me replaced by Henri Laurentie, an idea probably supported by the British government." In other words, British impatience on matters of rubber was starting to "to express itself a bit too loudly."[43] For our purposes, it seems worth underscoring the point, clearly understood by Eboué, that the British conceived of Free France's colonies mainly as rubber purveyors.

And yet on balance, Free French-British cooperation seems to have functioned reasonably well in the realm of latex, at least. For instance, the two administrations exchanged technical advice. On October 15, 1943, with the support of local Rubber Control Board officials, Eboué asked his headquarters to apply pressure on the British Ministry of Supply to deliver a machine analogous to the one that was being used to considerable effect in South Africa. The device mechanically transformed root and vine rubber into more classic rubber crêpes. He also requested two thousand handheld machines for beating the rubbery roots in the forests. He contended that this machinery was essential "if we want to maintain

<hr>

[41] ADN 116PO/1/71, rapport politique Pool, 1943.
[42] ANC GGAEF 126, file on rubber.
[43] ANC GGAEF 126, file on rubber, Eboué to London, April 14, 1943.

and increase our current production."[44] It also presented the advantage of removing a laborious and painful manual stage of wild rubber extraction, involving the beating of the roots to render them useable.

## Extraction and Its Consequences

The intensity of wartime demand meant that rubber was being sought by all means and from all sources possible. Administrators who failed to grasp the importance of rubber production were admonished. The head of the Nyanga department in Gabon committed the fatal mistake of writing in his 1942 report that "the native is content to remain idle; we shall see what the 1943 rubber collection campaign yields." In the margins, an apoplectic official in the governor's office in Libreville nearly broke his pen in anger: "It is unimaginable for the head of a department to write such a thing. I demand that Mr. Bousquet immediately improve his district's economic situation, especially by having the people in his region collect the rubber which we have been exhorting everyone to collect in no uncertain terms – a rubber so vital for the cause of Allied victory."[45] Passiveness on matters of rubber was no longer an option.

The official log of the post at Carnot in the heart of Western Oubangui-Chari records everything from aircraft passing overhead to medical visits to assemblies of chiefs. One can therefore be virtually certain that the rubber market recorded on April 26, 1942, in this cotton-producing region was the first of its kind in a long time. That day, inhabitants brought 880 kilos of wild rubber to the authorities. As of September 1, 1942, the market became monthly. The maximum quantity collected – 8,036 kilos – came in the month of May 1943.[46] Throughout FEA, rubber was outpacing other production. In Gabon in the fall of 1942, workers who had previously been employed in the logging business now shifted to rubber collection.[47] They were directed toward vines that had been sighted in the Abanga Noya area. In November 1942, the governor learned that many loggers had been enticed to collect rubber in the Bacoula region.[48] In point of fact, rubber collection paid far better than timber, cotton, or even gold extraction.

---

[44] ANOM GGAEF 5B 720, Eboué to London, October 15, 1943.
[45] ANOM GGAEF 4(1) D50, annual political report for 1942, department of Nyanga.
[46] ANOM GGAEF 3Y3.
[47] ANOM GGAEF 5B 715, Eboué to Libreville, September 5, 1942.
[48] ANOM GGAEF 2H 18, Brazzaville, November 20, 1942.

Wild rubber, whose wide-scale colonial exploitation in FEA had dramatically decreased in the 1920s and 1930s, made an officially sanctioned comeback. In August 1942, Pleven evoked the target of "tripling or even quadrupling" wild rubber collection that same year.[49] By 1943, the governor of Cameroon was reporting that wild rubber was growing scarce.[50] Eboué's team in Brazzaville did assuredly show concerns for worker well-being. In a September 15, 1942, telegram, they ordered local rubber collection companies to pay workers in multiples of 25 centimes, and to round fractions up systematically.[51] The reality on the ground, however, was often far removed from such good intentions.

Wild rubber actually encompasses a wide range of plant varieties that tended to be grouped into the categories of vine, grass, and root. In a report on an inspection visit he conducted in the region of Eséka in Cameroon in 1942, Lieutenant Henri Relly drew up an inventory of rubber-yielding plants. In the vine category alone, he observed that local populations distinguished between "some ten different species." Among the most exploitable he listed Ngo Yok (or "beautiful woman's milk"), Ndoumbe, and Nbongé. They produced very different latex in texture and color. Some featured blue, others white and pink accents. Then he explained how as "soon as the disaster in Malaya and the Netherland Indies became known," he personally took the initiative to seek information from the Cameroonians around him. It was they, he wrote, who "were the real specialists of vine rubber" and they helped him determine the latex's properties and elaborate the best extraction methods. He also pored over old reports from the region, especially those from the 1920s, to rediscover methods used at a time when Cameroon still produced forest rubber. Armed with all of this knowledge, Relly decided to "impose on each man present in the village a quota of six kilos of dry rubber per trimester. Every village chief, every family head, knows how many kilos of rubber they need to bring to the market." However, upon reflection, Relly reconsidered the amounts. "Given that only about a third of the population is actually present in the village, with so many currently employed in private and public works," he decided to lower the quota somewhat. Even with this adjustment, he expected to receive 24 tons per semester from the six sections of his subdistrict.[52] Relly evidently relied

---

[49] AOL 4B2, Pleven, August 7, 1942.
[50] AOL 4B2, Douala to Pleven and Langlade, April 19, 1943.
[51] AOL 4B2, Eboué Brazzaville, September 15, 1942.
[52] ANCMR 2AC 21, Eséka inspection reports.

on local knowledge, forced labor, and also personal initiative to wage the rubber campaign in his region. In March 1942, authorities from nearby British Nigeria even came to inquire about his methods, especially with respect to processing and conditioning techniques.[53]

There seemed to be few restrictions on what could be done to promote latex output. Some methods had been used for decades. Tamara Giles-Vernick cites recruitment at gunpoint and imprisonment as methods of choice to incite populations to collect wild rubber in Oubangui at the dawn of the twentieth century. Rubber was also used in many settings as a liquid tax. This particular practice was one of many retained by the Free French. Thus, the department chief in Alima reported in 1942 that: "the methods employed by the natives to fulfill their tax obligations remain palm oil and rubber."[54]

However, in most cases Africans were paid for the rubber they brought the authorities at market, even paid relatively well. In Cameroon, for instance, wild rubber jumped from one franc a kilo before the war to twelve francs a kilo in 1944.[55] At Carnot in Oubangui the first payments to rubber pickers between November 1942 and February 1943 were of 8.4 francs a kilo, before rising to a high point of 13.4 francs a kilo in June 1943. They would eventually taper off to 8.5 francs in July 1943, a level at which they would remain until January 1944.[56]

Contrary to certain previous practices, where in some regions the chiefs alone profited from rubber collection, under Free France pickers were generally paid individually (in cash or sometimes by barter).[57] A few exceptions do dot the archival record. Thus, in the subdistrict of Damara in Oubangui in 1943, village chiefs demanded one rubber basket from "every strong man in the village." The method must have proven effective, for this subdistrict that only produced 198 kilos of rubber in 1941, generated 18,247 kilos the year following, and 13,093 in 1943.[58]

Middlemen and entrepreneurs rushed to profit from this new windfall. Sometimes their initiatives literally crossed the line. In 1943, the Gabonese businessman Benoît Bitoura "raced ahead of the subdistrict chief" from village to village in the Minvoul region, buying up all of the rubber he

---

53 NAUK FO 859, file 6, wild rubber, note from the Consul General of Great Britain to Douala dated April 2, 1942, referring to a letter from March 9 of the year prior.
54 ANOM GGAEF 4(2) D76, Alima political report, second semester 1942.
55 Lachenal, p. 147.
56 ANOM GGAEF 3Y3.
57 ANOM GGAEF 4(1) D 52, political report for Ogooué-Ivindo, first semester 1944.
58 ANOM GGAEF 5D 168, report from the subdistrict of Damara, first semester 1943.

could. He then passed the border into Spanish Guinea where he sold a ton of the rubber. The Spanish authorities paid far more handsomely than the going rate in Free French Africa. However, on returning to Gabon, Bitoura was charged and sentenced to two months in prison, a sentence largely intended to set an example.[59]

Remuneration and profit do not necessarily imply a lack of coercion. A Congolese man interviewed in 1978 recalled that "the authorities picked up the rubber in the village. The day when militiamen arrived, they took a roll call during which everybody had to present their rubber. Whoever failed to bring the proper amounts or brought poorly prepared rubber could face a whipping."[60] In his history of the Central African Church, Father Carlo Toso tactfully depicts rubber collection under Free French rule as "practically forced labor." Historian Pierre Kalck considered the return to rubber picking in Oubangui-Chari under Free France to represent a major step backwards, accompanied by considerable violence.[61] In Cameroon, wild rubber collection featured high degrees of coercion. One subdistrict chief observed in 1944: "everyone is off to collect rubber, for the chief has used strong-arm methods: all village heads are either jailed or made to fear jail sentences."[62] On a smaller scale, one should not lose track of village dynamics. As with military recruitment, outsourcing was widely practiced. Thus, in their selection of workers for the Dizangué plantation in Cameroon, village chiefs in the Mbam region deliberately selected inhabitants whom they disliked.[63]

Some annual reports suggest that coercion was meted out to some while others profited. In his report on the Nyanga region in Gabon, the department chief noted, "Heading to Tchibanga in December 1943 to settle certain matters and attend the rubber market, I passed through the village of Miguembi 32 kilometers from Tchibanga." There, he explains, "several native chiefs came to welcome me. One spoke as follows: 'Monsieur Chaleil puts people in jail, he forces us to plant rice, to pick rubber and collect palm oil, but now we have money, we are rich.'"[64] In the eyes of the French official, this relative satisfaction on the part of an African chief seemed to confirm and justify the use of force. Of course, the women

[59] ANOM GGAEF 4(1) D51, report from Woleu-Ntem, first semester 1943, p. 16.
[60] Ollandet, p. 125.
[61] Kalck, p. 269.
[62] Lachenal, p. 149.
[63] Memoli-Aubry, p. 248.
[64] ANOM GGAEF 4(1) D51, Nyanga annual report, 1943.

and men who had actually undertaken the rubber picking were not consulted, and we can only surmise that their reaction to imprisonment would have been less positive.

The politics of the stick thus accompanied those of the carrot. Inhabitants of regions that failed to meet rubber expectations were most often punished. This included heavy fines, like those imposed on the Gabonese villages of Oveng and Obello (Estuaire département) in 1943 for "failing to meet production expectations." With chiefs constantly called on to justify the slightest anomaly, Victor Obame Essonne explained that his subjects steadfastly refused to take up rubber collection. To which the governor-general's services in Libreville scrawled menacingly in the letter's margins: "individuals must be warned that if they persist in refusing to pick rubber, they will be severely punished."[65] According to colonial officials, the slim output of these two villages could be attributed to the lack of authority of their chiefs. This perceived problem haunted the traditionalist Félix Eboué, whose idée fixe involved revalorizing the status and authority of chiefs. One way or another, many colonial officials seemed persuaded that without a combination of guidance and threats, rubber production would wane. "If we opted overnight to stop imposing rubber-picking on the natives, while still buying what they chose to pick on their own, it seems likely that the department's tonnage would plummet,"[66] observed a report from Ogooué-Ivindo in 1944. Latex served as a prime index for these officials to gauge the degree of capitalism, or for the most racist, the degree of "evolution," of local populations.

Several methods coexisted or were used in succession: imposition, coercion, threats on the one hand, financial incentives on the other hand. Nevertheless, most authorities in Brazzaville seemed persuaded that the availability of finished goods could prove a valuable incentive for rubber collectors, arguably the greatest motivation of all. In cases where there was payment but no shop or other outlet, the desire to pick rubber was lacking, argued some officials. The head of Ogooué-Ivindo complained in 1942 that the first rubber market he organized was something of a failure. When he tried to shift to a new scheme, by imposing rubber collection in lieu of taxes in cash, the situation hardly improved. "None of this would happen if Booué possessed a well-stocked shop that practiced normal pricing," he lamented.[67] In other words, according to some, consumer culture could achieve the goal of stepping up rubber production. Already

[65] ANOM GGAEF 4(1) D51, Estuaire first semester, 1943.
[66] ANOM GGAEF 4(1) D52, Ogooué-Ivindo report, 1944.
[67] ANOM GGAEF 4(1) D50, Ogooué-Ivindo report, 1942.

attempted prior to 1940, this strategy seems to have born fruit. According to Tamara Giles-Vernick, it allowed local populations to integrate international networks and for companies to stimulate production.[68] However the situation shifted fundamentally with World War II. The nature of the finished goods and the scale of exchange had changed. Suddenly, American consumer products flooded the region, either traded directly for rubber, or obtained in small stalls located near the rubber markets (see Figure 15).

This helps to explain how and why the Free French sought to obtain manufactured products from the United States and the United Kingdom in exchange for wild rubber. In March 1943, Pleven reported to Eboué that he was doing his utmost to procure merchandise that could fill the stalls in shops located by rubber markets across FEA. Another document sheds light on some of the goods offered: sweaters and jackets, short-sleeve shirts, lamps, pots and pans, plates, kettles, forks, locks, basins, and socks all figure on these lists.[69]

Colonial officials recognized that rubber collection was sometimes met with resistance. A report from the Pool area near Brazzaville for 1943 reads, "The collection and processing of rubber encountered quite a bit of resistance, despite the relatively good prices offered for it (10 francs a kilo for grass rubber, and 12.5 francs for vine rubber). However, thanks to a policy of persuasion and generosity, accompanied by numerous bonuses for producers, production has risen rapidly." On occasion, local officials remarked that success came back to haunt them. Between rubber picking, other harvests and mandatory roadwork, some Congolese areas were left exhausted and depleted. With reason. According to one report, "the natives walk 50 kilometers to go fetch the vines." Which led its author to recommend the following solution: "certain subdistricts that do not produce rubber could help those that do with their manioc supply, which would assist our subdistrict considerably and would allow it to completely devote itself to rubber."[70] In other words, the labor offices that were intended to distribute workers were now being called on to facilitate the mono-extraction of wild rubber.

While recognizing the war imperative, some officials seem to have considered the wild rubber campaign of 1942–44 to be a kind of Faustian pact serving neither the interests of Africans nor those of French colonialism.

---

[68] Tamara Giles-Vernick, *Cutting the Vines of the Past: Environmental Histories of the Central African Rain Forest* (Charlottesville: University Press of Virginia, 2002), p. 163.

[69] ANC GGAEF 126, rubber file, Affaires économiques, Brazzaville, February 15, 1943 and ANOM GGAEF 6B 69, Governor-General to London.

[70] ANOM GGAEF 4(2) D 76, Pool political report, 1943.

The head of the Mayana subdistrict near Brazzaville noted in 1943 that the collection of rubber from grasses "constitutes a particularly thankless task, that natives don't like, and for which the pay does not match the special effort required."[71] In 1942, his colleague in Northern Oubangui had remarked that in his department of N'Délé, "the wax harvest runs from March to June, the collecting of rubber from October to December. These two activities have created a kind of legal vagabondage, and obliged each man to leave his sedentary life, to camp in the bush. He wanders from river to stream, days away from his village. He is forced to eat savanna plants, fish from the rivers, and consumes home-made alcohol."[72] In 1943, the head of the subdistrict of Bitam in Gabon warned that "all of our results obtained through years of sedentarizing the native will be compromised if the rubber campaign continues."[73] He added that miserable campsites were slowly replacing "quaint villages."[74] In short, the run on rubber brought social consequences at the very antithesis of those desired by colonial authorities. On paper, Eboué and Laurentie espoused shining new worker villages.

Between 1942 and 1944, the rubber production curve was on a very steep rise. Establishing totals is complicated by the fact that rubber specialists used so-called conventional years that ran from July to June. FEA's production alone (not accounting for Cameroon) rose from 2,500 tons for the conventional year 1941–42 to 4,000 tons the year following, then 4,008 tons in 1943–44. Moyen-Congo and Oubangui-Chari account for most of this output: of the 4,008 tons generated in 1943–44, 1,841 came from Congo and 1,814 from Oubangui-Chari, with Gabon only generating 349 tons. FEA's goal for 1944–45 was set at 5,000 tons.[75] Cameroon went from extracting 1,000 tons in 1941 to 2,900 tons in 1942, then 3,000 tons for the standard year 1943, and finally 3,300 tons in 1945.[76]

The boom was such that by 1944, some officials felt the need to temper their subordinates' appetite for latex. In French Congo, Governor Gabriel Fortuné congratulated the head of the department of Sangha on May 13,

---

[71]  ADN 116PO/1/106, Mayana, political report, 1943.

[72]  ANOM GGAEF 4(3) D53, N'Délé political report, 1942.

[73]  ANOM GGAEF 4(1) D51, cited in the 1943 political report for Woleu-Ntem.

[74]  Ibid.

[75]  ANOM GGAEF 3B 2384, report to the commissaire aux colonies, July 24, 1944.

[76]  Sah, p. 488. According to the *Annuaire statistique du Cameroun*, the Cameroonian numbers work out to 2,013 tons in 1942, 2,262 for 1943, and 2,191 tons for 1944. Ministère de la France d'outre-mer, *Annuaire statistique du Cameroun*, Vol. 1, 1938–45, p. 63.

1944: "It is remarkable that thanks to your activity the production of wild rubber will soon reach roughly 1000 tons." But, he added, "it is nevertheless important for us to remain vigilant that this intense effort leave populations enough respite to tend to their own crops."[77] Similarly, a 1944 economic report for the Cameroonian region of Nyong and Sanaga attests to the population's exhaustion due to the intensity of the rubber campaigns. Perhaps predictably, the resource was also growing scarce. The document reads, "Increasingly, latex must be harvested on the edges of the subdistrict, or even in neighboring areas. . . . Entire families, whole villages become nomadic for months on end. A deep weariness reigns among the local populations. It is both likely and desirable for the end of the war to bring a close to this irrational practice."[78] In the subdistrict of Mayana in Congo, an administrator noted that same year, "The collection of wild rubber begun here in June 1942 has totally dried up local deposits. While it lasted, it certainly brought considerable wealth to the villages."[79] Finally, in the outskirts of Brazzaville in 1945, one official announced, "The rubber campaign was cancelled mid-year as it was rendered very difficult because of the disappearance of the rhizomes near the villages."[80]

This second golden age of rubber in FEA and Cameroon had lasted from 1942 to 1944. In 1944, Fighting France leaned on its new colonial acquisitions previously controlled by Vichy in West Africa and Madagascar for wild rubber. Thus, Côte d'Ivoire exported 1,412 tons of rubber in 1944, whereas it had only produced 18 tons in 1939. Entire Ivorian villages now emptied or fled to Liberia to avoid the horrors of forest rubber collection.[81] FEA and Cameroon's scenario from 1942 to 1944 was being replayed in French West Africa.

### Experiences, Reactions, and Testimonies

Thanks to interviews conducted in 1982, Léonard Sah was able to reconstitute the unusual school trips that marked the Free French era in rural Cameroon. "Teachers deserted the classroom to find rubber," he observed. Sah added: "at the head of their classes, they moved like nomads, from one corner to another of the tropical forest to collect the

---

[77] ANOM GGAEF 4(2) D 76, Fortuné to the head of Sangha, May 13, 1944.
[78] ANCMR APA 11655, economic report for 1944, p. 3.
[79] ADN 116PO/1/106, Mayana subdistrict, economic report, 1944.
[80] ADN 116PO/1/71, Brazzaville subdistrict, political report, 1945.
[81] Lawler, p. 98.

product.... Once they had amassed enough forest rubber, they returned to the village."[82]

Local populations typically found this work difficult and many sought to avoid it. On July 15, 1942, the chief of Fort-Rousset (modern-day Owando) in French Congo scrawled in his official diary: "Lengthy discussion with the chiefs about increasing the production of palm and rubber. The latter seems not to be in favor with the natives here. I will have to exert close control to ensure that rubber production takes place on a large scale."[83] The head of the department of Alima in Congo recounted in 1942 that the collection of rubber grasses took him back twenty-five years, to a time when he had served as subdistrict chief in Bambari in Oubangui-Chari. He knew from past experience that rubber grass collection and conditioning involved "the most thankless work one could find." He added, "I witnessed the policing and mobilization of populations for months on end. Under the surveillance of militiamen, men, women and children were assembled, left their villages for five or six days to collect rubber. Around the middle of the month, they brought bundles of roots out of the forest before beating them in unison in hangers." He concluded that the work "removed all initiative" from Africans. Mercifully, he wrote, international outrage had put an end to these practices: "FEA was pleased to declare one day, triumphantly, that the collection of wild rubber had ceased." Now the wild rubber chase was back on. The administrator was willing to recognize that "the rubber issue is vital for the Allies to win the war . . . so there is an excuse." But he added, "Yet it is without any enthusiasm that I am witnessing this turning back the clock a quarter century." To this grizzled official, wild rubber conjured up terrible demons, intolerable and obsolete practices reminiscent of the most odious abuses perpetrated by concessionary companies between the late nineteenth century and World War I.[84]

This great leap backwards also involved serious health concerns. A number of reports raise the question of medical consequences linked to the pounding of wild rubber. More worrisome still, sleeping sickness reappeared with a vengeance in several rubber-picking areas. In the Niari region of Congo in 1943, "Sibitti reported that the intensive quest for wild rubber had brought about a recrudescence of trypanosomiasis. It is certain that the natives seeking vines in dense forest galleries or near streams risk

---

[82] Sah, pp. 485–86.
[83] ANOM GGAEF 5Y5, journal de poste, July 15, 1942.
[84] ANOM GGAEF 4(2) D76, economic report for Alima, second semester 1942.

being stung by tsetse flies."[85] Similarly, according to Guillaume Lachenal, the large-scale return of rubber collection in the Upper-Nyong area of Cameroon was certainly linked to the recrudescence of sleeping sickness in this same region between 1943 and 1946.[86]

As the producers of *Autour de Brazzaville* seemed to recognize implicitly, it required a leap of faith for an audience to accept the camera panning from piles of dried rubber to footage of warplanes. The distance between this raw material and the finished military product is almost unfathomable. In this sense, wild rubber seems the true "roots of the sky," to borrow Free Frenchman Romain Gary's beautiful phrase. Although administrators certainly tapped into African know-how concerning wild rubber plants, were Africans considered and did they consider themselves full partners in the war for rubber and the broader war effort? What was their perception of their place in this global chain? Cameroonian historian Léon Kaptué seems skeptical of triumphalist colonial reports suggesting that the local population collected rubber enthusiastically "having understood the necessity of producing this substance to the Allies so that they might crush the Axis as quickly as possible."[87] Retrieving 1940s' African perceptions of this matter is a virtually impossible task. I would suggest, however, that an alternate African reading of a resource's utility can prove revealing in itself, even, or perhaps especially, if it is fabricated, appropriated, or diverted. Consider recent anthropological work on the idea that rubies might possess a military function.[88] In other words, some Africans likely did not believe the explanations they were given about the final destination of the rubber they brought to the authorities. However, in her interviews conducted in the Sangha Valley in the Central African Republic (former Oubangui-Chari), Tamara Giles-Vernick observes, on the contrary, the pride that one of her interlocutors displayed on this very score. He stressed the point that before producing it themselves, "white people" first came to the Sangha's forests to "make feet for their cars."[89]

At the time, Germaine Krull captured the effects of the rush on wild rubber in FEA, especially on women and children.[90] Her memoirs and

[85] ANOM GGAEF 4(2) D76, political report for Niari, second semester 1943.

[86] Lachenal, pp. 149–50.

[87] Léon Kaptué, *Travail et main-d'œuvre au Cameroun sous régime français, 1916–1952* (Paris: L'Harmattan, 1986), p. 169.

[88] See Andrew Walsh, "In the Wake of Things: Speculating in and about Sapphires in Northern Madagascar," *American Anthropologist*, 106, 2, 2004, pp. 225–37.

[89] Giles-Vernick, p. 163.

[90] On Germaine Krull, see Kim Sichel *Germaine Krull, Photographer of Modernity* (Boston: MIT Press, 1999); Kim Sichel, "Germaine Krull and *L'Amitié Noire*: World War II and French Colonialist Film" in *Colonialist Photography: Imag(in)ing Race and Place,*

photographs stored at the Folkwang Museum in Essen reveal little of the brazen confidence in Free French Africa's productivity that permeates *Autour de Brazzaville*. Indeed, this volunteer for the Free French information services seems to have taken stock of the growing disjuncture between what her propaganda services trumpeted, and the reality on the ground. Her reaction to the rubber market she witnessed at Mayana, outside of Brazzaville, in September 1943, is worth citing in detail:

> The market at Mayana is a kind of crossroads; a large ceiba tree, a few leaf huts, the hanger of Antonio's [rubber] company, the trucks awaiting the rubber, and that is all. Some hundred women and men crouch under a burning sun. The market runs like cotton markets in other places. There is a large scale, across from which are seated two elders, generally the village chiefs, wearing well-buttoned uniforms and a helmet... Next to them is an employee of the company who weighs each parcel; another notes the weight in a large register, and a third hands the woman a piece of paper indicating the weight of the rubber she has just deposited. The rubber is then heaved into trucks and the woman goes to join the line of others waiting for their pay. They are given half or a third in cash, and for the rest they are handed merchandise they never asked for: storm lights, shovels, spoons, all sorts of things that are completely useless to them, but which are a way of profitably liquidating stocks in various hangers... The women leave much as they came: resigned and silent. In fifteen days, the region's commander will once again send militiamen to tell the local people how many kilos of rubber they must bring to the next market. I spend part of the morning taking photos of the market, but the expression of sadness and resignation of these people moves me deeply. There is a *je ne sais quoi* that wounds me.[91]

Evidently, entire villages received the order to hunt for wild rubber and to bring it to the authorities for a set price. Krull also highlighted what she considered the useless barter materials being exchanged for rubber.

This testimony is all the more precious given that Krull's pictures engage with her texts and vice versa. What is more, Krull was no ordinary photojournalist. None other than Mann Ray once addressed her as follows: "Germaine, you and I are the greatest photographers of our time, myself in the primitive genre, you in the modern one."[92] Krull's camera captured individual expressions. Among the photos she took but were not utilized by the Free French information services, Figure 10 shows an

edited by Eleanor M. Hight and Gary D. Sampson (London: Routledge, 2002); Kerstein Meincke, "Unter Brüden und Stiefbrüdern: Mythos und Ambivalenz im Afrikabild Germaine Krulls (1942–1944)," Diplomarbeit, Folkwang Hochschule, 2010.

91  FLK Germaine Krull manuscript, pp. 125–26.

92  Cimathèque française brochure held at the FCDG, fonds personnalités, 10.

FIGURE 10. Germaine Krull. Woman seated on the ground at the Mayana rubber market. Photo 147/657/95-1. © Germaine Krull Estate, Folkwang Museum, Essen.

African woman waiting at the Mayana market with her rubber parcels. The picture conveys the woman's fatigue and drawn expression exactly as Krull writes in her text. But it also places a spotlight on the mass of wild rubber at her feet – rubber that is quite literally being brought to the Free French. Other Krull photos held at the Folkwang Museum show children carrying piles of rubber to market. Contrary to mine

FIGURE 11. Germaine Krull, August 1943. Mural fresco photographed in a "Banda village" in Oubangui-Chari, likely depicting the harvesting and sale of wild rubber. Photo 147/604/95-1. © Germaine Krull Estate, Folkwang Museum, Essen.

work, rubber collection involved women and children as well as adult men.

During one of her travels in Oubangui-Chari, Krull trained her camera on a fresco painted on the front of an African dwelling (Figure 11). The photo's legend remains unfortunately vague: "Oubangui-Chari, Banda village, native drawings on the homes, August 1943." It is therefore impossible to ascertain with certainty that the painting on the photo dates from the Free French era. It is even impossible to assert that the commodity being brought to the authorities, before being taken away on an open truck, is definitely rubber. However, much evidence points in this direction. The bags, baskets, and pouches being carried by the Banda women and men in this scene seem too small and variable in size to be cotton, the other Oubangui staple. Beeswax, which was also being harvested in the area, was not carried on one's hip in this way or on one's head in a raffia bag. If this were indeed wild rubber, its extraction had practically ceased in the area by the 1920s, while it massively resumed in 1942 (the truck seems more likely from 1942 than 1919). For all of

FIGURE 12. Africans arriving at the Lebango wild rubber market, French Congo, 1943. Library of Congress, LC-USZ62–130448.

these reasons, it appears likely to me that Krull captured a rare Central African reading of the very same rubber collection campaign she was busy photographing for the Free French authorities. The fresco's right side shows the market and the rubber being weighed. On the left, Banda women and men can be seen carrying the roots and vines. In the center, we witness the rubber's departure by truck to parts unknown. This fleeting testimony speaks to a local experience of the scramble for resources that no doubt defined the Free French period for rural populations.

Another set of photographs (Figures 12–15) held at the Library of Congress, and taken in the French Congo the same very same year, sheds further light on the markets described and photographed by Krull. The first one (Figure 12) shows a column of rubber pickers with their trade instrument, a machete. It also highlights their manner of transporting the product, on their heads, as in the Oubangui fresco. Figures 13 and 14 reveal the business of the Lebango rubber market and the lengthy queues that formed as Congolese rubber collectors waited to receive a ticket for finished goods and a set amount of cash. A "majordomo" operates the

FIGURES 13 AND 14. Weighing of wild rubber at the Lebango wild rubber market, French Congo, 1943. Library of Congress, LC-USW33-031073-D and LC-USW33-031074D.

FIGURE 15. Lebango, French Congo. "A store where the natives buy what they need after they sell the wild rubber they have gathered at the monthly rubber market." Library of Congress, LC-USW3-031609-D.

scale, while colonial officials – the only white people in the scene and not coincidentally the only ones seated – meticulously record the weights. A wooden rack in the foreground serves to stock and dry the rubber. A truck in the background stands at the ready to depart with the precious substance.

Figure 15 in this same Library of Congress series shows a shop outside the rubber market. We have seen that these stores were designed to incite rubber production among local populations. Its shelves featured cotton textiles, which we know were being acquired from America through the Lend-Lease program.[93] The stall also sold American cigarettes (Albert brand), tin containers, and blankets. Above the counter, a series of posters presented an impressive display of American air and sea power. Each image of bombers and destroyers was accompanied by a French-language

---

[93] AOL, France libre 4B colonies, France Libre to Washington, May 31, 1943.

text. President Franklin D. Roosevelt's likeness appears on the right. The exchange that Congolese rubber collectors undertook here visually implicated them in the war effort. But it also exposed them to a propaganda battle brewing between America and Free France: the stall presented no image of General de Gaulle, no Cross of Lorraine to match the confident portraits of Roosevelt.

### Financing Free France

In the wake of negotiations between Free French, British, and U.S. authorities, on April 29, 1942, René Pleven compiled a list of goods whose production Free French Africa was supposed to step up. These ranged from rubber to oils and tin – the latter reserved for the United States. Gold occupied an altogether separate place in this ranking. Pleven indicated, "Note that from the standpoint of our allies, gold is not mentioned. However, we have a particular stake in maintaining its production for it contributes to our financial and monetary independence."[94]

In the endless commodities lists the Allies dispatched to Brazzaville that invariably began with rubber, gold was conspicuously absent. Yet for reasons of sovereignty, Gaullist authorities considered it essential. In late August 1940 de Gaulle wrote to British authorities that he hoped to get hold of Bank of France gold stashes in French West Africa in order "to cover the purchase of war material from the United States. Gold would cover the purchase of material that would be undertaken with my agreement, by the British government in order to arm forces under my orders."[95] The failure of the Anglo-Gaullist operation on Dakar in September 1940 meant that the precious metal would need to be found elsewhere. Already, gold figured at the heart of a strategy for financial autonomy.

To be sure, Charles de Gaulle and Winston Churchill reached an August 7, 1940, agreement on funding the Gaullist movement. But the general clung to his desire to maintain as much independence as possible. The August 1940 accord granted a right of control to the British ministry of finances and therefore masked an "original inequality" between the two parties. It also stipulated that Free French expenses would have to be reimbursed after the end of the conflict. This was a British loan and

---

[94] ANOM GGAEF, 6B 712, Free French London to Brazzaville, April 29, 1942.
[95] Charles de Gaulle, *Lettres, notes et carnets (1940–1941)*, London, August 26 or 29, 1940, p. 99.

not a gift, and one more reason for the maverick French general to fund his movement as much as possible with gold drawn from colonial regions under his control. In December 1941, the Caisse centrale de la France libre opened on Threadneedle Street in London. It is there that Free French gold was dispatched. After the war, this link with Africa would endure, for the Caisse would turn into the French development agency (Agence française du développement).[96] What is more, as Philippe Oulmont has demonstrated, the first printing of Free French banknotes depended on this gold.[97]

Because of its special significance to the Free French cause, gold was deliberately kept out of the commercial agreements ratified between Free France and Great Britain. "I consider that our deal with the British government on the use of gold must not be included in the agreement on FEA because of possible repercussions on Free France's monetary and financial situation,"[98] wrote de Gaulle on January 8, 1941, to the high commissioner of Free French Africa, Edgard de Larminat.

In fact, FEA and Cameroonian gold was filling several different coffers. The Free French administration in Africa taxed it at its source. This proved rewarding as the precious metal became nearly twice as important to the Free French treasury between 1940 and 1942 as timber, the golden egg of years past.[99] But the balancing act proved tricky. Indeed, Gaullist authorities sought to obtain sufficient foreign currency for Free French Africa to purchase U.S. and British material. But they still needed to heed General de Gaulle's instructions, according to which "FEA and Cameroon's gold exports aimed at acquiring dollars ... need to be reduced to a minimum and tightly controlled ... by the Free French administration." Mostly, the general insisted on "a percentage being reserved to General de Gaulle's use."[100] A decision dated April 26, 1941, specifies. "As of now, half of all of FEA's gold production shall be ceded to the head of the Free French as a contribution to the war effort of the allied governments."[101]

---

[96] Crémieux-Brilhac, *La France libre*, pp. 85 and 88; Jay Winter and Antoine Prost, *René Cassin* (Paris: Fayard, 2011), p. 154; and the brochure entitled *La caisse centrale de la France libre: de Gaulle's bank in London*.

[97] Oulmont, *Pierre Denis*, p. 201.

[98] ANOM GGAEF 5D 290, de Gaulle, January 8, 1941.

[99] ANOM Cab 55, Valentin-Smith report, 1942. Indeed, timber exports dropped precipitously under Free France, with Cameroon's falling from 41,000 to 20,400 tons between 1938 and 1944. Catherine Suzanne Mpandjo Sombé, "Le commerce extérieur du Cameroun, 1930–1980," PhD thesis, University of Bordeaux, 2013, p. 285.

[100] ANC GGAEF 539, Note for the director of finances, Brazzaville, August 19, 1941.

[101] ANC GGAEF 539, decision of April 26, 1941, signed Eboué (file entitled 1942).

This decision raised some eyebrows in Brazzaville, where tensions once again arose between the high commissioner and the governor-general. In March 1941, the former contended to the latter that "the funds deriving from the sale of gold to the British government" were partly reinvested into British war bonds. The treasury in Brazzaville countered with the hope that the gold could help Free French Africa itself. High commissioner Adolphe Sicé retorted, in General de Gaulle's name, that the acquisition of the bonds "would render an additional service to Great Britain, which is the cause we should be ceaselessly helping. Our policy is directed to winning the war, a task we are undertaking in concert with Great Britain, with the objective of expelling the Germans from our national territory."[102]

In the summer of 1942, the Caisse centrale de la France libre proved more flexible on the matter. It seemed to bend slightly on the policy of African gold as Free France's financial touchstone. On July 31, 1942, it telegraphed the following message to Brazzaville:

> From the standpoint of the war effort of the United Nations, it is undeniably illogical for us to be devoting roughly twenty thousand workers in Africa to extract gold, when the United States possesses abundant stockpiles. We are examining ultra-confidentially and in a purely hypothetical way whether it might be possible for the Caisse Centrale to obtain from the U.S.A. the equivalent of FEA's war production or to be more precise, the amount we would no longer be extracting from FEA were we to cease gold mining. Gold workers would then be transferred to more useful occupations associated with the war effort.[103]

Thus, Free French officials in London readily recognized that gold mining made no sense from an Allied standpoint. A rogue local administrator in FEA thought much the same, and in July 1942 began channeling laborers from gold mines to road works, before having his wrists slapped for doing so.[104] Having reached a similar conclusion himself in January 1943, the consul general of the United States in Brazzaville indicated to the State Department that the focus on gold in Gabon was hampering that territory's ability to produce rubber. He consequently advised Washington to supply Free France in gold, so that FEA and Cameroon might better concentrate on rubber.[105] However, relations between Free France and

---

[102] ANOM GGAEF 3B 1091, Sicé to the treasurer, March 31, 1941.

[103] ANC GGAEF 82, Caisse centrale to Brazzaville, July 31, 1942. The same telegram is in ANF 3AG1 167.

[104] ANC GGAEF 82, Brazzaville, July 17, 1942, telegram 564 DDF.

[105] NARA RG 84, Classified general records, 1942–44, U.S. Consulate Brazzaville, UD 2519, box 2, telegrams from Taylor, January 12, 1943.

the United States never proved warm or stable enough to justify changing Free France's policy. Félix Eboué's compromise solution involved concentrating gold production in large mines starting in 1942.

## Output and Working Conditions

Beginning in 1941, gold production in Gabon experienced "meteoric growth."[106] Mines in Gabon and Moyen-Congo were the sites of frenetic activity answering Free France's call for the precious metal. Thus, a political report from the region of Franceville in Gabon in the second semester of 1941 reveals, "much labor has been provided to the gold mines. They employed some 500 workers all from Franceville...By year's end we registered a serious amount of gold produced."[107]

Statistics confirm the rapid rise in gold production in FEA. While the federation only produced 668.4 kg of raw gold in 1937 and 1,738.1 kg in 1939, it reached the following levels under Fighting France: 2,476.4 kg in 1940, 2,993.2 kg in 1941, 2,943 kg in 1942, 2,772.8 kg in 1943, and finally 2,580.3 kg in 1944. Within FEA, Gabon led the way, followed by Oubangui-Chari until 1943, at which point Moyen-Congo vaulted into second place.[108] Cameroon's totals mirrored those of Oubangui-Chari, rising from 544.6 kg in 1940 to 710 kg in 1941, 717 kg in 1942 before dipping to 678 kg in 1943.[109]

FEA and Cameroon's gold mines were above ground and fairly rudimentary.[110] Conditions often proved more trying still than those in the rubber sector. The governor of Gabon recognized in January 1941:

> One cannot count on the natives for seeking out gold. They have an insurmountable repugnance for this form of work. It is indeed very difficult since miners must spend the whole day semi-immersed in muddy and often nauseatingly disgusting water. The washing techniques presently used do not allow for any other solution. One can readily understand why natives would want to avoid this form of work.[111]

In other words, strenuous manual labor endured because mechanization had not reached FEA. In the department of Sangha, administrator Marius Camp observed in August 1942, "[mining mogul] Ménard must make an effort to replace manual labor with machinery. In this regard, the method

[106] Ebako, p. 281.
[107] ANC GGAEF 134, Franceveille political report, second semester 1941.
[108] Ibid, p. 128.
[109] *Annnuaire statistique du Cameroun* Vol. 1, 1938–45, p. 82.
[110] Sah, p. 502.
[111] ANOM GGAEF 2H 18, governor of Gabon to governor general, January 4, 1941.

I witnessed his company using to wash the sand and stones in the sluice could be performed differently; at the very least, simple brooms made on location, would help prevent silex from slicing open the hands of workers."[112]

To the inherent difficulty of this line of work, one should add the countless vexations, abuses, and humiliations endured by African mine workers. In 1942, the head of the Moyen-Congo learned that "the workers we provide Mr. Ménard only remain in his service by force and are paid ridiculously slim salaries next to what they could earn collecting rubber."[113] Moreover, this same Ménard often withheld pay as a method of punishment against those whose gold quota was not reached (this on an already "minimum" wage). The governor reacted vigorously to this news, inquiring about Ménard's food allowance to his employees, no doubt suspecting abuses in this realm as well. Yet physical abuse of all kinds persisted. In March 1942 during a tour of gold mines, Governor Valentin-Smith reported to Félix Eboué that he found it difficult to persuade mining operators not to beat their African employees. A certain Hepcée apparently told him that "the native considers the mine to be a penal colony, and we must therefore act accordingly." The governor of Gabon specified, "European personnel is persuaded that output can only be achieved through physical constraints exercised upon laborers."[114]

In August 1942, officials interrogated thirty-five "deserters" from the S.M.K. mine in Congo. They claimed to have left their quarry for the following reasons. First of all, their employers "beat them continually at work." Secondly, "they were not allowed to seek treatment in Kayes when they were ill." Thirdly, they possessed no paperwork and received a meager "fifty francs by month's end, which is not enough for people living far from home." Caught by S.M.K.'s private police, they sought the colonial administration's help, insisting that "under no circumstances do we want to return to the gold mine."[115]

Other testimonies provide helpful outside corroborations of practices in Free French African gold mines. Again, Germaine Krull proved rather more circumspect toward FEA mining practices than her 1947 film would suggest. In her unpublished manuscript, she described in considerable

[112] ANOM GGAEF 2H 18, Camp to the head of the subdistrict of Wouanke, August 12, 1942.

[113] ANOM GGAEF 2H 18, letter to Fortuné.

[114] ANOM GGAEF 2H 31, report from Valentin-Smith to Félix Eboué, March 31, 1942.

[115] ANOM GGAEF 2H 18, head of the subdistrict of M'Vouti to the head of Kouilou, August 25, 1942.

detail the gold mines at Eteké and N'Djolé in Gabon. In the case of the former (opened in 1937),[116] she noted the mine's isolation, which meant that it needed to be supplied by porters. She added that the mine's operator was carried by a team of eight Africans. Krull estimated that portering cost hundreds of lives, especially women's. Work in the mine was perhaps even less enviable yet. She noticed that the mines stirred terror among the Gabonese. She spoke at length with a local official and a doctor who tried in vain to reduce the mine's insatiable appetite for African laborers, limiting the number of workers recruited in the villages, and removing the ill from service. They were ultimately rebuffed when the mine operators complained to Brazzaville that the war effort was being undermined. The war, it seemed, could be invoked to justify all excesses.[117]

At Armand Vigoureux's operation in N'Djolé, Krull described conditions as follows:

> Here is the mine. Hundreds of blacks dig the ground, collecting it with a shovel and throwing it into small carts. From there, the precious earth is transported to a sluice. This sluice is a kind of wooden conduit in which the blacks throw the earth from the cart. A rudimentary water system runs like a stream through the sluice and washes this earth. This earth cascades down, large stones are caught by the first sieve, smaller ones in a second sieve, then a third, until we reach a very fine sieve that captures the gold... Surveillance of blacks is very strict. Even though they are already nude, except for a kind of cloth around their waist, when they return to the village they are thoroughly searched. Their mouths are examined, their teeth, under their tongues. Some occasionally manage to make off with gold, but when they are caught they are beaten almost to death, therefore theft occurs only very rarely. They work twelve to fifteen hours a day. The work is exhausting. The shovels full of earth are heavy to throw up to the sluice, which is higher than the riverbed. Once the gold is washed, collected and sorted, the powder is blown and collected in boxes, then transported to Brazzaville... Mortality rates are high among the blacks in the mines. The food is insufficient. They eat only manioc and occasionally dried fish, rarely meat. The administration says meat cannot be found; when in fact the forest is full of game. This waste of humanity is the reason for which the mine's administration must so often renew its labor and call on new recruits. The human waste is terrible.[118]

Once more, Krull's camera and words offer overlapping perspectives. Figure 16 shows two young African workers throwing earth into the

---

[116] Gray, p. 207.
[117] FLK Germaine Krull manuscript, p. 70.
[118] Ibid, pp. 96–97.

FIGURE 16. Germaine Krull. Workers toiling in the M'Vouti gold mine, April 1943. Photo 147/447/95-1. © Germaine Krull Estate, Folkwang Museum, Essen.

sluice at another locale, the M'Vouti mine in Congo, also belonging to Vigoureux. As in the mine of N'Djolé, the workers are barely clothed so as to avoid them pocketing nuggets. Just as Krull describes, they are clearly struggling to shovel the earth upwards. The legend specifies, "M'Vouti, Mr. Vigoureux's mining operation. The earth containing gold is brought near the 'table' to be washed." In the upper background one can make out a waterspout designed for this purpose.

The French colonial archives further flesh out this picture. Workplace accidents were common at Armand Vigoureux' mine. On November 28, 1942, Kinga Mouele, a former employee of Vigoureux's M'Vouti operation, launched a grievance against his manager. He had lost a leg in a mine accident. From Poto-Poto he addressed his complaint to the top, right to Governor Eboué. Mouele flatly refused the 1,500 franc payout that Vigoureux offered by way of indemnity, for he preferred to continue working, something his boss "refused." The worker pursued, "Instead of receiving a lump sum, I only want him to keep paying me every month, in keeping with the rules." The governor of Congo suggested referring the matter to arbitration.[119]

Little wonder, then, that mining operators struggled to find and keep laborers in their service. Between 1940 and January 1941 alone, 76 of Vigoureux's 1,764 mine workers had managed to flee his operation at M'Vouti.[120] The terror the mine instilled was certainly nothing new; what had changed since 1940 was the owner's ability to circumvent all rules in the name of the war. One report advocated three solutions to help stem desertions: establishing a contract for every employee, improving dialog between the administration and the mine operators, and finally, "treating the native firmly."[121] And yet, there was no stopping the hemorrhage of workers. In September 1942, Vigoureux and his colleagues from M'Vouti seized the opportunity presented by the visit of an official to complain that their workers were deserting to go collect rubber for the Compagnie française du Congo occidental. This was "a less difficult form of work for the same salary," they added. In reality, rubber was generally more lucrative than gold for African workers. Vigoureux and his consorts also suggested amending work permits so that they could include photographs, as well as improving worker housing.[122]

Recruitment proved as challenging as retention. On May 8, 1942, Vigoureux complained to the governor of Moyen-Congo on just this score, noting that he had no better luck recruiting in Mossendjo than he did in Komono. His middleman had only been able to scrounge together eight and twenty-eight men, respectively, in these two locales. Three days earlier, Henri de Suremain, the head of the subdistrict of Mossendjo, had reached a telling conclusion. It was hardly surprising that Vigoureux

[119] ANOM GGAEF 2H 25, Fortuné, December 18, 1942, and Kinga Mouele, November 28, 1942.

[120] ANOM, GGAEF 2 H 25, "Compte-rendu" on labor, February 26, 1941.

[121] ANOM, GGAEF 2H 25, February 26, 1941.

[122] ANOM GGAEF 4(2) D75, Kouilou inspection report, September 21–23, 1942.

struggled to recruit workers for his M'Vouti operation, he noted. For in this subdistrict, more than a thousand workers were already toiling in the region's gold mines, roughly the same number of public works projects, private companies demanded roughly a hundred porters a day each, and all of this while the area was asked to increase its output of rubber, palm oil, wax, and rice for the Allied cause. In sum, explained Suremain, "The truth is that we have pressed this orange so hard that we can no longer draw any more juice from it."[123]

Refusals left Vigoureux unfazed. On July 5, 1941, he requested one hundred workers from the Niari department, "in order to complete our staffing and to open a new mine" at M'Vouti.[124] The administration rejected this request, suggesting that Vigoureux might try again the year following.[125] In reality, administrators were beginning to band together to stem the mine's insatiable appetite for workers. On June 16, 1942, the head of the subdistrict of Divénié in the Niari department had sought his superior's support in matters of gold. He had insisted that recruitment from outside Niari be halted, given that Niari was struggling to fulfill its own agricultural, portering, and road needs. According to this official, the roughly hundred men Vigoureux had recruited there through an intermediary were the straw that could break the camel's back.

In November 1942, the department head of Niari openly complained of Vigoureux's helter-skelter recruitment practices. He demanded that his middlemen be reigned in. That same month, the head of the Pool department, also contacted by Vigoureux, responded that he could not provide him with a single worker because of the needs of other sectors, including the transport of lead ore.[126] These stands flew in the face of the Office du Travail, instituted in 1942 to facilitate the transfer of workers. They suggest that the demands of the gold magnates had become untenable to many government officials.

Indeed, colonial officials often thwarted the most outrageous demands of the mining operators. The Eboué administration even attempted to reform the entire sector by limiting portering work and by insisting that mine workers be accompanied by their families and lodged in new villages. However, even these seemingly liberal measures could end in coercion. In July 1943, the governor of French Congo issued the following message

---


[123] ANOM GGAEF 2H 18, H. de Suremain to Vigoureux, May 5, 1942.
[124] ANOM GGAEF 2H 18, M'Vouti, July 5, 1941.
[125] ANOM GGAEF 2H 18, Brazzaville, October 16, 1941, and Brazzaville, April 13, 1941.
[126] ANOM GGAEF 2H 18, head of the Pool department, November 4, 1942.

to the head of the department of Franceville: "Kindly ensure that the labor rules are strictly applied, watching especially that the wives of those recruited [to work for Vigoureux] be forced to accompany their husbands, except in circumstances of exceptional emergency (in which case I wish to hear about them)."[127] In seeking to maintain family cohesion, the administration seemingly opened the door to forcible abductions in the name of a patriarchal reading of the African family. Henceforth, not only would the freedom of movement of workers at the mine be circumscribed, that of their spouses would be as well.

The gold magnates' production imperative thus clashed almost systematically with the administration's bid to uphold safeguards. In the old conflict that pitted civil authorities against colonial entrepreneurs, the latter most often emerged victorious. On January 28, 1941, the head of the department of Sangha, Marius Camp, addressed the following letter to a certain Lecompte, who ran the gold mine at Kangamatoko in Moyen-Congo: "Out of the twenty or so Europeans who employ laborers in this department you are pretty much the only one . . . not capable of retaining your employees." The official continued, "Some veteran colonial hands have so many workers that they employ them in shifts . . . Elsewhere I find myself obliged to stem the desertion of villages to other operators . . . All of this tells me that there is something flawed in the way you treat your workforce." In spite of his repeated warnings, he nonetheless agreed to Lecompte's request for a revealing motive, "because it is currently in the colony's interest to extract gold, I am ready once more to give you my support to recruit your labor force and those who will supply it with food."[128]

Indeed, gold had become as sacrosanct as rubber, although for very different reasons. In a firmly worded May 20, 1942, letter denouncing abuses in Gabon's gold mines, Félix Eboué emitted the following theory to the governor of Gabon:

> Among the psychological origins of the current crisis that is shaking our mines, I think I was able to discern an interesting point in your report and from conversations I had with various officials: a propensity on the part of mining operators to consider the gold mines as somehow taboo, as lying outside the law precisely because they operate in the national interest. This, in turn, leads the miners to believe they possess special rights, especially with respect to labor practices.[129]

[127] ANOM GGAEF 2H 18, Fortuné to the head of the departement of Franceville, July 31, 1943.

[128] ANOM GGAEF 2H 18, Camp to Lecompte, January 28, 1941.

[129] ANOM GGAEF 3B 2382, Eboué to Libreville, May 20, 1942.

According to the governor general, mining operators deemed themselves invulnerable. In a letter to Pleven dated November 1942, Eboué did not mince words. He drew the following bleak picture: "Gold mining is undertaken in defiance of common sense. Dozens of incapable misfits, presenting a range of different forms of incompetence, have hurled themselves on this new vein. Rather than dissuade them, the administration has encouraged them." The governor-general even perceived in this new gold rush an echo of the okoumé timber madness that had once gripped Gabon. He therefore asked for "a step backwards." Since mid-1941, he noted, he had refused to grant any new mining permits. He hoped to impose limits on current operators, most notably by undertaking family grouping for workers. Finally, he received permission from General de Gaulle in person to punish the operators who were guilty of the worst abuses.[130]

Yet the mining magnates held their own. Eboué's measures may have prevented the opening of new operations, they did not fundamentally change matters in existing ones. On February 2, 1942, geologist P. Tkatchenko of the Hausser mining group addressed an intemperate letter to the head of the Fougamou-Sindara subdistrict. Deploring the many "desertions" from gold mines, he invoked one episode in particular, during the administrator's previous visit to the mine: "Each of the mine workers asked you the same question when you last visited: 'when will our contract end?' You answered that in wartime, Europeans are forced to stay at their posts and that natives must do the same." Whereupon the geologist remarked, "This is true, but if such is the case, then the administration must take very serious steps to stop deserters and inflict exemplary punishment on them, punishment that would dissuade anyone from deserting. Why not consider natives deserting from the gold mine as tantamount to military desertion in time of war?"[131]

### Weighing Gold Against Rubber

The administration recognized gold's terrifying cost. A July 1941 report reads, "One point jumps out from our data: the extreme instability of labor in Gabon. The situation is more or less the same in every gold mine across the territory." Certain parallels emerge between this gold rush and the concurrent rubber fever. In his 1942 report on the Nyanga region

130 ANOM GGAEF 3B 2382, Eboué to Pleven, November 10, 1942.
131 ANOM GGAEF 2H 18, P. Tkatchenko, Ikoy, February 2, 1942.

of Gabon, the region chief complained of the bottomless appetite of the gold mines for local laborers. He then segued to the trypanosomiasis epidemic gripping his region: 400 new cases in 1942.[132] The recruitment and movement of miners across the forests was likely linked to this recrudescence, much as the collection of rubber was.

Finally, the gold rush confirmed Eboué and Laurentie's worst fears. They who fretted above all over the "uprooting" of Africans must surely have cringed on reading the report of the head of the Ouham department in Oubangui-Chari, who noted that the increase in mining activity was "creating a proletariat." Governor André Latrille countered with the measures at his disposal: attenuating change by ensuring that workers be accompanied by their families, grouping "natives of a same race" in the same neighborhoods, and so on.[133]

While gold and rubber served different purposes, both commodities are profoundly revealing of the run on resources that occurred under Free French rule. Serving the Allied cause, rubber played a major role in Gaullist strategy. In 1945, the French ministry of foreign affairs presented France's role in the war as follows to the U.S. ambassador: "As you know, France brought to the war effort its production of African rubber."[134] Gold, conversely, played the opposite role by guaranteeing Free France's financial autonomy and a degree of emancipation from the United Kingdom and the United States. In fact, the failure of the 1942 scheme to stop gold mining in FEA so as to focus totally on rubber production highlights that Free French authorities ultimately deemed Free France's foundations too fragile, its international situation too precarious, to rely on the United States for its gold supply.

For Africans, the consequences of the gold and rubber races proved ambivalent. Local populations were connected into the global economy through rubber sales. However, work in the forest and in the mine also involved a range of abuses and suffering, not to mention flashbacks to the harshest eras of colonial rule in the region. The semi-nomadic lifestyle that wild rubber collection entailed caused a recrudescence in sleeping sickness. Mine workers toiled in dreadful conditions while their managers suddenly became untouchable by virtue of the war effort. In a terrible irony, Eboué and Laurentie realized that FEA and Cameroon were being "proletarized" on their watch. Their subordinates reported moreover that

---

[132] ANOM GGAEF 4(1) D50, political report Nyanga region, 1942.
[133] ANOM GGAEF 4(3) D52, Latrille, May 1, 1942.
[134] ADN 378PO/C/2/172, letter to the U.S. Ambassador, June 16, 1945.

Free French Africa was reaching its limit, as it was literally being bled dry. Free French Africa was an orange from which the last drop had been squeezed, remarked Suremain. In this sense, the entry of French West and North Africa, as well as Madagascar and the French Caribbean, into the fray in 1943 must surely have seemed long overdue from the vantage point of Brazzaville.

# Chapter 7

# Colonial Practices and Wartime Imperatives

FEA and Cameroon had certainly experienced forced labor and abuses for decades prior to 1940. Catherine Coquery-Vidrovitch has described how FEA's entire economy had long been "founded on coercion" and "based on crime." In the late nineteenth and early twentieth centuries, wholesale murder was commonplace in colonial Central Africa. Hostage-takings, corporal punishments, sexual violence, and legions of other crimes constituted a kind of "exploitation method" predicated on terror.[1] In the 1920s and 1930s, Albert Londres, André Gide, and Marcel Homet among others, deplored some of the abuses committed in the region and testified to the devastating human effects of the Congo to Ocean railway construction project. Organizations like the League for the Rights of Man regularly denounced timber and rubber companies. Whether formulated by the League of Nations, by journalists, or by concerned travelers, such criticisms shone the spotlight of international public opinion on Central Africa. The Komintern and anti-colonial nationalist groups also seized the image of colonial slaughter along the Congo River Basin.[2]

The interwar years brought some change, but no revolution in labor practices. Despite its unique status, the situation in French mandate Cameroon did not differ fundamentally from that in FEA. As J. P. Daughton has shown, in 1926 the World Labor Organization received a report suggesting that working conditions were actually harsher in

[1] Coquery-Vidrovitch, *Le Congo*, pp. 178–80.
[2] J. P. Daughton, "Behind the Imperial Curtain: International Humanitarian Efforts and the Critique of French Colonialism in the Interwar Years," *French Historical Studies*, 34:3 (2011), p. 517.

Cameroon than in its colonial neighbor.[3] FEA also struggled to reform. Other than a brief respite under the more liberal Governor François-Joseph Reste between 1935 and 1939, it remained in Elikia M'Bokolo's words: "The domain of brutal economic exploitation and uncompromising political domination."[4] Gaullist rule ushered in a recrudescence of surveillance and control and a redoubling of forced labor in the wake of the Governor Reste hiatus, all for the sacrosanct war effort. In its name, colonial authorities stepped up production, and developed transport routes in a veritable binge of coercion.

In the realm of labor, two decisive turning points can be identified in Cameroon and FEA. The first took place in September 1939 with the declaration of war, the second in August 1940 with regime change and the advent of Free French Africa. The state of war brought about a tightening of labor practices. In May 1940, FEA reached an agreement with mining groups, stipulating that African miners would no longer enjoy weekends off. The accord also extended the workday by thirty minutes and shortened lunch breaks by the same amount of time.[5] Other sectors followed suit. In the logging business, that same month notices announced the extension of the workday to twelve hours.[6] This answered the request of miner Armand Vigoureux, who dabbled in timber as well as gold. He contended that the measure mirrored metropolitan war acts extending work hours in certain key areas.[7] Yet labor practices in FEA only distantly resembled those in France, if at all. In fact, the head of the Kouilou district expressed complete consternation at the comparison, noting that French workers were paid by the hour and not by the month, as was the practice in FEA. In Equatorial Africa, then, the measure was tantamount to lengthening the workday significantly, without any commensurate salary increase.[8]

Was the Gaullist discourse of increased productivity after August 1940 but a mirage? Quite the contrary. In January 1943, the head of the Djambala region in Congo wrote Governor Eboué to tell of a remarkable agricultural success. He boasted of having predicted three years earlier

---

3  Ibid, p. 520.
4  Elikia M'Bokolo, "French Colonial Policy in Equatorial Africa in the 1940s and 1950s," in Prosser Gifford and W. M. Roger Lewis, eds., *The Transfer of Power in Africa, Decolonization, 1940–1960* (New Haven: Yale University Press, 1982), p. 173.
5  ANOM GGAEF 2H 25, Ordre de service, May 23, 1940.
6  ANOM GGAEF 2H 25, Scieries et placages d'Afrique, May 25, 1940.
7  ANOM GGAEF 2H 25, A. Vigoureux to the head of the M'Vouti subdistrict.
8  ANOM GGAEF 2H 25, Jacoulet, May 25, 1940.

that the region would one day become FEA's breadbasket. The official suggested that this regional success story, measured in beans and potatoes, hinged on a single factor: the hardening of colonial practices and the 1940 decision to redouble the war effort. Whereas in 1937 Djambala raised a "mere" 279,000 francs in taxes (130,000 in cash the rest in prestations or labor), in 1943 he bragged of collecting 980,000 francs (600,000 in cash). He concluded that since the colony had joined Free French ranks "the production curve has shot up almost vertically."[9]

Even from a purely productivist standpoint, not every picture was as rosy as this report suggests. Already in 1939, tensions had arisen between the dual necessity to step up output on the one hand and recruit soldiers on the other. In December of the same year, the governor of Gabon expressed satisfaction that the colony, already strapped for labor, would "only" have to contribute another 1,540 fighting men and 3,600 workers to the war effort in 1940.[10]

This was not the only delicate balancing act. The civilian administration of FEA lamented that vital equipment was being commandeered by the military. Thus a 1943 report observed that less timber had been exported than the year prior because of a shortage of vehicles.[11] This particular shortage also flew in the face of attempts in Brazzaville to increase mechanization and guarantee some safeguards for African workers. Indeed, in 1942 Henri Laurentie had sought to curtail the practice of portering, replacing it with mechanized transport.[12] But with the scarcity of trucks, mine operators in particular continued unabashedly to rely on large-scale overland portering. Modern means of transport were all being assigned to General Leclerc's forces.

Eboué and Laurentie's overarching objective, though, remained in theory one of social amelioration, indeed social engineering. Their vision was one of nostalgia for a precolonial, hierarchical, and rural Africa infused with aspects of colonial modernity. In particular, they were wedded to the idea of creating employee villages within short distances of workplaces, a notion likely inspired by similar schemes for worker towns in Europe and America. In August 1942, Laurentie explained, "Stabilizing the workforce means building team spirit, emulation; it also implies facilitating the formation and development of veritable worker villages around

---

9  FCDG, F22, 17, Djambala to Brazzaville, January 8, 1943.
10  ANOM GGAEF 2H 25, Masson, Libreville, December 3, 1939.
11  ANOM GGAEF 5D 299, Brazzaville, October 9, 1943.
12  ANC GGAEF 126, Laurentie, March 7, 1942.

worksites."[13] That same month, Germaine Krull photographed one such nascent village near a mine. She jotted in her journal that previous practices had involved tearing men from their villages, which had resulted in depopulating vast areas.[14] Laurentie and Eboué's reform was thus presented as favoring family units, encouraging stability and sedentariness. It was consequently believed to boost both African societies and the war economy. While some such villages were created, Eboué and Laurentie were the first to recognize that work in the mines remained thankless and indeed murderous. In this realm as well, Free France faced its broken utopia: it proved impossible to reconcile social reform and total war in Africa.

## Forced Labor

Coerced labor had a long history in FEA and Cameroon. Catherine Coquery-Vidrovitch has shown how it lay at the heart of the concession system in Congo, even though it was not inscribed in law per se. Two texts from 1903 and 1907 did attempt to strike a balance by recognizing freedom of work while at the same time criminalizing "desertion." However timid and contradictory, these rules went unheeded on the ground. Since the dawn of the twentieth century, force was almost explicitly recognized as a modus operandi by both the colonial administration and by the concession companies.[15] Historian Léon Kaptué paints an equally somber picture of French labor regimes in Cameroon, based on the chasm separating European and African conceptions, on abuses, and a manifest desire to organize labor distribution for the benefit of European corporations. In early twentieth-century Gabon, forced recruitment in the road construction and okoumé sectors brought about famine through forced population migrations.[16]

The statute labor practiced so widely in FEA until 1946 presents its own implications in the realm of memory. Tamara Giles-Vernick cites an African woman from the Sangha Valley (southern Central African Republic) who asserted that it was her husband, and not the Europeans, who ran forced labor in colonial times. In other instances, Giles-Vernick

---

[13] ANC GGAEF 126, Laurentie to the head of Kouilou province, August 20, 1942.

[14] FLK "Hallo, Hallo, Brazzaville vous parle," p. 71.

[15] Coquery-Vidrovitch, *Le Congo*, pp. 103–15.

[16] Kaptué, *Travail et main-d'œuvre*. Christopher Gray and François Ngolet, "Lambaréné, Okoumé, and the transformation of labor along the Middle Ogooué (Gabon), 1870–1945," *The Journal of African History*, 40, 1999, pp. 97–104.

registers inhabitants recalling forced labor as the monopoly of German colonialism, thereby demonizing the short German era in the region.[17] In other words, the Free French episode constituted but a short phase in a much vaster forced labor phenomenon possessing its own complex, contradictory, and fluctuating memories.

At the time, statute labor assumed a wide range of forms. It was common to demand so-called *prestations* or *corvées* from Africans who could not afford to pay taxes. Penal labor was also widely utilized. In Mokolo, Cameroon, in 1944, a visiting British official was awed by the work accomplished by 400 prisoners who erected houses, maintained roads, and cultivated vegetable gardens.[18] In Chad, those conducting *prestations* toiled on endless road construction projects, while prisoners were assigned to cleaning or public works. Colonial power relations, twinned with the war imperative, served to justify practices that were banned in principle, which is to say forced recruitment and the maintaining of Africans in private-sector posts against their will.

In theory, several international conventions from the 1930s prohibited this last form of forced labor.[19] However, in practice, it occurred on a vast scale in Free French Africa. Courts accommodated the theory and the reality on the ground. On May 15, 1941, the head of the Cameroonian region of Noun informed his subordinates that judgments rendered by the court of Bamiléké "repressing the abandonment of work on European plantations have raised eyebrows from the office of political affairs." In order to avoid "the annulment of these verdicts whose legal basis is undeniably flimsy," he recommended, "Only citing infractions whose materiality cannot be questioned, in particular the offense of vagabondage that tends to fit most cases." This charge "allows an effective repression of infractions in verdicts criticized by the bureau of political affairs." In other words, officials were asked to treat Africans who left the workplace as vagabonds rather than escapees, in order to avoid disapprobation from those fretting for Free France's image.[20]

In Cameroon, the advent of Free France and accompanying war imperatives, provided an opportunity to implement particularly harsh labor regimes that had previously been concocted in the 1930s. In the case of Upper-Nyong, a region as large as Switzerland entirely ruled by colonial

---

[17] Giles-Vernick, pp. 96–97.
[18] BD, Mss Afr. S 940, p. 12.
[19] Kaptué, *Travail et main-d'œuvre*, p. 69.
[20] ANCMR 2AC 5940.

doctors, this implied putting patients to work, even victims of leprosy and sleeping sickness. Guillaume Lachenal has shown how Dr. Jean-Joseph David assigned patients to land clearing and to plantation work. The medic was determined to end what he termed, "the failed principle of freedom of work."[21] The Nola region of Oubangui also proved rife with such abuses. Carlo Toso writes, "As if sleeping sickness were not enough, the chicote was used widely, as were ropes, chains and prison sentences, and the sick were subjected to unremunerated forced labor. Women and girls were subjected to the most serious humiliations. Sunday rest was abolished and the workday lengthened to become exhausting, far surpassing twelve hours a day."[22] Did the advent of Free France in 1940 mark a quantitative or qualitative change in such practices? To be sure, abuses had been legion in the past, recruitment intense. But the scale changed radically in 1940. In the Mbam region of Cameroon, women who had previously been spared were now mobilized to extract rutile in the Mayo-Darlé mine.[23]

In some cases, administrators boasted to their superiors of having recruited workers for private companies. In 1943, the head of the department of Alima proudly reported that he had enrolled a hundred laborers on behalf of the Kouilou mining society. The mines in question were renowned for their abuses, and consequently struggled to attract workers. The governor of French Congo did mention in his response that "the administration's intervention should not go as far as using coercion." But he added that given the war effort and the flouting of such rules in other regions, he considered it "normal" for the head of Alima to "have lent support to the recruiting agent." Two imperatives clashed. On the one hand, one sees a clear desire to heed London's legal concerns, and on the other hand a very strong imperative to recruit laborers at any cost. In the case of the Alima district, the clash between the two resulted in a blind-eye policy.[24]

The tone for such complacency was set high up the ladder. In February 1942, Henri Laurentie sent a secret telegram to the governor of Gabon, Victor Valentin-Smith. He indicated that "the moment was perhaps poorly chosen to pay close attention to infractions to labor law."

---

[21] Lachenal, p. 146.

[22] Carlo Toso, *Centrafrique, un siècle d'évangélisation*, (Bangui: conférence épiscopale centrafricaine, 1994), p. 175.

[23] Memoli-Aubry, p. 245.

[24] ANOM GGAEF 4(2) D76, G. Fortuné, to the head of Alima department, March 11, 1943.

Laurentie deemed that settlers and entrepreneurs "needed to be prepared for the application of the new regime involving the establishment of women and children on worksites." He added, "I know abuses exist, but aren't you concerned that by pursuing them today you might compromise the governor general's reform that will yield much greater results?" Thus, in his bid to implement his pet project of worker villages, Laurentie was willing to ignore a deluge of abuses in the gold-mining sector.[25] Valentin-Smith would not last long. He was replaced in June 1942 by Charles Assier de Pompignan.

Meanwhile, Jean Charles André Capagorry, the head of the Kouilou department, found himself on the receiving end of Armand Vigoureux's insistent requests for labor. Gabriel Emile Fortuné, the head of Moyen-Congo, was brought into the conversation to reject the mining magnate's nervy suggestion of criminalizing "native ill-will or the refusal by native workers to undertake work of national interest for private companies." Fortuné did mention to his interlocutors that the proposal was unnecessary, given that officials could already draw on Félix Eboué's December 12, 1940, circular, which stipulated that "mine deserters should be tracked down and returned to the workplace, after applying disciplinary measures in keeping with the indigénat, whose relevance I accept in matters of desertion from work."[26] Thus, forced labor was not merely tolerated, but fully authorized in the mining sector.

Fortuné did ask his subordinate not to make systematic use of corporal punishment on deserters, as Capagorry had recommended. He also rejected the even cheekier suggestion of criminalizing "disrespectful remarks or attitudes addressed to whites." Here too he opined that the idea was needlessly redundant. Officials could handle such situations with an existing December 1939 decree cracking down on "speech that can provoke disorder."[27] Clearly, high-ranking officials attempted to impose a modicum of textual restraint on rapidly escalating private-sector demands. The war effort had taken on a life of its own, emboldening the likes of Vigoureux. Consider the incredible temerity of proposing to criminalize African irreverence to whites.

Many an official reported that the situation on the ground seemed to be lurching out of control. On his scheduled visit of the Kribi region of

[25] ANOM GGAEF B 712, secret telegram 93/SG, Laurentie to Valentin-Smith, February 1942.
[26] ANOM GGAEF 2H 25, labor, gold mines of Kouilou.
[27] Ibid.

Cameroon in 1941, a stunned administrator found a series of deserted villages. He sought in vain an African chief who could help him with his census.[28] The latter would have served no purpose anyway, for the official in question realized that all inhabitants, chiefs included, had absconded to the rutile mine. Some sleuthing revealed that entrepreneurs had contacted village chiefs directly to recruit laborers, bypassing the colonial administration entirely.[29] In this case, control was exerted entirely by the private sector on its terms.

## The Labor Office and the Eboué-Cassin Clash

In a bid to implement a *dirigiste* war economy and to put in place a tightly controlled labor network, Félix Eboué and Henri Laurentie proposed a significant reform to labor laws. Yet as we have seen, Eboué's labor policy in many ways mirrored that of Pierre Boisson, Vichy's proconsul in West Africa: nostalgic essentialism, a glorification of the peasantry and of traditional hierarchies, a refusal to recognize labor freedom, and a shared belief that the clock needed to be turned back. Obsessed by decline and degeneration, fearing that uprooted villagers might mutate into a dangerous proletariat, Eboué deemed that rural Africans required order, hierarchy, and stability, the European chief taking on the role of an "aristocrat" at the summit of the local pyramid. Finally, Eboué and Boisson shared the "myth of the African traditional community,"[30] to borrow Frederick Cooper's phrase. Eboué's directives to the governor of Gabon in July 1941 confirm these impressions. In order to remedy the labor shortage, Eboué recommended "preventing as much as possible the mix of races and tribes on a single workplace."[31]

In December 1941, Félix Eboué began his vigorous defense of some sweeping reforms to indigenous policy that he had requested from London. His ideas for change, he argued, were not new. They drew from Hubert Lyautey in Morocco, from the British, and others; if his reforms were not passed, he implied, even the Belgians would seem more progressive than the French in FEA. He added that he had used the "pretext" of the labor question to in order to tackle the topic that was dearest to him:

---

[28] Such visits centering on the census had once been the "daily bread and butter" of local colonial officials. See Francis Simonis, *Le Commandant en tournée: Une administration au contact des populations en Afrique Noire coloniale* (Paris: Seli Arslan, 2005), p. 33.

[29] ANCMR 100092, Brette report.

[30] Cooper, *Decolonization*, p. 158.

[31] ANOM, GGAEF, 3B 2381, Instructions for Valentin-Smith.

African demography and quality of life in rural Africa.[32] Eboué's initial proposal expressed "regret" that statute labor could not be suppressed in wartime. But, he hoped, he could rationalize labor and ensure that villages were constructed near workplaces, and families not separated by forced labor practices.[33] While he cited Belgian and British examples, the centerpiece of his reforms, the creation of the Office du travail, likely drew inspiration from a similar system elaborated in French mandate Cameroon in 1937.[34]

To say that Free French in London were unconvinced would be an understatement. It certainly did not help that High Commissioner Sicé had told London that he opposed the scheme.[35] On May 19, 1942, Eboué nudged Pleven, indicating that he had not yet heard back about his project born of "his thirty years of colonial experience that enabled him to prescribe the right remedies [for Free French Africa]."[36] Precisely a month later, London telegraphed Eboué that his sweeping reform of indigenous policy had been blocked by Free France's Justice Minister René Cassin. In reality, as James Lewis has shown, de Gaulle's social adviser Henry Hauck, as well as Free France's Commission de législation, also had a say in the decision.[37] On June 16, Cassin had already expressed reserves. He deemed that the proposed labor reform contravened "international conventions signed and ratified by France on colonial labor."[38] Far from sugarcoating the verdict, the short dispatch from London to Eboué on June 19, 1942, flatly announced, "The main objections are that [your proposals] reinforce the reign of forced labor and end up limiting the administration's powers, by obliging it to accede to any reasonable labor requests from employers."[39] Cassin's commission also rejected the status of "evolved native," a project particularly dear to Eboué, on the grounds that "its very name seems ridiculous."[40] The Free French were deeply uncomfortable to see forced labor and hierarchies formally codified. This echoes a similar trend in the British imperial context in which, as David Killingray has shown, London expressed far greater apprehension about

---

[32] ANOM, 1Affpol 873, Eboué to London, December 20, 1941.
[33] ANOM, 1Affpol 873, decrees presented to the governor-general of FEA.
[34] Kaptué, *Travail et main-d'œuvre*, p. 50.
[35] Weinstein, p. 274.
[36] ANOM, 1Affpol 873, dossier 1, Eboué, May 19, 1942.
[37] James I. Lewis, "Félix Eboué and Late French Colonial Ideology," *Itinerario*, 2002, 26:1, pp. 145–49.
[38] ANOM, 1Affpol 873, dossier 1, Cassin to Pleven, June 16, 1942.
[39] ANOM, GGAEF, 6B 712, London, June 19, 1942.
[40] Ibid.

increasing forced labor circa 1942 than did settlers and other colonials on location in Africa.[41]

The law that Free France finally enacted in January 1942 proved to be a compromise between Eboué's original vision, and Cassin and Hauck's qualms. It did, crucially, establish "in each territory of Equatorial French Africa, an *Office du travail et de la main d'oeuvre indigène* intended to better ensure the principle of liberty of work, and to control recruitment and the use of indigenous labor."[42] As with the laws of 1903 and 1907, labor freedom was paradoxically invoked in a text that actually enabled forced labor. Yet Eboué and Laurentie's undiluted influence also shines through in this 1942 law. For instance, Article 7 reads, "The Office du travail ensures that hiring for a single company take place as much as possible within a same tribe, in order for workers to constitute homogenous villages, composed of natives of a single origin sharing the same customs."[43] This curious mix of preservationism and Taylorism sought to reconcile war imperatives, conflicting visions in London and Brazzaville, a vague tutelary sensibility, and the pressing need to cover labor needs in a territory spanning from the Congo River to the Sahara.

This new instrument ultimately worked to facilitate the movement of workers according to the needs of the war economy. Eboué explained to his subordinates on September 5, 1942, that the delicate balance between local and interregional labor needs had been dangerously compromised. He asked to be henceforth "kept abreast as closely as possible of the labor needs" of each department. He demanded a statement from both commercial and agricultural companies, indicating their number of laborers, specifying their rank, as well as outlining future hiring needs, the possibilities of local recruitment, and so on.[44]

The July 1942 text also created arbitration mechanisms for disputes over so-called desertions. It called, moreover, for regular meetings of the Office du travail. The latter ended up providing the opportunity for mining operators and other entrepreneurs to present their desiderata to the administration. Indeed, mining interests were represented on this body by none other than Armand Vigoureux, in the name of the 20,000 Africans mining in FEA.[45]

[41]  Killingray, p. 70.
[42]  *Journal officiel de l'Afrique équatoriale française*, November 1, 1942, p. 572.
[43]  Ibid, pp. 572–74.
[44]  ANC GGAEF 126, Eboué, September 5, 1942.
[45]  ANOM GGAEF 2H 37.

With the establishment of the Office du travail, local authorities regularly informed Brazzaville of the number of able-bodied Africans they could provide to operations in other regions. Many tempered their reports with reservations, even warnings. In November 1942, the lead administrator of Ouham-Pendé (Oubangui) indicated that "at the current time the population of Bocaranga is barely sufficient to follow the normal rhythm of its economic survival. Any change provoked by the slightest recruitment risks breaching a delicate balance." That same month, in the N'Délé subdistrict of Oubangui, another official reported that "the entire eligible male population of 5,000 men is already working on the wax and rubber harvests." In the Baguirmi department of Chad, a functionary explained in January 1943 that he could not part with a single worker, given that all laborers in Baguirmi were already toiling on the immense strategic road project.[46] Local reports confirmed the challenge of reaching a balance between Free France's clashing imperatives.

These examples were certainly not isolated. According to Etienne Pelissier's January 1943 calculations, out of the 26,332 prestataires registered in Oubangui's Lower-M'Bomou region, "one can find about 7,000 men physically able and available to work on European plantations." He had to consider the local needs for coffee collection, brick-making, and road construction, among other imperatives. His report then swiftly turned gloomier. The 7,000 men he mentioned were the only "relatively healthy ones" available, because of the ravages of leprosy and syphilis. Losing these workers, he warned, would quite simply "finish the disappearance of the Zacara race." He presaged ominously that "this situation will only grow more dire because of the race's exhaustion. We will soon see the day when recruitment in this department will no longer be possible."[47] Inspired by medical reports, steeped in a preservationist ethos, such admonitions reflected as much the local administrator's eugenic logic as his conviction that FEA was exhausting its human resources.

Following the creation of the Office du travail, companies approached the administration with their labor requests. Given the number of "desertions" it was experiencing, the Kouilou mining corporation requested a thousand laborers from the governor-general in February 1943.[48] Now

---

46 ANOM GGAEF 2H 25, Ouham-Pendé, November 14, 1942; N'Délé, November 2, 1942; Bousso, January 21, 1943.
47 ANOM GGAEF 2H 25, report dated January 4, 1943.
48 ANOM GGAEF 2H 25, Pointe-Noire office, February 22, 1943.

intercessors at best, human traffickers at worst, some officials emitted grave concerns. On the advice of the mining office, on November 17, 1942, Félix Eboué threatened to suspend recruiting for Menard's mines in Souahnké, so long as the latter "did not treat workers better."[49] Such episodes speak to ongoing tensions between private and public sectors. In 1941, the head of the Borkou, Ennedi, and Tibesti regions in Northern Chad betrayed serious annoyance at local firms:

> Private companies seem to have no oversight. They think of themselves as the administration itself. A transporter comes to me smiling, requesting 300 rowers. Employers fail to establish millet reserves for workers, when there is a granary program in place. Employers neglect to cover the food needs of their workers, which makes it very difficult for us to find rowers for example.[50]

Such grievances concerning food constituted an ongoing concern for government officials. The problem was not new. In 1930s Cameroon, the administration had struggled to impose a workers' dietary minimum on companies.[51] In his 1941 report on the Upper Sangha region of Oubangui, one official observed that the workers of the Eastern Oubangui Mining Company consumed 70 tons of manioc a month. According to him, this was only possible thanks to a "close surveillance of plantations." He ordered for 1942, "for companies to force the wives of workers to grow supplemental crops, like corn, peanuts, sesame and vegetables."[52] While coercive agriculture was not a new phenomenon in FEA, Free France's *dirigiste* economy served only to accentuate the trend.

### Road Work

It may well be in the realm of road construction that colonial officials proved the most zealous. Results quickly followed. General de Gaulle's priority as early as October 1940 involved creating new strategic arteries linking FEA and Cameroon with British Sudan and Nigeria.[53] Like rubber, roads constituted an area in which Free France could concretely support the British war cause. However, some projects proved too grand. In 1942, General Hutchinson suggested carving out a road from Bangui

---

49 ANOM GGAEF 2H 25, Pointe-Noire office, note for the political affairs bureau, November 17, 1942.
50 ANOM GGAEF 4(4) D51, 1941 report.
51 Kaptué, *Travail et main-d'œuvre*, p. 113.
52 ANOM GGAEF 4 (3) D 52, political report for Haute Sangha, second semester 1941.
53 Weinstein, *Eboué*, p. 255.

to El Obeid in Sudan. The plan was rejected because of the "grave" consequences it would entail for already exhausted FEA workers, given the collective effort they had already undertaken on other roads linking Chad and Sudan, as well as Southern Chad and the Saharan front.[54]

A Vichy report dated June 1942 provides an unsurprisingly skeptical outlook on the vast road works undertaken in Free French Africa. It begins by pointing out that the first plan for FEA and Cameroon's transport routes dated from 1936. It rested on the "spinal column" of the Congo Océan railway, and its extension by river up to Bangui.[55] At the war's outset, it adds, only Oubangui disposed of a decent paved road network – essential for year-round as opposed to seasonal travel. While the report expressed admiration for the work undertaken since August 1940, which it attributed largely to the help of British organization and American machines, the author of the secret report observed bitterly and correctly that the new undertakings tethered FEA and Cameroon to British colonies. He even predicted that if Britain lost the war, the new roads would serve as a welcoming red carpet for Italy to invade FEA in one fell swoop. Despite this outlandish prediction, the report was well-informed overall, drawing knowledge from tran-Saharan travelers. It noted that since 1940, the "dissidents" (read Gaullists) had transformed a great many paths into paved roads, chiefly in Chad, Cameroon, and Oubangui, and that they had succeeded in connecting Chad to Cameroon with a high-quality road. The artery between Fort-Lamy and British Sudan had also been upgraded: "During the second semester of 1941, thousands of workers toiled on the paving of the road between Bokoro and Amguéréda." While "numerous worker desertions" occurred in August and September 1941, the final results could not be denied. By October 1941, paving had been completed on three main routes leaving Fort-Lamy, for Faya, Abecher, and Fort-Archambault.[56]

Chad presented obvious strategic importance, as the point of departure for Leclerc's troops and as the neighbor of British Nigeria and Sudan. It therefore saw the lion's share of road construction. From August to December 1940 in Bas-Chari, emphasis was placed on the roads between Fort-Lamy (N'Djamena) and Moussoro on the one hand, and Fort-Lamy

---

54 On the Bangui-El Obeid road project, see ANF 3AG 167, telegrams dated September 19, 1942.

55 On the extensive road work undertaken with forced labor in the 1920s, see Giles-Vernick, p. 91; and Libbie Freed, "Networks of Colonial Power: Roads in French Central Africa after World War I," *History and Technology*, 26: 3, 2010, pp. 203–23.

56 Secretary of the State to the Navy, study #26 (secret), *Le réseau ferré et routier du bloc AEF, Cameroun, Congo belge*, June 23, 1942 (ANOM Bib AOM B 13827).

and Mogroum on the other hand. Between October and December of that year, 1930 inhabitants of the district were put to work on these roads. A colonial official witnessed and reported multiple abuses along the way: the recurring problem of low or late wages, routine beatings on construction sites, and significant food and water shortages.[57] For the road linking Fort-Archambault and Fort-Lamy, 3000 men were recruited in Logone in 1941.[58] The road works were fast exhausting human resources, noted the head of the Moyen-Chari department:

> Over the course of the second semester, road construction required 2,000 men, two waves of reinforcements, and another 250 men to maintain the roads. They were all supplied. That would be nothing if at least we knew what happened to last year's workers, or to those from the first semester of 1941. Admittedly a few returned here, but the vast majority must still be on some construction site or in big towns [like Fort-Lamy]. I am told that labor is needed in so-called Arab areas, but that does not change the fact that the land of the Sara is rapidly losing its young people.[59]

Indeed, military recruitment had hit the Sara particularly hard. Local companies also requested "hundreds of workers and rowers."[60] And now road builders joined the queue. Interestingly, this report also suggests frustration at losing tabs over workers after they left the region to join public works projects.

Although Chad undertook the largest road effort, it was not the only region concerned. Between 1940 and 1942, the road network in N'Gouiné province of Gabon expanded from 276 kilometers to 635, a 77 percent increase. According to the head of this same province, "Roads should come first, roads above all else."[61] He was reacting in part to the perception that previous administrations had overemphasized gold at the expense of infrastructures. But this also suggests that the military imperative was something of a pretext: like Eboué, Rogué wanted to achieve the "penetration" and "development" of Gabon, reducing portering through road construction.

As a harrowing and nonlucrative activity, roadwork generally failed to attract workers. And yet, tax pressure forced some to enroll. A December 1941 report by missionaries near Pointe-Noire reveals, "Taxes are becoming a growing concern for the natives. Many are leaving for

---

[57] ANOM, GGAEF 4 (4) D 50, Bas-Chari report for 1940.
[58] ANOM GGAEF 4(4) D 51, Lapie to the head of the Logone department, October 4, 1941.
[59] ANOM GGAEF 4(4) D 51, department of Middle-Chari, second semester 1941.
[60] ANOM GGAEF 4(4) D 51, department of Middle-Chari, first semester 1941.
[61] AFDG, F22, 17, report on N'Gouinié, p. 7 and 98.

public works to make a little money. The administration will have a hard time collecting the head tax at the level it has set."[62] Under the Cross of Lorraine, head and cattle taxes climbed significantly in Chad. In Fort Lamy, the head tax rose from 20 francs in 1939 to 30 francs in 1942–43, before reaching 50 francs in 1944.[63]

In many cases, workers did not have to make the trip to the public works department. Instead, it came to them. Recruitment provoked abuses of all sort. When in 1941 the Chadian department of Baguirmi was called on to contribute to the Fort-Archambault to Fort-Lamy road, an official reported that "in the Misselini villages" some were paying Saras to go on their behalf. The Saras then tended to desert.[64] On roadworks, official remuneration hovered around 2 francs a day, while portering usually earned 6 francs a day, to give one comparison.[65] Furthermore, when road workers failed to meet set objectives, their food rations were frequently withheld.[66] All of these factors no doubt help to explain the waves of desertions observed by the public works department. In the Lower-Chari (Chad), one official wrote of "numerous desertions; periods of calm are followed by massive departures. I sometimes register a surplus of fifty men, followed a day later by a shortage of 150 men."[67]

Roadwork sometimes met active resistance. On February 12, 1941, in the village of Isseirom near Lake Chad, associate chief Barma M'Boudou was stabbed repeatedly as he attempted to recruit laborers. Two days later, when armed native guards appeared, they were met with spears instead of daggers. The native guards promptly opened fire, killing one villager. The others were condemned to three years in jail and fined 10,000 francs as punishment for "armed rebellion."[68]

### African Reactions

Resistance took many forms. As some five hundred men were being recruited near Saa, the bishop of Cameroon François-Xavier Vogt

---

[62] CSE 3J1.19B, Mouyounasi diary, entry for December 12, 1941

[63] Bernard Lanne, "Chad, the Chadians and the Second World War, 1939–1945," *Africana Journal*, 16 (1994), p. 314; and Bernard Lanne, "Le Tchad pendant la guerre (1939–1945)," in Charles-Robert Ageron, ed., *Les chemins de la décolonisation de l'empire français, 1936–1956* (Paris: CNRS, 1986), p. 448.

[64] ANOM GGAEF 4(4) D 51, political report for Baguirmi, second semester 1941.

[65] ANOM, GGAEF 4 (1) D 50, rapport for Woleu N'Tem, p. 31. The same sum of 2 francs was reported at Logone in Chad, in 1941. ANOM GGAEF 4(4) D 51, Lapie to the head of the Logone department, October 4, 1941.

[66] ANOM GGAEF 4(4) D 51, Baguirmi, second semester 1941.

[67] ANOM GGAEF 4(4) D 51, Bas-Chari, political report, first semester 1941.

[68] Ibid.

reported that "a young man cut off his own fingers with a machete" so as not to be taken. Others then began clamoring their refusal to go. The administrator finally managed to round up the recruits thanks to the help of a missionary. But when it came time to board the trucks, revolt broke out. According to the bishop's diary, "They all lay on the ground and refused to board." Then, after the authorities tried to move them forcibly, "they began hurling rocks on police." In the end, the official was forced to back down. An inquiry revealed that in this same area, a previous round of recruits had been abused and poorly fed when they were last enlisted two years prior.[69]

On balance, however, such acts of overt resistance failed more often than they succeeded. Conversely, escape and stealth constituted ideal tools for escaping prestations and other forms of statute labor. Departure to a neighboring territory, be it Spanish Guinea, British Nigeria and Sudan, or the Belgian Congo, represented a radical response, insofar as it halted pursuers in their tracks. Such migratory strategies across porous colonial borders were nothing new. In the Upper Sangha region of Oubangui neighboring German Cameroon up to 1916, French and German colonial authorities long adopted ambivalent approaches, sometimes fostering and sometimes blocking transborder movement.[70] Starting in 1940, such migrations from Free French Africa often reflected the fact that FEA and Cameroon were at war, whereas Spanish Guinea and Portuguese Angola were not, and were hence spared some of the fever that consumed Gaullist regions. On occasion, colonial authorities brokered agreements to stem the hemorrhaging. In May 1940, British and French in Cameroon agreed to coordinate repression so as to "corner escapees and direct them like game into the nets of recruiters."[71]

However, colonial authorities also sometimes lost at the border game. Consider a case that transpired in 1942 in an area where Oubangui-Chari met the Belgian Congo. On the French side, the zealous new head of the Ouango subdistrict sensed somehow that his predecessors had missed registering half the population in their censuses. Sniffing out fugitives both real and imaginary, he dispatched his forces to the isle of M'Bomou, where he had "dissidents" arrested, stole livestock, and set fire to forty-nine dwellings. A few days later, he learned that the martyred village

---

[69] CSE, 2J2.3A, September 24, 1942.

[70] Tamara Giles-Vernick, "We Wander like Birds: Migration, Indigeneity and the Fabrication of Frontiers in the Sangha River Basin of Equatorial Africa," *Environmental History*, 4:2, April 1999, p. 173.

[71] Kaptué, *Travail et main-d'œuvre*, p. 173.

actually lay on the Belgian side of the border. Indemnities, goat returns, and excuses ensued.[72]

On a vaster scale, in October 1943 Governor of Chad Jacques Rogué alerted René Pleven of a regular "hemorrhaging" of Saras leaving Chad for neighboring British Sudan and Nigeria. According to the governor, a simple solution would help stem the tide: "abolishing prestation labor. The Saras need to be paid. They like money, if they get some, they will stay."[73] In this instance, British colonial practices appeared more attractive than French ones, creating an asymmetry that Brazzaville came to recognize, although it would only be redressed after the war.

Similarly, in November 1941, administrator Jean Brette had observed the significant discrepancy between the sum an agricultural worker earned per day in French Cameroon (1.58 francs), as opposed to Spanish Guinea (4.90 francs). Here lay the "real cause of emigration" to Spanish Guinea, explained Brette.[74] The disparity had not escaped the attention of British observers either. In a report on French Cameroon dated September 1942, a British official familiar with British colonial daily wages of roughly 5 francs registered surprise at French planters who grumbled about having to hike daily salaries to 2 or 3.5 francs.[75]

The threat of massive departures to foreign territories exerted an impact on local administrators, like the head of the Mayo Kebbi region of Chad. In March 1943 he laid bare to his superiors in Brazzaville that he had no workers at his disposal for transfer to other regions. He added that "these recruitments for other [parts of FEA] have always provoked trouble in the native population. They take the form of numerous escapes, especially to Nigeria, which preciously holds on to these migrants."[76] In some cases, the very possibility of migration served as a pretext to corporations not to draw up proper contracts. "Given the proximity of Belgian Congo and their propensity for escaping," workers could vanish at any time, contended some employers in the Likouala area of French Congo in December 1943.[77]

---

72 ADN 116/PO1/115 border incident file, as well as ANOM GGAEF 4(3) D53, Oubangui political report for Bas M'Bomou, second semester 1942, p. 3.

73 ANOM Cab 55, dossier AEF, Memo for Pleven, October 9, 1943.

74 ANCMR 100092, Brette report.

75 NAUK, FO 859, dossier 6, Political report on the Cameroons under French Mandate, September 3, 1942.

76 ANOM GGAEF 2H 25, report from Mayo Kebbi, dated March 30, 1943.

77 ANOM GGAEF 2H 25, Pointe-Noire report on the Likouala department, December 29, 1943.

Kaptué identifies a phenomenon he describes as the recourse to ruse, a weapon of the weak that some used to escape the clutches of forced labor.[78] For instance, in Free French Africa, some managed to put private and public sectors in competition, by claiming that they were already serving the one to the other. Until 1945, the relatively rudimentary nature of some identification devices (especially the absence of photographs) facilitated this kind of subterfuge.[79] In its response to an inspection tour of the Babimbi sector of Sanaga Maritime in Cameroon in 1942, the office of the "governor" of Cameroon attempted to resolve the problem of Africans "who accepted a work card with the sole aim of escaping administrative public works requisitions." After much consideration, the head of French mandate Cameroon recommended that local authorities "crack down by applying the dispositions of article 68 of the decree of November 17, 1937, that punishes any native who consents to a fictitious work contract." He congratulated the local official for having "taken the census at people's place of residence," contrary to past practice that had either involved outsourcing the task to local chiefs, or conducting roll call on the village square.[80] Caught between a rock and a hard place, some Cameroonians decamped; others turned to alternate oppositional practices.

Beyond escape, resistance, and ruse, what other recourse did local populations have? Letters of grievance constituted a genre with a rich local history and well-defined tropes, although results varied. Jeremy Rich has shown that in the 1880s and 1890s already, complaint letters played a crucial role in Gabon, allowing authors to promote and defend their interests. For instance, Chief Félix Adende made frequent and wide use of either a republican or a Christian lexicon, depending on his audience. Again, actual results could prove spotty, but the device and medium were well entrenched by 1940.[81]

Regime change in August 1940 introduced new possibilities. The advent of a black governor-general, a recrudescence of coercion, the

---

[78] On the concept of "weapons of the weak," see James Scott, *Weapons of the Weak: Everyday Forms of Peasant Resistance* (New Haven: Yale University Press, 1985); James Scott, *Domination and the Arts of Resistance* (New Haven: Yale University Press, 1990), p. xiii.

[79] Kaptué, *Travail et main-d'œuvre*, pp. 180–81.

[80] ANCMR 2AC 158.

[81] Jeremy Rich, "King or Knave? Félix Adende Rapontchombo and Political Survival in the Gabon Estuary." *African Studies Quarterly* 6, no. 3, http://web.africa.ufl.edu/asq/v6/v6i3a1.htm.

war effort as a new mantra, all variously conditioned and encouraged grievances. The complaints I consulted, stored in a carton at the national archives in Brazzaville, offer at once precious testimonies on the experiences of individual Africans, and a window onto some of their recourse strategies.

In August 1941, Mr. Tchioula, from Booué, Gabon, wrote to Governor-General Eboué in Brazzaville to complain of ill treatment on the part of the Booué district chief. His words must have sent a chill down the spine of Gaullist officials. He stated that prior to 1940, previous local administrators had been good men, concerned for the plight of Africans, and eager to "develop the country." However, "since de Gaulle took over Gabon, the [people] sent here have treated us like beasts." Tchioula proceeded to explain that the new chief routinely whipped Africans for no apparent motive, sometimes using the chicote fifty times a day on a single soul, and jailed inhabitants seemingly at random for between eight days and a month. According to this testimony, the local official accompanied this fierce violence with racist outbursts that included, "Blacks are monkeys who must be killed." Prestations were imposed for a period of one month, those enlisted were obliged to work on Sundays and holidays, even on July 14, "day and night without meals."

Tchioula described a system of organized pilfering that relied in part on African militiamen. On market days, he claimed, twenty to thirty chickens needed to be brought "to the whites." Booué's blacks were not the only ones to be called monkeys, he noted. When villagers responded to his invective by pointing out that Eboué was black, the tyrannical administrator retorted, "Yes, the governor general is a monkey like you." Here, Tchioula clearly sought to establish a common ground of racial victimhood, while no doubt also inciting Eboué to react. He also warned the administration in the following terms: "If you leave these whites in power in Booué, we will all flee to N'Djolé." Flouting the administration's power to direct population movements was a bold and no doubt effective menace. On more than one occasion, Tchioula deliberately tapped into the administration's discursive register. He argued, for instance, that the people of Booué wanted what the Free French were bringing elsewhere, namely roads. "We want roads like [neighboring districts] where the whites don't just care about eating our chickens, eggs, goats and sheep." The complaint thus struck at the core of Gaullist wartime efficiency; it embraced the Free French language of progress and development while portraying the local administrator as a counterproductive, depraved, and bigoted leech.[82]

Booué was no isolated case. In April 1941, roughly eighty inhabitants of the Gabonese town of Lambaréné signed a petition that chronicled their suffering under the reign of another administrator Pierre Duvergé, who had been at the helm of the subdivision since December 1940. Interestingly, a second version of the text, this one anonymous and more detailed, was also sent to Eboué, probably through different channels. Both documents signed by "the population of Lambaréné" depict a vicious circle. It began with the prestations. After twelve days of tough labor, skeletal "prestataires" were then dispatched to prison, where they were promptly whipped, beaten, and "tortured." The following day, they were sent to work on Mr Casteig's operation – the latter refusing to provide even a pot in which to prepare food. They survived on a few grains of raw rice. Whipped relentlessly and starving, many fled. Those who were caught were jailed for desertion, Duvergé adding for good measure "subdue and kill those monkeys." In unspeakable conditions, out of either despair, resolve, or some combination of the two, some jailed women performed abortions on themselves.[83]

This letter to Eboué was consciously termed a "cry of distress" aiming to rid inhabitants of "a pirate commander whose spirit is Nazi." In the unsigned version of the document, even more specific arguments are deployed. First of all, Pierre Duvergé utilized methods that even armies did not typically employ in conquered territories. Here Duvergé was clearly branded a criminal. Next, by employing such conduct against civilian populations, Duvergé was seeking "his revenge against African Gaullists, because Duvergé had been a Pétainist before."[84] Unfortunately, Duvergé's personnel file does not reveal whether he had indeed sympathized with Vichy. It does show that during the time of regime change in FEA (August 26–28, 1940), this 35-year-old official was located at Fort-Archambault, where the swing to de Gaulle did indeed prove arduous.[85] What seems certain is the Duvergé affair was connected to the many aftershocks of the civil war in Gabon between Vichy and Free French forces in the fall

---

[82] ANC GGAEF 378 Tchioula file, Booué. I have not reproduced the partly phonetic French that was used in the original, in part to facilitate the reading, in part to limit the effect of othering, and in part because of the challenges that a translation from phonetic French would involve.

[83] ANC GGAEF 378.

[84] ANC, GGAEF 379, the inhabitants of Lambaréné to Eboué.

[85] ANOM EEII 6562, Duvergé.

of 1940. Local populations, fully grasping the stakes of the conflict, were now in a position to utilize the language of the pan-imperial civil war that pitted Free France against Vichy.

On July 23, 1941, an "alliance of Lambaréné's population" drafted a collective grievance against Duvergé. It opened with the same observation as that of Booué concerning the African experience before 1940: "Before the war," wrote the petitioners, "administrators were good to us." However, things had soured since December 1940: "we are surprised that administrator Duvergé mistreats blacks, especially in wartime." Duvergé was described as a closet Vichyite, "whose job is to jail blacks." If Duvergé "were a real Gaullist," the inhabitants explained, "he would not make blacks who want to fight by de Gaulle's side suffer." Here Gaullist strategies were appropriated, in particular the broad-stroked discrediting of Vichy. Clearly and keenly aware of the colony's short-lived civil war in 1940 between Gaullists and Vichyites, the inhabitants of Lambaréné played on this French quarrel, and on the Gaullist rhetoric of liberty and anti-Fascism in their bid to condemn an abusive local official.[86]

It goes without saying that the colonial methods described in these touching complaints were nothing new in Gabon or in AEF more generally, which had been the theater of ghastly violence since the nineteenth century. A British report on Gabon from September 1942 suggested that old colonial hands were usually responsible for the worst abuses. In place for what seemed like an eternity in the colony, these were "men whose administrative talents seem to be concentrated almost exclusively on the more presentable section of the female native population and whose sole principle of native policy appears to be *flanquer en prison* [toss in jail] any unfortunate natives with whom they come into contact."[87] In this context, one can question what really changed in 1940. The answer is twofold. Firstly, one discerns a new sense of omnipotence among some Europeans who seemed to think the war effort conferred them virtually absolute immunity. Secondly, one witnesses the manifest determination of victims to seek redress against "torturers" and "Vichyites." This quest, coded in the language of the war, anticipated the equation of fascism and colonialism that Aimé Césaire would later draw in his *Discourse on Colonialism*. The moral landscape of AEF was briskly shifting.

---

[86] ANC GGAEF 378 Lambaréné files.
[87] NAUK FO 859, dossier 8, Political impressions of the Gaboon.

Naturally, the authorities in Brazzaville did not endorse the abuses. In a January 11, 1941, telegram, Félix Eboué reminded governors of AEF that "the firmness which we must show towards our subjects and the discipline we must impose upon them, especially in the realm of labor, still do not justify or excuse methods that could only anger and distance our subjects from us, compromising both moral health and tranquility." In particular, Eboué asked that an immediate end be brought to "brutalities and abuses that the natives still suffer from far too often."[88] This was a delicate balancing act, when orders called for resource extraction practically at any cost. In practice, then, the war imperative continued to "cover" many abuses.

How did the Gaullist authorities react to the calls for help from Booué and Lambaréné? In the case of Lambaréné, we know that Félix Eboué asked the governor of Gabon for an inquiry on May 25, 1941. Eboué observed:

> I fear…that in a region like Lambaréné, where the indigenous population was profoundly shaken by the events of last October [the civil war in Gabon], where it is no doubt important to restore order, where the issue of *prestations* and paid labor is becoming pressing, that these complaints are the expression of a state of mind that we need to take seriously, even I might say a reaction against inappropriate administrative methods that it may prove necessary to correct.[89]

Implicitly, Eboué seems to have recognized that the hell described by the plaintiffs of Lambaréné was no fiction. While he conceded the impact of the civil war in Gabon on the local situation in Lambaréné, he also seemed to admit that his administrators were utilizing excessive force. Subsequently in 1944, Eboué would strongly condemn such practices, while remaining mum on the fact that they had raged while he was in office.

And yet, while Free French Africa was striving for maximum productivity, at a time when the administration complained of a shortage of European personnel, the hour of reform had not yet rung. This is borne out by the fact that Duvergé's sole reprimand seems to have involved a prolonged holiday in South Africa (from November 1941 through March 1942), then a transfer to Oyem, before finally being moved to Ngouiné on April 1, 1943. In August 1941, his direct superior at Port-Gentil even

---

[88] ANOM GGAEF 5B 712, Eboué to the governors of Chad, Oubangui, Gabon, and Moyen-Congo, January 11, 1941.
[89] ANC GGAEF 378, grievances from the population of Lambaréné.

applauded his firmness: "He brought the population of Lambaréné back into line," he noted."[90] Admittedly, a review of his conduct in 1944 evoked his "difficult nature that makes his relations with everyone very complicated."[91] But beyond his vacation and transfer, nothing resembling a punishment appears in Duvergé's file.

Perhaps unsurprisingly, Duvergé did not reinvent himself in Ngouiné. On July 17, 1943, an African guard serving in the colonial administration, Honoré Mokononé, wrote Governor-General Félix Eboué in person from Mouïla in Gabon. He began by describing the decision to replace the previous official in Mouïla, Jacques Rogué, as "ill advised." He related that the new official, Duvergé, had entrusted him with some twenty prisoners, tasked with conducting leveling work on a road. When Duvergé realized that Mokononé had given the prisoners a lunchtime break, he became livid, and opened fire on Mokononé, barely missing him. He then psychopathically proclaimed that he was "going to kill everybody." Viciously punished, Mokononé only miraculously escaped Duvergé's crosshairs. In his grievance, the soldier implicitly invoked a common black victimhood in a bid to have Duvergé punished. "A black man cannot intervene to defend another black man in front of a white,"[92] he noted bitterly, hoping no doubt to stir Eboué into action. Here the fault line of conflict hinged on Gaullist road obsession, on war imperatives versus rights, dignity, and working conditions. Invocation of race served as a shorthand for underscoring Eboué's contradictory position as a black man at the head of a particularly extractive colonial organization.

Eboué's skin color surfaces frequently in this carton of complaints. I will close this section as I opened it, with the town of Booué. On December 10, 1941, a letter signed "the inhabitants of Booué" reached Governor Félix Eboué's office in Brazzaville. The grievances against administrators Numa Sadoul and Maurice Grandperrin were numerous.[93] They made the dead pay taxes or rather extracted taxes from living relatives well after a death. They put the "elderly" to work – which is to say those

---

[90] ANOM EEII 6562, Duvergé file, grades for August 1941.

[91] ANOM EEII 6562, Duvergé file, individual bulletin for May 1, 1944.

[92] ANC GGAEF 378, file of complaints against Duvergé, head of N'Gounié department.

[93] Sadoul's personnel file shows him to have been a loyal Free French administrator. He was depicted in April 1941 as having "rallied at the very first hour, and he continues to assert his personality." In October 1943, he was presented as "firm," possessing a "capacity for making decisions" and equipped with "a very good general education." ANOM EEII 7230.

between the ages of forty and fifty – beat them, and deprived them of food. They collected "taxes" without issuing receipts. And finally, Sadoul and Grandperrin allegedly stated that de Gaulle had made a mistake in appointing Eboué, who was nothing more than a "bush monkey" who should occupy at best the rank of canton chief. The text features revealing marginalia from the Governor-General's office in Brazzaville. The mysterious reader in Brazzaville – perhaps Eboué or Laurentie in person – scrawled next to the racist reference, "I would be surprised if Sadoul expressed himself this way in front of his charges." This left open the possibility that he would do so in private, or that he held such beliefs. Again, the inhabitants of Booué had cracked open a contradiction in a Gaullist hierarchy whose alleged color-blindness, embodied by Eboué, was belied by local realities. To the inhabitants of Booué, Sadoul and Grandperrin's attitude toward Félix Eboué was inextricably linked to their deeply abusive and exploitative practices toward them. Further along, the petition reveals, "Mr. Sadoul and Mr. Grandperrin tell us that General de Gaulle was wrong to name you, Eboué, as Governor General, and he was also wrong to continue the war against the Germans." Here, the same margin writer fumes, "unacceptable."[94]

These letters present the advantage of retrieving African voices, not to mention African experiences and strategies, under Free French rule. To be sure, they emanated from a specific and slender slice of the population, that is to say, literate rural elites. In some cases, as in the collective petition from Lambaréré, a scribe drafted the text on behalf of all signers. In all the other examples presented here, the spelling and phonetic nature of the texts (which I have not rendered here, for multiple reasons, not the least of which is the daunting task of translating phonetic French into phonetic English), suggest that it was indeed African soldiers, villagers, and other figures who articulated their complaints in person, usually bypassing the canton chief in the process. Naturally, these artifacts should not be seen as the reflection of some collective experience, but are rather the product of specific situations. Yet, we can still draw some conclusions from these remarkable sources, most notably with respect to their recurring formulae. Especially noteworthy is the capacity of these texts to target weak spots in the colonial apparatus. Consider the enumeration of racist attacks directed toward Eboué, the identification of practices that could be deemed counterproductive for the war effort, the perception of colonial practices as Nazi-influenced or inflected. These points were likely all

---

[94] ANC, GGAEF 379, the inhabitants of Booué to Eboué, December 10, 1941.

true; what is significant is that they were expertly plucked over others from a much larger body of grievances so as to deliver the maximum impact on a colonial state in flux.

## Carding

Up to now this chapter has dealt mostly with rural Africa. U.S. journalist Dudley Harmon, who worked for the Gaullist information services in Brazzaville, provides some insights into everyday life in Free France's African capital. Harmon captured a wide range of social interactions: take the reception she attended to mark the end of a mourning period. Her Congolese cook, the widower of the deceased, had invited her. Harmon's eye caught the bright green suit worn by her domestic Ozamba for the occasion. She also commented on her host's generosity given his paltry wage. She added that several white French people had sought to dissuade her from attending the event, so as to safeguard a color line they wished to reinforce.

Despite these streaks of lucidity, Harmon sometimes displayed less empathy. On May 25, 1942, for instance, she wrote to her father: "The funniest things keep happening here. The other day, just before lunch, we found our boy [African servant] had been thrown into jail for stealing bananas – so no lunch. Then the other morning he was arrested for not having his work card – so no breakfast."[95] Harmon seemed less concerned by the strict control that was being exerted on her domestic than for the regularity of her meals. But for our purposes, despite its anecdotal nature, this testimony speaks to the growing control and surveillance that urban African working classes experienced under Free French rule.

The colonial archives in Aix-en-Provence reveal that the Brazzaville work card Harmon mentioned had only just been introduced at the time of her letter. On December 22, 1941, Brazzaville's chamber of commerce contacted the governor-general to suggest several measures that could repress "vagabondage" in the capital, which constituted "a detrimental situation in wartime." One of the solutions involved "using the individual work booklet for workers and keeping it up to date." The suggested work booklet was not to be confused with "a contract book that would require many complicated formalities. The work booklet, complete with a set of dimensions, a photo, fingerprints and spaces for annotations and the

---

[95] SSCSC, Dudley Harmon papers, box 1, folder 2, letters dated January 11 and May 25, 1942.

list of employments should suffice." Among the other initiatives, one proposed, "preventing workers from leaving their employment without sufficient cause."[96]

The measure seems to have lived up to its promise. In September 1942, the governor of Oubangui-Chari invited one of his subordinates to copy the model that had recently been introduced in FEA's capital: "In Brazzaville, the implementation of an individual identity card validated each month by employers, and controlled by the local administration has rendered great services." He added that he had already asked Governor Eboué for a specimen that he wished to copy in Bangui.[97] Emulation continued. In 1943 with thefts on the rise in Bongor, Chad, the governor recommended, "We must purge Bongor. Make the work card mandatory for all employees."[98]

The use of identity cards, a major trend since the late nineteenth century, does not necessarily imply an authoritarian bent. Similarly, the presence of cutting-edge surveillance devices in the colonies need not automatically reflect a "colonial modernity."[99] Indeed, such projects often possessed ambivalent geneses. Initially, the work booklet had been intended to improve the fate of FEA's workers, by forcing employers to provide contracts to them.[100] But the instrument in question could also become dystopian in colonial hands. In a Free French context where labor shortages were chronic, where the civilian administration endlessly fended off Leclerc's efforts to siphon resources toward the military, the attraction of technological and bureaucratic shortcuts met a desire for increased social control.

Identity and work cards elicited different reactions in various settings. In France's old colonies of Guadeloupe, Martinique, and Réunion, they tended to rekindle the memory of slavery. They were rapidly imposed in the so-called new colonies as well. In Madagascar, which France conquered in 1895, a circular from 1898 already established "an individual booklet for natives." A 1906 decree (effective the following year) forced

---

96 ANOM GGAEF 2H 18, vice-president of Brazzaville's chamber of commerce, December 22, 1941.

97 ANOM GGAEF 4(3) D53, Bangui, September 30, 1942.

98 ANOM GGAEF 4(4) D53, Rogué, Fort-Lamy, October 12, 1943.

99 Clifford Rosenberg, *Policing Paris: the Origins of Modern Immigration Control Between the Wars* (Ithaca: Cornell University Press, 2006); On the use of modernity in colonial and postcolonial studies, see Cooper, *Colonialism*, p. 115.

100 Coquery-Vidrovitch, *Le Congo*, p. 112.

every Malagasy of sixteen years or more to carry said booklet, intended to "trace the native's tax situation" but also to serve as a laissez-passer for any trip "outside of the province in which the individual resided." The booklet featured a number, the holder's place of residence, age and address, as well as columns on which provincial authorities registered the carrier's movements.[101] Booklets and cards in turn generated administrative units to tend to them. In Indochina, a substantial identification service photographed and carded suspects and prisoners, utilizing both phonetic and finger imprints. In this same colony, a judicial identity laboratory was instituted in 1924. Drawing on the most cutting-edge police methods, it practiced photography and anthropometry, and possessed some 800,000 cards.[102]

The close connection between such instruments of control, the *indigénat* code, and forced labor created a veritable triptych of colonial coercion. Both work cards and laissez-passers were introduced in Cameroon. The former found its origins in the German era; at the beginning of the French mandate, it was mostly utilized for medical control purposes, which also involved curtailing freedom of movement. The colonial administration used the laissez-passer, officially implemented in 1925, to repress what it called vagabondage, most often "desertion" from statute labor.[103]

Yet as we have seen, the work card proved vulnerable to subterfuge and was in fact relatively easily skirted. In 1944, deserters from a Moyen-Congo gold mine simply altered the names on their papers before fleeing from the mine.[104] In 1941, the head of the Cameroonian region of Wouri complained of the time it was taking to come up with a more reliable identification method than the laissez-passer. Noting the existing system's vulnerability to fraud, he insisted on numbering the documents, and prohibited collective laissez-passers. He arranged for the duration of time spent away from home to be reported in letters and not in numbers, so as to reduce fraud (presumably a reflection of low literacy rates). Lastly, the document would henceforth have to bear the signature of a

---

[101] *Bulletin officiel de Madagascar et dépendances*, 1906, pp. 299–301.
[102] Patrice Morlat, *La répression coloniale au Vietnam, 1908–1940* (Paris: l'Harmattan, 1990), pp. 49–50.
[103] Léon Kaptué, "L'Administration coloniale et la circulation des indigènes au Cameroun: les laissez-passer, 1923–1946," *Afrika Zamani*, 10–11, December 1979, pp. 160–81.
[104] Kaptué, *Travail et main-d'œuvre*, pp. 180–81. On Moyen-Congo, see ANOM GGAEF 2H 18, Pointe-Noire December 1, 1944.

European.[105] On a local scale, then, a Free French representative was busy testing an identification and carding system meant to improve previous dispositions.

In neighboring FEA, a decree dated May 27, 1944, introduced a "mandatory card," likely inspired by the Brazzaville model. The head of the Alima-Léfini department in Congo welcomed this initiative as a mechanism for reducing tax fraud and for facilitating manhunts. The identification card drew from other antecedents as well. An "individual card for rubber work" had been imposed on the same region for many years. The new card, however, would be used much more widely. An official hoped that it would prevent "natives from constantly changing names" thereby stabilizing designations that colonial sources considered frustratingly mutable. Indeed, he added, "it often happens, as I have seen myself, that Congolese not remember all of their names; they then turn to their comrades who remind them of one of them." According to this official, many Congolese possessed four names, one personal, another familial, a third related to their village, and a final one reserved for tax purposes.[106]

In June 1945, as various liberal reforms were underway, Cameroon's commissioner decided to implement a multilayered identification system across the entire country. He certainly drew inspiration from the Wouri example, but also from the Southern N'Tem region where another carding system had been introduced on a local scale over the previous years. In order to extend the measure to all of Cameroon, the commissioner set aside budget space for ten million "family census forms." He also ordered three million metal plates, modeled on French military "dog tags." He decided, moreover, that the cards would only be delivered after the census was taken. Regional officials seem to have been delighted to add these new weapons to their arsenal. Each Cameroonian would receive a metal plate, an identity card, and a record containing their ten fingerprints. Administrators hoped that the new instruments would facilitate tax collection, the search for recidivist criminals, the surveillance of workers, as well as "ethnographic, demographic and medical studies." Although it was implemented in 1945, one can trace the source of this deluge of carding back to the Free French era, in particular to individual initiatives by officials in N'Tem and Wouri. As for the metal plates, their

---

[105] Léon Kaptué, "L'Administration coloniale et la circulation des indigènes," pp. 166–68.
[106] ADN 116PO/1/68, Alima-Léfini department, 1944 political report.

ancestry goes back to medical units that had pioneered sophisticated control and surveillance techniques for their vaccination and treatment programs over previous decades.[107]

## Outside Perspectives

How did outsiders react toward coercive colonial methods? Some like Germaine Krull expressed shock over slavery-like practices in the gold sector. But the photographer certainly never pleaded for racial equality. This is attested by the disdain she displayed in her writings toward her African assistant, and by the gaze she cast on Félix Eboué, whose phenotype became her idée fixe. Finally, Krull seemed persuaded that one had to be white to be a true Gaullist.[108]

Labor practices in Free French Africa generally failed to generate dismay among Americans who witnessed them. After all, parts of the United States presented even more rigid racial divisions. Far from condemning the administration's practices in their vicinity, Americans serving the Christian and Missionary Alliance in Gabon practiced coercion themselves. According to their 1943 annual report, Gabonese women frequenting their bible school in Bongolo "would all have withdrawn long ago had we not literally forced them to remain in school."[109]

Diplomats generated equally surprising reports. In January 1944, U.S. consul in Brazzaville Laurence W. Taylor began by pillorying "the trained native who is too good for manual labor and not good enough for anything else." According to the consul, the only missionaries who had obtained results in FEA and Cameroon were the ones content to teach hygiene and respect toward women and children. This was in his opinion the moral ceiling to which Africans could aspire. He then opined that in Free French Africa "there is injustice from time to time, short tempers, favoritism...temporary abuse of some natives...Where do these things not exist?" Hence his verdict: "The colonial system now in operation...fits the needs of the area as well as any." His parting sentences were nothing short of chilling: "Either the white man rules the area until the native intelligence develops to a point where it can absorb abstract ideas or he gets out completely. In the first case I would allow 500 to 1.000

---

[107] ANCMR APA 11316.
[108] FLK, "Hallo, Hallo, Brazzaville vous parle," pp. 50, 60, 110.
[109] CMA, RG 820 Gabon, annual report 1943, p. 2.

years. Then the subject of self-government can be opened. In the second case the native will revert inside a year to savagery and cannibalism."[110] Such were the impressions received by the State Department on FEA and Cameroon.

## Censorship

While Africans experienced an era of generalized coercion and constraint, some restrictions on freedoms impacted FEA and Cameroon's small white population as well. On November 27, 1943, the newspaper *AEF* published an unusually frank tirade against double postal censorship. As its name suggests, this system involved opening and reading correspondence at both its point of departure and arrival. The newspaper asked rhetorically, "Do you think that a letter leaving Brazzaville for Bol, Rig-Rig or N'gouré in Chad, where there is only one European, would be censored on arrival by said European?" Interestingly, the article implied wrongly that censorship only concerned Europeans. It went on to cite the case of one FEA official writing to his wife also in FEA, only to have the letter struck out, cut, and otherwise adulterated at both its point of departure and arrival. In another instance, a postal bag was actually burned in Pointe-Noire. This led the author to question, "Are the authorities afraid that we might change our mind [about supporting Gaullist cause]? If they take us for children, then they should also confiscate our radios, for they too can influence and modify our sentiments." The article concluded with the following admonishment: "We should remember that the word *liberté* remains French."[111]

Every territory at war need of course consider its security. This is precisely what General Leclerc asserted in a June 28, 1942, letter to de Gaulle. He wrote, "Surveillance of public opinion...is more than ever justified" in FEA.[112] Yet postal censorship in Free French Africa proved strict even by the standards of the day. In January 1942, the pious Henri Laurentie complained to Free French military authorities that the apostolic delegate in Belgian Congo was "a bit troubled to notice that the letters he received were opened by FEA censors." To make matters worse, this Monsignor Giovanni Dellepiane had rendered considerable services

110 NARA, RG 84, Classified General Records, U.S. Consulate Brazzaville, box 3, Taylor January 4, 1944.
111 "La censure postale" *AEF*, November 27, 1943, p. 2.
112 ANOM, Cab 63, Leclerc June 28, 1942, note on the questions asked to General de Gaulle.

to Free France at the time of the three glorious days, and continued to act as a mediator to improve the conditions of Free French prisoners of war. Spying on him so overtly therefore seemed impolitic at the very least. In December 1942, it was Félix Eboué's turn to grieve over such a matter, this time involving the opening of the Swiss consul's correspondence. This placed the governor "in an embarrassing situation," he remarked flatly. Religious and foreign authorities were not the only ones to complain. The head of the Pool region that encompassed Brazzaville lamented in a 1942 political report: "The only glimpses we have of the war here are the abuses of censorship and the misdeeds and spurious suspicions of intelligence services that hatch outrageous conspiracy theories, which negatively impact relations between honest French people."[113] In other words, postal control represented merely the visible tip of a vast and paranoid spy mania.

In February 1944, the Fighting French commissioner to the colonies in Algiers waded into the issue of postal censorship in FEA and Cameroon. Those at the helm of the censorship office alleged that it offered "a reasonable insight into public opinion." They added that a complaint stemming from Cameroon, asking for postal censorship to be abolished should be flatly rejected, for it masked an elaborate attempt at philatelic fraud. Some clever individuals apparently attempted to infiltrate stamps bearing Pétain's image into Cameroon to have them postmarked, which would obviously have created extremely rare pieces. Despite these arguments, the minister of the colonies determined that postal control "constitutes a considerable infraction of freedom that can only be justified by reasons of crucial public safety." It consequently abolished the practice and recommended that governors in French West Africa and Madagascar follow suit.[114]

Press censorship proved as stringent as its postal counterpart. In October 1942, London pointed out to Brazzaville that page 12 of the June 30, 1942, issue of *France d'abord* had been entirely censored, leaving only a starkly blank page. Carlton Gardens noted that such a measure might be tolerable were the periodical's circulation limited to FEA; then one could see in the matter merely "an example of the classic conflict between the press and the censorship office." However, this publication also served as Free France's vitrine to the world, meaning that the incident could

---

[113] ANC, GGAEF 126, Laurentie letter dated January 15, 1942. ANOM GGAEF, 3B 2382, Eboué, December 21, 1942. ANOM GGAEF 4(2)D75, Pool, political report for 1942.

[114] ANOM, 1Affpol 873, file on postal control.

be read as the sign of "a despotic and fascist tropical regime." London therefore urged Brazzaville to consider "the way Marion at Vichy would utilize this page if it fell into his hands" (Paul Marion served as Vichy's secretary general for information).[115] Censorship could evidently prove detrimental to a Free French movement suspected sometimes with reason of running roughshod over individual liberties.


## Taking Stock

Free France certainly invented neither forced labor, coercion, nor abuses in Central Africa. Yet far from abolishing them, it often reinforced them. In his April 1941 Brazzaville proclamation, High Commissioner Edgard de Larminat explained that the time for reform had not yet come: "We are taking the machine as is. We will improve its operation by any means at our disposal, but we do not aspire to disassembling it and rebuilding it under a better form."[116] In his eyes, Free French Africa was evidently a war machine. But as he readily recognized, it was not industrialized. One can only deduce that the machine whose output Larminat wished to increase was a human one.

Coerced labor, carding, censorship, colonial arbitrariness, and the indigénat code lay at the heart of the colonial system inherited by Free France in 1940. In the case of surveillance and identity control, Free France undertook significant breakthroughs. It also sought to better organize corvées, most notably in the road sector, and created labor offices intended to spike productivity. Results proved mixed. Gaullist retrenchment fuelled migratory movements and mountains of grievances piled onto the desk of a governor-general deemed naturally predisposed for sympathy toward Africans. In this sense, the Free French era in Africa mostly marked a difference of degree rather than a difference in kind. It was characterized above all by concurrent imperatives: military recruitment, gold and rubber extraction, and road construction were all considered vital priorities that had to be waged with equal intensity.


[115] ANOM, GGAEF 6B 713, London, October 6, 1942.
[116] CHETOM, 18H 138.

# Epilogue

Can the memory of World War II in Francophone Africa be disentangled
from that of the colonialism more broadly? Although the Free French
period introduced changes in scale, it did not bring about as many shifts in
kind. Take Edgard de Larminat's insistence that he retain the "machine"
he inherited in 1940, and simply focus on increasing its yield.

Many researchers have examined the memory and afterlives of the
French empire in Africa. Jennifer Cole notes that in northwestern Madagascar ritual sacrifices serve to reverse the effects of colonization. This
involves rewriting the colonial era while siphoning agency, authority, and
domination from the colonial authorities to transfer them to the ancestors
of the colonized. Achille Mbembe posits that in Cameroon the colonial
period was experienced through the prisms of disease and misfortune.
People grappled with it through this same interface, which is to say the
allegory of cure and recovery. Cole adds that the memory of colonialism
can be likened to a subterranean river, invisible for the most part until it
periodically bubbles up to the surface.[1] These readings are in some ways
reminiscent of the so-called Vichy syndrome identified by Henry Rousso.
Indeed, like the latter, the memory of colonialism has proven to be at
once ubiquitous, variable, malleable, and usable.

Schemes of resistance and collaboration were polysemous in the setting
that concerns us, given that the colonial era was overlaid with a Free
French one. Thus, one could be simultaneously an African collaborator

---

[1] Mbembe, pp. 403–05; Jennifer Cole, *Forget Colonialism? Sacrifice and the Art of Memory
in Madagascar* (Berkeley: University of California Press, 2001), pp. 215; 281.

with the French and a Free Frenchman resisting the Axis. Or conversely, one could be a Cameroonian Germanophile resisting the Gaullist war effort.

Does this mean that one can discern a memory specific to the Free French episode in Africa? The Gaullist years have been regularly evoked, both before and after the decolonization wave of 1960. In the 1950s, General de Gaulle reactivated a myth born around 1944. In the words of Henry Rousso the myth in question ran as follows: "The history of France from 1940 to 1944 had been made in London and Algiers."[2] This obviously left out a large proportion of the first Free French ranks, those having rallied to de Gaulle in the Pacific Ocean, French India, Cameroon, and FEA. This is not to say that one should necessarily speak of a "Free French syndrome" for FEA and Cameroon, any more than an undifferentiated "Vichy syndrome" can be applied to French West Africa. While the intensity and chronology of memorial ebbs and flows vary, there can be no doubt that various groups manipulated and shaped specific Free French African memories over time.

The goal of this epilogue is not so much to uncover a collective memory of Free French Africa, but rather to suggest the silences, appropriations, and distortions brought about after the war, around the issue of Free France's Africanness. I will therefore consider specific points in time when these memories were reactivated, as well as memorial vectors and actors. These include networks, individuals, organizations, and official commemorations.

## Brazzaville, 1944

This story begins long before the dusk of empire. The conference that was held in the capital of FEA from January to February 1944 presented at once ruptures and continuities with the Free French years that had preceded it. Not a single African delegate was involved in the event. It is also striking how many former Free French leaders in Africa took part in it: Pierre Cournarie (former "governor" of Cameroon), Pierre de Saint-Mart (same role in Oubangui), Charles Assier de Pompignan (at the helm in Gabon), Jean-Charles André Capagorry (Moyen-Congo), Henri Sautot (Oubangui), Henri Laurentie, Félix Eboué, and Jacques Rogué (Gabon, Chad). In short, these longtime Gaullist decision makers in Africa were

---

[2]   Henry Rousso, *The Vichy Syndrome: History and Memory in France since 1944* (Cambridge: Harvard University Press, 1991), p. 72.

about to prohibit the very practices that had underpinned their war effort. Much more than an end in itself, the Brazzaville conference constituted an about-face.

While some historians have hailed its "implicit universalism," others have viewed the Brazzaville conference as a cynical attempt to counter American anticolonial pressure.[3] What is certain is that participants did pronounce the rejection of forced labor and of the notoriously arbitrary *code de l'indigénat*. The conference established theoretical equality before the law. However, the foundations of this reformist spirit remained deeply conservative. The future Africa envisioned on the banks of the Congo River remained rural and hierarchical; the amelioration of "races" endured as a dominant concern expressed by the delegates.[4] A few of the more audacious proposals, like a vast imperial federation advanced by Pleven and Laurentie, were ultimately rejected.

The Vichy authorities collected information about the Brazzaville conference and were left unimpressed. A report from the political affairs bureau of the Ministry of the Colonies, dated February 12, 1944, asserted that the conference had mostly reaffirmed the principle that "the evolution of indigenous society" should take place "within the framework of a traditional milieu." As it happened, Vichy shared this quest for authenticity. This, in turn, no doubt explains the final Vichy verdict on the Brazzaville conference: "One has to admit that the Brazzaville conference is situated on a political line that has already been well trodden."[5] Others would seize on this notion of a counterintuitive continuity between purported reform and the policies of Pétain's regime. Indeed, the Brazzaville conference led to many disillusions in Africa. These were encapsulated by the Senegalese politician Lamine Guèye's complaint to the ministry of the colonies in May 1945: "The Brazzaville conference... had raised much hope. It has been dashed since the publication in West Africa of the indigenous legal code inspired from its recommendations." Indeed, according to Guèye, "this code retains many of the least popular and most tyrannical dispositions of the indigenous legal code promulgated by the Vichy government in French West Africa in 1941."[6]

---

3 Cooper, *Decolonization*, p. 178; Marc Michel, *Décolonisations et émergence du tiers monde* (Paris: Hachette, 2005), p. 94. The idea that the conference served to counter U.S. goals is not unanimously shared. See Institut Charles de Gaulle, *Brazzaville, aux sources de la décolonisation* (Paris: Plon, 1988), pp. 65–70.

4 Cooper, *Decolonization*, p. 181.

5 ANOM 1Affpol 883, file 21, rapport on the Brazzaville conference.

6 ANOM Cab 42, file 232, Guèye to the minister of the colonies.

Too timid for Africans like Guèye, the Brazzaville reforms appeared dangerously reckless to many Europeans, starting with settlers. Some administrators joined the ranks of the indignant. Thus, on August 9, 1944, the head of the Nyong and Sanaga region in Cameroon pleaded to the head of the bureau of political affairs: "The weakness that we are displaying by tolerating the creation of entirely native labor unions is sure to turn against us in the near future."[7] Given such competing interpretations, not to mention the teleological reading that many would make of the Brazzaville moment, it is hardly surprising that Elikia M'Bokolo evokes "myths" surrounding the conference.[8]

## Douala, 1945

This being said, by calling for the abolition of forced labor, by accepting the principle of freedom of labor and of labor unions, the Brazzaville conference marked a clear break from Fighting French practices. Indeed, under Free France, strikes had been illegal and were rapidly repressed, as when the employees of the Congo Océan railway halted work in Pointe-Noire on February 13, 1942.[9]

The major strike, followed by riots, that consumed Douala in September 1945 have several origins. The newly authorized unions played a role, as did nationalists, the influx of migrants from rural areas into the New Bell district, and the settlers themselves. A steep rise in the price of foodstuffs should likewise be considered a root cause. I would add that the impact and memory of the Free French era, and the war more generally, also shaped the riots, and mostly the reading of them after the fact. While most historians have considered the events of 1945 in Douala as a sort of dress rehearsal for the protests of 1955 in Cameroon, it seems to me that a reading back in time makes as much, if not more sense, than a projection into the future.[10]

The tense climate stemmed also from the dual radicalization of colonial and anticolonial sides, whose respective expectations of the Brazzaville conference brought matters to a head. On September 2, 1944, the "estates general of colonialism," a colonial platform expressly reserved

---


7  ANCMR APA 10658.
8  Elikia M'Bokolo, "La réception des principes de Brazzaville par les populations Africaines en AEF" in *Brazzaville, aux sources de la décolonisation*, pp. 246–252.
9  ANC, GGAEF 126, telegram dated March 4, 1942.
10  Coquery-Vidrovitch, "Emeutes urbaines," pp. 494–96; Joseph, pp. 63–68; Mbembe, pp. 177, 195–221; Sah, pp. 628–54; Deltombe, et al., pp. 43–45.

to "non-African citizens" (in a sure sign that race marked the divide, foreigners were admitted but not "natives, even ones possessing French citizenship").[11] This assembly served as a soapbox for settler interests. They roundly rejected the Brazzaville conference's recommendations, deemed "demagogical."[12] So irate were the settlers that they dispatched a delegation to General de Gaulle in person to "protest against the Brazzaville policies."[13]

On the other side, on September 12, some twenty-eight district chiefs and assorted other Cameroonian notables from the Wouri region handed the local administration a memorandum. In it, they outlined their reasons for boycotting the coming elections for the consultative assembly in Paris. They contended that "the rights of natives are not sufficiently safeguarded" by the judicial system in Cameroon. They also protested against numerous electoral restrictions. Finally, they complained that Cameroon was to be represented at the new assembly under the title "French Cameroon," unlike Togo, another former German colony under French mandate. They added that General de Gaulle, High Commissioner Sicé, and "Governor" Brunot had all accepted the principle that Cameroon was tied to the League of Nations rather than France.[14] Over the ensuing days, Douala language tracts circulated around town. They cited the meager social benefits reaped by Senegalese and Gabonese who had acquired French citizenship. Soon, posters appeared bearing a much more explicit message: "Free Cameroon for the natives. The whites must go."[15]

Several sparks lit the tinder keg. One was a strike at the rail works of Bonabéri, in the suburbs of Douala, which erupted on September 21, 1945. Strikers demanded higher wages. Three days later, the movement had spread. According to a gendarmerie report, in New Bell, some thousand rioters besieged the prison. They chanted "Free Cameroon for the natives." The other trigger came in the form of a tragic incident that unfolded that same day in New Bell. That afternoon, a military vehicle

[11] Martin-René Atangana, *Capitalisme et nationalisme au Cameroun au lendemain de la seconde guerre mondiale (1945–1956)* (Paris: Presses universitaires de la Sorbonne, 1998), p. 34.

[12] Joseph, pp. 62–63.

[13] ANOM Cab 64, file 454, note for the minister of the Colonies.

[14] It is interesting that there was no mention here of Free French leaders Leclerc and Cournarie who both bore the titles of "governor," which implies colonial, rather than mandate, rule.

[15] ANOM DSM 74, Douala September 1945, and Sah, pp. 637–39.

struck a Cameroonian girl. It was immediately set ablaze by an angry crowd. Other Cameroonians descended on downtown Douala, armed mostly with clubs. This, in turn, led roughly two hundred Europeans to scramble for weapons. Later that afternoon, the authorities began arming Europeans. Some of these vigilantes went on to assassinate Cameroonian protesters. At the airfield, a military aircraft opened fire on a crowd. In the center of town, Cameroonians were shot in the back as they left the train station. Others were struck by bullets fired by groups of whites roaming around town on trucks. The official casualty estimates from colonial records are no doubt far too conservative: they stand at fifteen dead and twenty-four wounded, all of them African. Historians tend to evoke higher figures, ranging from eighty to one hundred fatalities.[16]

Contrary to appearances, the French community was deeply divided at the time of these events. What had begun as a white lynch mob intent on crushing what it saw as a black riot soon turned into a rebellion by settlers against the government. It, in turn, was overlaid by a settling of scores against unionists deemed responsible for mounting Cameroonian political demands. On September 25, a group of armed Europeans laid siege to the house of French union leader Pierre Lalaurie. According to Achille Mbembe, this leading figure of the C.G.T. constituted merely a first target, the larger goal being a settler putsch against the colonial authorities. One of the attackers, the secretary of the chamber of commerce Ollivier, was shot dead as he tried to enter Lalaurie's dwelling.[17] The rioters then attempted to exact revenge on the unionist, and remove him from the hands of tirailleurs who had come to arrest him. On the governor's orders, Lalaurie and two other men were then evacuated on board an aircraft bound for Pointe-Noire. However, the dissidents managed to overturn the order and have the aircraft return to Douala. The prisoners then came within a hair of being hanged by a furious European crowd.[18] That same day, a delegation of the white faction demanded the arrest of the "native chiefs, signatories of the memorandum."[19] The goal thus involved crushing the political demands at the root of the unrest. The days of September 21 through 25 were laden with consequences: Cameroonians

---

[16] This paragraph is based on ANCMR 1AC 123 as well as Coquery-Vidrovitch, "Emeutes urbaines," pp. 494–96; Joseph, pp. 63–68; Mbembe, pp. 195–221; Sah, pp. 648–52.

[17] Lalaurie would be released a year later. The jury deemed that he acted in self-defense against men armed with machine guns who had declared their intent to kill him.

[18] This paragraph rests on ANCMR 1AC 123 as well as Joseph, pp. 63–68 and Mbembe, p. 219.

[19] ANOM 156 APOM 3, Douala events.

were massacred, union demands made way for nationalist ones, colonial authority was publicly flouted, and the French community revealed deep schisms.

There was more. The events of September 1945 also conjured up ghosts. The Free French era was subject to widely divergent readings. During the so-called estates general of colonization, intended to counter the Brazzaville conference reforms, FEA and Cameroon's settlers proved especially virulent. They invoked the war effort in their argument to maintain forced labor and the indigénat code.[20] They contributed an important spark to the events of September 1945, precisely by enrolling the memory of Free France in Africa.

The other side also ascribed to the wartime paradigm. In seeking to pinpoint the origins of the Douala riots, colonial administration Genin described "a panicked atmosphere" – he might have added a logic of racial besiegement – that prevailed among Douala's Europeans. He then concurred with another inspection report explaining the September events as a "fascist putsch." In this reading, the settlers who massacred African civilians, who tried to lynch Pierre Lalaurie, and who hijacked a government aircraft, were but another manifestation of the Nazi scourge that the Gaullists had fought. Here was a daring, though not particularly convincing, hypothesis.

The reasoning was suspect even by Genin's own admission. Firstly, the attempted putsch, if such a putsch was ever conceived, had been dictated by anguish. Phenotype and chameleonic transformation are blurred in Genin's testimony. One of Douala's Frenchmen is depicted as "green with fear," another "white like laundry" in the face of a black uprising. Genin also investigated some of the personalities of the criminals. He noted that during the events of September 24 and 25, "ordinarily peaceful people" were "suddenly transformed into fanatics." We seem far removed from Mussolini's black shirts vaunting gratuitous violence. For instance, Genin cites the case of Giraud, the head of accounting, who was one of the first to try to harm Lalaurie. And yet, remarked Genin, the man was ordinarily peaceful and cautious, "a good citizen, a good husband and fine head of his family." Moreover, his son had served in the Free French ranks. Genin elaborated a theory to elucidate the seemingly inexplicable settler position. He suggested that Douala's Europeans had been cut off from the motherland since 1939. Consequently, they "were not able to follow the union actions that spurred the resistance in France during the

---

[20] Joseph, p. 62.

occupation." According to him, the spirit of reform had been imported from the metropole in 1944. Introduced to the colonies, it acted as a kind of detonator. The Brazzaville conference reflected just such a rupture. The anachronistic, retrograde attitude of Douala's whites was thus imputed to the fact that Free French Africa had not been exposed to the Communist wind that blew over the French resistance. This was the reverse image of African troops teaching lessons to the maquis. Genin deemed that the metropolitan maquis ought to serve as a model in the first bastion of African resistance.[21]

Mostly, the notion of a fascist putsch seems problematic insofar as one of the coup leaders, Captain Jean Viazzi, had served in the first Free French division. At the funeral of his comrade Ollivier, he read a speech of which a few lines seem especially pertinent: "In the name of the Free French. . . . I come to give you our last salute. We are proud of you. You are deserving of France, which you have served with enthusiasm and joy since 1940. You were one of the youngest and dearest among us. . . . Never again will your beloved Provence see you. But we will go there and tell those you left behind: 'your son, your brother, died a Free Frenchman.'" Despite being killed by a C.G.T. union delegate in Douala as he tried to break into his home, Ollivier received a Free French homage, as if felled by German bullets.[22]

On October 12, 1945, the Resistance newspaper *Combat* added its stone to the edifice. It hinted that the troubles in Douala were imputable to enduring old quarrels between Gaullists and Pétainists. The newspaper pointed to "the adjudication of all transports in Cameroon to a notorious Vichyite, just released from the internment camp of Batchenga." It added the case of "a functionary revoked in Paris by a purge commission, who was maintained in the post of labor inspector by the governor."[23] Thus, according to both the supporters and detractors of the white insurgents in Douala, the fundamental cause of the September events involved the region's unhinging during the war. For some, the purge process had not been thorough enough. For others, the Free French had been deprived of salutary contact with the progressive domestic resistance.

In 1998, former Free Frenchman Pierre Messmer offered an intriguing explanation to account for the harsh stand by Douala's Europeans against the Brazzaville conference. "During the war, they had been cut

---

[21] The last two paragraphs are drawn from ANCMR 1AC 123.
[22] ANOM 156 APOM 3, Douala events.
[23] ANOM 156 APOM 3, Douala events, excerpts from *Combat* dated October 12, 1945.

off from the metropole, and were subject to the influence of South Africa, where apartheid reigned."[24] Likely inspired by a point raised by American political scientist Richard Joseph, this interpretation allowed Messmer to dismiss any link between Free France on the one hand, and the racist settler uprising of Douala on the other hand.[25] He thereby denied any continuity between the values of the September 1945 movement and the system of carding, the rule of exception, and the forced labor campaign that Free France had overseen in Africa in the name of the war effort. In his eyes, Free France had fought Nazism; it therefore could not embody colonial repression.

### Veterans and Recipients of the Resistance Medal

If some settlers proclaimed their links to the Free French past, it goes without saying that African veterans did the same. Like the Free French in London, those in Free French Africa consistently underscored the precocity of their engagement in the movement. It carried much weight among the Free French: a fighter who joined the Gaullist side in 1943 did not enjoy the same prestige as his brother or sister in arms who had enrolled in 1940. Competition of this sort sometimes reached absurd lengths. Thus, Alain Savary remembers that for the very earliest Gaullist volunteers in London, every day of seniority mattered.[26] This hierarchy of precedence would endure.

Precocity was one thing, agency another. Was it even possible for individuals to claim the status of "volunteer" when the entire territory to which they were posted swung over to Free France in August 1940? Robert Paxton noted this ambiguity in 1972, when he mentioned the "more or less 'automatic' Gaullists" of Free French Africa.[27] Already in November 1941, the idea of a bonus was hatched for Free French volunteers, to be paid after the war. In a wrinkle reminiscent of Ancient Roman practice, the bonus could take the form of a land plot in the colonies or protectorates. The plan was specifically restricted: "The decree is aimed only at Free French volunteers; soldiers who rallied by force of circumstance would be excluded."[28] Adding to the question of "automatic"

---

[24] Messmer, p. 117.

[25] Joseph, pp. 62–63.

[26] Savary's testimony in Daniel Rondeau and Roger Stéphane, *Des hommes libres*, p. 68.

[27] Robert Paxton, *Vichy France: Old Guard and New Order* (New York: Columbia University Press, 1972), p. 44.

[28] ANOM Cab 63, London, November 21, 1941.

engagements was the issue of Africans enrolled without consent. In any event, the projected decree of November 1941 opened up Pandora's Box. Who exactly was a Free French volunteer and who was not?

The question resurfaced in 1943, in another context, tied to the creation of the *Médaille de la Résistance*. The latter was intended to "recognize remarkable acts of faith and courage, which in France, across the empire and abroad, contributed to the resistance of the French people against the enemy and his accomplices since June 18, 1940."[29] In a letter addressed to Henri Laurenie on May 6, 1943, the representative of Moyen-Congo's functionaries, Jean Colsenet, contended, "It is untenable to suggest granting the medal of the Resistance to officials simply because they answered present when Colonel de Larminat took power. It would no longer be a *Médaille de la Résitance*, but merely a *Médaille du Ralliement* [Medal for rallying]."[30] Requests were therefore based on personal engagement and chiefly on the three glorious days and the Battle of Gabon. Very few Africans were nominated by European administrators in FEA and Cameroon. Of the hundreds of nominations preserved in a thick file in Brazzaville, I was able to find only three names bearing African markers. To give a sense of scale, there were as many Belgians nominated from FEA. The Africans in question were Amadou Seck, Adolphe Diagne, and René Diagne (the latter for having helped swing the Senegalese community of Bangui over to the Gaullists). Adolphe Diagne, son of the deputy Blaise Diagne, enjoyed full French citizenship. On this score, the file reveals deep confusion over the requirements for the medal, with many letters wrongly citing citizenship restrictions. And of course, the vast majority of FEA and Cameroon's African population were French subjects and not citizens. This erroneous reading therefore excluded nearly all African applicants. In 1945 and 1946, several proposals were turned down on this basis. Thwarted, a few determined officials then formulated fallback requests for the medal of honor of the colonies. Among those nominated were Congolese translator Alphonse Moutou, warrant officer Akoundou, Poumali of the indigenous guard, and Piti, Bongo, and Matchoulou, all canton chiefs.[31] In Cameroon as well, native recipients of the *Médaille de la Résitance* can be counted on one hand.[32]

---

29  http://www.ordredelaliberation.fr/fr_doc/medaille.html.
30  AC GGAEF 504, letter dated May 6, 1943.
31  AC GGAEF 504.
32  Sah, p. 728.

Although Africans were manifestly underrepresented among the recipients of this medal, the ministry of veterans' affairs did recognize their status of volunteers in the wake of the war. Indeed, this status seems to have been accorded across the board to FEA and Cameroonian Free French veterans. The issue was no mere formality. The rank carried with it considerable social capital and consequences with respect to pensions. The quality of "volunteer combatant in the Resistance" constituted another badge of honor. In 1957, the office of veterans' affairs in FEA indicated that the latter was systematically attributed to Free French veterans.[33] The balance sheet is therefore somewhat mixed.

The category of active combatant posed nearly as many vexing problems as the status of volunteer. It was also overlaid onto questions of seniority. Thus, starting in 1945, Free French tirailleurs having fought prior to November 8, 1942, received a demobilization bonus of 1,000 francs. Those incorporated after said date were ineligible for the bonus (which, by way of comparison, remained low next to the one granted by the British army).[34] One complaint pointed out that the rule excluded some African troops of the very first hour. Indeed, the proviso concerning active combat ruled out the entire B.M. 6 from Congo, which was never sent to the front because of the 1943 "whitening." Facing several such grievances from veterans, on August 29, 1946, the ministry of overseas France emitted the following instructions to Brazzaville and Douala: "The circular is to be applied leniently. Tirailleur paperwork and files were shoddily maintained between 1940 and 1944, and many have disappeared, which renders verifications difficult. In these conditions, all you need to establish is that the native in question has served for at least three months outside of his group of colonies." Even with this call for an expansive reading of the rules, the exclusion remained in place. A veteran had to prove that he had faced enemy fire or had been posted outside of Free French Africa.[35] Some could not.


## A Self-Made Hero

Jean-Bedel Bokassa, president (1965), then emperor (1977) of Centrafrique, was a dictator whose excesses and especially his Napoleonic self-coronation led even Mobutu Sese Seko to describe him as a

---

[33] ANOM 1Affpol 2217.
[34] Sah, p. 593.
[35] ANS 4D 60 (89).

megalomaniac.[36] Yet as a younger man, he served as NCO in the Free French. Like many other heads of state in Francophone Africa, Bokassa was therefore a product of the French military.[37] Specifically, Corporal Bokassa played an important role in the capture of a munitions depot in Brazzaville on August 27, 1940. He thereby contributed to rallying Congo to Free France the next day. In this sense, he actively participated in the birth of Free French Africa.

One wonders whether the memory of the August 28, 1940, putsch in Brazzaville crossed his mind as he staged his own coup in 1965 in Bangui? More generally, did the theatricality of the three glorious days leave any traces in Central Africa? This is what Cameroonian intellectual Mongo Beti posited when he evoked the circumstances and the stage in Cameroon in August 1940. He deduced that the *mise en scène* of regime change in 1940 prefigured some postcolonial practices. "Today still," he wrote in 1972, "current events in Cameroon are presented as a succession of prodigious and stunning *coups de théâtre*."[38]

In any event, up to this point, the official Bokassa story matches that told by the archives. It is the second phase of Bokassa's war that has long fooled historians and journalists. The official story runs as follows: Bokassa participated in the 1944 landings in Provence, and then in the campaign to liberate France. Two weeks after the December 31, 1965, coup that propelled Bokassa to power, the official government mouthpiece *Terre africaine* described the new leader to his people. In an article titled "Who is Colonel Bokassa?" the newspaper steered from ambiguity toward untruth. "Jean-Bedel Bokassa.... continued to fight by General de Gaulle's side until the landings on the Riviera."[39] The myth took root. In 1973, to mark the anniversary of de Gaulle's radio call of June 18, 1940, Radio-Bangui declared, "Remember, it was June 18, 1940, and the world war was entering its final phase. France was in peril and its fate was also that of its overseas colonies.... On the battlefields, a young son of Oubangui-Chari was being noticed for his acts of courage. Leaving the French army with the rank of captain, he is now an army general who presides the destiny of our country."[40]

---

[36] On the Mobutu comment, see Jean-Pierre Bat, *Le syndrome Foccart: la politique française en Afrique de 1959 à nos jours* (Paris: Gallimard, 2012), p. 377.

[37] One could cite for example Gabriel Ramanantsoa, president of Madagascar, Seyni Kountché in Niger, and Gnassingbé Eyadema in Togo.

[38] Mongo Beti, *Main basse sur le Cameroun* (Paris: Maspero, 1977), p. 56.

[39] *Terre africaine*, January 14, 1966, p. 5.

[40] ADN 68PO/1/167, transcript from Radio-Bangui on the June 18, 1973, ceremonies.

Biographers took up the myth, some actually propelling Bokassa as far as Germany in 1945.[41] Veterans in the know were not duped, however, even those who supported Bokassa. The memoirs of his former captain, Joseph Freitag, sang the praises of the future president (earning Freitag the title of officier de l'ordre national du mérite centrafricain). Yet even they limited themselves to describing the actions of Bokassa in Brazzaville on August 27, 1940.[42] Only in 2000 did Géraldine Faes and Stephen Smith reveal the contents of Bokassa's files in the French military archives. Their verdict was clear: "Bokassa never left the African continent" over the course of World War II.[43] Nor did he participate in any battles in North Africa, I might add. Indeed, the Vincennes archives confirm that Bokassa first faced enemy fire during the Indochina War. Between 1940 and 1944 he certainly served in the French army, first in Congo, then in Bangui where he honed his radio technician skills, before returning to Brazzaville. Yet he never saw action. He first landed in France in the port of Marseille in April 1950, rather more peacefully than the myth would have it. The Vincennes file does chronicle his rapid ascent through the ranks. He enrolled in the military in Brazzaville in May 1939, was promoted to corporal a year following, then sergeant in November 1941, and sergeant-chief in 1944.[44]

In and of itself, the fiction of a Provence landing can seem rather banal. After all, a great many heads of state have covered up or obfuscated far more troubled wartime pasts (consider François Mitterrand or Kurt Waldheim). Indeed, the future emperor's war can hardly be considered dishonorable, quite the contrary. Very few can claim to have joined de Gaulle's movement as early as August 27, 1940. What is intriguing, however, is Bokassa's apparent need to invent an even more heroic wartime experience. Was it a matter of eliding the 1943 whitening that kept many units in FEA? Or negating the 1945 rules that only rewarded Africans having seen combat?

---

[41] So tells us his only English language biography, which adds erroneously, "During the Second World War, he proved to be an able soldier, courageous in combat, and received the Légion d'honneur, the Médaille militaire and the Croix de Guerre." Brian Titley, *Dark Age: The Political Odyssey of Emperor Bokassa* (Montreal: McGill-Queen's University Press, 1997), pp. 9–10.

[42] Freitag, p. 67.

[43] Geraldine Faes, Stephen Smith, *Bokassa 1er un empereur français* (Paris: Calmann-Lévy, 2000), p. 66.

[44] SHD 2831/67.

The character's megalomania no doubt played a role, but cannot explain everything. Without providing a definitive answer, I would like to suggest three other explanations for Bokassa's accommodations with history. Firstly, the Bokassian shift reflects another. In the postwar, the feats of the mainland resistance, not to mention Allied actions, left little room to celebrate the three glorious days, symbols of the African effort, and Bokassa's main contribution to the war. The war was then perceived on a Franco-French scale, or on a truncated global one, favoring Stalingrad, Midway, and D-Day. Representing Free France in Africa lacked cachet. This is in essence what Bokassa signaled in 1977. In the preface to Freitag's book, he declared, "we Africans, as Free Frenchmen and companions of General de Gaulle, condemn the fact. . . . that France today has not officially and solemnly recognized this history. Free French Africa took risks to wage war and to achieve the final victory and the restoration of France." He then shifted the focus to his personal actions on August 27, 1940: "Having survived this tragic moment where the slightest error could have led me to be executed, I require more by way of acknowledgement than merely the flame of the unknown soldier. I also need the recognition of my former officers. Isn't that human nature?"[45] The slide toward the beaches of Provence was thus part of an unfulfilled wish for recognition.

Secondly, as paradoxical as it may sound, Bokassa was also consumed by a strong nostalgia for the French army and by boundless admiration for General de Gaulle. In 1961, it was "with bitterness" that Officer Bokassa left the French military to join the ranks of Centrafrique's. In fact, after his destitution by the French military's operation Barracuda in 1979, Bokassa first sought asylum in France by trumpeting his dual citizenship. Long before this episode, Jacques Foccart finally managed to soften General de Gaulle toward Bokassa by invoking the fact that the latter "considered himself not merely a Francophile, but as French."[46] As for de Gaulle, the story of his encounter with Bokassa in 1966 is well established. While most have commented on the title of "father" that Bokassa conferred on him, Jacques Foccart's testimony contains lines that strike me as far more revealing. He wrote of the 1966 *tête-à-tête*: "With official ceremonies over, I went to give . . . [Bokassa] an autographed photo of the General . . . Once he got back home, he had two giant photos mounted in his presidential office, each more than two

---

[45] Preface to Freitag, pp. 19–20.
[46] Faes and Smith, p. 112.

meters high. On the left, Bokassa as a barefoot tirailleur; on the right, Bokassa by General de Gaulle's side, wearing the insignia of the Legion of Honor."[47] Bokassa was thus able to constantly revisit the days of Free France through a photo presenting him as a "simple *tirailleur*." He thereby contrasted his memories with the tangible sign of his success, materialized by his presence as a head of state flanking the former leader of Free France. The fantasy of the beaches of Provence elevated the soldier and helped produce this meteoric ascension.

Finally, Jean-Bedel Bokassa felt a constant competition with Lieutenant Georges Koudoukou, who fell gloriously at Bir Hakeim in 1942. Koudoukou was the first officer and one of only three Compagnons de la Libération from Centrafrique, along with Dominique Kosseyo and Paul Koudoussaragne. In 1971, and again the year following, a delegation of Centrafricain veterans convened in Bangui to mark the anniversary of de Gaulle's June 18, 1940, radio declaration (interestingly, the three glorious days were not celebrated). The procession followed a carefully planned route that included three highlights: it left a first wreath of flowers on the memorial to French Lieutenant-Colonel Robert de Roux, followed by a second one on the Free French monument of the N'Dress cemetery, then a third at the foot of the stele depicting Lieutenant Koudoukou. In 1971, President Bokassa attended only the part of the ceremony at N'Dress. The following year, he bypassed the event entirely.[48] A French military note hinted that Bokassa was avoiding the sites dedicated to the hero of Bir Hakeim: "Koudoukou was the first officer from Centrafrique (Bokassa was the second)."[49] Being relegated to a parenthesis did not please the dictator. With Koudoukou dying in combat in 1942, none could reinvent him, like Bokassa, into a liberator of France in 1944.

### Compagnons Like the Others?

Besides the matter of his untimely death, Bokassa had every reason to envy Koudoukou. The Order of the Libération, in which the latter was admitted posthumously, was surrounded in a halo of prestige and camaraderie. Thierry d'Argenlieu had initially contemplated terming its members "crusaders," before René Cassin rejected the term in favor

---

47 Philippe Gaillard, *Foccart parle*, Vol. 1 (Paris: Fayard, 1995), p. 298.
48 ADN 68PO/1/167, note de service (1971) on the commemoration of June 18; notes to the ambassador (May 1971) and report from the French Ambassador to the Central African Republic, June 19, 1972.
49 AOL, Koudoukou file. Letter from Colonel Massip, dated June 26, 1991.

of "companions."[50] The order and its members nevertheless remained something of a "chivalry of modern times."[51] Its membership conditions were defined as follows: "People or collectivities both military and civilian who stood out during the process of liberating France and its empire."[52] The order's prestige was such, its character so sacred, that two French prime ministers, Jacques Chaban-Delmas and Pierre Messmer bear only the mention of "compagnon" as the sole title on their graves.[53]

The Order of the Liberation was founded in Brazzaville on November 16, 1940. Over the course of the war, it admitted eleven combatants and five civilians from sub-Saharan Africa, out of a total of 1,038 individual compagnons. The five African civilians hailed from French West Africa, and were all executed by Vichy for their Gaullist convictions and actions. The soldiers, meanwhile, were from Chad and Oubangui, save for two or three of them (Noukoun Kone from Mali, and Adolphe Diagne of Senegalese origin; the identity of another compagnon, Gargué, or Ngargué, who is presumed to have been African, has never been established). No known Congolese, Cameroonian, or Gabonese was ever admitted to the order. Neither Brazzaville, nor for that matter London, feature among the cities recognized by the Order – Grenoble, Paris, and Nantes being the only large urban centers commended in this way. Furthermore, the total number of African members seems miniscule given the preponderance of colonials in the early Free French ranks. It nevertheless remains higher than the number of women compagnonne, who total six.

And yet, for the first "class" introduced into the order in November 1940, de Gaulle had sought nominations from the "council of the crusaders of liberation" on the basis of quotas. He had requested fifty files from the Pacific, six from the French territories in India, and "roughly two hundred for Free French Africa."[54] In point of fact, it was Europeans posted in these territories who constituted the bulk of the nominees. Out of 1,038 compagnons, 140 were present in Free French Africa in August

---

[50] Jean-Christophe Notin, *1061 Compagnons. Histoire des Compagnons de la Libération* (Paris: Perrin, 2000), p. 10. Vladimir Trouplin, *Dictionnaire des Compagnons de la Libération* (Bordeaux: Elytis, 2010), p. 12.

[51] Guillaume Piketty, "L'Ordre de la Libération," in François Marcot, *Dictionnaire historique de la Résistance*, Paris, Robert Laffont, 2006, p. 1015.

[52] Trouplin, p. 13.

[53] Bernard Lachaise, "Qu'est-ce qu'un compagnon?" in Serge Berstein, Pierre Birnbaum, Jean-Pierre Rioux, *De Gaulle et les Elites* (Paris: la Découverte, 2008), p. 65.

[54] ANOM GGAEF 5D290, de Gaulle to Larminat, December 11, 1940.

1940, but only eight or nine were natives of these lands.[55] Subsequent nominations followed the same trend. When René Pleven cabled Brazzaville to obtain the names of additional "resistors of the first hour in FEA" on November 7, 1944, Henri Laurentie's list in response contained no African nominee. Conversely, it featured men like Henri Le Thomas, from Le Havre, who had emitted the telegram pronouncing Félix Eboué's adhesion to General de Gaulle in August 1940.[56] Thus, only Europeans having orchestrated or impelled regime change in 1940 were recognized as compagnons. Africans, including the ones who carried out the operation, were excluded. This imbalance grew over time. Although certainly present in the first wave of nominations, Free French Africa finished largely underrepresented when the Order ceased taking new members in January 1946.

This said, since 1945 the Order of Liberation has undertaken considerable follow-up with African compagnons and their families. Dense correspondence files attest this. They chronicle the Order's facilitation of pension payments and medical coverage for African members and their families. The Order achieved this through a variety of channels and connections, as it possessed only a limited budget and was not theoretically tasked with assisting its members. The Order's chancellery also maintained and sometimes even designed the graves of deceased African members. Finally, the Order's lexicon tended to undercut and even subvert colonial and neocolonial dynamics. Letters from Chadian and Centrafricain members addressed to Paris, and responses back, systematically bear the egalitarian marker "dear compagnon."[57] However, in practice, pension regimes differed radically for African and French veterans in general. African compagnons therefore experienced material conditions incommensurate with those of their metropolitan comrades (note that this state of affairs was hardly the Order's doing). Prior to his death in 1994, the last African compagnon, Dominique Kosseyo, collected the meager sum of 2.26 francs a day from the French government.[58] A letter from Kosseyo, dated August 25, 1960, shows that at that juncture, he

---

[55] Trouplin, p. 16. The uncertainty over the exact numbers derives from the same doubts over Ngargué/Gargué.

[56] ANOM GGAEF 6B 725, Pleven telegram, Brazzaville, November 7, 1944.

[57] AOL files of African compagnons.

[58] "Kosseyo, le dernier Compagnon de la Libération originaire d'Afrique est mort. La France lui envoyait une pension de 2,26F par jour," *Journal des Combattants*, December 16, 1995.

was receiving no pension whatsoever, contrary to some of his comrades in arms in his same town.[59]

## Monuments and Commemorations

Few memorials have been erected to celebrate African compagnons. The stele and fresco in Bangui honoring Lieutenant Koudoukou constitute exceptions that prove the rule. More generally, scant markers celebrate Free French Africa. In the thick of the war, Leclerc himself ridiculed the idea of naming a Yaoundé street after himself. He anticipated the perplexity of a young Cameroonian decades later asking of the putative street name, "What citizen was he?"[60] Conversely, Leclerc did toy with the idea of erecting a monument in Douala to the Free French who fell in Gabon, before retracting the proposal. It had elicited mixed feedback at best from his superiors.[61] The Free French naturally preferred to celebrate their victories over the Axis rather than this fratricidal campaign.

In the immediate postwar, during what Henry Rousso calls the "mourning phase,"[62] it was mostly Free French leaders who were exalted and commemorated. In 1949, a memorial ensemble to Philippe Leclerc was erected in Douala with much pomp and ceremony. It included a statue of the marshal posed in front of a vast bas-relief, recalling his victories from his point of departure in Douala through to Kufra, Strasbourg, and Colmar (see Figure 17).

In 2000, historian Marc Michel noted how this monument had endured while so many other "statues of French personalities had been disassembled elsewhere, as with that of Gallieni in Antananarivo." He then hypothesized, "No doubt it is because Leclerc's memory is not burdened by 'colonial ignominy'" (note the quotation marks). He nevertheless concluded that "In Black Africa, even in Cameroon, the memory of Leclerc risks becoming only a French one."[63]

Over recent years, this same Douala monument has come under attack. In May 2009, on the eve of Cameroon's national day, the nationalist militant Mboua Massock targeted it. He covered it with spray-painted slogans that read, "Our heroes and martyrs first" and "After fifty years after independence, this is too much." As head of the Nouvelle Dynamique

---

[59] AOL files of African compagnons.

[60] Notin, *Leclerc*, p. 126.

[61] Ebako, p. 256

[62] Rousso, p. 10.

[63] Marc Michel, "Leclerc et l'Afrique Noire," pp. 269 and 272, note 49.

FIGURE 17. The Leclerc monument in Douala, Cameroon, date uncertain (1950s?). Author's collection.

Nationaliste Africaine, Massock publicly called for the Leclerc monument's destruction. At his trial, he explained his actions as reflecting "a civic and political engagement." Massock deemed that Cameroon lacked memorials celebrating its own historical figures. In lieu of Leclerc, he wished to see statues to Rudolf Douala Manga Bell (a Cameroonian king and resistor to the German occupation who died in 1914), Ruben Um Nyobè (nationalist leader killed by the French army in 1958), and Ernest Ouandié (Cameroonian nationalist, executed by Cameroonian authorities in 1971). Moreover, Massock considered that the Leclerc monument embodied "the remains of the French colonial administration in Cameroon."[64] This reading privileged Leclerc as a representative of the French government.[65] It was also colored by the painful war that began in Cameroon in 1955 – a civil war characterized by the forceful intervention of the former mandatory power against the backdrop of the Cold War.

[64] "Querelle autour des monuments Leclerc," http://www.makea-world.com/fr/bnnews .php?nid=3197. Also see: elestinnkwetchoua.over-blog.com/article-cameroun-mboua-massok-et-le-monument-leclerc-a-douala.
[65] Indeed, he had served as "governor" for six weeks in 1940.

The Leclerc monument controversy mostly reveals a dual othering process. In France, the model for the Douala statue is curiously preserved at the Quai Branly Museum, devoted to "primitive arts."[66] This seems odd, for the piece's sculptor Evariste Jonchère was not African, and his work appears bereft of any African content or influence. One might far more logically expect to find it at the Invalides military history museum than in its current location. In Cameroon, conversely, the monument evokes colonialism and Françafrique, at least for some. The effect is no doubt reinforced by the fact that French tourists tend to congregate around the landmark to photograph it. It bears repeating that Massock does not intend to replace Leclerc with Cameroonian heroes of World War II, like Dangsalla, Raphaël Onana, or Manga Fabien. Nor does he propose honoring the memory of Cameroonian sacrifice more generally during World War II. Instead, he intends to celebrate nationalist Cameroonian figures from three distinct eras: German, French, and post-independence. Yet an opportunity is being missed to mark the place of Cameroonians in a global war effort that was also theirs.

In his novel *La Saison des prunes*, Patrice Nganang undertakes a similar spatial and chronological sweep. He depicts Yaoundé's post-office square as follows: "This square has seen so many heroes of national liberation pass before it:.... Leclerc! De Gaulle! Um Nyobé! Ouandié! Pouka! Mebga! Who can do better? And yet, on the sly, someone named it after Ahmadou Ahidjo, the name of a tyrant."[67] Here, postcolonial and Free French stakes and claims intermingle.

## A Living Memory in Central Africa

Has the Free French referent in Africa changed or lost its meaning? Over the twenty years that separated regime change of 1940 and the wave of independence in 1960, the Free French moment in Africa remained a potent reference that shaped events and vice versa. Thus, in 1949, Cameroonian nationalist Ruben Um Nyobè insisted on the sacrifice of his compatriots during the war years. He cited the figure of some 3,000 Cameroonians who perished building the strategic road linking Douala and Yaoundé. He also lionized the wartime efforts of Cameroonian workers, soldiers, and dockers.[68]

---

[66] http://www.quaibranly.fr/cc/pod/recherche.aspx?b=1&id=75.15555.1.4 and
http://www.quaibranly.fr/cc/pod/recherche.aspx?b=1=id=75.15555.1.2.
[67] Patrice Nganang, *La Saison des prunes* (Paris: Philippe Rey, 2013), pp. 137–38.
[68] Joseph, p. 48.

French officials also exploited the memory of the war, although for other ends. Two Cameroonians were decorated during the victory celebrations in Yaoundé in May 1947. One we have encountered before: Raphaël Onana, who fought and lost a limb at Bir Hakeim. In a solemn ceremony, he received the *médaille militaire avec croix de guerre*. Also decorated that day was André Fouda. This civilian received the Résistance medal, largely for having impelled the Spitfire purchase campaign in Yaoundé. The choice of Fouda may also reveal political considerations. He had been a militant for Jeucafra, a pro-French movement founded in 1938. In 1945, Fouda advocated France's pure and simple annexation of Cameroon. A conservative, he was soon elected mayor of Yaoundé, while remaining an important ally of the French authorities in Cameroon.[69]

The Gaullist R.P.F. party was obviously intent on keeping the Gaullist legend alive in postwar FEA. It rekindled clichés surrounding the Brazzaville conference. This incidentally allowed it to gloss over some of the darker aspects of the war in Free French Africa. The party regularly dispatched emissaries to the Congolese capital. There, they leaned on old Free French networks, including Dr. Staub in nearby Leopoldville, who had already supported Larminat in August 1940. In Brazzaville, beginning in 1949, the R.P.F. rested on four African pillars: the Cameroonian Radio Brazzaville reporter Faustin Mouasso-Priso, Gaston Gaïna, a former sergeant who had joined the R.T.S.T. in August 1940, municipal employee Jacques Bankaites, and propagandist Maurice Kéké. Gaïa held considerable sway among veterans, as he had fought in the Saharan campaign. Historian Jean-Pierre Bat and novelist Guy Menga alike have underscored the crucial support that Free French veterans lent General de Gaulle in FEA as of 1944.[70]

After independence, the Free French referent endured, although it experienced shifts. Elikia M'Bokolo writes, "Once independent, [the Republic of] Congo never ceased to reactivate the Brazzaville myth. The three days of riots that chased Abbot Fulbert Youlou from power in 1963 were baptized 'Three Glorious Days,' not to copy the Paris revolution of July 1830 but in reference to the three days of August 1940 over the course of which the Free French tore Brazzaville from the hands of Pétain."[71]

---


[69] Ibid, pp. 57–58; Serge Enyegue, *André Fouda, Itinéraire politique d'un bâtisseur, 1951–1980* (Paris: l'Harmattan, 2008), pp. 36–39.

[70] Jean-Pierre Bat, "De Gaulle brazzavillois, Brazzaville gaulliste" (chapter 1), of "Congo An I. Décolonisation et politique française au Congo-Brazzaville (1958–1963)," thesis at the Ecole des Chartes (2006), pp. 106–35. On Gaïna's wartime service, see the Ecochard database online. Guy Menga, *Case de Gaulle*, Paris, Karthala, 1984, p. 121.

[71] Elikia M'Bokolo, "Brazzaville," pp. 148–49.

I should add that the Fifth Republic's foreign affairs officials were completely taken aback by these new "Glorious Days" of 1963, which they approached through the prism of the Cold War. They vowed to stem any "contagion" to Gabon and Chad.[72] Here was an astonishing flashback to the events of August 1940, save for the fact that this time the Gaullists played the role of counterrevolutionaries.

### Commemorations as "Reunions"

French and African official memories of the Free French period frequently intersect. In such cases, the Gaullist line tends to dominate. Thus, in late September 1990, on the occasion of Free France's fiftieth anniversary, a delegation composed of former Free Frenchmen set off for Brazzaville. There, they commemorated simultaneously "the fiftieth anniversary of the June 18, 1940, speech and the creation of Brazzaville as capital of Free France (August 28, 1940)." This two-headed tribute was no doubt intended to bridge Londoner and African realities. As for the choice of August 28, 1940, it obviously elided Chad's rallying two days earlier, and Cameroon's on the 27th. Indeed, with FEA now dismantled and replaced by four sovereign states, each of them commemorates the Free French saga separately with the former motherland. Admittedly, the ambassador of the Central African Republic served on the organizing committee for the Brazzaville events of 1990; but this still left Gabon, Chad, and Cameroon out of the proceedings. Over the course of its six days in Brazzaville, the delegation participated in the decoration of Congolese veterans, laid wreaths at the feet of the Eboué and de Gaulle monuments, and attended an "ecumenical mass" at the Sainte-Anne du Congo cathedral. It also enjoyed several tourist activities, including a cruise on the Congo River and a visit to the Poto-Poto painting school.[73] On balance, these commemorations mostly stand out for their silences.[74]

More recently, in October 2010, the de Gaulle Foundation assembled a delegation of some "hundred personalities," accompanied by ninety military personnel. They undertook a vast tour to commemorate the three glorious days. The expedition left Paris aboard an Airbus A 340, bound for N'Djamena, Yaoundé, then Brazzaville. The whirlwind tour, undertaken in just five days, left out the Central African Republic and Gabon

---

[72] Jean-Pierre Bat, *Le syndrome Foccart*, pp. 183, 219–31.

[73] AMB, comité national congolais pour la commémoration du cinquantenaire de l'appel du 18 juin 1940 et l'installation de Brazzaville, capitale de la France libre.

[74] On this "heavy silence" see Rousso, p. 26 (the word "silences" is more explicit in the French original, p. 41).

entirely. Over the course of the visit, the foundation distributed pamphlets to Africans, invited veterans to ceremonies, and gathered before the monuments of Eboué, Leclerc, and de Gaulle.[75] In N'Djamena, the delegation read a text from President Nicolas Sarkozy, evoking the "thousands of Africans [who] fought for the freedom of Europe and the world." Interestingly, the text added, "No Frenchman worthy of the title can forget it."[76] This must have seemed something of an enigma to the audience, given that the wartime sacrifices of FEA and Cameroon remain scarcely known in France.

This forgetting is precisely what one of the characters anticipates in Guy Menga's 1984 novel *Case de Gaulle*. "The African contribution to the war," he writes, "is something we must not regret. If one day France were to forget the blood of our brothers that was spilled over there... then we should not seek to remind it, but we reserve the right to consider them martyrs to liberty." Whereupon the character N'Kenko retorts, "Forgetting sometimes betrays contempt. Justice requires that blood be the same color for all men."[77]

The 2010 tour also elicited tensions, chiefly in Chad. In N'Djamena, President Idriss Déby Itno chided the delegation. He reminded his audience of colonial crimes that ravaged his land in 1912, insisted on Chadian sacrifice during World War II, and asked for the restitution of historical archives. Finally, he expressed the wish that N'Djamena, former Fort-Lamy, be named to the Order of Liberation.[78] This would indeed have been a logical undertaking, had nominations to the order not been definitively shut in January 1946.

## Hypotheses

In geostrategic terms, the Free French legacy almost certainly shaped the famous French *pré carré* of influence in postcolonial Africa. This zone, whose contours have shifted over time, is generally conceived as being bounded by the Sahel to the North, which is perceived as a kind of "rampart."[79] Over the decades, this space has more specifically come to be seen as a buffer against Libya, the same idée fixe that consumed Eboué and

[75] See the special issue of the journal *Espoir* (Fall 2010), #162, pp. 8–22.
[76] http://tchad24.unblog.fr/2010/10/27/tchad-commemoration-du-70e-anniversaire-de-la-france-libre/#.
[77] Menga, pp. 126–27.
[78] Raymond Césaire, "L'Afrique centrale au cœur des ceremonies du 70ème anniversaire de la France libre," *Bulletin de l'AROM*, 22 (November-December 2010), pp. 8–9.
[79] Bat, *Le syndrome Foccart*, p. 233.

Leclerc in 1940. Without excessively leapfrogging, I would suggest that the Second World War conditioned future "special relations" with Chad, Centrafrique, and Gabon, most notably in the military realm. Within the ranks of the French army, operations in Chad in the 1980s seemed regularly to rekindle the ghosts of actions launched from Chad in World War II. Moreover, the networks of "Françafrique" – a nebulous web of French financial and political influence in Africa – rest at least in part on the myth of sub-Saharan Africa as fervently and faithfully Gaullist. The myth was shaped in part by the three glorious days of August 1940, in part by the kind of personalization of politics encapsulated by the Ngol rites, and finally by Brazzaville's role as a guarantor of French legitimacy during the war.

One is struck, ultimately, by the malleability and ambiguity of Free French memory in Africa. Which Free French Africa? For the settlers at Douala in 1945, Free French Africa represented a gilded age of colonialism that preceded what they conceived as Gaullist treason in the form of the Brazzaville conference and its concessions. Later on, other settlers in Algeria would elaborate a similar theory of Gaullist colonial betrayal. For some African soldiers and NCOs, an early commitment to the Cross of Lorraine led to spectacular ascensions; to others it amounted to bitter disappointment in the end. Many found that they were ineligible for the Résistance medal, others saw bonuses withheld because of their unit's whitening, others still experienced flagrant disparities in pensions, and limited recognition within prestigious institutions like the Order of Liberation. Attitudes toward the sacrifice of thousands of inhabitants of Chad, of the Central African Republic, of the Republic of Congo, and of Cameroon during World War II remain equally ambivalent, inasmuch as their contribution is remembered at all. While Ruben Um Nyobè sought to elevate fallen workers into national heroes, nowadays Mboua Massock fails to consider representing a Cameroonian Free French combatant on the pedestal presently occupied by General Leclerc in Douala. Like Franco-African relations more generally, the legacies of Free France in Africa are complex, made of silences, echoes, forgetting, and periodic reinventions.

# Conclusion

In a speech at the Palais Chaillot, in the shadow of the Eiffel Tower, on January 26, 1945, Henri Laurentie observed that never before had a motherland been liberated by its empire. Far-flung Roman provinces had not retaken Rome after its fall, he noted. Parenthetically, he thereby linked the sacking of the City of Light by the Germans in 1940 to that of the Eternal City by the barbarians in 476. No doubt Laurentie was conveniently forgetting the role of other colonial empires in World War II and even I. Yet this does not change his fundamental point about the actions of Free French Africa, or the risks the region took, and the human cost the area paid to remain in the war when the rest of the French empire had not. The situation was indeed unusual: the British Crown had not fled to Canada – a contingency plan that was never pressed into service – nor had the French government relocated to North Africa in June 1940 (although some certainly attempted this undertaking, only to be labeled traitors for doing so).

In this sense, Laurentie was correct to underscore the importance of FEA and Cameroon as seats of Free France. He was also right to insist on the singularity of this liberating army that departed from the equator to fight first in the Sahara, then Europe. This arrow running from south to north constitutes one of the defining features of the Free French war effort. As troops were madly being recruited in FEA and Cameroon, Free France was registering its first victories against the Italians in the heart of the Sahara. These triumphs would be followed by others in the northern reaches of the desert, at Ksar Rhilane for instance. Some of these same troops would then contribute to the liberations of Italy and France.

Lucidly, Laurentie went further still, when he maintained that the Free French effort in Africa rested largely on the shoulders of the colonized. He declared, "In their own way, black Africans were pure Gaullists." The phrase "in their own way" gives pause. Yet if Laurentie had been less diplomatic, he could also have added that Free French Africa's entry into resistance occurred four years prior to that of most of his Parisian audience. As for the territories of FEA and Cameroon, he contended, the victories of Kufra and the Fezzan would "not have been possible had Free French colonies not served as the starting point for the French columns. And far more than a starting point. It was essential that these territories be working in unison for the war and the liberation."[1]

The evidence I have provided here certainly does not contradict the bold arguments of FEA's former secretary-general. In terms of human resources, 27,000 men from FEA and Cameroon (or posted there in 1940) served as foot soldiers, drivers, NCOs, radio experts, artillery men, and so on between 1940 and 1943. They fought countless battles, despite the two waves of "whitenings" that struck in 1943 and 1944. In civilian ranks, women, men, and children all collected vast amounts of wild rubber; others built thousands of kilometers of roads linking Allied colonies, others still dug for rutile and gold. In terms of natural resources, while in December 1940, the Germans seized some 30,000 tons of rubber in metropolitan France, while in 1941 the Germans purchased another 20,000 tons of Indo-Chinese plantation rubber from Vichy (of which at least 17,000 reached the Reich),[2] while in 1944, 161,000 tons of rubber languished in stockpiles across Vichy-controlled Indochina,[3] the inhabitants of FEA and Cameroon toiled to extract latex from roots and grasses for a war effort that was desperately running short of rubber. Their contribution of 7,000 tons per year in 1943 and 1944 can appear incommensurate with Asian quantities at first glance. But every drop counted for British and American war machines that had exhausted their stockpiles now that Southeast Asia's rubber lay out of reach. Much the same observation holds for military recruitment figures. At first blush, the 27,000 combatants from Free France and Cameroon can seem like a drop in the bucket compared to the more than 100,000 recruited in French WestAfrica between 1939 and

---

[1] Laurentie, *L'Empire au secours de la Métropole*, pp. 3, 16, 18–19.

[2] Chantal Metzger, *L'Empire colonial français dans la stratégie du Troisième Reich, 1936–1945* (Brussels: Peter Lang, 2002), pp. 496–98.

[3] Jacques Martin, "L'Economie indochinoise pendant la guerre 1940–1945," *Revue d'histoire de la Deuxième Guerre Mondiale*, 138 (1985), p. 75.

the Battle of France in May 1940.[4] However, the point is that because of the armistice, the Third Reich, and Vichy, these West African combatants were held out of the war between 1940 and early 1944.

In all of these respects, Free French Africa weighed in the balance, especially during an early phase that proved so critical for a still fragile Gaullist movement. This contribution was undertaken under trying circumstances. The reorderings of 1940 triggered a pronounced deterioration in material conditions. Mostly, the effort constituted a poignant inversion captured by an official in Gabon who noted "the rather paradoxical situation of a French colony wanting to do something for France against the wishes of metropolitan authorities."[5]

In this way, FEA and Cameroon were called on to replace other colonies that remained in Pétain's orbit, but also the motherland itself. The most striking dimensions of Free French Africa include its contributions to the Allied cause, and the long underrecognized Africanness of the Gaullist movement between 1940 and 1943. This last point presents a correction to the myth of an essentially Londoner and metropolitan resistance.

[4] Echenberg, *Colonial Conscripts*, p. 88.
[5] ANOM GGAEF 4(1) D50.

# Bibliography

## I. Archives

*Archives nationales d'Outre-mer, Aix-en-Provence*

**Fonds GGAEF (*Gouvernement général de l'Afrique équatoriale française*)**


3B 192 to 196, Correspondence from the governor-general to the minister.

3B 1082 to 1104, Correspondence from the governor-general to the governor of Moyen-Congo.

3B 2381 to 3B 2384, Governor general's confidential correspondence.

5B 352 to 359, Telegrams from the governor-general to Oubangui-Chari.

5B 710 to 720, Governor-general's confidential telegrams.

6B 65 to 6B 75, Incoming telegrams from Pleven.

1D 120 to 122, Correspondence with the governor of Moyen-Congo.

4 (1) D 48 to 4 (1) D 54, Local political reports for Gabon.

4 (2) D 74 to 4(2) D 76, Political reports for Moyen-Congo.

4 (3) D 52 and 4 (3) D 53, Political reports for Oubangui-Chari.

4 (4) D 50 to 4 (4) D 53, Political reports for Chad.

5 D 86, Relations between Nigeria and French West Africa.

5 D 117, Counter-espionage in FEA.

5 D 168, Various incidents in Oubangui-Chari and Chad.

5 D 182, Indigenous policy.

5 D 187, World War II.

5D 194, Incidents at Abéché 1939–42.

5 D 195, Territorial and administrative organization.

5D 202, Eboué's indigenous policy, 1941–43.

5D 205, Assorted grievances, 1942.

5D 206, Indigenous policy, "notables évolués."

5D 289, Organization of Free France, relations with Great Britain.

5D 290, FEA's rallying to Free France.

5D 291, Correspondence.

5D 295, Censorship and postal control.

5D 299, Economic affairs.
5D 300 and 301, Various.
5D 302 and 303, Military affairs.
2H 18, 25, 26, 41, 34, and 37, Labor policy.
2Y 11 to 15, High commissioner to Free French Africa, 1940–42.
3Y 3, Diary of the post at Carnot, Oubangui-Chari.
5Y 4, Diary of the post at Fort-Rousset, Congo.

*Fonds Cabinet*
C 15, Organization of Free France.
C 37, Recruitment.
C 48, Origins of Free France.
C 49, Radio Brazzaville, Chad, 1940–44.
C 55, Tchad, Gabon, Cameroon, 1940–45.
C 62, Military affairs.
C 63, Military situation in FEA, Leclerc.
C 64, Colonial troops.
C 66, Mines & transport.

*Fonds Direction des affaires militaires*
DSM 74, Douala, 1945.
DSM 159, FEA Troops.
DSM 262, FEA's military effort, 1940–45.

*Fonds 1Affpol (Affaires politiques)*
AP 873, Naturalizations, alcohol, Prisons, postal control.
AP 885 and 891, Vichy's perception of Free French colonies.
AP 2136 d 6 Justice in FEA, 1941–55.
AP 2136 d 9, Discriminations and social demands.
AP 2217 B5 FEA veterans.
AP 2557 The empire rallying to Free France.

*Fonds privés et papiers d'agents*
27 PA, Pierret papers
156 APOM 3, Douala events, 1945
217 APOM Géraud de Galassus papers.

*Fonds AGEFOM (Agence économique de la France outre-mer)*
AGEFOM 357, dossier 91 bis, FEA during the war.

*Fonds Togo-Cameroun*
Cameroun 29, on the situation in Cameroon in 1940.

*Fonds AOF (Copies of the originals, which are located in Dakar at the
National Archives of Senegal)*
14 Miom 2284, 14 Miom 2289, 14 Miom 2324 all dealing with French West
    Africa from 1940–45.

### *Archives nationales de la République du Cameroun*

1AC 123, Douala, 1945.
1AC 4789, Monument in Yaoundé.
2AC 21, 2AC 158, 2AC 5202 and 2AC 5294, Local inspection reports.
2AC 433 Abuses, 1940.
2AC 3258, Public works.
2AC 4427, Workplace accidents.
2AC 5186, Justice.
2AC 5868, 5871 and 5893, Files on tirailleurs.
2AC 5940, Workplace "desertion," 1941.
2AC 5956, Work on plantations, 1945.
2AC 6324, War matériel.
2AC 6332, Relations with London.
2AC 6431, Intelligence.
2AC 7411, Financing the war.
2AC 9446, Victory celebrations.
2AC 11190a, De Gaulle movement.
APA 10068, Justice.
APA 10117, Capital punishments.
APA 10209, Tirailleur recruitment and desertions.
APA 10267, Courts.
APA 10658, Justice.
APA 11230, Postal control.
APA 11316, Identification cards.
APA 11324, War.
APA 11655, Labor 1944–45.
APA 10092, 11657, 11766, and 11801, Local inspection reports.
APA 11714, Rapport on Cameroon, 1941.
NF 382/2, Legislation.


### *Archives nationales de la République du Congo*

**Fonds GGAEF (*Gouvernement général de l'Afrique équatoriale française*)**
GGAEF 82, 255, and 258, Personnel.
GGAEF 84, Telegrams, 1940–42.
GGAEF 110, Arriving correspondence, 1940–48.
GGAEF 126, Belgian Congo, Moyen-Congo, Gabon, Cassin.
GGAEF 128, Public works.
GGAEF 134, Reports from Haut-Ogooué.
GGAEF 138, Secrtariat général.
GGAEF 379, Grievances.
GGAEF 502, Military cabinet.
GGAEF 504, Médaille de la Résistance.
GGAEF 539, Gold.
GGAEF 553, Exports.
GGAEF 596, Taxes.

Centre des archives diplomatiques de Nantes

**Fonds de Brazzaville**
116PO/1/68, 116PO/1/71, 116PO/1/95, and 116PO/1/106 Local reports.
116PO/1/115, Border with the Belgian Congo.
116PO/1/166, Veterans.

**Fonds CFLN London**
378PO/C/2/172, Rubber.
378PO/C/2/264, FEA's economy.

**Consular Fonds**
68PO/1/167 Bangui.
743PO/2/71 Yaoundé.

CHETOM, Fréjus

15 H 50 d. 9, The rallying of FEA.
15 H 152, Free French forces, 1940–45.
15 H 153, First Free French division.
15 H 153 Journaux de marche of the B.M. 4, 5 and 11.
15 H 156 JMO brigades du Cameroun et du Tchad.
15 H 158 Colonial units, Atlantic pockets, 1945.
18 H 138 Edgard de Larminat.

Service historique de la défense, Vincennes

11P 21, L. Force.
12P 259 Régiment de marche du Tchad.
12P 268, Colonial infantry.
12P 269, Cameroon.
1K 289 Mémorial du B.M.2.
2831/67 Bokassa file.

Archives de la Fondation Charles de Gaulle, Paris

F 22, 17 Eboué Collection.
F11 and FAA 10 Desjardins and Krull Collections.

Archives du Mémorial Leclerc, Paris

Leclerc 5a (Cameroon, Gabon, Chad), 5b (Cameroon, Chad), 6a (Kufra),
   6b (Kufra), 15 (Free French Africa).

Archives de l'Ordre de la Libération, Paris

B, 4B, 4B1 FEA to 4B4 Congo.
René Pleven papers
Files of the Compagnons de l'Ordre de la Libération.

*Archives nationales, Paris*

3 AG (1) 164 to 170, De Gaulle papers.

*Archives de la Fraternité des Capucins de France, Paris*

3R2 Berbérati bishopric
3R42 Berbérati diocese
T3R29 Correspondence, 1940–42
3R16a, Chad.

*Archives de la Congrégation du Saint-Esprit, Chevilly-Larue, France*

CSE 2J2.3A, Monseignors Vogt and Graffin.
CSE 3J1.19B, Journal of the Mouyounasi community.

*Centre des archives du personnel militaire de Pau*

Dangsalla personnel file.

*Archives du Mémorial de Caen*

Boislambert papers

*Archives of the Folkwang Museum, Essen, Federal Republic of Germany*

Germaine Krull collection, manuscripts, and photos.

*National Archives of the United Kingdom (Kew)*

FO 371, FO 859, FO 892, Foreign Office files on Free French Africa:
WO 178, WO 892, War Office files on Free French Africa.

*Bodleian Archives, Oxford, United Kingdom*

MSS. Afr. s. 424, folios 240–54.
Godfrey Allen, Report on the political situation in the Cameroons under French
mandate, July–Aug 1940.
MSS. Afr. s. 424, folios 292–94.
Herbert Llewellyn Cole, report for the acting British consul at Douala regarding
introduction of Free French troops into the French Cameroons, 1940.
Mss Afr. S 940, A.A. Cullen, report on visit to Cameroun, 1944.
Mss Afr. 1085 Memorandum by L. C. Giles, "First British Contacts with Eboué,
1940" Mss Afr s 1334 (9–10).
Mss Afr.s.1814 Papers of Sir Frederick Johnson Peder.

*Archives nationales du Sénégal, Dakar*

4D 60 (89), Requests from Free French veterans.

*National Archives and Records Administration, USA*

U.S.Consulate in Brazzaville: RG 84, Classified General Records, 1942–44, boxes 1, 2, and 3, as well as General Records (Brazzaville, 1942), declassified.

*Smith College, Sophia Smith Collection,*
*Northampton, Massachusetts*

Dudley Harmon papers, boxes 1 and 2.

*Archives of the Christian and Missionary Alliance, Colorado*
*Springs, Colorado*

RG 820, Gabon.

*Archives of the Magnum Photo Agency, New York*

George Rodger photo collection.

## II. Period Newspaper and Periodicals

*L'AÉF*
*Le Courrier d'Afrique* (édition AEF)
*La Catapulte* (Brazzaville)
*L'Eveil du Cameroun*
*France d'abord*
*Journal officiel de l'Afrique équatoriale française*

## III. Bibliography

*Memoirs and Testimonies*

Ackermann Athanassiades, Blanche. *France libre capitale: Brazzaville*. Paris: Editions La Bruyère, 1989.

Béné, Charles. *Carnets de route d'un 'Rat du Désert' Alsacien de la France libre*. Raon-L'Etape: Imp. Fetzer, 1991.

Boislambert (de), Claude Hettier. *Les fers de l'espoir*. Paris: Plon, 1978.

Boisseau, René. *Les trois glorieuses de l'empire, 26-27-28 août 1940*. Office français d'édition, 1945.

Burman, Ben Lucien. *Miracle on the Congo: report from the Free French Front*. New York: John Day Co., 1942.

Cassin, René. *Des hommes partis de rien*. Paris: Plon, 1974.

Churchill, Winston. *The Second World War*. Boston: Houghton Mifflin, 1949.

Davis, Hassoldt. *Feu d'Afrique*. Paris: Fayard, 1945.

De Gaulle, Charles. *Mémoires de Guerre*. Paris: Plon, 1954.

Dronne, Raymond. *Leclerc et le serment de Koufra*. Paris: éditions du Temps, 1965.

Freitag, Joseph. *Histoires vécues*. Paris: Bernard Neyrolles, 1977.

Ingold, François. *L'Epopée Leclerc au Sahara*. Paris: Berger-Levrault, 1945.

Laigret, Christian. *Sur les chemins de l'union française*: Châteauroux: éditions Novelty, 1949.

Lapie, Pierre-Olivier. *Le Tchad fait la guerre*. Algiers: Office français d'édition, 1943.

Lapie, Pierre-Olivier. *Mes tournées au Tchad*. Algiers: Office français d'éditions, 1945.

Larminat (de), Edgard. *Chroniques irrévérencieuses*. Paris: Plon, 1962.

Laurentie, Henri. *L'Empire au secours de la métropole*. Paris: office français d'édition, 1945.

Messmer, Pierre. *Les blancs s'en vont: récits de decolonization*. Paris: Albin-Michel, 1998.

Moynet, Paul. *L'épopée du Fezzan*. Algiers, Office français d'éditions, 1944.

Onana, Raphaël. *Un homme blindé à Bir-Hakeim, récit d'un sous-officier camerounais qui a fait la guerre de 39–45*. Paris: l'Harmattan, 1996.

Rodger, George. *Voyage au desert*. Paris: La Colombe, 1956.

Saurat, Denis. *Watch over Africa*. London: J.M. Dent and sons, 1941.

Sicé, Adolphe. *L'AEF et le Cameroun au service de la France*. Paris: Presses universitaires de France, 1946.

Soustelle, Jacques. *Envers et contre tout*. Paris: Robert Laffont, 1947.

Travers, Susan. *Tomorrow to be Brave*. London: Transworld publishers, 2000.

*Free France*

Azéma, Jean-Pierre. *1940, l'année terrible*. Paris: éditions du Seuil, 1990.

Barré, Jean-Luc. *Devenir de Gaulle, 1939–1943*. Paris: Perrin, 2003.

Broche, François, Caïtucoli, Georges and Muracciole, Jean-François. *La France au combat: de l'appel du 18 juin à la victoire*. Paris: Perrin, 2007.

Crémieux-Brilhac, Jean-Louis. *La France libre*. Paris: Gallimard, 1996.

Lacouture, Jean. *De Gaulle*. Paris: le Seuil, 1984.

Levisse-Touzé, Christine ed. *Du capitaine de Hauteclocque au général de Gaulle*. Bruxssels: Complexe, 2000.

Maguire, G. E. *Anglo-American Policy Towards the Free French*. Oxford: Macmillan Press, 1995.

Muracciole, Jean-François. *Les Français libres: l'autre résistance*. Paris: Tallandier, 2009.

Notin, Jean-Christophe. *1061 Compagnons. Histoire des Compagnons de la Libération*. Paris: Perrin, 2000.

Notin, Jean-Christophe. *Leclerc*. Paris: Perrin, 2005.

Oulmont, Philippe. ed., *Larminat, un fidèle hors série*. Paris: LB.M., 2008.

Oulmont, Philippe. Philippe Oulmont, *Pierre Denis, Free Frenchman and Citizen of the World*. Paris: Nouveau monde, 2013.

Prost, Antoine, and Winter, Jay. *René Cassin and Human Rights*.Cambridge: Cambridge University Press, 2013.

Rousso, Henry. *The Vichy Syndrome: History and Memory in France since 1944*. Cambridge: Harvard University Press, 1991.

Simonin, Anne. "L'Eléphant français libre: Babar, Romain Gary et la France libre," *Vingtième Siècle. Revue d'histoire*, 112 (2011), pp. 70–82.

Trouplin, Vladimir. *Dictionnaire des Compagnons de la Libération*. Bordeaux: Elytis, 2010.

Weinstein, Brian. *Eboué*. New York: Oxford University Press, 1972.

White, Dorothy Shipley. *Seeds of Discord: De Gaulle, Free France, and the Allies*. New York: Syracuse University Press, 1964.

### Free France in the Colonies


Clarence-Smith, William G. "La SOCFIN (groupe Rivaud) entre l'Axe et les Alliés," in Hubert Bonin, Christophe Bouneau and Hervé Joly, eds., *Les entreprises et l'outre-mer français pendant la seconde guerre mondiale*. Bordeaux: Maison des Sciences de l'Hommed'Aquitaine, 2010.

Dinan, Desmond. *The Politics of Persuasion: British Policy and French African Neutrality, 1940–1942*. Lanham: University Press of America, 1988.

Dubois, Colette. "Internés et prisonniers de guerre italiens dans les camps de l'empire français de 1940 à 1945," *Guerre mondiales et conflits contemporains*, 156 (October 1989), pp. 53–71.

Ebako, Eliane. "Le ralliement du Gabon à la France libre: une guerre franco-française," PhD thesis, University of Paris IV, 2004.

Fondation Maréchal Leclerc de Hauteclocque, *Le général Leclerc et l'Afrique française libre, 1940–1942*. Paris: Fondation Leclerc, 1989.

Kaptué, Léon. "L'Administration coloniale et la circulation des indigènes au Cameroun: les laissez-passer, 1923–1946," *Afrika Zamani*, 10–11 (December 1979), pp. 160–81.

Kelly, Saul. "Ce fruit savoureux du désert: Britain, France and the Fezzan, 1941–1956," *The Maghreb Review* 26: 1 (2001), pp. 2–21.

Lanne, Bernard. "Chad, the Chadians and the Second World War, 1939–1945," *Africana Journal*, 16: (1994), pp. 311–25.

Lanne, Bernard. "Le Tchad pendant la guerre (1939–1945)," in Charles-Robert Ageron, ed., *Les chemins de la décolonisation de l'empire français, 1936–1956*. Paris: CNRS, 1986.

Lawler, Nancy. "Reform and Repression under the Free French: Economic and Political Transformation in the Côte d'Ivoire, 1942–1945," *Journal of the International African Institute*, 60: 1 (1990), pp. 88–110.

Lewis, James I. "Félix Eboué and Late French Colonial Ideology," *Itinerario*, 2002, 26: 1 (2002).

M'Bokolo, Elikia. "Brazzaville," in Claire Andrieu, Philippe Braud, and Guillaume Piketty, eds., *Dictionnaire de Gaulle*. Paris: Robert Laffont, 2006, pp. 148–49.

M'Bokolo, Elikia. "French Colonial Policy in Equatorial Africa in the 1940s and 1950s," in Prosser Gifford and WM Roger Lewis, eds., *The Transfer of Power in Africa, Decolonization, 1940–1960*. New Haven: Yale University Press, 1982.

Memoli-Aubry, Crécence. "Le Mbam dans la Seconde Guerre Mondiale: contribution d'une région administrative du Cameroun à l'effort de guerre français," *Outre-mers, revue d'histoire*, (2009), pp. 241–66.

Munholland, Kim. *Rock of Contention: Free French and Americans at War in New Caledonia, 1940–1945.* New York: Berghahn, 2005.

Nnang Ndong, Léon Modeste. *L'effort de guerre de l'Afrique: le Gabon dans la deuxième guerre mondiale, 1939–1947.* Paris: L'Harmattan, 2011.

Ollandet, Jérôme. *Brazzaville, capitale de la France libre: histoire de la résistance française en Afrique, 1940–1944.* Brazzaville: Editions de la Savane, 198c.

Sah, Léonard. *Le Cameroun sous mandat français dans la deuxième guerre mondiale*, PhD thesis, Université de Provence, 1998.

Thomas, Martin. *The French Empire at War.* Manchester: Manchester University Press, 1998.

Vincent, Jean-Noël. *Les forces françaises libres en Afrique, 1940–1943.* Vincennes: Services historiquede l'arméede terre, 1983.


### African and Colonial History

Akpo-Vaché, Catherine. *L'AOF et la seconde guerre mondiale.* Paris: Karthala, 1996.

Bat, Jean-Pierre. "Congo An I. Décolonisation et politique française au Congo-Brazzaville (1958–1963)," PhD thesis, Ecole des Chartes, 2006.

Bat, Jean-Pierre. *Le syndrome Foccart: la politique française en Afrique de 1959 à nos jours.* Paris: Gallimard, 2012.

Berenson, Edward. *Heroes of Empire: Five Charismatic Men and the Conquest of Africa.* Berkeley: University of California Press. 2012.

Bernault, Florence. *Démocraties ambiguës, Congo-Brazzaville, Gabon: 1940–1965.* Paris: Karthala, 1996.

Bonhomme, Julien. "Masque Chirac et danse de Gaulle: Images rituelles du blanc au Gabon," *Gradhiva* 11, 2010, pp. 81–97.

Cantier, Jacques. *L'Algérie sous le régime de Vichy.* Paris: Odile Jacob, 2002.

Chafer, Tony. *The End of Empire in French West Africa: France's successful decolonization?* Oxford: Berg, 2002.

Cooper, Frederick. *Citizenship between Empire and Nation: Remaking France and French Africa, 1945–1960.* Princeton: Princeton University Press, 2014.

Cooper, Frederick. *Colonialism in Question: Theory, Knowledge, History.* Berkeley: University of California Press, 2005.

Cooper, Frederick. *Decolonization and African Society: The Labor Question in French and British Africa.* New York: Cambridge University Press, 1996.

Coquery-Vidrovitch, Catherine. *Le Congo au temps des grandes compagnies concessionnaires, 1898–1930.* Paris: Mouton, 1972.

Coquery-Vidrovitch, Catherine. "Emeutes urbaines, grèves générales et décolonisation en Afrique française," in Charles-Robert Ageron, ed., *Les chemins de la décolonisation de l'empire français, 1936–1956.* Paris: CNRS, 1986.

Daughton, J. P. "Behind the Imperial Curtain: International Humanitarian Efforts and the Critique of French Colonialism in the Interwar Years," *French Historical Studies*, 34: 3 (2011), pp. 503–28.

Deltombe, Thomas, Domergue, Manuel, and Tatsitsa, Jacob. *Kamerun! Une guerre cachée aux origines de la Françafrique, 1948–1971.* Paris: la Découverte, 2011.

Faes, Geraldine, and Smith, Stephen. *Bokassa 1er un empereur français*. Paris: Calmann-Lévy, 2000.

Frémeaux, Jacques. *La Sahara et la France*. Paris: Sotéca, 2010.

Giles-Vernick, Tamara. *Cutting the Vines of the Past: Environmental Histories of the Central African Rain Forest*. Charlottesville: University Press of Virginia, 2002.

Ginio, Ruth. *French Colonialism Unmasked: The Vichy Years in French West Africa*. Lincoln: University of Nebraska Press, 2006.

Gray, Christopher. *Colonial Rule and Crisis in Equatorial Africa: Southern Gabon ca. 1850–1940*. Rochester: University of Rochester Press, 2002.

Jennings, Eric. *Vichy in the Tropics: Pétain's National Revolution in Madagascar, Guadeloupe and Indochina, 1940–1944*. Stanford: Stanford University Press, 2001.

Joseph, Richard. *Radical Nationalism in Cameroun: Social Origins of the U.P.C. Rebellion*. Oxford: Clarendon Press, 1977.

Kalck, Pierre. *Histoire centrafricaine des origines à 1966*. Paris: L'Harmattan, 2000.

Kaptué, Léon. *Travail et main-d'œuvre au Cameroun sous régime français, 1916–1952*. Paris: L'Harmattan, 1986.

Koerner, Francis. "Le contrôle de l'industrie française du caoutchouc par l'Allemagne nazie (1940–1944)," *Guerres mondiales et conflits contemporains*, 240: 4 (2010), pp. 43–61.

Killingray, David and Rathbone, Richard, eds., *Africa and the Second World War*. New York: Saint Martin's Press, 1986.

Lachenal, Guillaume. "Le médecin qui voulut être roi: Médecine coloniale et utopie au Cameroun," *Annales, Histoire, Sciences Sociales*, (January–February 2010), pp. 121–56.

Lefebvre, Camille. "Territoires et frontières: du Soudan central à la République du Niger, 1800–1964," PhD thesis, Université de Paris I, 2008.

Martin, Phyllis. *Leisure and Society in Colonial Brazzaville*. Cambridge: Cambridge University Press, 2002.

Mbembe, Achille. *La naissance du maquis dans le Sud-Cameroun, 1920–1960*. Paris: Karthala, 1996.

Metzger, Chantal. *L'Empire colonial français dans la stratégie du Troisième Reich, 1936–1945*. Brussels: Peter Lang, 2002.

Rich, Jeremy. *A Workman is Worthy of his Meat: Food and Colonialism in the Gabon Estuary*. Lincoln: University of Nebraska Press, 2007.

Saada, Emmanuelle. *Empire's Children: Race, Filiation and Citizenship in the French Colonies*. Chicago: University of Chicago Press, 2012.

Simonis, Francis. *Le Commandant en tournée: Une administration au contact des populations en Afrique Noire coloniale*. Paris: Seli Arslan, 2005.

Sombé, Catherine Suzanne Mpandjo. "Le commerce extérieur du Cameroun, 1930–1980," PhD thesis, University of Bordeaux, 2013.

Suret-Canale, Jean. *Afrique noire occidentale et centrale*. Paris: Editions sociales, 1964.

Toso, Carlo. *Centrafrique, un siècle d'évangélisation*. Bangui: Conférence épiscopale contrafricaine, 1994.

White, Owen. *Children of the French Empire: Miscegenation and Colonial Society in French West Africa, 1895–1960*. Oxford: Oxford University Press, 1999.

### African Troops in World War II

Aubagnac, Gilles. "Le retrait des troupes noires de la première Armée à l'automne de 1944," *Revue historique des armées*, 2, (1993), pp. 34–46.

Echenberg, Myron. *Colonial Conscripts: The Tirailleurs Sénégalais in French West Africa, 1857–1960*. Portsmouth: Heinemann, 1991.

Echenberg, Myron. "Les migrations militaires en Afrique occidentale française, 1900–1945," *Canadian Journal of African Studies*, 14: 3 (1980), pp. 429–50.

Fargettas, Julien. *Les tirailleurs sénégalais: les soldats noirs entre légendes et réalités, 1939–1945*. Paris: Tallandier, 2012.

Frémeaux, Jacques. "Les contingents impériaux au cœur de la guerre," *Histoire, Economie et Société*, 23: 2 (2004), pp. 215–33.

Killingray, David. *Fighting for Britain: African Soldiers in the Second World War*. London: James Currey, 2010.

Mabon, Armelle. *Prisonniers de guerre "indigènes."* Paris: La Découverte, 2010.

Mann, Gregory. *Native Sons: West African Veterans and France in the Twentieth Century*. Durham: Duke University Press, 2006.

Rives, Maurice. *Héros Méconnus, Mémorial des combattants d'Afrique noire et de Madagascar*. Paris: Association française Frères d'Armes, 1990.

Scheck, Raffael. *Hitler's African Victims: The German Army Massacres of Black French Soldiers in 1940*. Cambridge: Cambridge University Press, 2006.

Zimmerman, Sarah. "Living beyond Boundaries: West African Servicemen in French Colonial Conflicts, 1908–1962." PhD thesis, University of California Berkeley, 2011.

### Novels

Gary, Romain. *La promesse de l'aube*. Paris: Gallimard, 1980.

Gary, Romain. *Les Racines du Ciel*. Paris: Gallimard, 1956.

Menga, Guy. *Case de Gaulle*. Paris: Karthala, 1984.

Nganang, Patrice. *La Saison des prunes*. Paris: Philippe Rey. 2013.

# Index

Printed in the USA
CPSIA information can be obtained
at www.ICGtesting.com
CBHW050422261124
18006CB00009B/244